HOPE-FOCUSED
Marriage
Counseling

A Guide to
Brief Therapy

Everett L.
Worthington Jr.

InterVarsity Press
Downers Grove, Illinois

InterVarsity Press
P.O. Box 1400, Downers Grove, IL 60515
World Wide Web: www.ivpress.com
E-mail: mail@ivpress.com

InterVarsity Press® is the book-publishing division of InterVarsity Christian Fellowship/USA®, a student movement active on campus at hundreds of universities, colleges and schools of nursing in the United States of America, and a member movement of the International Fellowship of Evangelical Students. For information about local and regional activities, write Public Relations Dept., InterVarsity Christian Fellowship/USA, 6400 Schroeder Rd., P.O. Box 7895, Madison, WI 53707-7895

Scripture quotations, unless otherwise noted, are from the New Revised Standard Version of the Bible, copyright 1989 by the Division of Christian Education of the National Council of the Churches of Christ in the USA. Used by permission. All rights reserved.

Table 10.1 taken from The Five Love Languages by Gary Chapman. Copyright 1995, Moody Bible Institute of Chicago—Moody Press. Used with permission.

Table 11.3 adapted from Andrew Christensen, N S. Jacobson and J. C. Babcock, "Integrative Behavioral Couple Therapy," in Clinical Handbook of Couple Therapy, ed. N S. Jacobson and A. S. Gurman, © 1995 Used by permission of Guilford Press.

ISBN 0-8308-1548-1

Printed in the United States of America ♻

Library of Congress Cataloging-in-Publication Data

Worthington, Everett. L. 1946-
    Hope-Focused marriage counseling a guide to brief therapy /
    Everett L. Worthington, Jr.
       p. cm.
    Includes bibliographical references.
    ISBN 0-8308-1548-1 (pbk. alk. paper)
    1 Marriage counseling. 2. Pastoral counseling. 3. Marriage—
Religious aspects—Christianity 4 Solution-focused brief
therapy.   I. Title.
BV4012.27 W668 1999
259' 14—dc21   99-18732
                                                                                          CIP

21   20   19   18   17   16   15   14   13   12   11   10   9   8   7   6   5   4   3   2   1

16   15   14   13   12   11   10   09   08   07   06   05   04   03   02   01   00   99

To Doug McMurry . . .
faithful to God's call,
worker in his service,
lover of his people . . .
pastor

CONTENTS

Acknowledgments 9

Preface 13

PART ONE: THEORY

1 Brief Marital Counseling.. 17

2 Bird's-Eye View of Hope-Focused Marriage Counseling 28

3 Using the Strategy to Promote Hope 45

4 Applying the Strategy to Eight Areas of Marriage 59

PART TWO: INTERVENTIONS

5 Precounseling Interventions 75

6 Assessment Interventions 84

7 Interventions for Drawing on Central Values.................... 101

8 Interventions for Revisioning a Core Vision 111

9 Interventions for Promoting Confession & Forgiveness........ 128

10 Interventions for Strengthening Communication *147*

11 Interventions for Aiding Conflict Resolution *168*

12 Interventions for Changing Cognition *195*

13 Interventions for Stimulating More Closeness *213*

14 Interventions for Cementing Commitment *238*

15 Interventions for Promoting Couple Commencement

from Counseling *252*

16 Essentials of Hope-Focused Marriage Counseling *260*

Appendix: Hope-Focused Marriage Counseling with a Young

Professional Couple: A Case Study (Terry L. Hight) *268*

Notes *285*

Author Index *304*

Subject Index *306*

Scripture Index *310*

Acknowledgments

I am grateful to many people in bringing this book to print. Most dramatically I owe a debt to clients who have stubbornly refused to get better when I persisted in working *my* program and not listening to *their* program. Clients force us to listen.

Over the years I have been blessed with extremely talented graduate students who have contributed ideas to the theory and practice we have shaped together through our interactions and joint publications. Many of these are now functioning as postdoctoral faculty members or practitioners, and many I have acknowledged in other books. Most recently I have worked closely with the following, who have moved to the postdoctoral level. Jennifer Ripley, Steve Sandage, Taro Kurusu, Kristin Perrone Shea, Wanda Bryant and Jeanne Face have contributed to my current theorizing. Jack Berry came to Virginia Commonwealth University (VCU) as a postdoctoral research fellow to work with me on studies related to hope-focused marital enrichment and FREE (Forgiveness and Reconciliation through Experiencing Empathy). Jack has been a competent theoretician and methodologist, a stimulus to my thinking and a friend.

Doctoral students en route to their Ph.D. have also contributed to my research and theoretical understanding. These include Terry Hight, Dawn Jones, Michelle Schmitt, Dee Drinkard and Nat Wade. In addition, eight other advanced VCU graduate students as well as counselors from Mike Flynn's Resource Guidance Services, Kent Radwani's Commonwealth Catholic Charities and Mark Yarhouse's coordinating efforts at Regent University have participated in our study of marital enrichment and have been generous with feedback on the approach within an enrichment setting. To a person, the graduate students and counselors with whom I have worked have functioned as collegial collaborators. We truly have worked together, learning from each other. I am pleased to count those collaborators as friends. Many former graduate students have remained close friends, some of them many years after they left VCU to further their professional careers.

Professional colleagues have also provided opportunities that have moved my research and thinking. In 1992 David Benner challenged me to write a version of my approach to help pastors counsel their parishioners. I was blessed to coauthor that book with my own pastor, Doug McMurry. That collaboration was extremely fruitful. Gary Collins and Tim Clinton, president and executive vice president (respectively) of the American Association of Christian Counselors, invited me to speak at many AACC regional conferences. Those conference workshops, and other invitations to speak that followed from those workshops, helped me clarify the model as I put ideas into words and reviewed the feedback from those who heard the talks.

Danny Ng in Singapore, Pam Guneratnam in Malaysia and Mervin van der Spuy in South Africa invited me to speak to professional counselors, lay counselors, university faculty and students, and media in their respective countries, which has challenged me to think more internationally and crossculturally. For example, in Malaysia, after I had spoken to a gathering of psychiatrists who were largely Muslim, a psychiatric resident in traditional Muslim garb rose to his feet when given the opportunity to ask questions. This guy was huge. When he jumped to his feet, I envisioned him leaping across the table, grabbing me by the throat and choking the "truth" out of me. His question: "I have a problem with my intrusive mother-in-law. Can you help me?" Many people share human concerns throughout the nations.

In South Africa I spoke at Durban-Westville University to practical theology pastoral graduate students. In spite of a bomb threat that caused the evacuation of campus just as I arrived (no connection, I hope), eleven graduate students and faculty met for my seminar. They challenged me to think about how my ideas applied to rural, poor, black Africans, whose marriages were under enormous strain. I have been forced to confront some of the cultural limits of face-to-face conjoint couples counseling, while being able to affirm the timeless biblical principles of promoting love, faith, work and hope in couples.

Other colleagues continue contributing to ways of helping marriages. David Larson and Michael McCullough, colleagues and friends, both at the National Institute for Healthcare Research, where I serve as a research fellow, have supported me and created numerous opportunities to investigate marriage and forgiveness within a Christian context. Les Parrott and Gary Oliver have been encouraging collaborators. Carl Rilee has been a faithful friend, supporter and colleague, as have Dale Berry and Don Danser.

I continue to be grateful to VCU and its Department of Psychology, led by

Steve Robbins, who have supported my research and writing throughout my twenty-plus years there. My colleagues on the faculty, especially Steve Danish, have challenged and supported me throughout the weeks and years.

I am particularly grateful to Sir John Templeton, Jack Templeton, Charles Harper and others at the John Templeton Foundation for having confidence to fund some of my research on forgiveness and reconciliation and on hope-focused marital enrichment with early married couples. Their encouragement, intellectual stimulation and financial beneficence have been a blessing. The financial support for my research by the General Clinical Research Center at Virginia Commonwealth University (grant NIH M01 RR00065) has also been greatly appreciated.

Two families provided a haven for writing this book. Without their aid, I couldn't have completed it. Thanks to Rena and Wayne Canipe and to Joe and Barbara Bausserman for providing places to get away from the office for extended periods to think and write.

Most of all, I acknowledge Kirby for all we have learned together in twenty-eight years of marriage; Jonathan, who has been a friend and colleague these last few years; all of my children (Christen, Steve, Jonathan, Becca and Katy Anna) for providing the opportunity to practice love; and Jesus, who has been gracious and merciful to love me and us.

Preface

I have dreamed of writing a book like this for over twenty years. When I began to counsel, I needed a brief book that succinctly explained a theoretical approach and compiled numerous practical techniques within a single resource. As I gained experience teaching, counseling and conducting research, my need did not diminish. It increased.

Over the years my theoretical approach to marital therapy has been refined in the fires of seeing clients, supervising graduate students and professional therapists, teaching courses, conducting research studies and speaking to professional therapists, researchers and pastoral counselors. Although I continue to refine the approach, as I suppose I always will, I believe you will read in this book about a powerful, yet brief, approach to helping couples. It draws flexibly and eclectically from interventions originally developed within disparate theoretical frameworks. Interventions drawn from other approaches and interventions I have developed are integrated under a unifying strategy for marriage, a focus on fostering hope in partners and a therapist's allegiance to the principles of Scripture and the working of the Holy Spirit in helping couples handle problems.

In hope-focused marriage counseling I integrate my Christianity and psychology at the level of principle. I believe the approach to be consistent with biblical Christianity as understood within the evangelical Christian tradition. However, the language of Christianity is soft-pedaled and the explicit use of Scripture is not stressed. Instead, I stress assessment before acting. Assess whether clients, Christian or not, can benefit by more (or less) explicit use of Christian concepts. Helping is effective to the extent that a therapist empathically joins troubled clients where they are rather than forces them to join the therapist where he or she is. Joining requires either assessment, luck or divine guidance. Only after empathic connection can a therapist move clients from their troubled trajectory to a new direction.

My decision to integrate faith and practice at the level of principle will probably trouble therapists who prefer a more explicit Christianity in their practice. They may criticize the approach as not Christian enough. It will also probably trouble therapists who do not share my Christian beliefs and values, who will likely criticize the approach as too Christian. However, the theory I commend to you can be readily adapted to function in either thoroughly secular or strongly religious settings with clients who are or are not Christians.

Hope-focused marriage counseling is intentionally brief. My shocking revelation about myself is this: I have always practiced relatively brief marital or couple counseling. (I used to be secretive about my addiction to brief therapy, but over time I have blurted it out.) Most couples want brief therapy. I have found brief therapy more suitable to my temperament and skills than I have found extended therapy to be.

This is not to say that all therapists should use brief therapy. I believe that there are both therapists and clients for whom brief therapy would be either a waste of time or positively harmful. My emphasis on careful assessment of clients and your own self-assessment should help you discern whether a relatively brief therapy is appropriate for you to use with a particular couple.

Hope-focused marriage counseling is truly a brief, flexible approach to helping couples that draws from both theology and psychology. I hope you will integrate it into your practice, research or ministry.

Part 1
Theory

Chapter 1

Brief Marital Counseling

You can help troubled couples quickly, compassionately and effectively. It isn't easy.

I build this approach to marital counseling on the basis of the honoring of marriage that we read throughout the Scriptures.[1] Marriage is a shadow of the relationship that we are expected to have with Jesus—permanent, loving, committed (Eph 5:32).

We will have the most success with marriage counseling[2]—indeed with all counseling and with life in general—to the extent that we develop a healing character. That healing character is the character of Christ bursting through our own personalities. We manifest that character in our relationships with our clients, coworkers, family members and peers. Christ's love shows up in our interactions with everyone. Christ's love produces faith and work, which provide the basis for hope.

WALKING THROUGH THE VALLEY OF THE SHADOW OF MARITAL DEATH
An Overview of the Book and Hope-Focused Marriage Counseling
In this book I describe a brief approach to marriage counseling called hope-focused marriage counseling. I emphasize building hope throughout the counseling. I recommend this book as a manual for treating couples with marital problems in less than ten sessions.

In the first part of the book I summarize the theory. Hope-focused marriage counseling, like other forms of counseling, is based on a good relationship. The goal of professional (and sometimes pastoral) marriage counseling is to produce stronger, less troubled marriages. I show how to use a three-part strategy to build hope through fostering motivation (willpower to change), showing couples tangible ways to change (waypower to change) and strengthening their resolve to wait on God's work in their marriage (waitpower). The strategy includes correcting weaknesses in love, faith and work. I discuss eight areas of marriage (of nine that I identify) in which problems might be concentrated.

In the second part of the book I present over one hundred in-session interventions and homework assignments to flesh out the theory. I concentrate on interventions that are physical rather than simply verbal. The physical manipulations—of objects, space or behavior—coupled with verbal processing of the interventions, are the ones that make changes seem *real* to couples. Real changes can be sensed. They are "sense-able," or sensible.

Hope-focused marriage counseling, thus, involves a blueprint for marital counseling that describes your goal (produce stronger marriages), focus (promote hope), strategy, potential target areas and interventions. I have summarized the blueprint in figure 1.1.

Hope-focused marriage counseling has been used for years with couples who have sought counseling for problems.[3] We have conducted substantial research on its use with couples who want to better their relationship (cleverly entitled hope-focused relationship enrichment).[4] I have even adapted the approach for couples who were planning marriage (would you believe, hope-focused marital preparation?) and couples who were newly married (you've probably detected the pattern). In my experience, the approach works well for each type of couple.

Effectiveness (or Ineffectiveness) of Most Marital Counseling

The goal of hope-focused marriage counseling is to strengthen marriages and reduce divorce. How effective are most approaches at accomplishing such a goal?

The longer I have practiced marriage counseling, the more I have appreciated how hard it is to do well. If you counsel couples, you may not have been very successful. Under the best conditions (that is, highly skilled and experienced counselors who follow a manual that describes an effective marriage counseling protocol), counselors have traditionally not been successful at helping troubled couples avoid divorce. *Consumer Reports,* in a survey of consumers, found that of all the problems for which people seek counseling, marriage counseling and

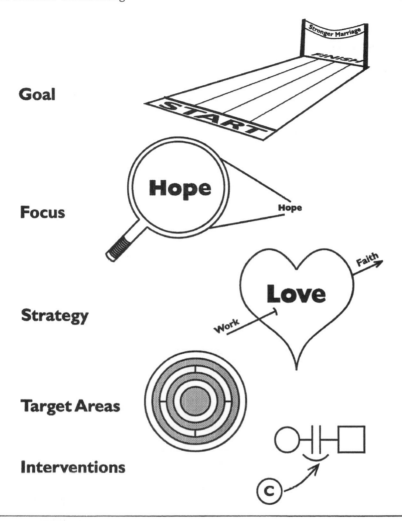

Goal

Focus

Strategy

Target Areas

Interventions

Figure 1.1. Blueprint of hope-focused marriage counseling

addictions had the least successful outcomes.[5] Only about fifty percent of the clients who seek professional counseling for their troubled marriages emerge with well-functioning marriages that last over three years. That fifty-percent figure is about the same as Neil S. Jacobson reported for behavioral therapy and about the same as others have reported for other types of marriage counseling approaches.[6] For counselors who are not experienced, well trained or skilled, the outcomes are worse. If some are worse, though, that suggests that some counselors have better outcomes. I want you to be one of those.

Marriage counseling is tough to do. If you are discouraged with your results, you are not alone. Most counselors dread dealing with troubled marriages even though troubled marriages often form the majority of their caseload.

Is the Goal I Stated Appropriate?

The goal of strengthening marriages and preventing divorce is difficult for any approach to achieve. Is the goal even appropriate for marriage counseling?

Professional marital counseling is different from (a) lay or friendship helping, (b) pastor-provided counseling within a congregational context and perhaps (c) professional pastoral counseling. The major difference is in the couple's goals. When a couple seeks help, they do so within a context, which implies specific expectations. From a friend or lay counselor, couples expect understanding, support and perhaps uncomplicated advice. From a pastor, couples expect Christian-oriented advice and counsel. From a professional counselor, whether explicitly Christian or not, couples primarily seek aid with the presenting problem. The professional counselor is obligated, within the bounds of morality and ethics, to embrace as his or her number one priority to help strengthen the couple's marriage (if that is what they want).

An explicitly Christian counselor might hold a secondary goal of strengthening the partner's faith or promoting more spiritual intimacy. However, clients who pay for professional marital counseling have a right to expect that the professional counselor's first goal concerns promoting stronger, less disturbed marriages (unless an explicit agreement is made to prioritize other goals ahead of that goal).

The professional pastoral counselor, as opposed to a congregational pastor who counsels, has the role with the most ambiguous expectations. This counselor is both a professional counselor and a member of the clergy. Which goal should take precedence? As an outsider to that profession, I do not presume to provide a definitive answer. I believe that pastoral counselors should provide a full a priori disclosure of their goals to the clients.

Earlier, I presumed one side of a continuing debate in the field of marital counseling.[7] I defined the goal of marital counseling as bettering the marriage. Some marital counselors would disagree. They define the married individuals as co-clients. Their goal is to help each partner develop optimally. In such an approach, divorce might be seen as a successful outcome of marital counseling if the counselor deemed it best for both individuals (or perhaps either individual). This makes the evaluation of the effectiveness of marital counseling almost impossible to determine, given the three participants (husband, wife and counselor). For example, if one partner adamantly wants divorce and the other does not, then can one determine whether counseling has succeeded, regardless of outcome?

However, I believe that divorce is always considered a failure of marital counseling. Of course, that does not mean that maintaining an intact marriage is the most important consideration in counseling. The counselor is first responsible to maintain the physical safety of the partners. So if the husband is physically abusing the wife and she is threatening to shoot him, the wise counselor might recommend separation; this would be considered a failure to strengthen the marriage and thus be a failure of marital counseling. Some might even recommend divorce; this would also be considered a failure of marital counseling.

Conjoint Marital Counseling: The Preferred Approach

The success rate for marital counseling is better (that is, improved marriage and less chance of divorce) if the couple comes to counseling together than if partners do not come at all, do not come together or seek counseling individually.[8] Couples do not have to come to counseling together. Good counseling can occur even if only one partner comes, if that person really wants to improve the marriage. If both attend counseling but only one wants to improve the marriage, success is possible. The best results occur if both partners attend counseling and if both partners are interested and involved in improving the marriage.

Hope-Starved Marriages

Few couples enter counseling with both partners fired up and eager to work. Wise counselors do not count on seeing a full caseload of highly motivated clients. Nor do wise counselors carp because their clients aren't motivated to work. Usually, both partners are discouraged and demoralized. They lack hope. One or both may be going through the motions of counseling simply to say that they have tried everything prior to divorcing. You must actively engage the partners in working on their marriage. That depends on your character, the relationship you can form with the partners and the interactions you have with the partners.

You must work the relationship magic fast. Hope-focused marriage counseling is one long assessment session plus five to eight intervention sessions. For many people who seek marital counseling, those few sessions will be enough to turn them around and send them in a more positive direction. For some clients, sadly, five to eight sessions won't begin to affect their marriage.

MARITAL COUNSELING: BRIEF OR BRIEFER

Brief marital counseling can be highly effective. Weigh carefully all the important factors before deciding whether to use brief counseling and if so how long it should be.

Who Benefits from Brief Therapies?

People who benefit from brief marital counseling aren't easy to distinguish from those who require longer marital counseling. Severity of the marital problems is not the distinguishing characteristic.[9] Some couples with very disturbed marriages benefit quickly, while less-troubled couples resist changes.

Initial willingness to work on the marriage is important.[10] However, some couples come to counseling with their heels dug in, fighting change with each step; and yet, after a good, hope-inspiring first session, they throw themselves into counseling wholeheartedly. Others seem hopeful at first, but after a few sessions, hope fizzles, sputters and finally goes *pffft*.

People's assumptions about counseling predispose some clients to be able to benefit from a few sessions and cause others to require longer. When people assume that counseling must be long, arduous and psychologically painful, they often have a hard time shifting gears. When people come to counseling seeking quick change and expecting it, they often find it.[11]

Thinking Brief

Managed mental health care has changed the expectations for almost all types of counseling. Most modern psychotherapies last less than ten sessions, and virtually all last less than a half year.[12]

Marital counseling is usually not covered under insurance plans, so most people who seek marital counseling must pay for it. Most are appalled at the cost. While they might have thought nothing of paying $10,000 or more for a wedding, they are often reluctant to spend about $800 (that is, $200 for a thorough assessment and eight sessions at $75 per session) on counseling that might help a derailed marriage headed for divorce get back on track.

Most marital counselors have responded to the pressure for briefer marital counseling, but generally this has meant counseling as usual, merely less of it. In fact, briefer counseling requires different therapeutic skills and a different mindset on the part of the counselor and clients if it is to succeed.[13]

A few counselors have designed intentionally brief (or briefer) therapies.[14] For example, using a book summarizing eight Christian marital therapies,[15] Jennifer Ripley and I found that most counselors aimed at between six and fifteen sessions for marital counseling with a motivated couple having quite a few marital troubles.[16]

Not Merely Time

The most common misconception about brief marital counseling is that the major difference between it and traditional marital counseling is the duration of the counseling. Brief counseling is briefer (muffled gasp of surprise) than the more traditional marital counseling.[17] Yet the major difference between the two approaches is that in traditional marital counseling most of the change was expected during treatment. Once treatment stopped, the improvements in the marriage either maintained or deteriorated slightly, sometimes substantially. In hope-focused marital counseling, the counselor aims to create a turning point in the couple's life together—one that will lead to continued improvement after the end of counseling.

Hope-focused marriage counseling seeks to arouse hope in couples. Thus, aim at creating the desire in clients to try to change, arming clients with concrete ways of changing and fortifying clients with a sense of eager waiting for change. Demonstrate to the clients that they can change using the ways they learn in counseling and thus give them the desire to employ those ways after marital counseling ceases. Help them ignore some of the inevitable failures that will occur while new patterns of marriage are practiced.

Does Brief Marital Counseling Change the Causes of Marital Discord?

Some critics of brief marital counseling worry that because it takes fewer than ten sessions, it can't address the deep causes of marital problems.[18] These critics' underlying assumption is that important and lasting change can only occur over a long period of time. That assumption is insupportable.[19]

Much change occurs briefly. Jesus healed numerous people of physical ailments in encounters that lasted only minutes. Peter spoke at Pentecost and over a thousand were converted soon after his brief speech. Paul interacted with people who were ailing physically and spiritually, and many were quickly healed.

True, in all these cases one change did not bring the people into total maturity. Jesus devoted three years to training his disciples. Peter pastored the church at Jerusalem for many years. Paul stayed in various cities to train the new converts. Yet real and lasting change occurred in brief encounters when God was at work in people's lives. Brief encounters launched a rocket ship of change that kept accelerating even after the launching.

My tennis serve was forever altered when one of my boyhood heroes, Sammy Darden, captain of the University of Tennessee tennis team, saw me (then a high-school junior) practicing my serve at a local park. Sammy demonstrated the American twist serve. He didn't delve into my past behavioral repertoire, my unconscious motivations or my cognitive structures that prevented me from hitting a twist serve. He demonstrated. I observed. When Sammy left the park that day, my serve was little different than it had been before he came, but my direction was different. I had a strategy for hitting my serve, and I had hope. I contend that promoting hope in couples and teaching the strategy of faith working through love will repair the root causes of marital problems.

Is Hope-Focused Marital Counseling Consistent with Scripture?

Scripture is not a counseling manual. Counseling is a recent description of ways to help people. As far as I can tell, there is no remote analogue to marital counseling within Scripture. That is, there are no cases in which a person set out to help a couple with a troubled marriage restore their marital relationship. Thus, Scripture can shed little light on the methods of modern marital counseling. However, we can evaluate whether any type of help is consistent with principles of Scripture. I believe that hope-focused marriage counseling is consistent with Scripture.

☐ It focuses on love, faith and work (Gal 6:5).

☐ It promotes marital commitment, which is important because the marital bond is used often as a metaphor for our relationship with Christ (Jer 31:32; Hos 2:16; 3:1; 1 Cor 6:16-17; Eph 5:25-33).

☐ It promotes harmony and reconciliation between people who are in conflict (Mt 5:9).

☐ It promotes love between Christians (Rom 12:9-21; 1 Cor 13; Eph 4:22—5:2).

☐ It uses methods of harmonious relationships that are emphasized throughout Scripture, in such books as Psalms, Proverbs and Song of Songs, and by such people as Jesus, Paul, Peter and others.

☐ It promotes covenantal commitment: the Abrahamic covenant (Gen 15:9-11, 17-18), the new covenant in Jesus' blood (Lk 22:20) and the marriage covenant (Mal 2:14; Mt 19:4-6).

What Are the Implications of Brief Marital Counseling for Practice?

Hope-focused marital counseling has a number of characteristics different from traditional marital counseling.

☐ The relationship between counselor and clients is vital. Relationship is at the center of the Godhead in the Trinity. People were created to live in relationships (Gen 2:18). Problems occur in relationships (Jas 5:14). Relationships provide a powerful mechanism for healing of problems (Jas 5:16; Heb 10:25). In hope-focused marriage counseling a strong relationship between counselor and couple must be formed within the first session to maximize change. In traditional counseling the demands for quick relationship development are not as stringent.

☐ Hope-focused marriage counseling needs to employ a strategy (faith, work and love) that is repeated frequently enough so that couples can learn easily.

☐ The emphasis is on rekindled hope rather than feeling perfectly happy now. That implies that the counselor assumes throughout counseling that the couple will continue to change their behavior even after counseling has ended. Homework is emphasized, which implies that the counselor is not the main change agent. Rather, God helps the couple change more at home than within sessions.

☐ Interventions should be focused and choreographed toward promoting the strategy of faith working through love. Every intervention should promote that strategy.

☐ Every intervention should promote hope in the couple. In traditional marital counseling, interventions are less focused and address more objectives. There is more tolerance for getting off track.

☐ Interventions should be active and involve observable behavior, emotion or effects. This emphasis on concrete observable interventions promotes powerful lasting change. In traditional marital counseling fewer techniques must be active and observable. Not every intervention in traditional marital counseling needs to make quite the impact of an intervention in hope-focused marriage counseling.

☐ Couples need to understand how interventions affect their love, faith, work and hope. Couples should not simply be manipulated into changing. The knowledge of the broader base behind change will affect the clients' motivation to apply the change efforts after counseling has terminated. In some traditional marital counseling approaches, many interventions (for example, reframing or paradoxical interventions) may be made without the clients' understanding the reason for the intervention.[20] Overall, clients cooperate better if they understand how interventions contribute to their goals.[21]

What Are the Major Differences Between My Previous Traditional Approach and the New Approach?

In 1989 I recommended a more traditional marital counseling, though it was briefer than most traditional approaches to marital counseling.[22] Table 1.1 summarizes some differences between that approach and the present approach. The 1989 approach drew eclectically from more sources (especially cognitive and family systems approaches) and provided a wider range of theoretical exposition and a critique of various theories. Hope-focused marriage counseling is more integrated, more focused, briefer and somewhat more explicit. Hope-focused marriage counseling will appeal more to counselors who want to intervene quicker but are satisfied with seeing less change during the time that the couple are in counseling. The 1989 approach will appeal to counselors whose

Area	Marriage Counseling: A Christian Approach	Hope-Focused Marriage Counseling
Theory	Eclectic: heavily influenced by cognitive-behavioral marital therapy, developmental life-transition theory	Eclectic: more integrated but less comprehensive; emphasizes a goal of producing hope and a strategy of increasing love, work and faith
Areas of marriage	intimacy communication conflict management hurt-blame-sin	core vision central values confession and forgiveness communication conflict resolution cognition closeness complicating problems commitment
Duration	2 assessment, 1 feedback, 6-12 interventions	1 assessment, 5-8 interventions
Assessment	2 assessment sessions, 1 feedback session	1 assessment session not as thorough as the two sessions could be
Interventions	Over 50, worked into the text within chapters on the areas of marriage that interventions address	Over 100, little overlap with the previous book; structured according to which of the areas of marriage it addresses; tied to producing hope and to which portion of the strategy it addresses
Analysis of other marital approaches	50-page appendix summarizing and critiquing major approaches to marital counseling	Minimal
Objective	Change within the sessions; maintenance terminates change	Initiate a fundamental change in direction in marriage, which will continue to improve
Target counselors	Professional therapists, therapists in training	Professional therapists, counselors, pastoral counselors, pastors who counsel, counselors in training, researchers

Table 1.1. Comparison of *Marriage Counseling* (1989) and *Hope-Focused Marriage Counseling* (1999)

theoretical orientation is closer to family systems approaches. The 1989 approach is appropriate for professional counseling; the hope-focused marriage counseling approach is also appropriate for professional counseling but is more easily adapted for use by pastoral counselors and pastors who counsel.

I hypothesize that hope-focused marriage counseling will produce a faster onset of change, more change by the ninth session (which is the end of most hope-focused marriage counseling), less change by the end of the fifteenth session (which is the end of most traditional Christian marital counseling) and equal change by six months after initiating counseling. Controlled studies are needed to investigate whether these hypotheses are accurate. (For graduate students and faculty members, there should be some good theses and dissertations in testing these assertions.)

Hope-focused marriage counseling will appeal more to counselors who enjoy and do well at brief approaches. It will also appeal to counselors who do not have the time or resources to devote to more traditional marital counseling. In addition it will appeal to pastors who want to adapt a professional model of marital counseling to their pastoral marital counseling. I believe it will strengthen (eventually) the scientific basis for Christian approaches to marital counseling.[23]

SUMMARY

Hope-focused marriage counseling is not merely less of a good thing. Like most brief counseling, it is a new way of conceptualizing marital counseling, its purposes and its methods. It requires quick relationship formation, a powerful overarching strategy, dynamic active methods that make change apparent and a focus on the hope of continued improvement. You can apply hope-focused marriage counseling by using this book as an intervention guide that informs your clinical judgment. I suspect you are wondering what happens in hope-focused marriage counseling. In the following chapter I sketch an outline of the counseling; in subsequent chapters we will fill that in.

Chapter 2

Bird's-Eye View of Hope-Focused Marriage Counseling

Before you get into the nitty-gritty of doing hope-focused marriage counseling, you need a mental map of the territory. So let's fly over the land and see what the counseling is all about. Hope-focused marriage counseling has six major aspects:

☐ Therapeutic relationship: The key to effective counseling

☐ Goal: To produce stronger, less-troubled marriages

☐ Focus: To promote hope

☐ Strategy: To correct weaknesses in valuing love, faith and work

☐ Target for change: Based on assessment, selected from nine areas of marriage

☐ Repertoire of interventions: Sensible, powerful, planned interventions that are employed flexibly

This chapter presents general guidelines for each aspect of conducting the counseling. Chapter three discusses the strategy in detail; chapter four takes up the target areas; and part two describes the interventions.

FORMING AND MAINTAINING A GOOD RELATIONSHIP WITH EACH PARTNER

Relationship is the key to effective counseling. If the counselor does not have a good relationship with each partner, counseling will not progress well. The foundation of counseling is not a strategy or interventions: It is the human relationships between a counselor and two people. Pay special attention to forming and maintaining a good relationship with each partner.

All counselors are not equally skillful nor effective. Skillful counselors have been found to be more effective.[1] But what do more skillful counselors do better than less skillful counselors? Skillful counselors[2]

☐ establish good relationships

☐ empathize with their clients

☐ make clients feel as if the counselor understands them and their problems

☐ inspire confidence in their clients

☐ provide structure without seeming to be authoritarian

☐ motivate clients to work toward change

☐ communicate clearly

☐ discern partners' agendas and harmonize them with a therapeutic agenda

☐ convey an impression that they are expert, attractive and trustworthy without being aloof and untouchable (Note: *Attractive* refers to a winsome personality, not physical beauty)

☐ appear natural and relaxed in providing activities for clients to try in-session and out-of-session

In addition, the counselor in hope-focused marriage counseling must have these skills: to form a positive working alliance *quickly,* to make a *rapid* assessment, to focus and keep the session on task while valuing each partner's expression of thoughts and feelings, to convey *love* (that you value both partners) and to *motivate and inspire* (that is, instill hope) without coming across like an insincere cheerleader.

The skill level of the counselor is crucial in this and any counseling. I hypothesize that failure to exhibit certain skills will result in failure of the counseling.

☐ If the counselor does not demonstrate a warm, competent, friendly demeanor to the clients and if the counselor does not engage the clients within two sessions, then counseling will fail.

☐ If clients miss one of the first four sessions, counseling has a poor prognosis. If clients miss (and have to reschedule) two or more sessions, regardless of reason, then counseling will fail.

☐ If the counselor senses that counseling is not going well and fails to be flexible and change, then counseling will fail.

☐ If clients do not perceive that counseling focuses on the problem that they present and if the counselor does not engage them in an effort to solve that problem, then counseling will fail.

❑ If the counselor does not empathize with the clients and let them know unambiguously that the counselor not only understands their specific problem but also cares about each of them as a person, then counseling will fail.

It stands to reason, then, that the effective counselor will be warm, friendly, empathic, flexible, focused and understanding.

GOAL: BETTER MARRIAGE, LESS DIVORCE

Hope-focused marriage counseling aims to produce stronger, less troubled marriages. That goal might be at odds with the goal of individual partners, who often covertly want vindication more than they want reconciliation. That goal might also be at odds with a partner's safety, in which case the wise counselor protects people's safety as a first ethical responsibility. That goal might rise and fall in salience depending on the setting (for example, pastor's office versus counseling office) or circumstance (for example, one partner having severe psychological difficulty or conversation focused on spiritual growth). In general, though, attaining the goal of stronger marriages will be the main measure of the effectiveness of hope-focused marriage counseling.

Specifically, most couples enter marital counseling scoring less than 90 on Spanier's Dyadic Adjustment Scale (DAS), which is considered to be the clinical cut-off for clinical marital distress.[3] One measurable goal is to raise each partner's DAS score to 90 or above. Furthermore, scores of 90 or above should be expected at follow-up measurements of one year or more.[4]

Specifically, too, about half of the couples who seek counseling ultimately divorce.[5] Thus, a second measure of the success of hope-focused marriage counseling would be to maintain a divorce rate of less than fifty percent at all subsequent follow-up periods up to five years postcounseling. Such an outcome would be similar to the effectiveness of other marital therapies.

FOCUS: PROMOTE HOPE

Hope-focused marriage counseling is focused on building hope. Working on the marriage requires hope. Hope provides the motivation to work. This hope can be explained in a three-part theory: willpower, waypower and waitpower. C. R. Snyder, in the *Psychology of Hope*, says that[6]

Hope = Mental Willpower + Waypower to Reach Goals

A person may have good communication skills, excellent coping skills and adequate knowledge, and be equipped in every way to have an excellent marriage (that is, the person has lots of waypower to reach goals), yet he or she might have little hope because he or she has become depressed. Depression is a sense of hopelessness, helplessness and powerlessness that saps mental willpower. Waypower without willpower spells no hope.

On the other hand, a person might have all the willpower in the world to make an excellent marriage, but might not know how to act, or might know but not have the skill. Willpower without waypower also spells no hope.

Beyond Snyder's approach to hope, though, is another message of hope. Hope is more than conquering obstacles. As Christian philosopher and theologian Gabriel Marcel has argued, hope involves perseverance.[7] Hope involves the certitude that God is with us *through* difficult circumstances, even when he has not made a way *around* those circumstances. Like Daniel's three Israelite friends, Someone walks through the furnace with us. Like the Israelites in captivity in Egypt, Someone works hand in hand with us. Like Stephen amid the stones of his enemies, we see that Someone. Hope involves a motivation to endure when we cannot change circumstances. Hope involves a vision of a way through suffering: willpower and waypower to endure, with the help of the Triune God. Hope is crucial to counseling.

Hope	=	Willpower to change	+	Waypower to change	+	Waitpower even if change is not happening

God is the author of hope. He builds both mental willpower and waypower. He provides waitpower. He is the source of all power—including the power to make and hold together a good marriage.

Samuel Johnson said, "The human mind moves not from pleasure to pleasure but from hope to hope." People were created for hope. We are fish out of water.[8] We are homesick for Eden.[9] Marital partners, despite their shared misery, have been designed for hope. That is the spark that the marital counselor must fan into flame.

As therapies have become briefer, they have become more focused, usually zooming in on one thing. Other aspects of the person's experience are not ignored, but less attention is paid to other areas. For instance, the counseling performed by the Mental Research Institute (MRI) in Palo Alto has become known as problem-focused counseling because it assumes that people embroil themselves in problem cycles, which make their difficulties worse and worse as they try to deal with the problem.[10] So MRI counselors focus on problem cycles. Solution-focused counselors pursue solutions to the problems with unrelenting zeal.[11] Emotionally focused counselors give primacy to emotional experience rather than to cognition or behavior.[12] In contrast to problem focus, solution focus or emotion focus, hope-focused marriage counseling targets hope through increasing love, faith and work. It attempts intentionally to stimulate hope. Whereas the other focused approaches undoubtedly stimulate hope in the couples they treat, stimulating hope is not as important to them.

STRATEGY: CORRECT WEAKNESSES IN LOVE, FAITH AND WORK

I do not suggest that a marital counseling room is like a battlefield. However, one of the graduate students in our program (not using hope-focused marriage counseling, I must add) said that he became convinced he needed to learn more about marital counseling when, in the final session of a year of marital counseling, the wife arose, walked across the room and hit her husband in the face. Then she strode out. It seemed a rather dramatic way to end counseling, but it was a clear communication to all that marital counseling had not been exactly successful.

Sometimes I have felt almost like I needed to don armor to deal with marital conflict. In fact, now that I think about it marital counseling *is* a lot like a battle.

A strategy is a counselor's battle plan. A model of counseling provides an understanding about how the strategy will be employed within different stages of the "battle" of counseling.

The Strategy

The strategy I use is applying *faith working through love*.[13] This strategy is God's pattern for helping people mature. In Galatians 5:5-6 Paul says, "But by faith we eagerly await through the Spirit the righteousness for which we hope. For in Christ Jesus neither circumcision nor uncircumcision has any value. The only thing that counts is faith expressing itself through love." The Revised Standard Version says "faith working through love."

☐ Faith working through love is prescriptive for good marital relationships (as it is of all mutual discipleship relationships).

☐ Weaknesses in love, faith or work (or combinations of the three) are seen as the general cause of marital problems.

☐ Strengthening weaknesses in love, faith or work (or combinations) is seen as the general strategic solution to marital problems.

Whether people understand faith working through love as motivated by

Christian values and beliefs or as simply an expression of their own relationship goals, they can strengthen their marriage to the extent that they use the strategy.

Definitions

Love is a willingness to value and to avoid devaluing people that springs from a caring, other-focused heart. The marital counselor wants to promote agape love. The basic task in a marriage is for spouses consistently to love each other, which will build trust and security and will provide a basis for solving practical problems.

Love is evident in all aspects of good marriages. In establishing a balance of intimacy and privacy, communicating, resolving differences, confessing their failings and forgiving the partner's transgressions, adhering to a lifelong commitment to marriage and working to make the marriage better, both partners seek to value each other and never devalue or put down each other. Love is the primary task of marriage.

Couples in different circumstances practice love differently. The newly wedded couple, with stars in their eyes, find that being willing to value and unwilling to devalue each other flows naturally from the heart. In a different way the loving older couple, married fifty wonderful years, find that being willing to value is a habit that reflects a heart of love without their even thinking about it. The couple who have a troubled marriage, though, must take a third pathway to a loving heart. They must put on love. They must *consciously* will to value their partner even when they do not feel like it. They must consciously will not to devalue their partner even when they feel the urge to bite back when gnawed at by being criticized or ignored. None of these pathways to love is the only right one. Each couple must use the pathway that fits their circumstances.

Faith is believing that things hoped for will come about. "Now faith is being sure of what we hope for and certain of what we do not see" (Heb. 11:1). Maritally distressed couples usually desperately hope for a healed marriage. They cannot "see" that healed marriage. The fog of rage, the rain of tears, the snowy bitter cold of unforgiveness blind them to a positive future. Sometimes they dare not admit hope, lest they set themselves up for disappointment. Yet hope simmers within.

Faith always has an object. In marriage, especially troubled marriage, faith has multiple objects. Faith involves trust in the character of a person. Faith may be faith in God through knowledge of his son Jesus. It may be faith in God through the witness of the character of the Holy Spirit. On a different level, faith involves a trust in the partner. When couples come to counseling for marital troubles, they usually have little faith in their partner. They have focused on the negative behavior, thoughts and interactions of their partner, and trust has evaporated.

Faith in a person is based on what a person considers sufficient evidence to justify the faith.[14] That is true when one becomes a Christian. One accumulates enough evidence and changes his or her mind, deciding to trust Jesus as Savior. Getting married is also based on sufficient evidence to merit faith in the partner. Partners interact until they believe that they have accumulated enough evidence to become engaged. Declaring a marriage a "troubled marriage" is similarly a statement of faith. A partner's conclusion that the marriage is troubled depends on the amount of evidence. This evidence that the marriage is troubled accumulates until one or both partners stumble over a threshold and declare the marriage in trouble.[15]

In the same way, believing that a marriage can be healed is a statement of faith, which is also based on evidence that partners accumulate. The marital counselor injects faith into a situation that marriage partners see—on the outside—as hopeless. By maintaining an attitude of faith and by working with the couple through love, the marital counselor can help build the conviction of things not seen. Partners who believe their marriage is troubled focus on the negative, overlooking positive interactions and qualities of their partners. You can help rebuild faith in the partner by calling systematic attention to the positive behavior of the partner, the positive interactions that the partners are having and the positive aspects of each partner's character.

As a marital counselor, provide evidence that can form a new foundation of faith in marriage. Use interventions that make love visible to the partners. Help partners provide undeniable evidence of love. Eventually, in successful counseling, the light bulb comes on, and partners reacquire faith that the marriage can be healed.

Faith not only involves belief that the marriage can be healed, but it also involves some degree of confidence that *counseling can help* partners improve their marriage. Many couples are so dejected and dispirited with their marriage that they see counseling as merely the last futile step before they plunge headlong into inevitable divorce. Counseling, they think, may simply grease the slope to divorce. Help them put on the brakes and lean away from the brink. That requires the partners to change their belief about the likely effectiveness of counseling.

Faith requires that partners believe that their effort to do tasks at home will improve marriage. Troubled partners believe that they have tried everything to improve their marriage. *Why bother trying something else?* they wonder. Help clients gain confidence that their actions at home can improve their marriage.

For explicitly Christian couples, faith connotes a faith in God. Their faith in God's sovereignty and his active intervention in their lives is a powerful healing aspect of their relationship. Help partners experience the working of the living God.

Faith depends on a history of fulfilled promises. Troubled marriages have few recently fulfilled promises. Where do they find the history of fulfilled promises from which they can draw faith? They can draw on early times in their marriages, when things were good. They can draw on the daily interactions, even in the dark times, when positive things do happen but get overlooked or explained away. Yet you, the counselor, can see the positive when it happens, and you can help build faith by focusing the partners' attention on those positive experiences that reveal the good intentions and good character of the partner. Look for exceptions to the negative. They will not be as hard to find as the partners think they will be.

Be realistic. Don't manufacture positive aspects of the marriage that do not exist. That will undermine the couple's confidence in you. Instead, merely see what the troubled couple cannot see through their dark glasses.

Work is energetic effort. One important principle of life is the second law of thermodynamics: unless energy (or work) is added to a system, the system will become more disorderly. An untended garden grows weeds, not vegetables.

Maintaining a good marriage, improving a marriage and solving problems in a marriage require that the partners exert effort, that they work on the marriage. Solving problems in marriage through marital counseling requires that the couple work on the tasks that the counselor assigns, both within the counseling hour and particularly between sessions. Inspire the couple to perspire to achieve what they aspire to. You cannot browbeat or coerce them into a work ethic.

Kingdom living requires love, faith and work. Hope-focused marital counselors should never consider themselves marital technicians or problem-solvers. Counselors are ministers of love. As such, they are part of the body of Christ. It is through his body that Jesus Christ moves people into closer relationship with God the Father. That is a high calling.

Teaching and Using a Strategy

If you have a general plan for counseling, you will be more likely to get that plan across to the clients. If you don't have a plan, you will leave clients confused. Interventions will be helter-skelter, or will appear that way to the clients.

In hope-focused marriage counseling, you have a strategy to guide your own behavior. At times, most counselors become exasperated with some of their clients. It is difficult not to devalue those clients in our minds or to colleagues. Yet love demands continual valuing. Love demands faith that the Lord can work—with us or apart from us. Love demands our highest effort. Convey the strategy to the clients. Whether you are training the couple in communication, trying to help them increase their intimacy, helping with sexual functioning or promoting confession and forgiveness, always work to build love, faith and work— especially love.

In hope-focused marriage counseling, teach clients a strategy by which to live. If you've ever gone through counseling, you know that it can at times be confusing. You might wonder what the counselor is up to and what—if anything—you are expected to retain from all the exploration, effort and pain you are going through. When the counselor gives clients a clear strategy, clients can understand what the counselor is doing in context and can know what is important and what isn't. That helps counseling take place more efficiently and more effectively, and it helps the clients participate most actively in their counseling. A clear strategy mobilizes the clients' resources to achieve their common objectives.

Promote love, faith and work to help the couple or individual with marital problems solve those problems. Do this by (1) *direct teaching,* (2) *training* the couple in applying faith working through love, (3) *stimulating practice* at forgiving the spouse for perceived wrongs, (4) *helping spouses forgive* each other, parents and others in their past for contributing to the roots of relationship problems, (5) *modeling* faith working through love and (6) *motivating* couples to work in hope, have faith and love each other.

TARGET: AREAS OF CHANGE

Hope-focused marital counselors have plans for conducting counseling. In fact, when I supervise trainees, I require each trainee to formulate a written plan prior to each session. Of course, clients don't read the counselor's treatment plan, so they persist in arriving at counseling with their own agenda.

Make each plan based on a thorough assessment of the couple. Tailor plans to the stage of counseling: encounter, engagement and disengagement. Use strategically informed tactics for conducting each session. Deal differently with couples conjointly or partners individually.

Assess and Give Feedback

To treat the clients effectively, you must know what is wrong. That involves knowing what the clients think is wrong, but it also involves going beyond the understanding of the clients—who often understand the problems as being due primarily to the spouse's behavior—and developing a larger perspective. Thus your assessment will involve

☐ self-reports of each partner

☐ results of written instruments

☐ tape recordings of their conversations

☐ your clinical observations

Assessment helps you and the clients know better what is going on. You will share the results of the assessments with your clients, and that sharing will empower your conceptualization because the results of assessment are objective. Do not skimp on assessment: it is an integral part of treatment.

Your assessment should consider nine areas of married life:[16]

☐ central values and beliefs

☐ core vision of the marriage

☐ confession and forgiveness

☐ communication

☐ conflict resolution

☐ cognition about the marriage

☐ closeness (intimacy, coaction, distance)

☐ complicating problems (such as abuse, alcohol or drug dependence, or mental health problems)

☐ commitment (including contentment with the marriage and compounding investments in the marriage compared with contentment with alternatives to the marriage such as other relationships, jobs, children, hobbies, friends)

I arrayed the areas like a target (see figure 2.1) with central values in the bullseye and commitment as the outer ring. I will discuss the areas of change in detail in chapter three.

The assessment culminates in an assessment report to the couple. That report includes a formulation of the problem as being due to weaknesses in love, faith and work in each of the nine areas above *that seem relevant for the couple* and a recommendation of the work needed to resolve the problems. The assessment

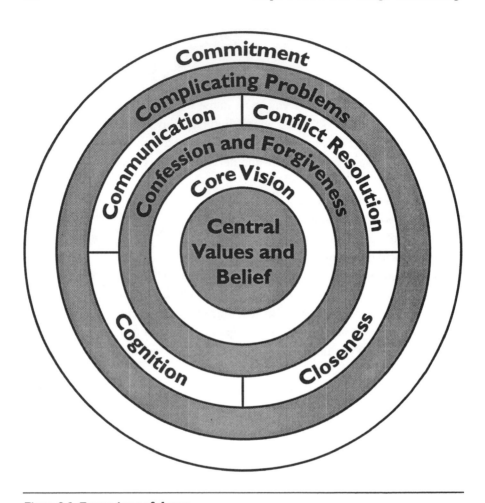

Figure 2.1. Target: Areas of change

report should mention the need for new hope. To begin to rebuild the mutual faith of the partners in each other's character, also include a summary of the marriage's strengths and weaknesses in equal emphasis.

INTERVENTIONS: PLANNING SENSIBLE COUNSELING

Planning a course of counseling for a couple involves following a set of basic principles, weighing a number of factors and taking at least several steps.

Making Change Sensible

You can promote hope more by showing the partners that change is possible than by telling couples to have hope. I call my approach *sensible* because I encourage interventions that are easily able to be sensed. They appeal to all the partners' senses, not just the sense of hearing.

Thus I use active strategies, written assessments and videotapes to provide information. Each intervention provides evidence that is more tangible than mere talk. When couples make concrete, active, observable changes, they demonstrate to themselves that they are indeed changing. That physical demonstration of change conveys hope when there was no hope before.

Planning Different Actions in Different Stages of Counseling

Hope-focused marriage counseling occurs in three stages: encounter, engagement and disengagement.17 (See figure 2.2.) Encounter includes two major tasks: (a) establishing and maintaining a working relationship in which counseling is initiated and structured and the marital counselor joins the partner or

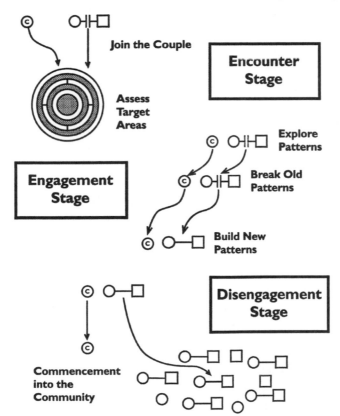

Figure 2.2. Actions in each stage of hope-focused marriage counseling

couple to attempt to solve the marriage problem and (b) assessing the appropriate targets for change. In each task, show that you value both partners and attempt to promote more valuing love between them.

Engagement is where most of the action is. Explore feelings, thoughts and behaviors in past relationships and in the present relationship. Help couples break negative patterns. Promote healing of memories and of current relationships. Build new patterns of acting, thinking and feeling both toward the partner and toward God. Engagement focuses the partner's or couple's efforts in changing their (a) values or beliefs about marriage and each other, (b) closeness, (c) communication, (d) conflict resolution strategies, (e) cognition about the marriage (that is, their tendency to blame each other and God), (f) confession and forgiveness, (g) complicating problems or (h) commitment. In each area of their marriage, help partners devalue the spouse less and value the spouse more.

In disengagement, consolidate changes within the marriage. In addition, because partners live in communities of faith and friendship, help partners remain involved in those communities so they will continue to feel valued.

Employing Strategically Informed Tactics

Always holding your overall strategy in mind, develop tactics for every counseling session. Tailor your treatment to each couple. In general, a typical session will follow this pattern:

□ Discuss homework. Find out what worked. If it didn't work, why not? If they didn't do it, why not and how could they succeed at doing it?

□ Employ new interventions (about thirty to forty minutes). Deal with a significant problem and make sure the climate of the session remains hopeful to the extent you can engender hope.

□ Recapitulate the learning that occurred during the session.

□ Assign specific homework for the coming interval between sessions and explain it clearly. Deal with any objections the couple has to the homework so you can agree on something that is likely to work.

Tailoring Treatment to Fit Clients

People respond best to tailor-made treatments. Tailoring a treatment directly to each couple respects and values them. Listening to the couple also values them. If they do not feel that you value them, your strategy of promoting love, faith and work will be undermined. They will view you as hypocritical. You must convey to the couple that you value them, and tailoring treatment to them is essential in doing so.

Hope-focused marriage counseling is based on various interventions that address nine common problems.[18] Select the interventions that are precisely appropriate for each particular couple. Adapt each intervention so that it fits each couple. Select homework that is tailored to each couple. Standardization of treatment is blended with individualized treatment.[19]

Setting Time Limits

Hope-focused marriage counseling is limited in time. Never decide prior to the end of the first session (the assessment) how many sessions you will recommend. Base your decision on your assessment. Frame your recommendation as tentative, saying that at the end of x sessions you will reevaluate in collaboration with the couple how they are doing at that time and what they would like to do then.

As a rule of thumb, prescribe a minimum of five sessions (assessment plus four) and about one additional session of counseling for every year (or substantial portion of a year) over one year that the problems have been severe. Use nine sessions as a maximum. For example, if a couple has had serious problems for less than one year, prescribe five sessions. For one and one-half years of serious problems, prescribe six sessions. For more than four years of serious problems, prescribe the maximum of nine. Like all these guidelines, this is not a hard and fast rule.

Once you make a recommendation, stick with that plan until those contracted-for sessions are complete. Having a time limit focuses the couple's energy. They know the target date and will exert more effort as the date to end approaches. Sessions do not need to be evenly spaced. In fact, the first two or three might be less than a week apart to deal with a crisis. The last two might be a couple of weeks apart. Don't think that counseling will be over just because you have "terminated." People will often return for additional help if you leave open the door.

You might wonder, *What can be done with a marriage in less than ten sessions?* You might even be thinking, *Nothing of consequence!* Some counselors think of counseling as curing people or as making people problem-free. Those counselors generally opt for long-term, time-unlimited approaches. Hope-focused marriage counseling does not hold this view. It adopts two goals of counseling: to solve problems and to help couples grow.

However, the goal of counseling cannot be to eliminate all problems. In fact, I don't believe it is possible to eliminate all problems. People will always have problems. When they end counseling they will still have problems. But they will be successfully dealing with them, whereas when they came to counseling they were not. When people leave hope-focused marriage counseling, they will

☐ have a better strategy for dealing with the problems

☐ have more hope that they can solve existing problems and other problems that arise in the future

☐ have solved the major problems to the extent that they feel comfortable continuing to work on those problems without the assistance of the counselor

☐ know how to handle future problems

☐ feel good about what they accomplished in counseling, and consequently

☐ feel free to consult with the counselor again in the future if they run into an insurmountable problem

The counselor believes in the ability of most couples to solve most of their own problems and fosters that view in both partners. The realistic view is that a couple will have problems that recur throughout the marriage and that the couple can solve those problems generally without help, but if necessary with a relatively brief series of consultations. This is more adaptive than creating the view that counseling has cured the couple or made them problem free. When problems occur, the new problems can knock the couple for a loop.

As with all parts of counseling, sticking to time limits, once agreed upon by counselor and clients, cannot be rigid. This is an ideal and will be adhered to most of the time, but there are always the other cases in which you have to use your good judgment and maintain flexibility in extending the number of sessions.

Planning Each Session *in Writing*

Before you begin a session, formulate a plan. Base it on the strategy of promoting faith working through love. Target one of the nine areas of marriage. Choose interventions to make up the plan. Then choose homework suggestions to maintain the couple's effort at home. People who formulate goals in writing accomplish more of their goals than do those who leave the goals formulated only in their heads.[20] If you want to help your couples achieve their goals, write down what you intend to accomplish. Be specific. Table 2.1 shows a sample plan for a typical third session.

As you can see, constructing a written plan takes less than two minutes. It will drastically increase your effectiveness.

Couple's main problem: Weakness in love. Namely, the partners complain of a dead relationship, no romance.	

Couple's main problem: Weakness in love. Namely, the partners complain of a dead relationship, no romance.
Session: Three
Area we intend to work on: Closeness
Intervention: Love bank
Homework: Have each partner write a list of ten behaviors that he or she could do that might please the other partner. Do not consult with each other. We will check out each partner's ability to know what would please the partner at the upcoming session.

Table 2.1. Typical plan for session three

Being Flexible

Be flexible enough to junk your plan within the first two minutes of a session if necessary and deal with an emergent crisis. On the other hand, though, most plans *are* flexible enough that they need not be junked—even in a crisis. For instance, if you had planned to work on communication and the couple arrive in heated conflict, then the counselor can discuss communication within the context of the hot conflict. If you had agreed to work on intimacy and they arrive in heated conflict, help them work on the conflict but examine the way that conflict affects their intimacy. Point out that successfully resolving a conflict increases their feelings of intimacy for each other. Sometimes, you must completely abandon the therapeutic plan.

Not every couple wants brief marital counseling. Some people prefer longer counseling (and will sabotage brief counseling), and other people simply have problems that do not yield to brief approaches, regardless of the approach's power. Hope-focused marriage counseling is flexible. It can accommodate different clients.

Counselors also have different resources, abilities and preferences. Pastors usually have little time to spend in counseling and have heavy demands for marital counseling. They may choose to limit the duration of their counseling to five sessions or less.[21] Some professionals have a well-developed referral base that provides fee-for-service clients who prefer long-term counseling.

Hope-focused marriage counseling is intentionally brief, yet it is flexible. Because you identify areas of concentration for each couple (for example, closeness or communication) and because numerous interventions can address those areas, you can extend the focus of counseling within each area—conducting hope-focused marriage counseling in few or many sessions.

OVERVIEW

You now have an overview of hope-focused marriage counseling: the goal, the strategy (building faith working through love), the stages (encounter, engagement and disengagement), the conditions of counseling, the necessary planning for each session, the focus on hope rather than on merely solving problems, the emphasis on making change sensible and the flexibility that comes from using interventions and homework assignments drawn from a variety of sources but still fitting into the general strategy of the approach. (See figure 1.1 for the blueprint of hope-focused counseling.) With that vision you are ready in subsequent chapters to delve more deeply into each aspect of hope-focused marriage counseling.

Many counselors have little success in counseling with couples. They become discouraged and demoralized. They groan when a couple calls for counsel because they don't have the success rate with couples that they do in treating people who are depressed or anxious or have low self-esteem. Hope-focused marriage counseling is hope-focused in terms of building hope in counselors as well as in clients. Throughout the first part of the book, I attempt to give you the will to treat couples and the desire to succeed. I try to show you that you can succeed in helping couples. In Snyder's language, I try to help you have more willpower to effect change in counseling with couples.

In the second part of the book I try to make the interventions very concrete so you can gain waypower to reach your goals as a marital counselor. I describe interventions and homework assignments so you will be able to visualize exactly what you can do to promote hope in your clients and to help them experience better relationships. In doing that, you can see that there is a way to help clients improve their marriages. You can thus gain a renewed sense of hope in your marital counseling.

Hope is willpower plus waypower to change and the added knowledge that God is with us even when change isn't happening. God is in control.

Chapter 3

Using the Strategy to Promote Hope

What causes marital problems? In this chapter I argue for a simple conceptualization of the cause of the marital problems, which implies a solution for those problems. That conceptualization provides an opportunity to help couples who are in emotional turmoil deal productively with their relationship and rekindle hope.

CONCEPTUALIZING THE CAUSE OF MARITAL TROUBLES
Couples build hope in their marriage by building love, faith and work in their marriage. Problems are generally related to losses in these areas.

Discipleship
Each Christian is commissioned to make disciples of others (Mt 28:19). Failure to promote the partner's spiritual maturity within the marriage relationship is a serious Christian problem.[1] It is difficult to want to help a partner better his or her relationship with God when feelings of hurt, fear and sadness run high. Partners who are demoralized and feel no hope generally focus more on their own survival than on the growth of the partner with whom they are actively having conflict.

One charge of the Christian counselor, though, is to move partners closer to fulfilling the Great Commission within their own marriages. To do that, help the partners build more hope by building love, faith and work in their marriage. You also can directly address the spiritual consequences of marital animosity. Usually pastors will directly address spiritual concerns more often in pastoral counseling than will licensed practitioners.

Nonetheless, the Christian marital counselor—whether pastor or professional counselor—can promote maturity in Christian and non-Christian clients by stressing issues that are foundational to Christianity such as love, faith, hope, forgiveness, commitment, moral integrity and faithfulness. While those personal characteristics won't make a non-Christian into a Christian, they are valued personal characteristics that form the basis for harmonious relationships. When those personal characteristics are encouraged with love and gentleness by a counselor who is known by the client to be a Christian, those characteristics can draw a non-Christian as well as a Christian closer to desiring to seek a relationship with Jesus. I don't believe that the counseling room is often an appropriate venue for explicit evangelism of clients (though this sometimes happens—usually at the initiation of the client, who is prompted by the Holy Spirit).[2]

The Primary Cause of Marital Problems: Loss of Love

Problems in marriage arise when partners do not love each other as much as they want to. They fail to value and they actively devalue each other.

In marriage people commit to value each other. In fact, the commitment of marriage is a particularly important type of commitment, a covenant lasting until death. The lifelong challenge of the marriage covenant is continually to find ways to value each other. Issues about which spouses differ (finances, in-law relations, child discipline) are occasions of challenge in which love can grow, but in which love is often bruised if partners fail to value each other.

When people do not feel loved (that is, valued), they may feel sad, angry, jealous, depressed, resentful or bitter. They may deal with the emotions in the flesh or in faith. When they deal with the emotions in the flesh, the emotions grow and transmute into even uglier emotions. When they deal with the emotions in faith, they work through love to heal the bruised emotions and promote an increased sense of value in the partner.

When people do not feel loved, they also act—either in the flesh or in faith. In the flesh, they desperately seek assurance of their value, working hard and sacrificing their own dignity at times to get evidence of their value from the spouse. Or they may seek revenge, become self-preoccupied or withdraw from the marriage psychologically or physically. They may attack, devaluing the spouse to elevate their own value.

It is nearly impossible to wrest a sense of love from an unwilling partner. It is impossible to bludgeon, either psychologically or physically, a sense of love from a defensive, hurt partner. Only through faith can a sense of love be won. God can give the grace for one partner to value the spouse even if the spouse is hurting or devaluing the partner. Then, as one partner begins to value the other, love can grow in the other. God can soften each's heart to make them receptive to mutual valuing.

When partners do not feel loved they blame the spouse, God and sometimes themselves.[3] They focus on their own pain and become self-centered—evaluating everything in terms of the impact it will have on them. As they think negatively, they act negatively. Negative thoughts feed on themselves, attracting other negative thoughts like a feeding frenzy of sharks. Troubled partners need to think more positively. Promote active valuing and discourage devaluing to focus the couple on love.

One Secondary Cause: Losing Faith

There are two secondary causes of marital problems that can be as destructive to the relationship as losing love. One secondary cause is losing faith. When people devalue each other and fail to value each other, the ratio of positive to negative interactions between the partners decreases. As John Gottman, perhaps the world's leading researcher in marital interaction, has shown through years of research, when the ratio of positive to negative interactions drops below five to one, the marriage suffers a drastic turnaround.[4] Partners begin to view the relationship as basically negative. Their attributions about the causes of problems change: problems are seen as global and stable. Negative interactions are expected and attention is paid to them, when in the past they might have been overlooked. The couple has lost faith in the future of the relationship. Counter that loss of faith to help the marriage survive.

Another Secondary Cause: Reducing Work on the Marriage

Marriages require work if they are to thrive—indeed if they are to survive. When marriages lose love and then faith, partners stop working on the relationship. *Why pour energy into a lost cause?* they might think. Efforts to improve the marriage often backfire. Soon those efforts are discontinued. People hope that if they avoid conflict, the marriage will heal itself. Not likely. Without work, the relationship will worsen. Rekindle the partners' motivation to work on the marriage.

Overall

In general, loss of love, faith or work spells disaster, or at least trouble, for a relationship. Regardless of the main cause, if the marriage is in trouble, the marital counselor must address all three causes.

MANIFESTATIONS OF THE LOSS OF LOVE, FAITH AND WORK

How does the loss of love, faith and work reveal itself? To examine this we begin with a brief study of people's basic needs.

People's Underlying Needs

People need a sense of meaning in life. That meaning is obtained through gaining senses of intimacy and of effectance. Effectance is the belief that one can cause events to happen. I discussed these needs in more detail in an earlier book, *Marriage Counseling: A Christian Approach for Counseling Couples*.[5] People are created to be in relationship with the Triune God. They receive senses of intimacy and effectance, and thus meaning, from their proper relationship with the Triune God.[6]

People also gain a sense of meaning by being in relationships. Through those relationships, they gain a sense of intimacy, acceptance and attachment.[7] They believe they can produce meaningful work, influence positive and affirming responses from their loved ones and produce the effect of feeling important or valued by their loved ones. When relationships with important people produce intimacy and effectance, the person usually feels that life is meaningful. The person feels loved, has faith and hope, and has a motivation to work.

Relationships can be disappointing, threatening or even harmful. When relationships do not provide a sense of intimacy, people feel unattached and have a weakened identity. When relationships do not provide a sense of effectance, people feel unattached and out of control. They do not sense love, have little faith and hope, and have little motivation to work.

Relationship Histories

Marriages are the oaks that began as acorns in families of origins. Through early family interactions the child will develop a mental picture (or schema) that provides either an adequate or faulty sense of attachment.[8]

Early family influences are important in forming the person's character, but schemas based on early influences can be modified or rejected as a result of more recent experiences. Later events are more likely to influence schemas to the extent that the later experiences are (a) emotional and (b) repeated or long-lasting.[9] People's previous romantic relationships meet both criteria for influential experiences. Mature romantic relationships that are characterized by love, faith, work on that relationship, and hope can repair early attachment traumas. On the other hand, romantic relationships that are characterized by anger, hostility, threat, rejection or violence can undermine good experiences or magnify traumatic ones within the family of origin.

The marriage is the most vital crucible for modifying a person's schemas. If the marriage is good, it can strengthen good schemas and repair poor schemas concerning the self in relationship. If the marriage is troubled, it can weaken good schemas and create poor schemas about the self in relationship.

Marital Interactions

Marital interactions, like interactions in all ongoing relationships, rapidly become patterned. When people have pleasing interactions, they pay attention to the partner's attempts to have pleasing interactions and they respond accordingly.[10] Pleasing interactions build on each other. Intimacy, good sex, good communication, successful conflict resolution, positive expectations and commitment beget more of the same. When interpersonal offenses occur, confession begets confession, and forgiveness begets forgiveness. On the other hand, when people have unpleasant interactions, those interactions quickly become patterns too. Several patterns are typical of troubled couples.[11]

Discuss-avoid. One partner might be more talkative than the other. One believes that only by talking about feelings can a problem be solved. The other partner believes that talking about feelings makes things worse. The more one partner discusses the problem, the more the other avoids it.

Demand-refuse. Partners may struggle over who can influence whom. At issue is a threat to the person's effectance. The more one partner demands, the more controlled the other feels and the more he or she refuses.

Criticize-defend. One partner may believe that the spouse is blameworthy. That partner might attempt to correct the problem by criticizing the spouse. The more the partner criticizes, the more the spouse is threatened and thus defends himself or herself. The more the spouse defends, the more the partner believes there is merit to the criticism.

Accuse-deny. Sometimes a partner might suspect that a breach in trust has occurred. If the spouse denies it, the accusing partner might become more convinced that the breach has indeed occurred.

Pursue-distance. The emotional pursuer fears rejection and demands more closeness, discussion and intimacy. The emotional distancer also fears rejection, but avoids closeness.

Attack-withdraw. Failures of each partner to yield to the other's demands might occasion criticism, accusation and contempt, or alternatively, withdrawal and stonewalling (that is, turning oneself into an unfeeling stone wall). Research by Gottman has shown that such attack-withdrawal patterns predict future marital dissatisfaction. When husbands are defensive and unresponsive, wives act critically and contemptuously of their husband, and those behaviors predicted marital separation four years later.[12]

Attack-attack or withdraw-withdraw. The attack-withdraw pattern usually does not continue indefinitely. Either the withdrawing spouse counterattacks or the attacking spouse gives up and both withdraw. Such marriages are usually in their terminal stage unless some drastic changes are quickly forthcoming.[13]

As conflict spreads and intimacy decreases in a marriage relationship, love that values each other is eroded. Faith in the future of the marriage and hope for a resolution of problems decreases. Work on the marriage decreases. Patterns may become more destructive.

People who are hurt protect themselves by adopting defensive strategies. These might include the following.

Mental defenses. The person might deny that problems exist or are hurtful, distort the marriage (usually by thinking of the other person as the culprit who has virtually all of the responsibility for the problems) or project his or her own dissatisfactions and hostilities onto the other person, thinking that the other person harbors dissatisfaction and hostility toward the partner.

The best defense is a good offense. The person might minimize his or her own pain through attacking and criticizing the partner. If both partners attack, conflict is frequent, heated and hurtful.

Avoiding the partner. When a person experiences pain whenever interacting with the partner, the person quickly learns not to interact with the partner.

Escaping conflict. Many people who have slid far down the slope of marital troubles will escape conflict once it starts. They leave, slam doors or clam up. Or they may stop having sexual relations if both partners are not instantly orgasmic (and of course such an occurrence is highly unlikely under the best of circumstances).

Stonewalling. People may numb themselves against feeling anything. Psychologist John Gottman says this is like turning oneself into a stone wall.[14] As

Simon and Garfunkel sang, "I am a rock. I am an island. And a rock feels no pain."

Defenses help people cope with pain. They also shove the partners farther down the slippery slope toward disengagement and divorce.

The Marital Relationship

When interactions become fixed into long-term stable negative patterns, partners conclude that the relationship is poor.[15] From then onward, they search for data that support their conclusion. They ignore data that disprove their conclusion. Whatever the partner does that might be construed as positive, the spouse discounts as being temporary, done at the instigation of the counselor, or failing to reflect the partner's true feelings. Conclusions about the relationship provide the backdrop against which the people interpret the next day's interactions.

THE SOLUTION

If the root of marital problems is insufficient love, then the solution to the marital difficulties is to help the partners love each other more. People marry because they love each other.[16] (Of course, other reasons figure into a decision to marry.) People stay married because they love each other. People become dissatisfied with marriage because they feel that they don't love each other any longer. One of the marital counselor's central tasks is to help people in troubled marriages fall back into love with each other.

Partners can't simply will themselves to love each other and expect the emotions associated with love to be reborn. But they can will to value and not to devalue each other, which are two essential ways to show love.[17] Having shown increased love to each other and having experienced increased love being shown to them, they can begin to feel more love for each other.

People choose to love through faith, even if they feel that their partner is unlovable. Faith is believing that the partners can restore love and that counseling can help the partners restore love and then acting on that belief. Loving feelings will follow acts of faith in which the partners value each other.

When people are distressed because they don't feel loved by their partner, they can manipulate or coerce, or they can act in faith. You, the counselor, must model faith working through love and help partners give up manipulation and coercion.

Faith working through love is active. To receive valuing from the partner, each partner must act in ways that promote valuing through faith. Faith-initiated and faith-sustained behaviors can then convey that one values the partner. Each partner does not wait passively to receive a gift of valuing from the spouse. Rather, each partner initiates valuing love.

Your therapeutic strategy is to help each person, by faith, work to love the partner more than previously. Accomplish this strategy through (a) helping partners see that they must act in faith and love and (b) modeling, teaching and training partners to apply faith-working-through-love to the marriage. Apply the strategy insistently and consistently with the aim of reinspiring hope.

PROMOTING HOPE

The problem with the troubled marriage—failure in love, faith or work—is not usually the largest problem for the counselor. The counselor's chief problem is to reinspire hope within the couple. Once the demotivation, demoralization and depression of the couple can be set on an upward slope by inspiring hope, progress can result. The counselor strives to inspire hope by promoting sensible love, faith and work in the couple.

Doubts are inevitable during marital counseling.[18] Doubts are countered through partners seeing concrete actions that show progress. Seeing builds hope, which fuels additional change. In the movie *Jerry McGuire*, Tom Cruise portrays a sport agent for a football star, played by Cuba Gooding Jr. Cruise is forced to shout, "Show me the money! Show me the money!" to the football star to prove his faithfulness. Yet the movie is really about "Show me the love!" Hope-focused marriage counseling is an attempt to show troubled couples their love for each other—concretely, in ways they cannot deny—until hope is rekindled.

THE COUNSELING RELATIONSHIP IN PROMOTING HOPE

To successfully promote hope in a couple's marriage, counselors must foster helpful interactions with each partner and avoid unhelpful ones.

Helpful Interactions Between the Counselor and the Partners

Knowing that partners of troubled marriages often feel deficient in love, hope and faith, and in motivation to work on the relationship, aim at restoring those characteristics. To restore love, the counselor must value each partner and value the relationship. Here are some types of statements that counselors might make.

Valuing each partner.

☐ "Susan, by your willingness to set up this appointment, you show how much you value the marriage."

☐ "Bill, by coming today, even though you feel discouraged about the marriage, you reveal that you have a sense of hope that won't lie down and quit."

☐ "Huong, your dedication to the Lord is amazing. I sense a real commitment in you. I know how sad you must feel because of Bonnie's affair. I know you want to give up on your marriage, yet I also see the steel within you that prompts you to want to fight for your marriage."

☐ "With the two of you experiencing a lot of conflict, it seems hard for you to see much positive in the other. You are each looking for the negative because that's been on the front burner lately. From outside the conflict, though, I can see a lot of positive things about each one of you. You, Evan, are . . . And you, Margaret, are . . ."

☐ "I can see by the way you worked on the homework this week that you each deeply care about your relationship."

☐ "Nadia, you are so tender with your children. You are kind to your friends. When you are angry at Thomas, it is hard to show that same love for him. Yet I know that your loving character is there."

☐ "Carlos, by confessing what you have done to hurt Tammy, you have shown a lot of courage. Few men feel secure enough to admit their failings. I know Tammy appreciates that courage. I'll bet that is one of the reasons she married you."

Valuing the marriage.
☐ "You both seem to have a similar vision for the marriage. You want to recapture the love from those early years of marriage, the passion, the times of good sex and hot romance. It has been my experience that when couples share such a vision, they can usually recapture their love—if they are willing to trust the Lord and work on their own behavior."

☐ "You share Christian values. You value the marriage and don't want it to disintegrate. You value your children and want to do what is best for them. You value forgiveness, and even though both of you have often been hurt by the other, I think you can forgive each other and experience that healing. You have a good foundation for rebuilding a loving, faithful marriage. I'm encouraged by your prospects."

☐ "You've told me a lot about the sexual problems that you are experiencing. Latisha, you can't seem to have orgasms any longer except by stimulating yourself, and you don't want to make love with Vic. Vic, you are frustrated and feel like you are a failure as a man because you can't satisfy Latisha. Those are serious problems, and I think we can improve things over the next couple of months. I don't want you to stop paying attention to the many positive parts of your relationship. I see many strengths. For instance, . . ."

☐ "You are fighting often, and I know you don't like that. You are happier when you don't fight. But I'm encouraged that you are at least still talking with each other. When love has eroded, people give up on the marriage. You have definitely not given up. You're still hanging tough, trying hard to improve the marriage by getting the other person to change. That is a good base to work from, even though you'll need to change strategy to build more love."

☐ "You both have worked hard during the past six sessions. You have rebuilt hope for the future and faith that God can work in your marriage. Most of all, you have experienced renewed love. I think you have done a lasting work. In the future, when you experience discouragement, as we all do at times, you can remind yourself about God's faithfulness and care for your marriage, and that will help pull you through difficulties."

Interacting with the couple to build love, faith, hope and work. In these statements that you might make, we see several themes. First, do not make positive statements about the people or the marriage that are not founded in truth. Ground your statement in behaviors that you have observed (and usually called the partners' attention to at the time you observed them). Second, use the framework of promoting love, faith and hope, and work to incorporate your observations and conclusions. Third, do not gloss over problems. Acknowledge problems as real and as difficult to solve. Yet help the couple view the mountaintops of hope beyond the parched desert dryness of loss of intimacy and the searing heat of conflict. Fourth, you are definitely on the clients' side. You are a staunch supporter, not an accuser. While you want clients to take responsibility for changing their marriage and themselves, you do not want clients to feel as if they are shamed by their actions.

Unhelpful Interactions Between the Counselor and the Partners

By your interactions with the partners, you can also inadvertently make the problem worse.

Recapitulating the marital dynamics. Consider the emotional distancer-pursuer couple. If you talk a lot with the emotional distancer, ask him or her to discuss feelings at length, give in-session directives that promote intimacy and assign homework that asks the distancer to initiate intimacy, then the emotional distancer will probably reject your counsel. By pursuing the distancer, you will repeat the pattern that characterizes the marriage. Consider also the couple in which one partner is Christian and the other is not. If that issue is a hot topic in the marriage, you can make the problem worse by challenging the non-Christian spouse in his or her religious position. That pattern also recapitulates the marital dynamics, making the problem worse.

Stimulating resistance. Fundamentally, there are two types of approaches to helping—those that stimulate people to resist the counselor and those that stimulate people to cooperate with the counselor. For example, interpreting people's motives promotes resistance, as does using paradoxical directives. Hope-focused marriage counseling is aimed at promoting cooperation. Most of the methods I recommend have been drawn from theories that promote cooperation or have been adapted to reduce the resistance-provoking potential of the method.

Failure to stimulate hope. Counselors must reinfuse troubled marriages with hope. Counselors do not have a magic hope pill that can be administered to the troubled couple. However, counselors can act as ambassadors of the living God, who is the God of hope. You can point couples toward the source of hope—sometimes without ever mentioning religion—humbly and sometimes directly. Strive to create a relationship characterized by love, faith, hope, mutual effort, trust, fairness and cooperation. Those characteristics grow from godly character and godly interactions. Those godly interactions, empowered by the Holy Spirit—not technical wizardry—produce lasting change within couples.

PRACTICAL ACTIONS IN PROMOTING HOPE

In these first three chapters I have repeatedly suggested that counselors should promote hope. How? Here are some practical ways.

☐ Use interventions from solution-focused therapy.[19]

☐ Name problems. That can build hope by a sort of "Rumpelstiltskin effect," in which naming the problem makes it self-destruct.

☐ Recognize long-standing patterns and describe convincing ways to change those patterns.

☐ Teach partners new ways to communicate or act with each other.

☐ Pray for (and perhaps with) a couple.

☐ Focus on the partners' emotions and show that softer emotions underlie the harder, angrier, more discouraged emotions.[20]

☐ When a problem cannot be changed, say so. A problem that cannot be changed might be accepted or coped with.[21]

☐ Provide a close, caring relationship for the couple.

☐ Help the couple find support from a community of friends, family members or church members.

☐ Call attention to the miraculous intervention of the Lord God when it occurs.

PRESUPPOSITIONS IN PROMOTING HOPE

Presupposition is one way that counselors of all persuasions focus couples on things that are likely to help them. R. Bandler and J. Grinder, in the book *Structure of Magic,* analyzed counselors of many theoretical schools.[22] Almost all made statements that presupposed beliefs when they counseled. Presuppositions tend to bypass the defenses of couples because they do not invite disagreement. It isn't that a single presupposition will change the couple's point of view. Instead, it is the accumulation of the presuppositions until the couple finds the idea palatable. Here are some practical examples of things that a counselor might say that presuppose hope.

☐ "I can see that you both want to make a positive marriage. The problem is you are going about it ineffectively. We need to work on ways that you can get what you want—a better marriage—more effectively." (Implications: You want to improve the marriage, and you can learn better ways of doing that.)

☐ "What are your hopes for counseling?" (Implication: You have hopes.)

☐ "What specifically are the changes that you each want?" (Implications: You each want some changes. You haven't given up hope on the marriage.)

☐ "Coming here is the first and perhaps the most important step in restoring your marriage." (Implication: There are other steps that you have not yet taken. When you take those steps, you will help your marriage. In that, there is hope. Another implication: You want to restore your marriage.)

☐ "Your continual fighting is, in a way, somewhat encouraging. The opposite of love is not fighting; it is noninvolvement. You are anything but uninvolved." (Implication: You are not as far from restoring your relationship into a loving marriage as you thought you were. You can have hope that the step is shorter than you thought.)

☐ "How did you act when things were better?" (Implication: You acted differently then. Another implication: Things were better once and they can become better again if you do the things that you did then. That can provide hope.)

Be pro-hope. Focus couples on hopefulness rather than have them continue to wallow in the mire of hopelessness. Once couples have hope, they can build love. Once they have love, they can renew their faith and thus find new motivation to put energy and work into their marriage.

DEFEATING DOUBT IN PROMOTING HOPE

DeLoss D. and Ruby M. Friesen suggest that in couples who have begun to work on their problems, doubt is prevalent.[23] Hope, the antidote to the snakebite of doubt, is needed throughout counseling.

At the beginning of marital counseling, partners usually doubt whether the spouse is willing to try to change. Hope is built in that early period by seeing the partner making attempts to act differently. By seeing the partner doing different things, people gain hope that the partner is willing to try to change.

In the middle of marital counseling, partners frequently doubt the spouse's ability to change. They may think, *Sure, he is trying. But I don't believe he can act differently.* Partners gain hope through seeing each other actually change. The counselor points out successes, and the sight of those successes make it hard for both partners to deny that change is happening. Partners gain hope that change is possible.

Near the end of counseling, partners often doubt that changes can be maintained. *She has made some changes,* they might think, *but the changes are temporary. They won't last. The changes have occurred because the counselor made her change.* Partners gain hope that changes can be maintained as they note that despite the normal ups and downs in relationships, the trend of the relationship is definitely up. The counselor can help the couple gain this hope through teaching the couple to look for the long-term trend and not get side-tracked by fleeting ups and downs. Partners can gain hope that changes can last and improvement can continue for the life of the marriage.

SUMMARY

Concentrate on the strategy of identifying failures in love and building successes in their place. Increase the couple's faith and willingness to work. Use the concept of building a loving marriage throughout counseling, and teach it explicitly to the couple. By emphasizing this strategy, you direct the couple's attention to areas that you know can make a difference in their marriage.

One of this book's reviewers was not convinced that failure of love is the primary cause of troubled marriages, suggesting that such a concept is simplistic. Actually, that is quite true. Marriages work for many complex reasons and fail for equally complex reasons. Any conceptualization of marriage is simplistic. But counselors and couples need a strategy that captures the essence of the problem and provides the opportunity to intervene in a way that might turn the marriage around. Adopting the strategy of promoting love, faith and work accomplishes that. It provides the opportunity for the couple to build hope.

There is no simple way for you to build hope. You must match your methods to the couple's level of disturbance and to each partner's personal style and willingness to accept the challenge of a rebirth of hope. Focusing on hope consistently will arm you with a will to continue when the partners become discouraged. That hope provides the couple with courage to adopt the necessary strategy of building love, faith and work in the nine important areas of marriage, which we will examine next.

Chapter 4

Applying
the Strategy to
Eight Areas of Marriage

The human body is fascinatingly complex. The brain, immune system, endocrine system, cardiovascular system, respiratory system and other biological systems I can't even pronounce are separate yet function together in coordination. When a physical problem occurs, the body feels its repercussions jolt almost every system. Medicine historically saw problems as located in single systems, but today it appreciates the interconnectedness of the body. Symptoms are signs of more systemic problems but are also often problems in their own right—such as high fever.

Marriages are like our bodies. When troubled, signs appear: in-law problems, financial problems, disagreements over toilet seats being up or down. In comes the counselor, the love doctor. Marital counseling cannot treat the millions of difficulties that arise in marriages. Too often novice counselors see themselves as referees or problem solvers who try to help troubled couples solve every issue they present. Focus on separate issues will paralyze the counselor. It is the *Hamlet* trap: analysis is paralysis.

Instead of zeroing in on individual issues—even common issues such as in-law problems, child-rearing disagreements, financial conflict or sexual troubles—intervene to promote love, faith and work in nine basic areas of marriage. (The astute observer will quickly note that I begin each word with a C, which can completely confuse counselors.) These nine areas are

☐ central beliefs and values
☐ core vision
☐ confession/forgiveness
☐ communication
☐ conflict resolution
☐ cognition
☐ closeness
☐ complicating factors[1]
☐ commitment

CENTRAL BELIEFS AND VALUES

Values are aspects of living that people deem important, some values more so than others. Mack Goldsmith and Betty Hansen[2] have characterized a person's values as a stronghold surrounded by a marsh, which is located within a hostile forest. The stronghold represents the person's core values, strongly held. Surrounding this stronghold is a marsh of uncertain footing. The marsh represents values that are less strongly held. The marsh in turn is surrounded by a hostile forest, representing rejected values. In crisis, people rarely change their stronghold or forest values. Crisis attacks the marsh values. Vulnerable core values near the marsh-stronghold border may also be eroded into the marsh.

Bolster endangered values concerning the permanency and importance of marriage through support and reassurance, and strengthen positive values by calling attention to things learned through the difficult experiences. Be warned though: a steady stream of positives from the counselor will usually be perceived as insensitivity to the couple's pain. Don't come across as if you are trying to put a Band-Aid on a major wound. Three values are often vulnerable to change during marital counseling: love, self and commitment.

Love

Love is a central value. Hope-focused marriage counseling deals with people's beliefs and values within the context of solving the marital problems so that the couple will be more loving. Counselors help partners value love more than when they enter treatment.

Self

Individuals generally implicitly hold one of three models of the self:

☐ Philip Cushman[3] suggests that we often have a view of self as an "empty self." We see ourselves as empty vessels that need to be filled—by the right mate, the right job, the right church, the right experiences.

☐ Kenneth Gergen[4] suggests that we live in a postmodern world in which we feel disconnected and deconstructed. Our view of self is often fragmented into numerous isolated roles—husband or wife, parent, worker, friend. We can see few connections across roles.

☐ The third view of self is as a connected self.[5] In that view, we define who we are by the commitments people make to us and the commitments we make to others.

How does each partner view the self: primarily as an empty self, fragmented self or connected self? Marital troubles rock people's sense of connection, fragmenting them and making them feel unfulfilled. Bolster their connectedness.

Commitment

Traditionally and in most Christian communities, commitment implies that people are walking hand in hand, unable to see into the future yet determined to remain together over time despite any changes. In modern thinking, though, commitment often is dissociated from time. Commitment means exclusivity. A commitment might last only days, but it is exclusive while it lasts. Commitment is an important value in marriage. But don't assume that you know what a person means by commitment unless you ask specifically. Commitment will be more fully addressed later in this chapter.

CORE VISION OF MARRIAGE

Each partner develops a vision of marriage.[6] Sometimes the vision is blurred. At times it is obscured by the haze of anger or the fog of depression. Occasionally, all too occasionally, it is crystal clear.

There are three parts of a core vision of marriage: the concept of the actual marriage (that is, the way a person perceives the marriage), the true marriage (that is, the way the marriage really is, which can never truly be determined) and the way a person thinks the marriage should be (that is, the ideal concept of the marriage).[7] In the perfect marriage, the three completely overlap. In reality, no one's concept of the actual marriage is completely the same as the true marriage would be. Everyone looks at his or her marriage to some degree as if through a toilet paper roll, focusing on some parts of the marriage and ignoring other parts. When things are going well, people train the toilet paper roll on the positive events and feelings. The concept of the actual marriage looks a lot like the ideal concept of the marriage. The toilet paper roll is a wonderful perceptual tool to keep a happy couple happy.

However, when marriages are sliding downhill, people train the toilet paper roll on negative events and feelings. They ignore and distort their marital history and much of the marital present, because they are looking mostly at the (limited) negative part of their marriage. Past events are actually transformed by the mind into more negative memories than were the real experiences. People *think* things aren't like they should be. Unhappiness is related to the amount of perceived difference between the concept of actual marriage and the ideal concept of marriage. Further, the partner firmly and strongly believes his or her perception to be absolutely correct. No negotiation. No discussion. Period.

As counselor, help partners form a different picture of their marriage than the negative toilet paper roll picture. Help them focus on the ways they do and can love their partner by actively valuing and avoiding devaluing the partner. Help them see the solutions they can pursue, feel the stirring of hope.

CONFESSION AND FORGIVENESS
Pain in marriage is inevitable, even good ones. Confession and forgiveness are crucial in healing.

The Road-Test of Love
The road-test of valuing love is in confession and forgiveness of hurts. When our mechanic repairs our car, before he sends us out into traffic he road-tests the car. He revs up the engine, corners at highway speeds and puts the new parts under the stress of daily driving to see whether the parts will stand up.

In hope-focused marriage counseling, the couple learns to apply love in faith through work. They practice under the counselor's supervision during counseling sessions, but the real tests of rebuilt love will occur when they hurt each other—as they are almost certain to do before they complete marital counseling. Instead of being discouraged that they have slipped back into old patterns, use the hurtfulness as a road-test for their valuing love, testing whether they can confess their failings and forgive each other for hurts they might have received.

Reconciliation
Hurts. Hurts are wounds inflicted by accident, through negligence or through

intention. Accidental hurts are usually easily forgiven—if the person who was hurt can be convinced that the hurtfulness was indeed accidental. Difficulties arise when hurts are perceived to have been inflicted through negligence or intention.

Hurtfulness. Marriages that have become troubled are usually not plagued by simple hurts. Troubled marriages are full of hurts; they are characterized by hurtfulness. Partners in hurtful marriages have forgotten most of the hurts. The history of hurts is too long, too bitter. There is no trust.

Attitude of softness. In cases of perceived intentional hurt or hurtfulness, confession of one's failings is essential for a healthy marriage. Confession paves the way for forgiveness. When a partner hurts the spouse, the spouse might confront the partner—asking for, and sometimes demanding, an explanation. The partner must decide how to respond. He or she can deny responsibility for hurting the partner or deny that hurtfulness was intended, ignore the hurts, excuse the hurts, justify the hurts or confess and apologize. Generally, relationship healing (reconciliation) is most likely when the partner accepts his or her responsibility, confesses and apologizes. At times, explaining that no hurt was intended can help heal the relationship. Ignoring, excusing or justifying the hurt will drive the wedge of anger and retaliation deeper between the partners. With confession, though, a partner says, in effect, "I value you more than I value my need to save face." That soft valuing statement opens the door to forgiveness.

Not justice, but forgiveness. Justice can never be achieved in a hurtful marriage. Justice involves balancing the scales of hurt. Yet each partner perceives his or her own pain more than the pain he or she inflicted on the partner, and people tend to seek punitive damages to balance their own suffering with that of the other person.

Clearly, restoration of trust—if it is to be achieved—must first come from each person's forgiving the partner's hurtfulness. Mistrustful people are wary of new hurts and thus hardened to becoming vulnerable again, so being first to confess is risky. Confession is crucial for healing a troubled marriage because the hardness must be penetrated before forgiveness can penetrate the heart. After confession, the burden falls on the partner to forgive or to harden the heart. Reconciliation, though, is more complex and also involves a mutual effort to behave with trustworthiness prior to the achievement of reconciliation.[8]

If people want to forgive someone who hurt them, they can be helped to do so by applying a program we have developed to promote forgiveness and reconciliation.[9] That program has empirical support for its effectiveness.[10] Chapter nine discusses it further.

THE DAILY OPERATION OF MARRIAGE

The daily operation of the marriage revolves around four areas: communication, conflict resolution, cognition and closeness. There is considerable mutual influence among the four; nonetheless, there is a logic that determines the order in which I address the topics. I first address communication, the bedrock of the relationship. Second, crucial to making the troubled marriage better is conflict resolution. Troubled marriages almost always are conflictual. Third, conflict is usually at the heart of negative cognition, and when conflicts are resolved, cognition usually becomes more positive. Fourth, once couples can communicate, resolve conflicts and think positively about their relationship, they can build greater intimacy. In one sense, intimacy (or closeness) is an outcome of a better relationship.

On the other hand, if you can help a couple become more intimate—even without addressing the other areas explicitly—the couple may begin to think more positively about the relationship, avoid or resolve conflicts more often than previously and communicate better. Changes in intimacy can change the remainder of the marriage. In counseling, the order in which you address the areas depends on your assessment of the couple. All areas of the marriage are interrelated, and interventions can be aimed at any area whenever it seems appropriate based on initial and ongoing assessment.

COMMUNICATION

A lack of love underlies many communication problems, especially the ones outlined below.

Types of Communication Problems

Focus on current communication. Most couples' problems began long ago. Efforts to find "who started it" may go back to Adam and Eve. Finding the first troublesome communication in a series will not help the couple solve their problems, though many couples seem to think it will. Don't get caught up in chasing the origin of the problem.

There are three ways that most counselors understand and intervene to solve marital problems. They may think of poor communication as being due to misunderstandings, poor communication styles or imbalances of marital power.[11]

Misunderstanding meanings. Some counselors think most communication problems occur because people do not understand each other's meanings. Perhaps the partners are distracted, tired, stressed or too focused on formulating what they are going to say next to listen to the partner. Counselors who view communication problems as being due to misunderstood meanings will try to help couples understand each other better. Misunderstandings are interpreted as lack of valuing. People often assume that if one's partner really cared, then the partner would exert whatever effort is required to try to understand. Thus, communication problems are viewed as failures in valuing love.

Unhelpfully "punctuating" the conversation. Other counselors assume that communication problems arise not because of what people say but because of how they say it. To use an analogy, problems occur because people punctuate their interactions inappropriately. Conversational punctuation errors also lead to misunderstandings. For example, if one person continually interrupts—cutting the other person's sentence too short—the person shows the partner that his or her own agenda is more urgent than the partner, which makes the partner feel less valued. It is as if the person continually intersperses dashes throughout the conversation. A partner who is too dogmatic makes every sentence end with a period, even when there are questions or doubts.

On the other hand, some people continually question their spouse, expressing doubt about the spouse's abilities, talents or behavior. Others use too much silence, failing to express themselves adequately, while yet others may communicate as if their entire life were a run-on sentence, making the important emotional events in their life indiscernible. Still others have one crisis after another, punctuating their experiences with so many exclamation points that it is difficult to take their emotional expressions seriously. In each case, the style of communication—regardless of what was said—makes the partner feel devalued.

Unintended effects of communication, usually the effect on relative power. Some counselors view couple communication as an attempt to determine who has marital power.[12] The power that energizes communication difficulties is not economic nor physical power; it is the power of who can say what the marriage is going to be like. On each decision the couple defines and redefines the balance of decisional power. On some issues the husband may have more power; on others, the wife; on still others, the power is shared.

Couples become locked in a power struggle over who has the power to say how their relationship will be conducted. The topic of the discussion is irrelevant. It might be a disagreement over sex, money, child discipline or visiting the in-laws. Or it might be as seemingly insignificant as whether to leave the toilet seat up or down during the night, whether to squeeze or roll the toothpaste or whether the toilet paper should be installed flap-out or flap-under. The important issue for the couple is defining who has the power to say. Such power struggles lead to poor communications.

Loving Communication

I believe that the root of all communication problems—whether they are understood as misunderstandings, poor communication styles or attempts to gain power within the marriage—can be understood as a deficit of love. The desire to be understood but not understand the other person is a lack of love. Poor styles of communication suggest, "My agenda is more important than yours." Such communications do not *show* the valuing love to the partner that the spouse might actually feel. The partner feels devalued, unimportant, unloved. When partners feel insecure, threatened or without power they want to prove that they are adequate, important and powerful—in short, valued and loved. So they try to control their marriage.

Communication difficulties will not be dealt with unless the root cause of deficient love is addressed. Partners must defeat pride and power and replace them with love through valuing the spouse, even if it means laying down one's own expectations and rights. Love is being willing to value and not to devalue the partner; this willingness springs from an other-oriented heart. People need to be reminded that in marriage they have a great opportunity to cultivate an other-oriented heart.

CONFLICT RESOLUTION

Most troubled couples have chronic conflict.[13] Styles of chronic conflict may differ radically. Some may shout, swear and physically abuse one another. Some may treat each other with cold disdain. Some may ignore their spouse, fume acidly or snipe at the partner with painful zingers. Some people never seem to fight but always seem to be in a cold war. Still others may be experts at character assassination. Some people start with small disagreements and work themselves slowly into heated arguments. Others explode from tranquillity to full-blown conflict. Regardless of style, troubled couples usually cannot resolve their differences. Power struggles and hostile devaluing characterize their interactions.

The counselor enters areas of conflict like a soldier in a mine field, fearing a sudden explosion, afraid that even if a mine is located it will explode when it is being defused. Yet despite the dangers, mines must be located and defused if the couple is to walk safely.

Conflict is the single biggest characteristic of couples who come to marital counselors. Each partner wants to get the specific answer to a particular issue about which they disagree. When they get an answer on that issue, they will want another. And another. And another. Although partners ask counselors for answers to their conflicts, the partners do not really want answers. They want affirmation. Each partner wants the counselor to decide that the partner is right. Both partners feel devalued and unloved. They want to wrest value from winning the conflict. They want to put the counselor in the role of value-giver.

Do not become a couple's referee. If you do, you won't be able to please them both; even if you could, you'd be necessary as their validator forever. You do not have to resolve a couple's conflicts. Instead teach them how to resolve their conflicts themselves.

□ When couples are in conflict, they don't value each other. Help them value each other even when they are disagreeing.

□ When couples are in conflict, they are interested in their own agenda, not in listening to their partner. Help them slow down and listen to each other.

□ When couples are in conflict, they are so interested in making their points that they don't check out misunderstandings. Help them explore misunderstandings and straighten them out.

□ When couples are in conflict, they don't want to compromise. They want to win. They want to prove that their position is best. Help them learn a strategy by which both can win.

Your success in counseling will usually rise or fall on how well you handle the couple's conflict and whether you can get them to practice faith, work and love in the midst of hot conflicts.

COGNITION

If partners do not change their thinking about their marriage, any other changes made in counseling probably will not last. Help couples change their mental activity in four areas:

□ negative thinking about the marriage

□ attributions that blame the spouse

□ expectations about the future of the marriage

□ assumptions about the marriage[14]

Usually, when the marriage has gone sour and partners have donned "dark glasses" through which they see every interaction as negative, the partners will be thinking negatively in all four areas. They have lost faith in the future and faith in each other. They cannot visualize their relationship as ever regaining love. They have lost hope. Help them remove the dark glasses and put on more apt prescription lenses by focusing the partners' attention more on the positive than perhaps is deserved without being insensitive to their complaints about what they see as "wrong" with the relationship.

CLOSENESS

Closeness is necessary for a healthy marriage, yet the types and levels needed varies from one marriage to another, from one partner to another and sometimes from one moment to the next.

Distance, Coaction and Intimacy

Closeness is composed of a balance of distance, coaction and intimacy.[15] Distance involves performing activities alone. Examples include listening to a radio headset, studying, reading and daydreaming. Coaction is performing activities with another person but without intimate interaction. Doing activities together is coactive. For example, going to the movies together, playing a sport or board game and talking about what to buy at the grocery this week are coactive activities. Intimacy involves activities that promote a sense of unity or bonding. Having sexual relations, talking about values, recalling pleasant times, discussing matters that both partners consider important, revealing positive feelings and sharing secrets are examples of intimate activities.

Each person needs to establish a unique balance among distance, coaction and intimacy. Generally, each person is comfortable within a band, or comfort zone, of each. People regulate their needs for each of the three through ways they spend time. Also, people select careers and mates with an unconscious eye to the demands they might make for distance, coaction and intimacy.

When people are not in their comfort zone on distance, coaction or intimacy, or any combination of the three, they will feel unsatisfied and will be motivated to redress the balance. They may change their time schedule, job or the like, or use indirect strategies to regulate closeness, such as complaining (thus driving people away), demanding more intimacy from someone already satisfied with intimacy (thus driving them away) or avoiding contact with someone who wants coaction (thus inciting the person to pursue).

Types of Closeness

Closeness comes in several varieties. It might be emotional intimacy (sharing emotions or feelings or expressing themselves), sexual intimacy, social intimacy (like coaction), recreational intimacy or intellectual intimacy.[16] Individuals may experience fulfillment differently in each type of intimacy. People place different values on each type of intimacy, but emotional and sexual intimacy seem to be two of the three best barometers for marital happiness. A third, which was not mentioned above, is spiritual intimacy, the degree to which partners approach religious and spiritual issues similarly, harmoniously and without conflict.

When partners don't meet each other's needs for distance, coaction or intimacy, they can feel devalued and unloved. If the needs are unmet for a substantial period of time, and if the partner doesn't seem to want to meet the needs, they can lose faith in the partner's love or in the future of the relationship.

Certainly people should rely on the Lord to meet all their needs. The fact is, though, that the Lord often meets some of those needs through (a) marital partners, (b) family members and (c) the body of Christ. Further, individual differences are great in the degree to which people *can* rely on the Lord. Instead of demanding instant spiritual maturity in our clients, we can help them move to an intermediate position of providing for more of each other's needs.

COMMITMENT

Commitment is generally based on either a contract or a covenant. The partners' understanding of their commitment has a profound effect on their marriage.

Contracts and Covenants

Two understandings of commitment permeate modern culture—one based on contract, one on covenant.[17] Covenantal commitment is more traditional, but contractual commitment is steadily prevailing.

People who treat commitment as contractual may be highly dedicated to their careers, marriages or friends. Their commitments may in actuality last as long as many who hold a covenantal view of commitment. They might be willing to sacrifice for the partner.[18] Yet for most people contractual commitment is more fragile than is covenantal commitment.

Contractual commitment depends on reciprocity or exchange.[19] Strong ties can be forged in relationships when partners exchange things valued positively or when partners share resources needed by the spouse. Contractual commitment is built on mutual need fulfillment and breeds mutual dependency. When needs are not fulfilled, though, contractual commitment can erode. Contract commitment is individualistic for some but mutual for others.[20] In individualistic contracts, each person meets his or her obligations only as long as there is a reasonable likelihood that eventually the other person will meet his or her obligations. Each person is mainly concerned with receiving the resources that the contract stipulates, which are (by contract) his or her rights. In mutual contracts, need fulfillment is more interdependent than in individual contracts. People want things for "us" as well as for "me." Yet commitment is still based on both people fulfilling their end of the contract.

Traditional marital commitment is built on a different foundation. In a covenantal commitment both parties treat each other as one flesh. They promise to love self-sacrificially, placing the other person's welfare at least equal to one's own welfare. The origin of this covenantal view of commitment is ancient. It is as American as blood brothers among the Native Americans who cut their wrists and let their blood flow together. It is as distant as African ceremonies where people cut their fingers and drop blood into a common cup, which they imbibe. It is as old as the Hebrew understanding of God's slaying of animals to seal his covenant with Abraham. It is as religious as the Christian understanding of Jesus' sacrifice on the cross as sealing a new covenant with believers in Jesus.

In a covenantal commitment, people care for and stay committed to a partner because they have staked their honor, their word and their identity on fulfilling their covenantal obligations toward the other person regardless of what the other person does or doesn't do. They feel deep within that marriage is sacred.[21]

Commitment's Components
According to social psychologist Caryl Rusbult, commitment is made of three components: satisfaction with a relationship, satisfaction with competing alternatives to the relationship (such as career, children, hobbies, other romantic interests, television or sports) and investments in the relationship.[22] Changing any component can affect commitment. Commitment can be strengthened by increasing satisfaction with the marriage, decreasing alternatives to the relationship or increasing investment in the relationship. Rusbult has also noted the role of willingness to sacrifice in commitment.[23]

Scott Stanley and Howard Markman, clinical psychologists, identify only two components to commitment: dedication and constraint.[24] Dedication is the desire to remain devoted to a loved one. Dedication is the pull, the attraction. Some commitments are based almost entirely on dedication. If dedication fades, the partners flit away as a bird from a noise. Constraints are the ropes that keep people tied to each other. Constraints are children, jointly held property, worry about what others might think. Some commitments are based almost exclusively on constraints. Mutually positive feelings have long evaporated and the partners stay together for the kids, for the fear of what others might think or for some other reason.

Marriages based mostly on a commitment of constraint can be fulfilling or dead.

Commitment gives the relationship integrity. It knits partners into a unit. Like our skin, commitment is a complex organic boundary. If commitment is rubbed away by the abrasives of hurtfulness, dissatisfaction or anger, then the relationship can disintegrate.

SUMMARY

Hope-focused marriage counseling is characterized mostly by employing two frameworks throughout: (1) the strategy of promoting love, faith and work and (2) the goal of building hope by increasing willpower (motivating), waypower (making changes highly noticeable to clients through active interventions or tangible materials, like written assessment reports or building a physical testimony to the couple's progress) and waitpower (the patience to persevere when progress is not yet evident). Apply the two frameworks within the counseling relationship with husband, wife and couple as you target whichever of the areas of marriage your assessments reveal to be the most critical for them. By zeroing in on the targets, you will help partners move toward their goal of a better marriage and less chance of divorce (see figure 4.1).

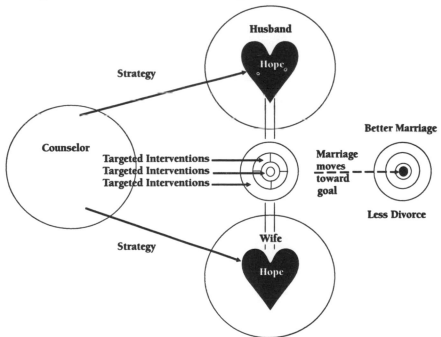

Figure 4.1. Counseling relationship

Part 2
Interventions

Chapter 5

Precounseling
Interventions

Counseling begins before you ever see your clients. By the time a troubled couple reaches your office, they have had thousands of interactions that have moved them apart. They are usually desperately unhappy, so unhappy that they might be ready to spend at least one whole session that they hope will move them back together again. (No counselor has ever seriously claimed that humans are completely rational beings.)

Don't wait until the first counseling session to help the couple. Follow these four steps: First, begin from the initial phone contact to direct the partners' attention to love, faith, work and hope. Second, get the partners to think strategically about their relationship through completing assessment instruments. Third, when partners arrive at your office, orient them to the type of counseling they will receive through using a videotape. Fourth, use a pamphlet about the counseling to reinforce the conceptualization of the marriage you hope to help them develop. Begin with those steps and at least the couple will move into counseling sensing a glimmer of hope.

INITIAL PHONE CONTACT
When you or your receptionist discusses counseling with a prospective client,

accomplish three tasks. First, go over the business you transact with all clients (for example, informing them about fees, attendance policies and the like).

Second, tell the partner who phoned that counseling will be more efficient and effective if the partners will complete some assessment instruments prior to arriving at their appointment. Each partner can complete the forms at home in about one hour or less. Partners should pick up the forms at least a day before the appointment. Inform the partners that when they pick up the forms, they will leave a refundable deposit to cover the cost of materials should they not attend the first session.

Ask partners to arrive at least fifteen minutes before the scheduled start of the first appointment to view an informative videotape about the counseling. Any partner who cannot complete the assessment forms at home prior to the first appointment, should arrive ninety minutes prior to the scheduled counseling session so that the forms can be completed by the beginning of counseling. (Tell the partners that they will not be billed for that time.)

Third, before ending the phone conversation, say (or have the receptionist say) something like this:

> Many people find that their marriage improves merely from the increased hope of scheduling an appointment for marital counseling. Would you each note any ways that things get better, even a small fraction better, after this phone call? During the first session I [or your counselor] will ask you about what you might have noticed.[1]

HAVING PARTNERS COMPLETE ASSESSMENT INSTRUMENTS
Having couples reflect on their relationship can change the relationship. That is especially true as the partners think about the strengths of the marriage, good times and things they can do to improve the relationship. Assessment instruments are chosen to provide a multifaceted picture of the marriage, but also to direct partners' thinking to positive aspects of the marriage. Assessment is covered in the following chapter.

PRECOUNSELING VIDEOTAPE
Have the couple view an informational videotape. Table 5.1 shows a sample script for such a videotape. You can easily make your own if you have a video camera-recorder.

Table 5.1. A sample transcript for a precounseling videotape

I'm Everett Worthington, a professor of psychology at Virginia Commonwealth University, and I want to introduce you to the type of counseling that your counselor is going to use with you.

How to Use the Videotape

This videotape lasts less than fifteen minutes and provides a lot of information. The best way to use the tape is for you and your partner to view the tape at one sitting. Preferably view it together, but if you can't find the time, make sure both have seen it before your first session. This should provide an overview of the counseling and give you an idea of what to expect.

Once counseling begins, you can view again selected portions of the tape. I cover eight parts of counseling:

☐ the initial assessment of your relationship,
☐ what to do with the assessment,
☐ the major cause of most problems and thus the areas you'll want to strengthen,
☐ how to be forgiven and to forgive,
☐ how to communicate better,
☐ how to resolve differences,
☐ how to build intimacy, and
☐ a final assessment of your relationship.

These eight parts are useful in almost every marriage. In your marriage, your counselor will have an individually tailored emphasis that deals with the things of most concern to you.

The Initial Assessment of Your Relationship

Your counselor needs to find out about your relationship so he or she can help you efficiently. If you respond frankly and honestly and provide the counselor with relevant information, your counselor will stand the best chance of tailoring help just for you. By using the questionnaires that you might have already completed or soon will, your counselor will find out a lot about your relationship. Then in your first meeting, your counselor will ask you many of the following things:

☐ to describe the current status of your relationship;
☐ to describe briefly how your relationship developed;
☐ to discuss, using an audiotape, a topic about which the two of you usually disagree;
☐ to discuss the quality of your communication and your ability to resolve differences;
☐ to discuss the ways you show closeness, affection and intimacy; this will include a discussion of your sexual relationship;
☐ to evaluate your commitment to the relationship;
☐ to discuss any complicating factors that might prevent you from bettering your relationship;
☐ to describe in some detail how you would know if your relationship were improved.

After that, the counselor will give you a brief initial summary of his or her opinion about your relationship. The counselor may ask you to complete some task at home between the first and second counseling session. In fact, the counselor may ask you to complete some task at home after each counseling session. At the beginning of the second session, your counselor will provide a written report to each of you on his or her expert view of your relationship and what can be done to improve it.

The Major Cause of Most Problems

The major cause of problems in relationships is failure or weakness in love, faith, work or some combination of those. The root difficulty is usually repeated failures in love. By love I mean valuing your partner at every opportunity and refusing to devalue or put down your partner regardless of how upset you might become. People often fail to show valuing love for a partner in the midst of conflict, in normal conversation, in mentioning the partner during interactions with others and in intimate interactions. Your counselor will want you to think continually about how to value your partner more and how to avoid devaluing your partner.

When most partners enter marital counseling, they are discouraged and have little hope that anything can be done to improve their relationship. They may not feel that the counseling will help. It is common to go through a period of discouragement in the midst of counseling, thinking that the relationship is not benefiting. When these times of discouragement happen, remind yourself that they are common, and keep the faith. Most people *do* benefit from marital counseling.

Discouragement about your relationship may result in your not wanting to work on the relationship. If you stop working on the relationship, it quickly deteriorates further. Also, when people take their partner for granted and stop trying to make their relationship more intimate and committed, when they stop trying to communicate better, when they stop forgiving their partner for hurting them, or when they stop seeking forgiveness for the times they have hurt their partner, the relationship runs downhill. A fundamental law of nature is that anything that we don't put work into will eventually run downhill. When we don't tend a garden, it produces vegetables for a while, but eventually the weeds will choke out the vegetables.

These weaknesses—in love, discouragement and not working on the relationship—cause most relationship problems. You can improve your marriage by showing more love. Your counselor will help you do that.

What to Do with the Assessment

Many people think of the problems in their relationship as being primarily due to their partner. They acknowledge that "both people are to blame for marital problems," but in their heart of hearts they think, *My partner is mostly to blame.*

Such thoughts are natural and normal. We look for the causes of our problems in what we see and hear, and, frankly, we see and hear our partner more than we see or hear ourselves. We see his withdrawal, her nagging, his long hours at work, her complaining. We blame mostly what we see and hear.

Although it is normal and natural to feel that your partner is mostly to blame for your marital problems, it isn't *helpful* to do so. We quickly find that we cannot make our partner change. Try as we might to get our partner to change, we simply become more frustrated. Many people come to marital counseling hoping that their counselor will change their partner.

In fact, we can only change our own behavior. Your counselor will try to help each partner change his or her own behavior. Your counselor will try to be fair in doing so, though at times the counselor might ask you to change more than he or she asks your partner to change. Over counseling, your counselor will generally be fair in asking each partner to change parts of his or her life that might help the marriage.

As you listen to your counselor's assessment of your marriage, think, *How can I value my partner more? How can I work harder to change? How can I have more faith?* Try to put aside your natural and normal tendency to think that your partner doesn't value you as much as you would like, doesn't seem to want to work on the relationship, or has given up. Blame is a dead-end street.

You, and only you, can change your behavior and thus affect your marriage. Don't wait for your partner to change first. Throw yourself into changing your own part and let your partner come along as fast as he or she is able.

How to Build Intimacy

Not everyone has the same need for closeness. Some people have more need for intimate talk, affection, sex and romance. Some people have more need for alone time. Some people have more need for social time with others and time spent merely being together as a couple. Each couple must work out a balance of intimacy, aloneness and social activity that satisfies both partners. The good news is that you can adjust your schedule so that you meet your needs from a variety of places. The partner does not have to meet all your needs.

To meet intimacy needs, I am going to use an acrostic to help you remember several main points. The acrostic is VALUE.

V = Value Your Partner
A = Affection
L = Love Making
U = Use Positives
E = Employ a Calendar

V: *Value your partner.* Nothing creates a feeling of closeness and intimacy like always valuing your partner.

A: *Affection.* Value your partner by showing him or her affection. Be tender with each other. Remember romantic occasions. Express your affection in words. It isn't always easy to put your feelings into words, but it usually helps your partner if you can say what you appreciate.

L: *Love making.* Your sexual relationship is important. If love making is not working as well as you would like, ask your counselor directly. Your counselor can give you helpful advice or a referral if necessary.

U: *Use positives.* Researchers have found that couples who have at least five times as many positive interactions as they do negative interactions usually have satisfying and stable relationships. If you want to improve your marriage, increase the positives and decrease the negatives.

E: *Employ a calendar.* How you use your time affects whether you meet your needs for intimacy, distance and social activity. Look hard at your calendar and see if you can shift or eliminate activities to make more time for each other.

How to Communicate Better

To communicate better, use another acrostic: LOVE.

L = Listen and Repeat
O = Observe Your Effects
V = Value Your Partner
E = Evaluate Both Partners' Interests

L: *Listen and repeat.* When your partner is on a roll and you'd like to say something or when the two of you are disagreeing and you want to interrupt to make your own point, you can get awfully frustrated. Our usual response is either to shut down or to interrupt. Either way, our partner feels devalued and misunderstood, which adds to the way we feel—devalued and misunderstood.

Instead of trying hard to get your own point across by thinking of what you are going to say next, by interrupting, by shouting or by leaving, try to understand your partner. Listen and repeat what your partner is saying until your partner is sure you understand. That will make your partner more willing to listen to you. If you summarize your partner's thoughts, you do several things:

☐ you show you care,

☐ you avoid many misunderstandings because the partner can correct misunderstandings right away,

☐ you slow down the rapid self-centered disagreements that can turn into fights.

When your partner feels that you understand, he or she usually doesn't feel as much pressure to keep talking a lot, and then you can have your say.

O: *Observe your effects.* When you say something and get a surprising reaction from your partner— such as a puzzled look, an argument when you expected agreement, a show of unexpected emotion—that should alert you instantly that there has been a misunderstanding. Gently say, "I'm sorry. I must have not communicated clearly. What did you think I was saying?" By seeking understanding, you can short-circuit a lot of misunderstandings.

V: *Value your partner.* Always. This is the number one key to keeping communication flowing and to resolving differences. If you can remember always to value and never devalue your partner, you will avoid most misunderstandings and increase your marital happiness.

E: *Evaluate both partners' interests.* When you disagree, instead of staking out win-lose positions on issues, learn to look behind the positions that you and your partner take to see what your real interests are. Usually, if you identify your interests and your partner's interests, you can arrive at a solution that meets both people's interests—a win-win situation.

How to Be Forgiven and to Forgive

Over time, in any ongoing marriage, hurts occur. If you can keep a short list of grudges over those hurts, your marriage will be happier. Quickly admit your wrongs and seek forgiveness from your partner. Be much more attentive to confessing your own hurtful behavior than to whether your partner needs to confess. If you or your partner has been hurt and has held onto the hurt, then before you end your marital counseling you will probably want to discuss the hurt with an eye toward forgiveness (not to punish the other person).

When you seek forgiveness, sincerely apologize and admit your wrongful behavior. Show that you regret hurting your partner and don't want to do so again. Ask whether you can in some way make up for hurting your partner. Don't offer excuses or blame your partner for something that provoked you. Say you're sorry and ask for forgiveness. Be patient. Sometimes it takes people awhile to forgive, so don't expect your partner to forgive instantly.

Final Assessment of Your Relationship

When counseling nears its end, the counselor will ask you to reassess your marriage. You'll consider intimacy, communication, ability to resolve differences and commitment, as well as how closely you have approached your ideal marriage as you described it in the initial assessment. At that point you can set some practical goals for your marriage about how to improve your relationship. For some that might be continuing counseling or seeking counseling with another counselor. For others it will be planning specific ways to keep working on building love and faith.

Closing

I hope this brief videotape helps prepare you for some of the ideas that you are likely to encounter in counseling and makes your efforts to improve your relationship more pleasant and more efficient. I wish you well in your work with your counselor.

What the Research Shows

D. E. Orlinsky and K. I. Howard summarized thirty-four studies and showed that, in general, orienting people to what to expect in counseling will improve the outcome of counseling.[2] In particular, twenty-one studies showed a positive effect of providing an orientation to counseling, and thirteen found no effect. L. E. Beutler, M. Crago and T. G. Arizmendi summarized a different collection of thirty-four studies, though many studies overlapped in the two summaries, and they found essentially the same thing as did Orlinsky and Howard.[3] Of the thirty-four studies, twenty-four were found to produce a positive effect and ten no effect. In most of those studies precounseling information was aimed at either reducing people's anxiety about counseling or at providing an orientation about what to expect during counseling.

How I View Precounseling Videotapes

Taro Kurusu and I have thought about precounseling instruction differently.[4] We use the theory of change developed by James Prochaska, Carlo DiClementi and John Norcross, which they call the transtheoretical model of change.[5] People might be at the precontemplation stage, in which they are not even considering changing. If they begin to think about changing and perhaps make a few brief attempts to change, they are in the contemplation stage. Once serious plans and attempts to change are begun, people are said to be in the preparation stage. Active and systematic effort at changing is undertaken during the action stage. Once successful change has taken place, people must prevent themselves from slipping back into old ways; this is called the maintenance stage.

Most people enter marital counseling in the contemplation stage, though sometimes a reluctant spouse might even be at the precontemplation stage. In Prochaska, DiClementi and Norcross's transtheoretical model, effective precounseling interventions would be those that might move partners through their stages of change faster than if counseling were begun from a standing start. Thus, precounseling interventions, such as videotapes or pamphlets, would get people to consider change if they had not done so already. Generally, when people enter marital counseling, they are not thinking about changing; they are thinking more about how to get their partner to change.

PAMPHLET

Because of the vast amount of television and large number of videotaped movies most people watch, most people are geared to learn from videotapes. Some people, though, derive more benefit from written material. Make available the material printed in table 5.2. It can be printed as a pamphlet, simply typed and copied on the front and back of a piece of paper or photocopied from this book. Allow people to take a copy with them.

SUMMARY

By the time couples begin their first counseling session, they should have already moved from the precontemplation stage of change to at least the contemplation stage of change. You will have started them on the road to the preparation stage through focusing their attention on their own marriage, on some things that might improve in their marriage and on the parts of the strategy you intend to employ—building love, faith and work—to create hope for change. Once they are on the road, they will be more likely to reach their destination.

Table 5.2. Pamphlet describing hope-focused marriage or couple therapy

Benefiting from the Couples Counseling You Are About to Receive
Everett L. Worthington Jr., Ph.D.
Taken from Hope-Focused Marriage Counseling: A Guide to Brief Therapy. *Downers Grove, Ill.: InterVarsity Press, 1999.*

Marriage Problems
It has been my experience that each couple is unique in the problems they are wrestling with. Nonetheless, certain roots seem to be at the base of almost all problems that couples have. Namely, troubled marriages usually show weaknesses in love. Love is being willing to value your partner and being unwilling to devalue your partner. Generally, troubled marriages are those in which each partner devalues the partner and fails to take opportunities to show and tell the other how much the partner is valued.

A troubled marriage is one in which partners devalue each other and fail to take every opportunity to value each other.
Generally, also, as love has lessened people lose confidence that the marriage can ever improve, and their demoralization and loss of hope prevent them from working on changing the relationship.

Marriage Solutions
If you are going to improve your relationship, you *must* do the following:
□ Regain a willingness to *work* on improving your relationship and sustain that willingness long enough so that the marriage can bounce back. The worse off your marriage is now, the longer you must be willing to work to change it before you give up.
□ Focus on the good things that you do. If you focus on the successes and try to ignore the failures for a period, you'll regain a sense of *faith* in the relationship and confidence that it can improve.
□ Increase your efforts to value your partner in *love* at every opportunity, and increase your efforts to avoid devaluing your partner.

To improve, love your partner more by valuing him or her.

Adopt a Helpful Attitude
Marital problems focus our attention on ourselves. It is easy to see the ways we are hurt, the things that the partner is doing to hurt and devalue us, the ways the partner seems to be avoiding work or showing a lack of faith, the unforgiveness the partner harbors. In short, what you see is your partner, not yourself. Your natural desire is usually to change your partner. Yet you cannot change your partner. You can only change yourself. You must, therefore, stop looking at what your partner does and doesn't do, and start focusing intently on how you can change your own behavior to make things better in your relationship.

Change what you can: your own behavior, thoughts and (eventually) feelings. Don't worry about what your partner is or isn't doing. Be the first to change; don't wait for your partner to change.
Be patient. Changes won't occur overnight. Give your partner a break. Don't expect perfection.

Take it as a given that 99% of all partners want their marriage to get better. Regardless of what you might now think, your partner is trying to improve the marriage. He or she might not be going about it effectively. That's one thing we'll work on in counseling. But your partner's motives are positive.

How to Benefit from Counseling
1. Realize that counseling is not a miracle cure for your marital ills. You will change your marriage,

mostly outside of the time you are with your counselor. The counselor will simply show you how to do that more effectively.

2. Be honest with the counselor.

3. Be honest with yourself. Try hard. Don't sabotage counseling because your confidence is at a low ebb.

4. Do the activities at home that your counselor asks you to do.

5. Understand that your counselor is not a referee for your arguments. Nor is your counselor a decision maker who will tell the two of you who is right or wrong. Instead, your counselor is a person who can show you *how* to resolve differences in a way that promotes valuing love and avoids devaluing. Your counselor will focus more on how you are communicating than on whether you arrive at a solution to all your differences. Frankly, there isn't enough time for the counselor to have you deal with all your differences. But if you learn a good method of resolving differences in valuing love, then you'll be able to resolve your own differences for the next fifty or more years.

6. Your counselor is not a hunter who seeks out your problems and shoots them. Rather, your counselor is more like a hunting guide, who will help *you* root out your problems and develop solutions that work to promote love, work and faith.

Chapter 6

Assessment
Interventions

As a psychological intern at the University of Missouri-Columbia, I attended a workshop by an eminent marital counselor. At one of the breaks, I rushed up to ask a question about a couple I was counseling. I explained their problems and my frustration, and I waited with bated breath for helpful advice.

"What did they score on the . . . ?" He named three instruments that were associated with his approach to counseling.

"I didn't give any assessment instruments," I said.

"I can't help you," he said. He turned and walked away. Maybe it was my bated breath.

I slowly recovered from the rejection. Life progressed. Usually, the couples I counseled didn't. After my rude encounter with Dr. X, though, I was determined *not* to formally assess. I'd show him! Of course, he certainly wouldn't remember me, and even if he did, wouldn't care.

I stumbled along for perhaps five years, thinking *win-some-lose-some* and not examining my euphemistically called "success rate" too closely. I remember when I decided to assess couples formally. I had just completed counseling a couple whom I had dismally failed to help. Okay, they brutalized me. The husband was a pastor and the wife a writer. They were verbally adept. The first session seemed to start well, but by the end of the hour, they had me answering questions about my position on divorce, women's leadership in the church and probably (I forget the details; call it trauma-induced repression if you like) pretribulation rapture. In desperation, I assigned some homework.

Of course, they didn't do it. They never did any of the homework I assigned. I changed toothpaste to do something about the bated breath.

By session three, I was already trying paradoxical directives and thinking of the couple as "resistant." I lasted seven sessions before I tossed in the towel and referred them elsewhere. As I sat drooling in my office pondering the couple, I realized that after trying to help them for seven weeks, I knew absolutely nothing about them except their position on fifty theological issues and their "resistant" nature.

The vision of Dr. X's face mocked me. I decided that I would assess my next couple before I tried to counsel them. A woman had phoned that day saying her husband refused to come to counseling, but could I see her? I had agreed. Mired in my postfailure depression over the resistant couple, I spontaneously phoned her and asked if I could speak with her husband about his coming to counseling. I could almost hear her sneer at the thought. She handed him the phone.

"Yeah, this is Bubba," he said. (In some parts of Virginia, we have whole families named Bubba.)

"Your wife, Shirley Mae, phoned me today, Bubba, and she wants to come in and discuss your marriage."

"Yeah, I know. It's okay with me, but we ain't got no marriage problems."

"You might be right," I said. "That's what I wanted to find out. But I realized that if she came in alone, I would just have her side of the story and she would probably tell me about all the things she thinks are problems."

"Yeah, she tells me about 'em all the time. We don't agree."

"Bubba, I was wondering, would you be willing to come in with her once, take some marriage questionnaires and talk with me about each of your sides of the marriage? You wouldn't be coming to get counseling—only to figure out why you and Shirley Mae might see things differently."

"That doesn't sound too bad," he said. "What'll it cost me?" My mouth fell open. I had never been hugely successful at getting husbands to come in for counseling.

I gathered several questionnaires and when Bubba and Shirley Mae talked about their marriage, I listened and bit my tongue to keep from doing counseling. At the end of the session, I gave them the questionnaires and asked them to return them by midweek so I could look at the questionnaires before the second assessment session.

Midweek Bubba dropped both envelopes by my office. "Yo, Doc. Those tests weren't so bad."

When I looked at the questionnaires, though, it looked as if they came from different marriages. Bubba and Shirley Mae certainly didn't see things the same way. I had amassed more information about Bubba and Shirley Mae than I had ever collected about any of the over one hundred couples I had counseled. The problem was how to tell them. There were so many differences that I did not trust myself to remember them. So I wrote them into a report, and I summarized their scores next to each other.

When they arrived for session two, I gave them a copy of the report, which Bubba took. It was clear that Bubba and Shirley Mae had many differences and that Shirley Mae was very unhappy and on the verge of divorce. That was news to Bubba, though I was sure (watching Shirley Mae talk with Bubba in session) that she had told him "about 'em all the time." But this time it was official. It came from a doc. It came in writing. Bubba practically pleaded with me to counsel them as a couple.

Bubba and Shirley Mae responded like most people with whom I have tried this method. Good assessment is the doorway to good marital counseling.

You are the major assessment instrument. Your clinical acumen will govern your interventions. You can use a variety of aids to effective assessment—the intake form, initial questionnaires, observation and tape recording of partners' conversations and self-report forms that might help you obtain specific information that you need. Assessment will occur in three contexts: before and during the first session, during the weeks of counseling sessions and prior to the end of counseling.

INITIAL ASSESSMENT

The initial assessment of the couple begins with their completing the intake form even before their first session. The initial assessment continues throughout their first session and culminates in a report.

Intake Form

When a couple arrives for counseling or even before that—after they arrange an initial appointment—have them complete an intake form. That form collects basic data about the marriage. Solicit information about the person, the relationship status and history, the person's evaluation of the marriage, the problems that each person believes brought them to counseling, one thing that the person might do to improve the marriage and other specific information. The intake also provides supplementary information to assess the person's evaluation of the nine different areas of the marriage outlined in chapter four. Have partners rate their relationship using brief ratings on your intake form and, if possible, use assessment instruments whose properties have been investigated scientifically. Following are my suggestions about what to ask on the intake form.

Relationship status. Ask directly about the relationship status—married, engaged or cohabiting.

Relationship history. One easy way to assess relationship history is to have each partner graph marital satisfaction beginning when the partners met. On the graph, partners note pivotal events in the relationship. Follow up with a discussion about the events.

Marital satisfaction. The graph referred to above allows you to assess current marital satisfaction as well as its historical fluctuation. Supplement that assessment with a standard measure. Have partners rate marital happiness using the Dyadic Adjustment Scale (DAS) if possible, or at least the following item from the DAS:[1]

The dots on the following line represent different degrees of happiness in your relationship. The middle point, "happy," represents the degree of happiness in most relationships. Please circle the dot which best describes the degree of happiness, all things considered, of your relationship.

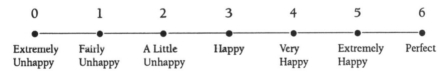

0	1	2	3	4	5	6
Extremely Unhappy	Fairly Unhappy	A Little Unhappy	Happy	Very Happy	Extremely Happy	Perfect

D. G. Cross and C. F. Sharpley showed that the single item accounted for over half of the item variance in the entire scale.[2]

Problems that brought the couple to counseling. Partners list (in free-response form) from their point of view what major problems with their marriage brought them to counseling, and they identify what they consider to be the most serious problem.

One suggestion for improving the marriage. Partners also list one thing they think they personally could do to improve the marriage regardless of what the partner does.

Other specific information. Ask the questions included in table 6.1 directly on the intake form, usually as the last page of the form. The questions are helpful in assessing the prognosis for successful marital counseling.

Table 6.1. Questions for the intake form that help in making a prognosis of the outcome of marital therapy

1. Have you ever been to counseling as a result of problems with this relationship prior to today? (Circle: Yes or No) If so, what was the outcome of that counseling?

2. Have either you or your partner been in individual counseling before? (Circle: Yes or No) If so, give a brief summary.

3. Do either you or your partner drink alcohol to intoxication or take drugs to intoxication? (Circle: Yes or No) If yes for either, who, how often and what drugs (or alcohol)?

4. Have either you or your partner struck, physically restrained, used violence against or injured the other person within the last three years? (Circle: Yes or No) If yes for either, who, how often and what happened?

5. Have either of you threatened to separate or divorce as a result of the current marital problems? (Circle one: Yes or No) If yes, who?

6. Have either you or your partner consulted a lawyer about divorce? (Circle one: Yes or No) If yes, who?

7. Do you perceive that either you or your partner has withdrawn from the marriage? (Circle one: Yes or No) If yes, which of you has withdrawn?

8. How frequently have you had sexual relations during the last month?
 _____ times

9. How enjoyable is your sexual relationship? (Circle one)

Terrible	More unpleasant than pleasant	Not pleasant, not unpleasant	More pleasant than unpleasant	Great

10. How satisfied are you with the frequency of your sexual relations? (Circle one)

Way too often to suit me	A bit too often to suit me	About right	A bit too seldom to suit me	Way too seldom to suit me

11. What is your current level of stress? (Circle one)

Extremely high	Very high	High	Moderate	Low	Very low	Extremely low

12. To what degree do you have family or friends that support you as a couple? (Circle one)

Extremely high	Very high	High	Moderate	Low	Very low	Extremely low

13. To what degree do the two of you share a similar basic worldview? (Circle one)

Extremely high	Very high	High	Moderate	Low	Very low	Extremely low

---

The First Session

I consider the first session to be an assessment session rather than a counseling session. The first session, though, is crucial to successful brief counseling of any kind, and I have given particular attention to it. I made a videotape describing and demonstrating how to conduct a first session (available from the Christian Association for Psychological Studies).[3]

Problem description. Couples come to counseling with lots of pent-up energy to tell their story. After a brief greeting to each partner, say, "I want each of you, in turn, to describe what you think, from your perspective, the major problems are with your marriage." Try to prevent partners from interrupting each other. If one blurts in, say, "Excuse me, Marty. As soon as Debra finishes giving her perspective, I will ask you to give your perspective and I'll ask Debra not to interrupt you."

Their descriptions should be brief. If someone rambles, say, "We are going to discuss these difficulties in detail if we decide to pursue counseling. For now, I'd like to get a brief overview of the main problems from each of your perspectives."

Videotaped discussion. Have partners discuss an issue about which they disagree. Videotape or audiotape it so you can analyze it later.

Brief history. Take a history of their relationship. You might start by saying, "You have each described the problems you sense in your marriage. But you didn't get to this point without a history. So I can understand how these problems developed, I'd like you to tell me about how your relationship developed. How did you meet?"

Continue to ask about their relationship: what attracted them to each other, how their courtship progressed, how they decided to marry, how their honeymoon went and so forth (see chapter eight, especially interventions 8-1 and 8-2). Focus more on the early positive aspects rather than on the negative. You want to hear the history, but you also want to call the partners' attention to some of the happier times. Later in the interview, you might ask how they could recapture those times.

Fleshing out the vision. Ask some variation of the "miracle question," which is used in many solution-focused therapy approaches.[4] Ask them, "If you woke up tomorrow and your marriage were perfect, what would be different?" (See chapter eight, especially interventions 8-3 and 8-4.) Then, depending on your judgment of what aspects of the marriage are crucial, ask about the nine areas of marriage.

Evaluations of the Nine Areas of Marriage

To assess the nine areas of marriage, use a combination of intake questions, initial interview, longer questionnaires and short-answer questions.

Central beliefs and values. Use the initial interview to ask directly about the couples' Christian values (or lack of adherence to Christianity) and to ask directly about the partners' view of commitment. Use the Religious Commitment Inventory (RCI) to assess religious commitment.[5]

Core vision. The first interview is largely aimed at fleshing out the current and ideal vision of marriage, including the realistic possibilities for achieving the vision. This includes the miracle question and a discussion of marital history.

Confession/forgiveness. As part of the intake, ask partners to complete a brief measure of marital forgiveness.[6]

Communication. Have couples describe communication difficulties and areas in which they communicate well. Supplement those descriptions by observing their communication during the interview and by audiotaping or videotaping two 5-minute discussions, one on an issue that they consider positive and one on an issue about which they disagree.

Conflict resolution. Ask partners to describe any difficulties in resolving differences and the extent and nature of their disagreements. Supplement those verbal descriptions by observing any conflicts during the interview and their attempts at conflict resolution during the five-minute taped discussion of the issue about which they disagree.

Cognition. During the first interview, note instances of the couples' negative thinking about the marriage, attributions that blame the spouse, expectations about the future of the marriage and assumptions about the marriage.[7]

Closeness. Have partners assess their intimacy, including their ratings of intimacy, using a pictorial representation of ideal and actual emotional, sexual and spiritual intimacy.[8] (We place pictorial assessments on our intake form. We have not substantiated that they are valid and reliable at the point of writing this book, but investigations are underway.) During the first interview have each partner describe how he or she uses time in a typical weekday and a typical weekend day. That description tells a lot about the couple's intimacy (or lack of it) and gives an idea how flexible the partners might be if you ask them to change their activities.

Complicating factors. There are four common complicating factors: affairs,[9] alcohol or drug abuse,[10] physical abuse,[11] and emotional or psychological problems.[12] Ask directly about each one on the intake form or in the first interview.

Commitment. During the first interview ask people directly about their level of commitment and their understanding of what it means to be committed to the partner.

First-Interview Observation of Communication and Conflict Resolution

As suggested above, during the first session instruct the partners to discuss for five minutes an issue about which they typically disagree. Audiotape or videotape that discussion and analyze it later. To help in assessing patterns of communication and conflict, answer the seventeen questions in table 6.2. Be specific. Use your answers to write your assessment report and plan how to help couples improve their conflict resolution and communication.

Table 6.2. Seventeen questions to answer for yourself after session one to help you understand communication and conflict resolution

What Couples Say

1. Does each partner seem to understand what the other is saying? If they were asked to repeat the other person's main arguments, do you think each partner could do so with fidelity? (Cue: Understand)

2. Do partners devalue each other? If so, how often and how do they devalue each other? (Cue: How Devalue)

3. To what degree is each person leveling with the partner (that is, sharing important information, feelings, thoughts)? To what degree does each partner seem to be editing information helpfully? (For example, are partners able to control expression of hurtful words and actions?) Unhelpfully? (For example, are partners clamming up or not passing along important information?) (Cue: Level-Edit)

4. Do partners seem bitter and unforgiving? (Cue: Unforgiving)

How Couples Say It

5. To what degree do the couples remain calm, especially when they get involved in a disagreement? (Cue: Calm)

6. Do couples make any attempts to regulate their negative emotion? That is, does one or both partners attempt to lighten the mood when it gets heavy or prevent the negative emotion from escalating? Do they have what John Gottman[13] calls self-soothing strategies? (Cue: Regulate)

7. To what degree do partners listen to each other? Is misunderstanding evident? Do they give verbal or nonverbal signals that communicate that they are not listening? (Cue: Listening)

8. To what degree do partners spend time defining the problem versus trying to solve the problem? (Cue: Problem/Solution)

9. How do the partners' problem-solving styles complement or oppose each other? Is one person primarily emotional and the other primarily rational? Can the couple's problem-solving styles work together easily? (Cue: Styles)

10. To what degree is each person able to express his or her emotions nondestructively? (Cue: Emotional Expression)

11. Who does most of the talking? Who commands the floor? Who exerts the most power? Does one person have veto power? (Cue: Talk-Time)

12. Do partners have patterns of communication that make it hard to resolve differences? For example, does one partner (or both) interrupt? Filibuster? Communicate dogmatically? Refuse to consider other points of view? (Cue: Patterns)

13. Do couples devalue each other by looks, gestures, interruptions and other styles of communication? (Cue: Looks)

What Effects Couples Have on Each Other

14. To what degree do partners stake out incompatible positions? Attempt to see behind their positions to the interests of the other person? (Cue: Positions or Interests)

15. To what degree do partners seem committed to winning the argument because their egos are on the line? (Cue: Ego Involvement)

16. To what degree do partners seem to be in a power struggle with each other? Does the argument seem more related to a struggle over who has the say regardless of the problem, or does the struggle seem to be localized to the content of the problem? (Cue: Power Struggle)

17. To what degree do partners devalue each other? (Cue: Degree of Devaluing)

Think systematically about the partners' communication. I recommend the following procedure. Type a cue sheet with seventeen cues corresponding to the questions in table 6.2. (See the last part of each question in table 6.2 for recommended cues.) While listening to or viewing the tape and reflecting about the session, use the cue sheet and jot answers or other notes on it.

Questionnaires

For Christian couples, I recommend using two questionnaires during the intake. Use the *Marriage Assessment Inventory* (MAI) to obtain self-reports on most of the nine areas of marriage.[14]

Use the Personal Assessment of Intimacy in Relationships (PAIR)[15] to assess five types of intimacy: emotional, sexual, social, recreational and intellectual.

Prognosis

At the end of the first session, determine the likelihood of your ultimate success with the couple. To help make your evaluation, refer to table 6.3 for a summary of factors associated with success or failure of marital counseling. If you think the chances of helping are extremely small, inform the partners so they can determine whether they wish to pursue counseling.

Your Written Assessment Report

At the end of the first session, write an assessment report. Constructing that report is an excellent use of your time. Present the basic data on the marriage, list the presenting concerns, summarize the history of the relationship, name strengths of the marriage (at least as many as weaknesses), list weaknesses of the marriage, enumerate treatment goals and write a concluding paragraph motivating the partners to work on the relationship to build love and to grow in faith and hope. (See table 6.4 for an example.) The assessment report is useful to you and to the couple for several reasons.

Information to the couple. The report summarizes your assessment for the couple and makes feedback efficient, an important consideration in brief counseling.

Intervention to solidify the conceptualization. The assessment report is not simply a report to the couple. It is an intervention. Throughout counseling, I emphasize the concepts of valuing love, work on the relationship and faith. Reread the assessment report in table 6.4. Circle each use of a theory-relevant concept—value, love, work or faith. That repetition solidifies the strategic conceptualization that you used in session one and prepares the couple for your continued use of the conceptualization throughout counseling.

Table 6.3. Information from the intake form and your observations during the first session on which to make a prognosis for hope-focused marriage counseling

The presence of any of these criteria indicate low likelihood of success. Presence of more than one criterion indicates extremely poor likelihood of success:

☐ severe psychopathology for either individual
☐ alcohol or drug abuse for either individual
☐ evidence of violence by either or each partner
☐ couples using coercion and threats of divorce
☐ either partner having consulted a lawyer about divorce
☐ either partner habitually withdrawn from the marriage
☐ either partner strongly committed ahead of time to a conception of counseling that stresses understanding of motives and insight as the solution for problems rather than active behavior as the solution

Presence of the following factors indicates good likelihood of success. The absence of a factor hurts likelihood of success but does not necessarily indicate a prognosis for failure.

Observable from Couple Interactions
☐ less dissatisfaction and distress rather than more
☐ ratio of positive to negative interactions that is 5:1 or higher
☐ emotional commitment to the specific marriage
☐ both partners' perceived-actual emotional intimacy relatively close to ideal
☐ both partners' profession that they want to resolve their problems and want practical suggestions
☐ couples still emotionally engaged with each other, even if they argue frequently and/or heatedly
☐ couples reporting that they are still having relatively frequent sexual relations, especially if those relations are usually enjoyable for both partners

Observable from Characteristics of Couple
☐ couple has good reasons for staying together (for example, long history together, children in the home, potential for being hurt in reputation or finances by divorce)
☐ younger couples rather than long-married couples
☐ fewer rather than more life stressors
☐ presence of a nonintrusive, noncontrolling social support system for both spouses

Partner Similarities
☐ both partners express high value of marriage
☐ partners agree in general on their worldview,[16] and that worldview is generally consonant with the counselor's worldview
☐ couples are both committed Christians
☐ couples are not offended by the counselor's Christianity
☐ both partners trust counseling and counselor

Involving yourself. By writing the assessment report, you help yourself assess the couple. In fact, I have found that writing the report is my greatest assessment instrument. When I must write my conceptualization in concrete words, I must think clearly about the couple. I find that those sharp conceptualizations of the couple's problems that I had prior to writing the report are sometimes revealed as shapeless shadows when I must write them. Writing sharpens my picture of

---

Table 6.4. A sample assessment report provided to each partner during the second session

CONFIDENTIAL
Carl and Sarah Simpson (fictitious names)

Personal Data
Carl (37) and Sarah (36), married seven years, have sought counseling because they want to improve a marriage that has recently been characterized by increasingly frequent conflict and lessened intimacy. They have three children: Michael (6), Paul (5) and Esther (2). Paul has recently been diagnosed with attention deficit disorder with hyperactivity (ADDH) by the educational psychologist in their school district. Carl reports a close relationship with his mother, who lives nearby. Sarah reports estrangement from her parents, who live in Illinois and are now divorced.

Presenting Complaints
Carl and Sarah feel discouraged by their marriage. They argue often over many topics, notably tensions about the amount of time involvement required of Carl at work and home, sexual relations (frequency), child-rearing concerns around Paul's ADDH and potential favoritism among children, differential religious involvement, household chores, degree of Carl's participation at home and whether they should move to a section of town that has a better school system and less risk of crime.

Both feel unappreciated and devalued, especially during times of conflict, but extending into many areas of the relationship. Both feel demoralized and do not believe that much can be done to improve their marriage. They feel that they must attend marital counseling to give it a try, but they don't believe that counseling will help. They complain about an eroded love between them, and they express little faith that any amount of work can restore their relationship.

Relationship History
Carl and Sarah met nine years ago on the production line at a local plant. Carl was line supervisor and Sarah was a worker on the line. Sarah initiated the contact, and they began seeing each other. Carl had been seeing another woman, but he was attracted to Sarah. He continued to see both women for a time. Eventually Sarah confronted him with needing to make a choice. He chose Sarah. The other woman moved, and soon thereafter Carl asked Sarah to marry. They had seen each other for two years before they married.

They conceived on their honeymoon in Jamaica, and Michael was born at the beginning of their tenth month. Neither felt ready for parenthood. Sarah quit work, and Carl felt increasing financial pressure to support the family. He began to spend more time at work. Sarah conceived Paul within two months after Michael's birth, despite their using birth control. With Paul's birth both parents felt an increase in demands on their time. At that time Carl sold his car (a Corvette) and entered a local community college. He received an A.A. degree after two years and transferred to a large state university within the city, where after three additional years he received a B.A. in business (management). The recent graduation has precipitated much new arguing.

Both are highly overcommitted to various activities, feeling intense pressure. The time strains place a burden on their lives, reducing the time they have for sexual and romantic intimacy. The time strains also intensify the feelings of annoyance that each feels when they disagree. Both mean well for their relationship. Both want the marriage to survive and thrive, but neither is happy with the relationship as it now stands.

Relationship Strengths
The relationship is strengthened by having two caring partners, both of whom are intensely interested in making the marriage work. Despite the conflict, there is obvious love between them. They are committed to their children and to providing a good home for them, as evidenced by Carl's concern about providing financial and other resources for the family and by Sarah's involvement in

teaching Sunday school and in active parenting. Both have the strength of a Christian faith to draw on. Sarah is more active in church than is Carl, but Carl professes an active support of the church and a willingness to provide his children with a good Christian example of a moral and hardworking man. Sarah is very concerned about helping Carl become a more involved husband and father. Carl recognizes the commitment that Sarah has shown in helping him and taking much responsibility for child rearing during the time Carl has been in school.

Relationship Weaknesses
Three weaknesses plague the marriage.
☐ The relationship is weak in love for each other. Pressure and conflict has intensified differences. Both Carl and Sarah feel devalued, and they do not have a sense that the partner really values what they do or who they are.
☐ The relationship is starved for work. Like a garden that needs weeding or a room that needs a paint job, their marriage has been neglected while each concentrated on other things: work and school for Carl and child rearing and church activities for Sarah.
☐ The relationship is short on faith. Both partners have lost faith in their ability to solve marriage problems. Both have little faith that counseling will help their marriage. Both have little faith that Jesus can intervene to make a difference in their marriage.

Recommended Treatment Goals
Carl and Sarah identified some goals for resolving their marriage difficulties. When asked how they would know if their marriage was better, they agreed that the marriage would be better if they
☐ argued less often and
☐ used fewer hurtful words when they disagreed (devalued each other less).
Instead they need to
☐ value each other more by
    a. making more statements that let each other know that they think the other person is valuable and is doing valuable things for the marriage and the family,
    b. telling each other what they like more often,
    c. simply sitting down and talking at least weekly,
    d. making love at least twice a month, if not more,
    e. have a special time together at least once a month,
    f. making more effort to do things that they know the partner wants them to do (for just one example, for Carl to pick up clothes more often; for Sarah to not remind Carl of what he needs to do as often),
☐ work on the marriage, especially concentrating on the next six months while the marriage is repairing itself, and
☐ have more faith that their work on the marriage will pay off by observing positive changes with an open mind and trying to say aloud what positive changes they have observed.

Overall
Carl and Sarah have a marriage that is troubled by conflict and low levels of intimacy. However, they have a good foundation to their marriage. They love each other and they share many common values. They have a commitment to the marriage and the family, and they have a faith that will empower them to continue to work on their marriage even through the hard times still to come. The problems can be resolved and the love can be restored *if Carl and Sarah are willing to work hard on their relationship.* The changes in their relationship depend to a large degree on how hard they are willing to work and on whether they are able and willing to love each other by treating each other as a precious pearl in as many ways as they can. They are encouraged to draw on their faith to help them *work with high energy on their marriage.*
Everett L. Worthington Jr., Ph.D.

what the couple is struggling with as well as what I want to do about their struggles. William Zinssner calls this writing to learn.[17]

Increasing hope. Throughout marital counseling you must increase the partners' hope. Hope is willpower to change plus waypower to change plus waitpower while God works change. The assessment report builds willpower to change by showing partners their positive vision for marriage including clear achievable goals. It creates waypower for change by serving as a concrete document suggesting a plan for change. The written report also provides a permanent record of the relationship status. The assessment report creates a sense of waitpower, to the extent that the counselor does not promise instantaneous change and stresses the necessity for the couple to work and wait on God to change them.

Counselors often bristle when I suggest that writing the report is so beneficial. *Why can't I simply discuss the assessment data?* you might wonder. Write the report so couples have something concrete to take home and read. (1) The report reinforces the conceptualization and goals. (2) Couples feel that they have received something of value when you provide a written report. (3) A written document does something that can never be done by a mere discussion of the marriage. It provides a permanent record of the initial status of the marriage and a plan for changing that status. If the assessment is discussed but not written, it is subject to reconstruction in the partners' minds. Later, couples tend to deny that they agreed to work on some goals. The permanent record minimizes that defense. Also looking back from the end of counseling, a successful couple often discounts improvement. "Our marriage wasn't that bad," they say. Such shifting standards are common. With a documentation of the status of the marriage, they have a permanent account of the initial status.

You might say, "I don't have time to write the report for every couple." Beginning counselors write their first report in only about two hours, which in itself is not long given the therapeutic benefits. Beginning counselors write subsequent reports much faster. Experienced counselors can usually write a good report in about an hour and fifteen minutes the first time they try. After having done numerous reports, I can write a report in fifteen to forty-five minutes regardless of the complexity of the case. (I wrote table 6.4 from scratch in less than forty-five minutes.) Any counselor can do the same. With computers, many counselors can write a good report, tailored to the couple, in fifteen minutes by composing standard paragraphs for common difficulties and using cut-and-paste computer commands.

Not only are costs low, but the benefits are high. In a controlled study of untroubled couples who received assessment plus a written report versus those who were assessed but given no feedback, the assessment and written feedback accounted for about one-fourth of the total gain usually experienced by couples who go through relationship enrichment procedures.[18] Written assessment without feedback did not produce changes in relationship satisfaction. (It is often more difficult to get changes in relationship enrichment than in couple counseling because the couples have less room to change.)

ASSESSMENT DURING ONGOING COUNSELING

Assessment continues throughout the entire course of counseling, as you observe the couple's communication, responses to in-session and homework assignments, and so forth.

Your Clinical Observations

During counseling, continually observe your clients. I have found to my dismay that most clients have not read my theory and don't know how they "should" behave, at least according to my theory. Clients upset our glib theoretical conceptualizations by their actual behavior. Thus, we must maintain humility with respect to our conceptualization of clients, and we must be open to revising our thinking based on the clients' behaviors.

Observations of their communication. As couples talk with each other, they sometimes surprise me. A harsh husband reaches out and tenderly caresses his wife. A sweet wife suddenly venomously lashes out at her husband. The natural tendency is to ignore such surprises. The mind is great at ignoring things that don't fit our preconceptions. Surprises are alarms that say, "Wake up, counselor. Pay attention to what is going on and see why you were surprised." Whenever a couple surprises me, I think long and hard about the surprising interaction. That thought often leads me to revise my approach to helping the couple.

Couples' response to in-session assignments, interventions or directives. When you make an assignment, you usually do so because you think you know what will move clients along therapeutically. When clients surprise you with their reactions, treat that surprise as an alarm that cues you to reevaluate your thinking. When I am surprised, I first ask myself, *What is wrong with those resistant clients?* I know from experience, though, that it is not "resistant clients" that lead to most surprises. It is my lack of clarity at giving directions or a signal that I may have missed something important in conceptualizing the couple.

Couples' response to homework assignments. Couples can respond to homework by doing it completely, partially or not at all. Even if couples do the homework you assigned completely, they might or might not feel that they are benefiting from it. At every session ask whether couples did the homework and what they got out of it, if anything.

Couples' Improvement or Lack of Improvement

If couples seem to be progressing, that suggests that *they* are doing something right. Sometimes couples improve in spite of what we counselors have them do, not because of it. Still, usually when couples improve, we generally proceed as if they were doing something right in counseling. On the other hand, the progress of few couples is steadily upward. Most marriages improve in fits and starts. Sometimes they improve dramatically, like turning on a light switch. Monitor the couple's mood to gauge whether you need to make a course correction in your counseling.

Your Own Reactions to the Clients

I usually can tell when counseling is not going well. I start not wanting to meet with the couple, disliking them or feeling as if I am a failure. Monitoring your internal reactions to clients may reveal that you need to change something in counseling.

Brief Summary

Assessment during ongoing counseling usually does not involve giving assessment instruments, writing reports or conducting videotaped, structured behavioral observations. Rather, progress is discernible from the outcomes partners experience and from your and their feelings during counseling. Table 6.5 shows some telltales for evaluating progress in counseling.

ASSESSMENT PRIOR TO THE FINAL SESSION

Prior to the final session, reflect on the marriage and write a report assessing its current status. Begin with the brief summary of the marriage that you wrote at the beginning of counseling. (By cutting and pasting, you can again produce a substantial report without exerting as much effort as you think.) Describe the couple's progress during counseling. Summarize the status of the marriage. Propose new goals for the couple and suggest ways for the couple to achieve the goals. Express your feelings about working with the couple in counseling.

You can use portions of the intake form part of as a postcounseling evaluation

---

Table 6.5. How do you know whether counseling is working?

Following are some indications that counseling is working.
☐ Partners give you the impression that you connected with them emotionally before the end of session one.
☐ Partners do not miss sessions.
☐ Partners devalue each other less often in your presence.
☐ Partners report that they are getting happier and their relationship is better.
☐ Partners attack each other less (especially the woman attacks less) and are less personal in their attacks.
☐ Partners withdraw less (especially the man withdraws less) but do not argue more as counseling progresses.
☐ Partners do the homework almost every time.
☐ Partners cooperate more as the sessions are progressing.
☐ Partners are more willing to acknowledge specific ways that they contribute to problems (not just general acknowledgments that "two people contribute to any marital problem").

Here are some indications that counseling is not working.
☐ You feel that you have not made emotional contact with either person during the session.
☐ There is evidence of a severe ongoing power struggle that does not seem to lessen with additional sessions.
☐ The main issue is lack of trust, which seems not to change.
☐ There is a low threshold for interpreting the mate's actions as being a threat.
☐ One person persistently argues with you.
☐ One person seems to accept what you say on the surface but can't seem to understand how to employ your suggestions. As a consequence, nothing seems to work.
☐ One partner or both partners are rigid and don't want to accept any responsibility.
☐ When one partner softens, the other does not soften but stays hard and combative.
☐ One partner is hostile, anxious and rigid and cannot seem to accept the other person's imperfections.
☐ You find that one partner criticizes the spouse to the partner's friends and those friends support the complaining partner.
☐ One partner persists in putting career, leisure, children or other activities in higher priority than marriage even though the spouse has requested that the marriage needs more attention.
☐ An affair that had apparently ended starts up again.
☐ Jibes, criticisms, put-downs and subtle and overt devaluing continue despite repeated encouragement by the counselor to cease those destructive habits.

---

of the couple. Particularly telling is the degree of change in marital happiness on the single-item measure or DAS.

Sadly, change produced in marital counseling does not always last. Wouldn't it be nice to think that any change in life would be so permanent that it never eroded or was upset by future catastrophes? If the marriage deteriorates two or three years later, many couples will say, "We went to counseling several years back, and it didn't work." They forget about the astounding gains they may have made. When you give the couple a written report summarizing the gains, you make it harder for them to discount the change that they worked hard to achieve. Provide a written account: it makes change sensible, and it makes couples more likely to seek help in the future (if they need it) rather than give up on their marriage.

LOOKING BACK, LOOKING AHEAD

Making hope sensible begins and ends with assessment. Assessment keeps you selecting effective interventions throughout the middle of counseling too. In fact, if you use the most powerful interventions in the world with couples whose problems are not related to those interventions, at times when couples cannot use them, or in ways that couples cannot receive, then the interventions will be impotent. Your assessment of the couple and your skill at intervening are crucial to your success.

The following chapters have summaries of many interventions you can use to help couples grow in love. These interventions by no means exhaust the possible interventions in hope-focused marriage counseling. In fact, I draw eclectically from many theoretical approaches to marital counseling. What makes the interventions and homework usable in hope-focused marriage counseling is that each one meets the following criteria:

☐ It is targeted at one of the identified areas of marriage (organized by chapter).

☐ It promotes hope by increasing at least one of the three aspects of hope: willpower to change (that is, motivation), waypower to change (that is, usually showing the couple clearly how to change and usually involving a behavioral or physical manipulation that makes change sensible to the partners) or waitpower (that is, promoting a sense that God can sustain the partners during a period of little or no change).

☐ It strengthens weaknesses in one of the three strategic objectives: love (increases deficient valuing or decreases excess devaluing of the partner), faith (in the marriage, in the future of the marriage, in the partner, in counseling as a potential help to change or in the Lord to produce or maintain changes) or work on the marriage.

These three characteristics define hope-focused marriage counseling interventions.

Chapter 7

Interventions for Drawing on Central Values

Susan and Paul's marriage slammed into the rocks of conflict when Paul's parents invited the couple and their daughter to the beach. Susan didn't want to go, and she didn't want her daughter to go either. Paul sided with his parents against his wife (almost always a bad move). He valued his parents more than he valued his wife.

A value is what one feels is important. Values order thinking and help make decisions by setting priorities. Beliefs are statements that one thinks to be true.[1] For example, a person may strongly believe Christianity to be true but may not value it.

In counseling, you discover that two of Paul's beliefs are in conflict: that his family of origin is important and that his nuclear family is important. His choice showed that, at least in the beach incident, he valued his family of origin more than his nuclear family. You become convinced that you need to challenge his values. Dare you? Are you imposing your values on Paul? If you do challenge his values, how should you do it and what will happen if you do?

YOUR ATTITUDE TOWARD CLIENTS' VALUES: RESPECT
Jesus held a firm standard throughout his life on earth. Whomever he touched, he respected their values. Yet he did not agree with opposing values, and he clearly and strongly confronted many people whose values were not in line with

the kingdom of God. While it is more difficult to infer what he did *not* do, I would bet that he did not confront every person with whom he differed. Instead, he chose his battlegrounds strategically to make the most impact on the person and on those who were involved with the person.

Jesus left a commandment for his disciples: "By this everyone will know that you are my disciples, if you have love for one another" (Jn 13:34-35). In John 15:12-13 Jesus said, "This is my commandment, that you love one another as I have loved you. No one has greater love than this, to lay down one's life for one's friends." Paul carried on with Jesus' theme. In Romans 12:9-10 he wrote, "Let love be genuine; hate what is evil, hold fast to what is good; love one another with mutual affection; outdo one another in showing honor."

Our clients are friends—not in the sense of being intimate personal acquaintances, but in the sense of being fellow humans of great value. Whether clients believe similarly to us, they are our neighbors and friends, and we must maintain the attitude of loving people genuinely, hating sin passionately, holding truth tenaciously, expressing mutual affection unashamedly and honoring our clients openly (to paraphrase Rom 12:9-10).

A counselor must respect the central values of the client couple. Some central values may be destructive, and if you believe that the values of one or both partners are destructive, you have an obligation and right to present your beliefs to the couple. The value issue should be clearly labeled as such, and the counselor should not attempt to coerce the client, unless the problem is immediately life or health threatening. For example, if one partner's drinking is not only affecting the marriage but is posing a health danger to the individual and perhaps to the partner (if violence or drunk driving is involved, for instance), then the counselor should address the issue. If you confront a client, use the five-step template identified in intervention 7-1, respecting the client's central values.

Intervention 7-1: Respecting Central Values

Use the following five-step template anytime that (a) you need to confront a client on a value-laden issue or (b) a client questions your authority to demand a change. Respecting the person's right to make his or her own value decisions, you must

1. identify your own important values
2. affirm the client's desire to do what is good and to make good decisions
3. identify problems arising from the client's values or behaviors

4. help the client examine the evidence of the consequences that will ensue if the behavior continues, including consequences to the person and to the spouse

5. respect the client's right to accept the consequences for his or her own value decisions

Strategy: Demonstrate valuing love; increase faith in counseling's ability to help

Hope: Increase willpower to change

REVEALING YOUR OWN VALUES

Counseling is value driven. It is impossible to keep your values out of counseling, though I believe that you should attempt to minimize using your values in counseling, especially values not relevant to the counseling.[2]

Sometimes it is helpful to reveal one's central values to the clients at the onset of counseling, especially if the clients have chosen to attend counseling with you *because* of your values. For example, some people attend counseling with an explicitly Christian counselor *because* Christian values are the counselor's central values. For explicitly Christian counselors, those religious values should generally be revealed early in counseling. However (except when clients want a fuller discussion of the beliefs and values), the counselor should not discuss the values at any length. In fact, some research shows that providing more complete information can actually harm the therapeutic relationship, because with only a label the client can "project" favorable values onto the counselor.[3] In your yellow-pages advertisement, advertising brochure or intake form, you could list "Christian counseling" as one option.

Jennifer Ripley and I studied Christian couples' preferences for explicitly Christian or non-Christian counselors who said in their advertisements that they did or did not use explicitly Christian interventions.[4] We found that strongly committed Christians (in the upper 15 percent of the entire population in Christian commitment) preferred explicitly Christian counselors regardless of whether they said they used Christian interventions.

Revealing Your Values During Counseling

Regardless of whether you have revealed your Christian beliefs or values prior to counseling, you should reveal important and relevant values when explicitly dealing with issues on which those values might have an impact. After the initial part of counseling, you should reveal your values especially on any issue in which you are going to make a value-laden recommendation.

Sometimes during counseling, you know that the partners are going to address a value-laden issue, one about which you hold a strong position. You realize that it is likely that your values will be detected by one or both of the partners. Perhaps you favor the position of one partner and are concerned that the other will sense your support and be defensive. Perhaps you merely want to help clients make an informed decision rather than one in which you might be unconsciously manipulative. The psychoanalytic concept of countertransference, in which you project your own issues onto clients, can sometimes be effectively countered if you make explicit your values about an issue touchy to you. By making your position explicit, you force yourself to be aware of the issue and to be scrupulously fair to the partners.

To reveal your position fairly, use the three-step method below. For example, suppose that partners reveal in the second session that they are considering divorce.

1. State your values succinctly.

> I, of course, am very promarriage. I believe that in marriage counseling we need to try as hard as we can to make the marriage work and not be wishy-washy about whether we are looking for a continued marriage or divorce. If we try as hard as possible to make this marriage work and if the marriage doesn't work, then we'll deal with that.

2. Tell why you are revealing your values.

> I tell you my position on marriage and divorce because I want you to understand my advice within the context of my values. I don't want you to think I'm neutral on this. I'm not.

3. Assure the partners that you encourage them to make informed judgments.

> You, of course, may disagree with my position, so knowing what my position is will help you make informed judgments.

ASSESSING CLIENTS' VALUES

The central values of marriage will differ for different couples. Here are some of the ways to discover the central values of the person or couple. First, ask directly about important values and listen carefully to what the client says. Second, look beyond the words to detect many other important values. Third, tentatively suggest that their tone of voice and body language might reveal values. For example, say something like "Frank, I observed that you made a face and moved around a lot when we began to discuss whether you should spank your children. Millie, you also showed signs of discomfort. Am I right in assuming that you disagree on this value?"

Be careful. You may have observed only a small sample of behavior and that sample may not represent the person's values. Or the person might feel a conflict and be showing one value while holding the opposite. The person might be unaware of how his or her behavior is coming across. In fact, the person might be unaware that he or she is even experiencing a value conflict.

Using Homework to Find Out About Central Values

A few instruments assess values, but I have found none good for assessing the values important in marital counseling. I have developed a questionnaire (see table 7.1) that asks people to rate each value; however, I have done no research on its reliability or validity, so interpret your results cautiously. Assign partners to complete the instrument at home, working independently.

Using Homework to Promote Awareness of Central Values

If partners seem unaware of values yet you can see that those values are substantially affecting the marriage and the progress of counseling, you can initiate a discussion of values during a session. Depending on how well the partners communicate with each other, you can assign partners to reflect individually or together about the values when they are at home between sessions. Having partners who are in chronic conflict discuss their basic values at home without supervision can threaten a troubled marriage in the early stages of counseling. Do not assign this to a couple unless you are sure they can successfully discuss differences in values without arguing. Usually that means that such an assignment will be made late in counseling with couples who have successfully undergone training in conflict resolution and communication. (See interventions 7-2 and 7-3 for two suggestions for homework.)

Intervention 7-2 *(Homework)*: Reflecting on Competing Values

Assign both spouses to consider separately at home the relative weighting of two or more values. Such an assignment is best for a person who is naturally reflective about values, but can be used for all clients if the issues are clearly defined at the time of assignment. It is helpful to have some clients write reasons why one value might be ranked higher than another.

Strategy: Work

Hope: Willpower to change

Table 7.1. A questionnaire to assess marriage-relevant values

For each issue below, rate how important it is to you *right now* using the following scale:
  CEN = One of the most central or important issues to me.
  IMP = Very important but not as essential as the central issues.
  MOD = Of moderate importance to me.
  LIT = Of little importance to me.
  NO = Of no importance to me.

1. My religious beliefs	CEN	IMP	MOD	LIT	NO
2. Money and things money can buy	CEN	IMP	MOD	LIT	NO
3. Having a common vision for our marriage	CEN	IMP	MOD	LIT	NO
4. Agreeing on important values	CEN	IMP	MOD	LIT	NO
5. Being able to forgive each other when we've been hurt	CEN	IMP	MOD	LIT	NO
6. Being able to admit to each other when we are wrong	CEN	IMP	MOD	LIT	NO
7. Spending time together	CEN	IMP	MOD	LIT	NO
8. Sharing a sense of being emotionally bonded	CEN	IMP	MOD	LIT	NO
9. Having a sense that we are about intellectually equal	CEN	IMP	MOD	LIT	NO
10. Sharing common interests in leisure	CEN	IMP	MOD	LIT	NO
11. Sexual satisfaction	CEN	IMP	MOD	LIT	NO
12. Shared social activities	CEN	IMP	MOD	LIT	NO
13. Expressing positive emotions	CEN	IMP	MOD	LIT	NO
14. Expressing negative emotions	CEN	IMP	MOD	LIT	NO
15. Keeping each other posted about little things that have happened throughout the day	CEN	IMP	MOD	LIT	NO
16. Not arguing	CEN	IMP	MOD	LIT	NO
17. Being able to resolve differences	CEN	IMP	MOD	LIT	NO
18. Not hurting each other when we disagree	CEN	IMP	MOD	LIT	NO
19. Not blaming each other for things that go wrong	CEN	IMP	MOD	LIT	NO
20. Holding basically the same expectations	CEN	IMP	MOD	LIT	NO
21. Fidelity	CEN	IMP	MOD	LIT	NO
22. Keeping our word to each other	CEN	IMP	MOD	LIT	NO
23. Being dedicated to each other for life	CEN	IMP	MOD	LIT	NO
24. Being self-controlled	CEN	IMP	MOD	LIT	NO
25. Time with friends	CEN	IMP	MOD	LIT	NO
26. Commitment to my job or career	CEN	IMP	MOD	LIT	NO

Intervention 7-3 *(Homework):* Discussing Values

Assign each partner to consider his or her values surrounding an issue. Tell the partners that you would like them to discuss the issues at home during the week prior to the upcoming session. Direct the couple to break off the discussion if either one feels as if it is turning into an argument. Then, direct the couple to set a time to discuss their respective values. At the following session, process the results of the discussion.

  Strategy: Love, work
  Hope: Willpower to change

CHALLENGING CLIENTS' VALUES

People choose their own values. Counselors can never force clients to change their values. In confronting a person concerning a self-destructive value, do not try to change the person. Aim to inspire reflection on values that will lead to continued reflection under the prompting of the Holy Spirit, which will eventually lead the person either to modify or reaffirm his or her values.

When people are challenged about their values, despite your best efforts, they often feel devalued and defensive. Research has shown that when Christians—and even non-Christians—observe a counselor challenging a client's religious values, the observers evaluate the counselor negatively.[5]

General Tactics for Challenging Values

You must challenge so that the person can consider what you say and not defensively shut down. That is a tough task. Use this guideline: Affirm before you challenge. Administer grace before truth.

Challenging values is like phoning long-distance. First, you enter the area code to make the connection with the proper interchange. Then, and only then, can you dial the number and connect with the person whom you are phoning. If you enter all the correct numbers but in the wrong order, you will not successfully communicate.

Sometimes the need to confront is clear, such as when a partner is abusing drugs or alcohol, abusing a child or spouse, or having an affair. We could use one of those cases to illustrate affirming and challenging. Instead, let's take a deliberately ambiguous example to see how this might work. Recall Susan and Paul from the opening of the chapter. Paul's parents want to take his daughter to the beach. Susan says no. Paul feels caught in the middle. He sides with his parents, and a loud argument ensues between Susan and the other adults. Do not get side-tracked with the issue of whether Susan or Paul was right, or whether a better compromise solution could have been worked out. (Undoubtedly, it could.) Instead, examine Paul's decision to support his parents instead of Susan.

Based on Genesis 2:24 we know that when partners marry, they are to leave their parents and cleave to their partner. Suppose you believe that once the issue became unresolvable, Paul should have sided with his wife rather than his parents. How would you challenge Paul's values?

Affirm Paul before you challenge his values. Affirm what you observed Paul did well, and affirm his motives. You might say,

Paul, I liked several things that you did during the episode. You did a good job of seeing everyone's point of view. You valued your parents by understanding their sacrifice in driving to see you and in offering to take the family to the beach. You valued Susan by acknowledging her commitments in town. You were considerate of Natalie's experience too, weighing what you thought she would enjoy more: a trip to the beach or a birthday party. You valued everyone involved and tried to make a good decision. You felt caught in the middle of three people you loved very much, and you felt that regardless of your decision you would disappoint someone. That's a terrible position to be in, frustrating, angering, distressing, but sometimes things like that happen.

Once you have affirmed the person, reflected feelings and acknowledged how difficult the situation is, offer the challenge.

I want you to consider a principle in case you get caught in the middle again. This principle comes from Genesis 2 and argues that when you marry, you are to leave your parents and cleave to your wife. Of course, that's a hard principle always to apply in practical daily situations, but it's an important one. I think that in this situation, your best decision might have been to support Susan even if you thought she was wrong in her decision. That united front of marriage is the foundation of all your other relationships with family and friends. That doesn't mean that you can never disagree with Susan about her decisions. In fact, I was glad that you were able to discuss with her the pros and cons of her decision this time. I think it is perfectly fine to share your views and to try convincing her to change her mind. But if it comes to an impasse, you might consider whether you value the solidarity of supporting your wife or making what you think is the best decision and supporting your parents.

I'm not trying to second-guess your decision. That's finished and past, and you and Susan have now worked through the disagreement. I want you to consider in light of your values what kind of decision you might make if such a situation arose about a different issue. I'd rather you not answer now. Instead, think about the issue in relationship to your own values. You may or may not change your opinions. What's important is that you think through your values so you can make a value-informed decision next time instead of being caught in an emotional situation to which you have to respond immediately.

Using Homework to Help a Partner Think About Your Challenge

When you challenge a person's values, sometimes the person gets caught up in reacting to your challenge, regardless of how much you affirm and support the person before you issue the challenge. People caught up in the challenge often cannot think rationally about their values. Help the person structure time to reflect on the challenge, as is suggested in intervention 7-4.

Intervention 7-4 *(Homework)*: Reflecting on Challenges to Values

After you have challenged one (or both) partners' values during the session, assign the partner to reflect on the challenge. Suggest that the partner take a blank piece of paper and pen and spend thirty minutes alone. The person should begin the quiet time by praying for the Lord to reveal his will during the quiet time. Suggest that the partner pray for the spouse's general welfare. Have the person enter a time of praise and follow that by a prayerful confession of sins. After a time of silence, the person may write the issue on the piece of paper. As the person thinks about the issue, have him or her write down thoughts that come to mind. At the beginning the partner should not try to resolve the issue. Instead, he or she should consider various sides, writing notes as they seem relevant. After about ten to fifteen minutes, have the person look at the paper and begin to consider whether a resolution of the issue is possible. If a resolution is reached, the person should write the solution down and bring it back to the next counseling session.

Strategy: Love

Hope: Waypower to change

Expect to Deal with This Value

Clients must work on their marriage outside of counseling sessions. Few clients embrace the value of homework. Some counselors observe a "rule of thirds" concerning couples and their response to homework. About one-third of the couples do homework conscientiously, one-third do homework sometimes, and one-third never do it. Those who never do homework claim to be too busy to complete the assignment. Some of those couples denigrate the value of homework.

I have not found the rule of thirds to hold in my practice or in the practice of the students I supervise. Much of the couple's response to homework depends on the seriousness with which the counselor takes homework. In fact, a literature has developed over about twenty years of research that suggests that clients' performance of homework depends largely on what counselors do.[6]

Help the couple see that homework is valuable. Sometimes you must address that value directly. I use metaphors and analogies when challenging couples to work at home. For most people a good metaphor seems to be more understandable and to produce less resistance than a direct statement of a principle. Intervention 7-5 describes a metaphor that I often use.

Intervention 7-5: Use a Metaphor to Justify the Agreement to Work at Least Five Hours per Week on the Marriage

Here are a couple of metaphors you can use to help persuade the partners to value doing homework.

☐ Many people wait for romantic feelings to emerge. They won't emerge on their own. Partners must act romantically, and that helps feelings grow. I could wait for garden-grown tomatoes to appear on my plate so I could enjoy them. The fact is, they won't unless I plant the seeds, nurture the seeds into small plants, plant the plants, fertilize the soil, water the plants, stake the plants and harvest the tomatoes. You need to work your marital garden. I'm asking you to spend time in that garden during the next months. Let's see if you can produce some pleasing fruit.

☐ If people put as much energy into saving their marriage as they did into recovering from divorce, they would be better off. Divorce devastates partners and children. It takes an emotional toll that research has shown to be experienced ten years after the divorce.[7] So putting a year or two of effort into saving the marriage is a great investment. I'm not even asking you for a year of effort. I'm asking only the equivalent of a single work week of effort for now—five hours a week at home for eight weeks. Are you willing to work one week to try to improve your marriage?

Strategy: Work

Hope: Willpower to change; Waypower to change

SUMMARY

You will frequently have to deal with central values—your own and your clients'. You will deal better with those issues you have contemplated in light of your own values. Clients will deal better with values to the extent that you can get them to think through their own values in light of Scripture.

Not all clients like to be reflective about general values, so tailor your interventions to your clients. With clients who are not reflective, help them think about the value issues as they arise during counseling. For clients who are more reflective, rely more on homework.

Chapter 8

Interventions for Revisioning a Core Vision

To help couples gain a vision that can guide their marriage is one target of hope-focused marriage counseling. Couples usually have a vision, but the vision they bring to counseling is disjointed. Their vision of their marriage is like a withered, deformed flower, and their unattainable dream-vision is like the most perfect flower garden in existence.

In the core of their vision is a prescription for distress. William James said that happiness is performance divided by expectation.[1] The couple with a troubled marriage has little happiness: high expectation and low performance. Help them change both their performance and expectation. In this chapter we tackle ways that the couple can change their vision of marriage—their expectation. The interventions are divided into two sections: those that assess the core vision and those that strive to change the vision of the marriage.

ASSESSING THE CORE VISION

Before you can help the partners change their core vision of marriage, you must first assess it.

Exploring the Core Vision Through Taking Histories

Find out about the core vision of the marriage over the course of counseling. Much of the core vision you can deduce after the first interview. You learn about it during the first session by taking a history of the partners' relationship and a brief history of each partner's parents' relationship.

Marital problems were not born full-grown. They developed through each spouse's repeated failures in valuing, repeated devaluing and repeated efforts to obtain valuing from the partner. Having clients describe the history of their relationship puts the marriage problems in context for you and the clients. It helps the partners see how their failures in love mounted over time; thus the myth that a solution should occur instantaneously is weakened, though not eliminated.

History taking also gives clients hope and increases their motivation to change.[2] In recounting the history of the relationship, people describe the good times in their marriage as well as the bad times. Listen to their stories, reflect strategically (calling attention to love, work and faith) and summarize by noting that good times in the marriage were characterized by mutual valuing and rocky times by devaluing.

Intervention 8-1: Taking a History of the Marriage Relationship

During the first session, immediately after you have asked each partner to give a brief summary from his or her perspective of the major problems with the marriage, take a history of the relationship. Follow these five guidelines.

Guideline 1: Introduce the history taking by describing its context, saying, "You have told me about the problems in your marriage, but I suspect that those problems didn't always exist. They probably grew as your relationship developed. It would be helpful if you described your relationship history beginning when you met. Then I can understand the context of your problems and what you can do to get over them." Match your exact words to your clients.

Guideline 2: Pay at least as much attention to the good times as to the problems. By attending to the good times, as well as the bad, you remind the partners that there are parts of the marriage that they would like to recapture.

Guideline 3: During history taking, help strengthen the conceptualization (that marital problems are due to failures in love) by attending to specific positive demonstrations of love and failures in showing love. Help clients see that a positive marriage embodies love and a troubled marriage fails to demonstrate mutual love.

Guideline 4: Listen actively. To help the couple understand their marriage as requiring love, faith and work, reflect portions of clients' stories often. For example, when a client describes a good time in his or her marriage, reflect such phrases as "During that period, you felt important to your spouse," or "At that time, you sensed that she cared for you," or "When he did that, you felt valued." After you have made such reflections several times, respond to other descriptions of good times by simply asking, "How did you feel about that?" The partner will usually answer that he or she felt valued, loved or important. Respond to descriptions of the bad times in the marriage by reflecting how the client did not feel valued (important, cared for and so forth).

Guideline 5: Close with a strategic summary. At the end of the history, say, "As you related your history, I noticed that a pattern might be evident. Whenever you felt valued, the marriage went well, but when you felt devalued or felt that your partner did not think you were important, the marriage was troubled. Is that accurate?" Helping clients draw such conclusions will prepare them for understanding one task of counseling as trying to love and therefore value the partner more than is currently evident.

Strategy: Love

Hope: Willpower to change

After the clients have described their history and you have concluded that failures in love have caused relationship problems, observe that those failures in love probably were learned when the client was young. Explore the histories of each partner's family of origin. Look for two things: (1) How did each client's mother and father treat each other? By finding such information, you can discover much of the client's core vision of marriage. What marriage is hoped to be often depends on trying to duplicate or avoid parental patterns. (2) How did each of the client's parents treat the client? The opposite-sex parent usually provides a model of how the person's partner should or should not behave within the marriage, but the same-sex parent teaches how to respond to a spouse. Additionally, the same-sex parent usually builds important patterns of rejection or acceptance in the client by the way the parent treated the client.

Rather than obtain a chronological history of the family of origin, elicit a description of a few critical events embodying ways that parents devalued or failed to value each other or the client. If such critical memories can be healed, the client can often be freed from their bondage. Thus, effect a healing of memories when appropriate.[3] Often people in troubled marriages have been deeply hurt as children. Help clients conclude that there are important differences between their relationships with parents and with their spouse. If they can't see the differences, help them.

Intervention 8-2 describes four steps for using each partner's history within the family of origin. Introduce the intervention (step one) by drawing on clients' accounts of their own marriage. "You each describe ways that you put the other down, ways that you hurt each other, ways that you do not try to encourage and build up each other. Usually, such patterns were learned from your parents. Do you see any evidence of this in your families of origin?"

Intervention 8-2: Supporting the Strategy by Asking About Parents

Use the history of the family of origin to bolster the conceptualization that problems occur through failures in faith, work and love. Follow these four steps.

Step 1: Note that poor behaviors in the clients' marriage might have been learned from their parents. Have partners describe any evidence of this in the families of origin.

Step 2: Ask how the parents treated each other.

Step 3: Determine how parents treated each partner.

Step 4: Summarize the similarities between patterns learned in families of origin and those partners described in their own marriage. Use the conceptualization of deficiencies in love, faith and work.

Strategy: Faith, work, love

Hope: Willpower to change

After the partners answer and perhaps give examples, continue with step two: "You probably learned a lot about how to act and how not to act as a marriage partner from observing your parents. How else did your parents treat each other?"

After the partners describe parental behaviors, progress to step three: "In a few words how would you describe your relationship with each parent?" After each partner answers, summarize (step four) the similarities between patterns learned in families of origin and patterns the partners described in their own marriage.

Assessing the Current Vision of the Marriage

As I mentioned briefly in chapter six, in the first interview you *must* ask, "If things were perfect between the two of you, what would be different than what exists right now?" Ask the question naturally in your own words rather than repeating a verbatim phrasing that seems awkward to you. Intervention 8-3 describes how to use this question. Because this is an important intervention, I will discuss it in some detail.

Intervention 8-3: Ask About Each Partner's Vision of the Perfect Marriage

Step 1: Ask, "If things were perfect between the two of you, what would be different than what exists right now?"

Step 2: Follow up negative, unclear or incomplete answers by helping each partner develop a specific concrete vision of the perfect marriage.

Step 3: Summarize, in behavioral terms, the two or three major changes each partner would like to see that would make the marriage more perfect.

Strategy: Love

Hope: Willpower to change

This is often called the "miracle question" because Steve de Shazer, founder of solution-focused therapy, usually introduces it by saying, "If you went to bed tonight and during the night, a miracle were to occur such that you woke up and your marriage were perfect, what would be different?" This miracle question was once considered *de rigueur* for solution-focused therapy,[4] though in recent years solution-focused therapists have not been as insistent as were earlier practitioners.[5] Gary J. Oliver and H. Norman Wright, who advocated a solution-based Christian marital therapy, recommend use of the miracle question.[6]

Partners tend to answer by defining the marriage negatively. They will say things like

☐ "We wouldn't argue as much."

☐ "We wouldn't avoid each other."

Or they will blame the other partner by saying things like

☐ "She wouldn't nag me."

☐ "He wouldn't drink."

Follow their negative statements by asking for the positive. If the couple says, "We wouldn't argue as much," ask, "What would you do instead of argue?" Then restate their answer positively. For example, if the wife says, "Instead of arguing, we'd have long talks without raising our voice; we'd really communicate," you might say, "So if things were perfect, you'd be able to talk pleasantly about important things."

Follow up additional unclear statements. For instance, in the previous example the wife said, "We'd really communicate." Ask, "What would you communicate about? How would you talk to each other if you really communicated?"

This activity, if done correctly, will take twenty to thirty minutes. Meticulously follow up on parts of each partner's "perfect" vision. Create clear ideas of how each person could make the marriage more perfect. I give an illustration of how to conduct such an intervention in videotape three of the videotape series entitled The Master's Counselors, which is produced by the Christian Association for Psychological Studies (CAPS).[7]

Solution-focused therapy stresses the positive answer to the question "How would you know if the marriage were better or if the problems were solved?" This answer becomes a goal that is focused on from that point onward. I believe the miracle question is effective not merely because it helps people select goals that they can work toward and behaviors they can change, but also because that question helps people identify their core vision rapidly and turn it into a concrete, behavioral, reachable vision. Its utility has as much to do with revisioning the marital vision as with setting behavioral goals.

Get a Summary Statement of the Marital Vision

In the initial interview, near the end of the hour after assessing how partners would know if their marriage were better, you might want a summary statement. Ask couples what they most desire from their marriage. Most people will say that they want the distress to stop. If they focus on the negative, say, "That is a good summary of what you would *not* like—you would not like so much pain and turmoil—but what would you like?" Most women will mention intimacy and most men—happiness. Use the words chosen by the partners in your written assessment that you provide at the beginning of session two.

Get to the core of the vision by continuing, "You've talked about doing many things differently. I sense that if even *some* of those changes could be made, you'd each be happier with the marriage. What do you desire most from your relationship?" Help partners focus on one target. Many partners cannot do so. If the partner has difficulty, don't press. Reflect specific changes that the partner named.

At the end of the session, solidify the gains in the session by assigning homework to attempt to move closer to the vision that has been elaborated in the first session. (Use intervention 8-4 for this assignment.)

Intervention 8-4 *(Homework)*: Looking to Get Closer to the Fleshed-Out Vision

In the first session, ask the question "If things were better in your marriage, what would be different?" The partners' answers to that question, which is posed several times in different ways during the initial session, will provide a rough fleshed-out behavioral description of the vision of the marriage. Ask partners to summarize what they could do. Instruct them to think of their own behavior. To paraphrase former President John Kennedy, "Ask not what your partner can do for you, but what you can do for your partner."

Step 1: Review the discussion of marital vision.

Step 2: Assign partners to see whether they can do some activities that they identified that would make their partner happier.

Step 3: Have them monitor the change in their spouse's reactions and the change in their own feelings when they do more of the behaviors that have been successful at making their marriage better in the past and that they want to recapture.

Step 4: Tell them you will have them report what they did and how their partner reacted to it at the next session.

Strategy: Love

Hope: Waypower to change

CHANGING THE CORE VISION

After assessing the partners' core vision of marriage, you can begin helping them change it.

Three Basic Steps in Changing the Core Vision

Help partners (1) replace unrealistic ideals with realistic ideals that are consistent with Scripture, (2) move their true marriage closer to the more realistic ideal and (3) move their concept of the actual marriage closer to their changed ideal concept of marriage.

Replace unrealistic ideals with realistic ideals. Throughout counseling, help clients develop a different ideal concept of marriage. You can help accomplish this in four ways.

First, after you begin with a solution focus to your initial interview, expand the discussion. Ask, "How would your friends know that things were different? What would they see?" Have the partners reflect on what they themselves would see if the marriage got dramatically better.

Second, gently help people recognize their unwillingness to take personal responsibility for their part in the marital problems. As they accept their own responsibility and imperfections, they will usually judge their partner less. Don't hammer this point home. If partners feel "hammered," they will "nail you" by resisting or failing to attend sessions.

Third, teach partners the scriptural pattern of marriage: faith working through love. Partners need that vision to modify their behavior toward each other. Help partners develop a realistic and biblical understanding of marriage. Teaching in counseling is rarely by lecture. Instead, help partners self-discover the principles by being alert to their mention of the principles and calling those instances to their attention.

Fourth, encourage partners to be involved with other couples in groups and in the community. As they interact with other couples, partners often lower their idealistic standards.

Move the true marriage closer to the ideal. Help partners move the true marriage closer to the ideal marriage by having them express more love. To the extent that partners value each other more and devalue each other less, the marriage moves closer to the ideal. Help them speak the truth in love (Eph 4:15) and live by faith working through love (Gal 5:6). By shifting people's behavior, you help them put off their old natures (Eph 4:22), be renewed in the spirit of their minds (Eph 4:23) and put on their new natures in Christ (Eph 4:24).

Help people develop an understanding of faith working through love and then try to act it out. To help partners understand faith working through love, describe marriage as God's crucible where people in close contact with each other can value each other despite any tensions between them. They must work constantly to refrain from devaluing the other person, to confess their own failures at love and to forgive the failures of their spouse. Your emphasis on (1) faith working through love, (2) confession and forgiveness and (3) covenantal commitment will solidify a healthy, productive concept of marriage. But go beyond promoting understanding. Help partners act lovingly toward each other, not just in counseling but also between sessions. Help partners act consistently with the biblical pattern of marriage.

Move concepts of actual marriage closer to ideal concepts. Most troubled marriages have many positive aspects within their history and even their current experience, but partners cannot see the positive because the negative clouds their vision.[8] Their concept of the actual marriage is blurred, out of focus. Correcting the vision requires that you focus on positive aspects of the marriage. Be careful how you do this. If you ignore the couple's negative experiences consistently and obviously, you disqualify yourself in their eyes. One way to begin to shake the totally negative vision is to direct partners to notice whether improvement occurs as a consequence of scheduling the first appointment (see chapter five).

Once you begin to interview the couple, though, be patient and empathic. Reflect the negative aspects of the marriage until you are sure the partners know you understand their pain. Clearly label partners' negative experiences as pain, sadness, hopelessness, mistrust and the like. Only then can they benefit by a different approach.

Once partners feel that you understand them, begin to shake their negative vision and create a more positive one. Even though in the very beginning of counseling, you are validating the couple's negative experiences,[9] you should pay attention to the positive because troubled partners are unlikely to notice the positive even when it occurs. Intervention 8-5 lists seven opportunities to focus on positive aspects.

Intervention 8-5: Help Couples Throughout Counseling Attend to the Positive in Their Marriage

a. During history taking, spend at least as much time having couples describe their joys, reasons for marriage and pleasant memories as their problems.

b. When you summarize the marriage at the end of assessment, mention at least as many of the marriage's strengths as its problems.

c. When couples communicate, point out instances of good communication and conflict resolution as well as correcting poor communication.

d. When spouses discuss intimacy, have them talk of successes as much as failures in intimacy.

e. Call attention to progress when couples work on their marriage, both in session and in completing homework.

f. Interpret partners' efforts to change, even if change is not completely successful, as evidence of their desire to improve their marriage and restore love.

g. Treat people's motives toward each other as positive. They want to reestablish a loving marriage even when they hurt each other. Treat hurtfulness as a failure to carry out their good intentions, not as evidence of lack of love.

Strategy: Love

Hope: Willpower to change, waypower to change

Dealing with Painful Memories

To help promote a healing of memories, help the client experience the memory differently.[10] You might want to lead the client through a guided imagery exercise of adding forgiveness and tenderness to the image of the hurtfulness. Do not attempt this until the spouses have begun to make some substantial changes in their behavior and they begin to soften toward each other. Some counselors have the client reconstruct one of the critical hurtful events in imagination. Alternatively, if the counselor and client are religious, one or both may simply pray for the people involved in the memory.

Using Homework to Get Closer to the Fleshed-Out Vision

Have partners work together to create a vision statement for the marriage. Intervention 8-6 has seven steps.

Intervention 8-6 (Homework): Writing the Statement of the Vision for the Marriage[11]

1. Describe the need for a vision statement.
2. Justify the assignment, appealing to common experience of needing to plan a trip or plan strategically how to run a business.
3. Describe what comprises the vision statement.
4. Describe a six-step procedure (on the accompanying pages) for concocting the vision statement.
5. Make provision for their not being able to do the task jointly.
6. Give an escape clause.
7. Discuss the vision in the following session.

Strategy: Work, love

Hope: Willpower to change, waypower to change

---

1. Describe the need for a vision statement. After the initial session we sometimes find that the couple has little notion of what they want for their marriage. Lacking a sense of vision can be disastrous. As Proverbs 29:18 admonishes, "Where there is no vision, the people perish" (KJV). Describe to the couple the necessity of fleshing out their vision for the marriage.

2. *Justify the assignment.* I use one of two analogies to justify the homework assignment to develop a vision statement: planning a journey or running a business. To liken a vision statement to planning a journey, say something like this:

Not having a vision for marriage is like being adrift in a sea on a cloudy night. You feel afraid, disoriented and paralyzed. Developing a vision statement is like charting a course across the sea. A person would never undertake a voyage without knowing the destination. Knowing the destination helps the traveler collect resources necessary to make the trip. As counselor, I'm your travel agent. With my help you can determine your ultimate destination and then break the journey into achievable segments.

You can develop one of two kinds of visions for marriage. Your vision can be a standard that will never be met, that you complain about or use to punish your spouse. That type of vision is like sighting on a cloud. Or, your vision for marriage can be a target to aim at, like sighting on a beacon of light. It can be used to motivate change or guide loving behavior. That's the type of vision statement that I would like you to develop.

Sometimes you can appeal to partners who are in business by saying, "Almost no business today would attempt to operate without a mission statement that includes its vision of the business. Most people spend more time each week in a marriage relationship than in a business setting, yet they have given almost no thought to what their mission and vision for the marriage are. I challenge each of you this week to concoct a vision statement for your marriage."

3. *Describe what constitutes the vision statement.* When you sense that the couple has accepted the need to create a written vision statement, describe what it should consist of. Following the recommendations of Neil Clark Warren,[12] describe three essentials for a marital vision by asking these questions: (1) Is the dream equally inclusive of each of them and their life together? (2) Is the dream broad enough? (3) Is there evidence that both partners are strongly committed to the dream of their life together?

4. *Describe a recommended procedure for concocting the vision statement.* Recommend that the partners follow the six steps below to formulate their vision statement. Also tell them that they are free to follow whatever procedure they choose as long as they bring a written statement next week. Here are the six recommended steps:[13]

a. Picture yourself ten years from now.
b. Talk about where you would like to be in ten years and where you would like your marriage to be.
c. Prepare a chart showing the ten-year period.
d. List obstacles you might encounter in implementing the plan.
e. Devise ways to hurdle each obstacle.
f. Each of you write a page about how you would feel ten years from now if you accomplished the plan.

5. Make provision for their not being able to do the task jointly. Because partners are often in conflict and may be in a power struggle, tell them it is more important that they complete the exercise than that they agree on every point. If partners disagree on only a few points, they should include disputed points and note whose idea each point is. If there are many disagreements, partners may write separate vision statements.

6. Give an escape clause. Emphasize that you do not intend this exercise to create additional conflict, so if an argument erupts, they should write separate statements.

7. Discuss the vision in the following session. When the partners have written a vision for their marriage, you must discuss it with them. Discuss it on its own merits, but you can be informed by substantial research on the qualities of long-term successful marriages. There is much agreement on the qualities that predict long-term satisfying marriages. Table 8.1 summarizes the literature on this topic. I identified twelve factors, grouped into four categories, and listed the references on which I based my summary.[14]

Dealing with Unrealistic Aspects of the Vision

When partners create a written vision statement (see intervention 8-6), you might challenge some of their goals when you discuss the vision. Minimize resistance by using an analogy. Tell them,

> Usually if we see a goal we walk toward it. In the desert, though, sometimes we can see a mirage of what we want. We idealize the marriage that we want, hoping it will be perfect. Marriages are never perfect. If you hold a perfectionistic mirage of marriage, it will retard your progress. Mirages draw us from the path of life (Ps 16:11). We follow the things we lust after—such as a marriage totally free from disagreement and characterized by complete unity—rather than walk the hard path to the real oasis. The real oasis is still hot and dry at times, but we have access to cooling water and shade in places.

Table 8.1. Factors predicting long-term successful marriages (a summary from research studies)

Planfulness (Category 1)

☐ *Theme 1: Intentionality, vision, mission, commitment, persistence:* Having a focused mission and core values, a plan for each child from the time it is born (or before); having dreams and translating them into goals (which are dreams that you do something about); recognizing that extraordinary outcomes require extraordinary effort. Never giving up when the going gets tough. Having flexibility of vision. Sharing a vision for life or a life-plan that you want your lives to follow. Many times throughout life, the vision may have to be changed or adjusted due to events or life changes, but the vision always exists and guides your life together.

Sense of Larger Perspective (Category 2)

☐ *Theme 2: Positive values and religious faith:* Having good moral values and a sense of your proper place in creation (humility). Blessing people. Dealing honestly with sin. Developing a sense of values that lasts forever, gives purpose and meaning to life and answers big questions. Attending church together.

☐ *Theme 3: Servant leaders:* Modeling service to family, church, community, coworkers and even people you don't know. Practicing self-sacrifice: a willingness to sacrifice one's own needs and pleasures for another family member's needs and pleasures.

☐ *Theme 4: Humor and fun:* Learning to laugh at yourself, even when things go wrong. Enjoying fun together. Never making jokes at the expense of the partner.

☐ *Theme 5: Able to relabel tragedy and difficulty, overcomers:* Being a victor, not a victim. Reframing and reprioritizing. Becoming vulnerable (letting tragedy open your eyes to your weaknesses and dependence on God). Becoming humble (not thinking of yourself more highly than you should [Rom 12:3]), adaptable and empathic.

Group Cohesion (Category 3)

☐ *Theme 6: Mutual meeting of each other's needs:* Gratifying each other's physical, spiritual, emotional and psychological needs.

☐ *Theme 7: Identity as a marriage:* Having a sense of identity as a couple, loyalty to and unity with the partner. Engaging in teamwork.

☐ *Theme 8: Experience of mutually agreeable amount of love, affection, intimacy, support:* Expressing love for each other, verbally and physically. Expressing appreciation for what a person is and does. Encouraging each other to be what God has ordained. Forgiving when a person violates social or family norms. Having positive feelings of being together. Showing an attitude of cooperation, mutual interest, agreement and mutual valuing. (No absolute amount of closeness is desirable; what is important is an amount people feel comfortable with.)

☐ *Theme 9: Networked and autonomous:* Being interconnected and interdependent. Having freedom to establish relationships outside of the family.

Healthy Interactions (Category 4)

☐ *Theme 10: Transparent and open communication:* Having honest and open communication with sensitivity and mutual respect for each other's feelings. Demonstrating trustworthiness and (resultant) trust.

☐ *Theme 11: Effective teaching of the new generation:* Taking parenting seriously.

☐ *Theme 12: Quality time together:* Spending time together. Time is like oxygen. There's a minimum amount required for survival. You can get by on a high mountain with a shortage, but if the shortage continues, the result is brain damage.

Changing the Emotional Climate of the Marriage

The vision of the marriage is often encapsulated by a stable affective feeling about the marriage.[15] While partners' emotions might run the entire gamut from moment to moment, the baseline affective feeling of a good marriage is generally pleasant. However, the affective feeling of a troubled marriage is often marked by mistrust, hostility, anger, frustration, distress and fear.[16]

If the marriage is good, a number of characteristics attend the positive emotional climate. If the marriage is troubled, a number of characteristics attend the negative emotional climate. These characteristics are interrelated. Much attention has been focused on Gottman's ratio of positive to negative interactions (see chapter four).[17] Often that ratio is treated as the causal factor in a good marriage. Instead, it is likely that Gottman's ratio is one of the constellation of interrelated factors surrounding the emotional core of the marriage. To change the troubled marriage, the couple, under the direction of the counselor or on their own, might grasp any of the strings and unravel the kinks and knots. Table 8.2 summarizes some of the likely aspects at the core of the emotional climate of the marriage.

One goal of counseling, then, is to change the emotional climate of the marriage from negative to positive. One way to accomplish this is to use emotionally focused marital therapy techniques.[18] Those techniques actively elicit from clients their feelings, which at first are usually hard and self-protective. Then the counselor evokes vulnerable (softer) feelings from the clients. Clients are encouraged to stay with the softer feelings despite clients' attempts to retreat to the more familiar harder feelings. The counselor works with one partner at a time, while the other partner observes the emergence of tender, vulnerable, softer feelings. Observing those vulnerabilities often makes that

Aspects of the emotional climate	Ways the aspect of the emotional climate shows up in positive marriages	Ways the aspect of the emotional climate shows up in negative marriages
Love	numerous examples of valuing the mate	numerous examples of devaluing or putting down the mate
Faith in the marriage	high belief in the spouse and marriage	low belief in the spouse and marriage
Work on the relationship	effort to maintain and increase love is evident	work to better the marriage is virtually nonexistent
Ratio of + : - interactions	>5:1	<<5:1
Valence of attributions about the mate and the marriage	positive	negative
Hope for the future	high	low

Table 8.2. Different aspects of the emotional climate of positive and negative marriages

partner more willing to be vulnerable himself or herself and less apt to inflict continued harm on the vulnerable partner.

When a partner expresses hard anger, say, "You must feel a lot of pain to act so angry. You must really have been hurt." Similarly, you can say, "Anger is our best weapon for helping us feel in control when we have felt out of control. You must have felt vulnerable, hurt and out-of-control to be so angry." Have the partner discuss the hurt, sadness and vulnerability that underlie the anger.

Expression of these tender emotions can embarrass some people. They want to run back to the hard emotions of anger, resentment, bitterness and suspicion. To counter that say, "You've been very honest and courageous in admitting how vulnerable and hurt you have felt and how you have used anger as a shield to ward off the pain of really feeling your hurt. I think, though, that it really helps for you to talk about those tender feelings. Rebecca probably hasn't seen much of that side of you."

Substantial evidence supports the effectiveness of emotionally focused marital therapy,[19] but it is not applicable to all couples. At particular risk are couples in which one partner, usually the male, might be embarrassed by his or her emotional expression. Nonetheless, for many couples, emotionally focused marital therapy methods can make a dramatic change in the emotional climate of the marriage.

Having Partners Express Their Love to Each Other

By expressing love to each other, the partners make their love real, which changes both their closeness and their vision of marriage. Thus, the following intervention can be used to promote closeness. (See also chapter thirteen for other ways to promote closeness.)

Assign a homework task of writing love letters to each other (see intervention 8-7). Those tangible expressions of love will remain permanent testimonies of love. Writing a love letter is seemingly more permanent than telling the partner of one's love, though both have a place.

Intervention 8-7 *(Homework)*: Write a Love Letter: The Hotter the Better

Assign each person to write an ardent love letter to the partner telling what each loves in the other.[20] Couples must write at least two pages and must avoid anything that is not completely positive and loving. This is not the time for the partners to try to change the spouse. Instead direct the partners to affirm each other and tell each other of the positive parts of their marriage. This can be attempted at any of three times during counseling.

☐ At the beginning of counseling, with the rationale that couples need to tell themselves why they are working to improve the marriage.

☐ When the couple deals with intimacy, with the rationale that expressing positive thoughts will promote a feeling of regaining intimacy.

☐ Near the end of counseling, as a reminder of their continuing love for each other.

Tell partners that at the following session they will read each other's love letters aloud. Ask them not to exchange letters during the week.

Strategy: Love

Hope: Waypower to change

In the session following the completion of the homework, have partners exchange letters and read them silently. Discuss their reactions. Deal with difficulties that arise. Partners sometimes make backhanded insults like "I wish I believed you felt this way" or (accusingly) "Why didn't you tell me this long ago?"

Keep the experience positive. Say something like this:

> We are not trying to gloss over the negative parts of your marriage by doing this exercise. Ignoring the negative can be devastating to a marriage. A marriage based on denial can be like a rotting wall beneath beautiful $1000 wallpaper. I'm convinced that you won't deny your problems. You certainly have not denied them to this point. In this exercise, each of you wrote what you felt. Some negative feelings might be mixed with these positives, and we'll work on them in counseling; but these positive feelings exist, and you need to accept that there is a basis for love in your marriage.

Revising the Vision Statement

As the last session approaches, focus the couple on future goals. Recall the necessity of setting attainable goals for the marriage. Tell the couple that you want them to revise their original vision statement to reflect their learning throughout counseling. (See intervention 8-8.)

Intervention 8-8 *(Homework)*: Revising the Vision Statement Before the Commencement Session

Step 1: Introduce the assignment.

Step 2: Describe why an updated vision statement is important.

Step 3: Review guidelines for creating the vision statement (see intervention 8-6).

Step 4: At the final session, compare the revised vision statement with their initial statement and ask whether the partners see much change.

Strategy: Love

Hope: Waypower for change

After introducing the assignment (step one), describe why you consider revising the vision statement to be important (step two). Some reasons might be because the updated vision statement (1) helps them envision what they want to accomplish, (2) helps them realize what they need to do differently to accomplish the goals, (3) organizes their thinking, (4) pools the resources of both partners and focuses both people moving in the same direction and (5) increases romance and intimacy.

Summarize guidelines for redoing the vision statement (step three).

☐ Describe what you want to accomplish rather than what your spouse is doing wrong.

☐ Describe your vision in behavioral or action terms (things you can do or observe).

☐ Break goals into small steps and, despite your success in marital counseling, don't expect too much too soon.

☐ Picture the end product and use that picture to figure out how to get there.

☐ Remember to be realistic. All marriages have ups and downs, so goals like "We won't ever fight" are unrealistic.

At the final session compare the revised vision statement with the initial statement and ask whether the partners see much change (step four). Congratulate the partners on how hard they worked throughout counseling.

SUMMARY

Partners are guided in their actions toward each other by their core vision of their marriage. You need to help assess the vision and change the core vision throughout marital counseling. Assessment of the core vision comes about through helping partners make their perfect vision concrete. You can help them explore that vision through looking at what the current relationship is, what they would like in the future, where their relationship was good in the past and what was good and bad about their parents' marriage.

Change the core vision by helping partners think and act differently about the marriage, both with and without your presence to cool the heat of conflict. Once changes begin, your task continues: helping partners see the changes and incorporate the revisions into their vision of marriage.

Chapter 9

Interventions for Promoting Confession & Forgiveness

T he central day-to-day skill of marital survival and growth is *reconciliation*. In marriages, partners will always hurt each other. Hurt is inevitable. What distinguishes good marriages from troubled ones is whether couples reconcile after inevitable hurts and how well they do it.

Reconciliation is rebuilding trust after a violation of trust. Trust is rebuilt by both parties showing trustworthy loving behavior. What moves people from feeling hurt to being willing to act in love? Two things: On one hand, the person who inflicted hurt needs to signal a laying down of the weapons, a softening of heart, a vulnerability. On the other hand, the one who received the hurt must signal a turning from revenge, a forswearing of aloofness and separateness, and an opening of heart toward the aggressor.

CONFESSION AND FORGIVENESS

Confession of one's wrongdoing is an important signal given by the aggressor. Experiencing and granting forgiveness are important signals given by the person who was hurt. In marital reconciliation, both are necessary by both partners.

Who's Responsible?

In marriage, hurting is virtually never one-sided. Sometimes one person hurts the other in more ways and in more obvious ways, but violations of love and trust are always present on both sides.

That does not mean, of course, that all hurts are equal or that both parties are responsible for any particular hurt. For instance, a husband who abuses his wife is responsible for that choice. Regardless of what the wife did or did not do, the abuser chose to act or to respond to the wife's offense through violent abuse. He is responsible. If the abusive event was triggered by an argument, that does not mean that the wife is to blame for the abuse. The husband could have made numerous other responses, such as discussing the issue rationally, leaving the room, calling a friend for help or seeking counseling. He chose to act abusively and thus bears the responsibility for the abuse. The counselor must work with him to prevent future abuse regardless of provocation. The counselor holds him responsible for his acts.

The counselor realizes that the wife might have insulted her husband immediately before he struck her, or she might have put him down the day before and when he came home drunk the next night he retaliated, or perhaps she did absolutely nothing to provoke the attack. She is responsible for her hurtful and unloving acts, even though her acts did not *cause* the abuse.

Becoming Experts

Both partners need to be experts in both confession and forgiveness—for offering and receiving the olive branch of reconciliation in their marital relations. If they are to reconcile, both partners must acknowledge when they feel hurt but put aside bitterness, revenge and a desire for separation. Much of this book is aimed at helping couples reconcile through revealing central values, developing a positive core vision of marriage, practicing loving communication, resolving conflict lovingly, engaging in loving cognition about the marriage and the partner, experiencing closeness and maintaining commitment. But I firmly believe that trustworthy loving behavior alone will lead to a soulless marriage and incomplete reconciliation after inevitable hurts. Reconciliation is aided immeasurably by expressions of confession and forgiveness.

Forgiveness is the glue that holds commitment together. Without forgiveness, commitment will unravel and the marriage will come apart. Confession helps promote forgiveness. Both are difficult.

Confession and forgiveness are rarely acts people can accomplish under their own power. If people bring their inadequacies to God and rely on his working in their lives, confession and forgiveness become roads to apprehend more of his grace and mercy. When partners feel inadequate to forgive or to confess their wrongdoing, that can be an invitation for them to learn to know better the prompter of confession and the author of forgiveness.

What the Counselor Has to Work With

Most people agree that forgiveness is necessary in a marriage in this sense: "*He certainly needs forgiveness for all the things he has done to me.*" They rarely believe at an emotional level that forgiveness usually follows confession of one's *own* hurtfulness. Much of what you do to promote forgiveness is to promote confession.

Most people are able to empathize with their partner. Empathy—being able to feel as the other feels and think as he or she thinks—is a key to forgiveness and confession.[1] The counselor needs to bring out the empathy that partners in chronic emotional conflict often try to suppress.

Most people are capable of experiencing humility, though some are better able to experience true humility than are others. Humility, the other key to both confession and forgiveness, is being able to think, *I am capable of doing such hurtful things myself,* and thus seeing one's own need of forgiveness. Humility is not obsessionally taking the blame for everything that goes wrong in the world; such blame-taking indicates a powerful self-focus, the antithesis of humility. As Andrew Murray said, "Humility is not thinking worse of yourself than you should. It is not thinking of yourself at all."[2] The counselor must be able to focus on the event, each person's guilt within an act and each person's capacity for such evil rather than allow a partner to dwell on excessive self-focus and self-flagellation. Then, the counselor must draw attention to people's experiences of being forgiven and to their gratitude for it.

Forgiveness is an altruistic act, an act of doing a nice thing that the other person does not deserve, helping the other person have the gift of gratitude. Forgiveness is where justice and mercy come together. Forgiveness does not excuse or minimize the hurtfulness of the other person's act. Rather, it says, "Yes, you did a hurtful thing to me. You did wrong." But forgiveness is then acting mercifully and saying, "I choose not to hold that against you. I forgive you."

I'm convinced that couples will survive many misunderstandings to the extent that they are able to have real empathy for each other, have a real sense of humility and conviction that they too are needy people and are able to confess when they hurt the other.[3] Only then will they be able to forgive each other.

PROMOTING CONFESSION

The first step in helping couples practice reconciliation is promoting confession.

Preparing Partners to Deal with Confession and Forgiveness

You must first prepare partners for dealing with forgiveness and confession. In the second session, as you review the assessment report with the partners, mention that each seems to have experienced numerous hurts as they have tried to resolve their differences. Suggest one of two books that will prepare the partners for dealing with forgiveness as it arises during counseling: Lewis Smedes's classic book[4] or Michael McCullough, Steven J. Sandage and Everett L. Worthington.[5] Both books are suitable for either Christians or non-Christians.

In an early session, also prepare couples in this way: when partners describe a conflict, ask, "What would happen if one of you had confessed the things you did that were wrong, said you were sorry and asked the other person to forgive you?" That might initiate reflection on how forgiveness applies to their situation.

Steps for Promoting Confession

Confession involves (1) seeing that the other person is hurt, (2) seeing oneself as a contributor to the marital problem, (3) agreeing that one's actions are wrong and (4) desiring to change hurtful actions. Help promote an attitude of confession, which is necessary for the healing of marital hurts.

Help individuals see the other person's hurt. Good counselors are empathic. They sense people's pain and reflect it in their conversations with the person. By making pain explicit, both partners benefit. The partner expressing the pain knows you have heard his or her story and that the spouse has heard it. Your empathy helps both partners take a fresh look at the suffering.

Help individuals see their responsibility. Most people will acknowledge that marital problems are partly both partners' fault, but most people rarely apply that abstract truth to their own marriage. They blame the partner. Help individuals see their own responsibility for contributing to marital problems. Intervention 9-1 shows several ways you can do this.

Intervention 9-1: Getting People to Focus on Their Part

Employ the following interventions as appropriate.

a. Preface comments to each partner by phrases such as "From your perspective, how do you see . . . ?" or "How did you experience . . . ?" This is done continually throughout counseling, not just once or twice.

b. Require each person to talk for himself or herself and not for the partner. You might say, "We can't always be sure what the other person is really feeling or thinking. What were *you* thinking during . . . ?"

c. Focus on each individual's story—not on an individual's blaming the partner or telling what the partner did that offended him or her. Some description of a spouse's perception of the other's behavior is necessary, especially to demonstrate a spouse's emotional reaction to the partner's offensive behavior. But discourage the person from simply complaining.

d. Ask, "What did you do that contributed to the problem escalating?"

e. In the face of a partner's (often frequent) demands that the spouse change, say, "You can't change the other person, regardless of what you do. Your partner can't change you either. Only you can change yourself."

f. After a description of an angry confrontation, reflect: "So neither of you admitted your own part and the anger and distress grew."

g. When blaming statements are made by a partner, ignore the blame and focus on the individual's behavior.

h. Do not accuse individuals of blaming their partner. For example, if a counselor says to Sharon, "You are avoiding taking responsibility for your own actions of overspending by blaming Seth," then Sharon will almost certainly become defensive. She may (a) argue with the counselor, (b) insist that she wasn't avoiding responsibility or (c) outwardly accept the counselor's interpretation while she harbors resentment. She will almost certainly feel devalued by the counselor, which is opposite to what the counselor is trying to teach (faith working through love). She will probably retaliate. This does not imply that you should never confront clients. At times you must confront, yet confrontation is more easily accepted by clients when they know you love and respect them than when they feel accused. The loving counselor-client relationship is the foundation on which successful counseling builds.

Strategy: Love

Hope: Waypower to change

Help partners see that their actions are wrong. No one likes to admit that he or she has done wrong. Gentleness is your guiding beacon. Gently promote self-reflection through any of the actions described in intervention 9-2.

Intervention 9-2: Stimulating Self-Reflection on a Partner's Own Culpability

a. Induce clients to reflect thoughtfully on their behavior. By bringing a person into contact with the reality of his or her hurtfulness, you can make confession more likely.

b. Refer to a situation in your own life and marriage when you struggled with similar problems. This helps eliminate partners' defensiveness and promote honesty. (Use examples of yourself judiciously. Some clients do not appreciate a counselor talking about himself or herself.)

c. Promote thoughtful self-examination by calling attention to the effects of communication on the partner. Suppose Patricia lashes out at Mark during counseling. "You're such a stupid, unfeeling dolt sometimes. It makes me want to scream, but it wouldn't do any good." Mark may snap back angrily, "You never let that stop you from screaming before. You have no self-control." Don't allow such hurtfulness to continue. Say something like "Just a minute. Those kinds of comments don't convey that you value each other, which is what you've been working on. Let's analyze this exchange. Patricia, when you said Mark was a 'stupid, unfeeling dolt,' what did you want to accomplish? . . . [Later] Mark, when you said Patricia had no self-control, what kind of effect do you think that had on her?"

Strategy: Love

Hope: Waypower to change

Promote a desire to change. Examining the effects of hurtful behavior, as in the case of the counselor's therapy with Patricia and Mark, can promote a desire to change perhaps because it stimulates a sense of guilt over a hurtful act. However, I prefer more often to stimulate an awareness of what partners *want* rather than what they guiltily think they *should* do. Promote a desire to change (see intervention 9-2c) by following any of several actions in intervention 9-3.

Intervention 9-3: Promoting a Desire to Change Hurtful Behavior

a. Show each person that he or she was not having the effect that he or she wanted to have. Instead, the effects of their communications were exactly opposite of their desired effects.

b. Call attention to their goals. Remind them that they had been working on valuing each other.

c. Don't insist that partners admit their wrongdoing, which can lead to a power struggle between you and the clients. Rather lead them to *consider* their behavior. Often, they will spontaneously confess their wrongdoing and express a willingness to change.

Strategy: Love, work

Hope: Willpower to change

PROMOTING FORGIVENESS

The second major step in helping couples practice reconciliation is promoting forgiveness.

Helping People Prepare to Forgive

Like confession, forgiveness can be stimulated as people consider their actions thoughtfully. This is especially true if you help committed Christians see their actions in light of Scripture. Several actions on your part can make forgiveness more likely.

The early part of counseling involves recounting family-of-origin histories, which will usually bring out an awareness of past hurtfulness within that family that each partner perpetuates in the marriage. As you lead the couple through the recalling and healing of memories, forgiveness of parents is common. Often when a spouse hears the partner's past, he or she can become more tender, understanding and forgiving.

Dealing with Difficulties in Forgiving

DeLoss and Ruby Friesen, marital counselors in Oregon, identify two problems people often have in forgiving their partners: misunderstanding forgiveness and having difficulty forgiving.[6] These were discussed also by David Augsburger.[7]

Misunderstanding forgiveness. Misunderstanding forgiveness comes in a number of varieties. Some think they have forgiven when they have not. They still harbor feelings of delight if evil befalls the person who hurt them, even though they do not want to perpetrate the harm themselves. That is incomplete forgiveness. Others think that to forgive, they must forget and act as if the hurt never happened. That is equally incorrect. Offenses are not forgotten, but when forgiven they should not be brought up again. Others think they can forgive only after the person has suffered or made restitution. Revenge, not forgiveness, requires suffering and restitution prior to forgiveness, for after the restitution has been paid there is nothing to forgive.

Forgiveness is not condoning an evil or harmful act. Condoning means that the person declares that the act was not really wrong or evil. In forgiveness a person admits that the act was wrong or evil but chooses to forgive anyway. One further distortion of forgiveness is to equate it with reconciliation. I commonly hear, "I must not have forgiven her because I don't want to get back together." One can fully forgive and still not choose to reconcile, especially when reconciliation would risk sustaining additional hurts. This might be the case, for example, with an unrepentant physical abuser. Help couples correct these misunderstandings of forgiveness.

I define forgiveness as an altruistic reduction in the desire to distance, seek revenge or defend oneself and a desire to reconcile if good moral norms can be reestablished. Altruism is the unselfish regard for the other person's welfare. Forgiveness is motivated by a heart touched by empathy and humility. You don't need to define forgiveness formally as you talk to clients; use the definition to inform yourself so you can correct misconceptions.

Having difficulty forgiving. Having difficulty forgiving is common in deep hurts. Perhaps every person has experienced at least a few deep hurts throughout his or her lifetime. Holding on to unforgiveness is bad for people physically, mentally and spiritually.[8] We realize that we shouldn't hold on to unforgiveness but struggle with turning it loose.

Assess the degree of confession of each partner's hurtfulness of the spouse and the degree of forgiveness that each exhibits. You can do that through simply asking, but you may be able to observe unforgiveness even without asking. Generally, it is better to ask directly about whether each has confessed his or her hurtfulness to the partner and about whether the partner has been able to forgive the spouse. You might find that your inferences and assumptions about the partners were incorrect.

When partners have difficulty forgiving, discover the barriers to forgiving and help partners deal with them. Assign intervention 9-4 to help the partners identify and remove barriers.

Intervention 9-4 (Homework): Helping with Trouble at Forgiving: Identifying Barriers to Forgiveness

In session ask, "What keeps you from forgiving your partner?" Here are some answers that people typically bring up.

lack of time to deal with the emotion of it
lack of trust that the partner won't hurt me again

don't want to feel pain again
takes a lot of effort
pride
guilt or shame
fear
distraction or busyness
past unresolved pain from childhood

If the person can identify no barriers, provide the above list and assign the person as homework to think about which barriers he or she might be facing.

In the following session, discuss the results of the homework. Then ask, "What would it take to remove those barriers? What would you have to do to remove those barriers? What would your partner have to do for you to be able to forgive?"

Strategy: Love

Hope: Willpower to change, waypower to change

Helping People Walk Through the Steps of Forgiving

When dealing with a fresh hurt, follow these steps:[9] (1) remind couples that their goal is to restore their marriage; (2) help them experience the pain rather than deny or minimize it; (3) help each partner empathize with the other; (4) help each person reflect on his or her own capability of inflicting hurt; (5) help each person recall times that he or she has been forgiven; (6) provide an opportunity for each person to say aloud that he or she forgives the partner; (7) discuss the maintenance of forgiveness.

Remind couples that their goal is to restore the marriage. People want to forgive for many reasons. For one, forgiveness can be good for the person. It can lower blood pressure; reduce free-floating hostility that is associated with an increase in risk for cardiovascular problems; give people a sense of control over their lives rather than being dominated by anger and hatred; help people feel less stressed, fearful and depressed; and restore the person spiritually to a better relationship with the Lord. All of those are valid reasons to forgive; I am not minimizing them.[10] However, in marital counseling people don't seek forgiveness per se: they seek a better marriage. Reconciliation in that marriage is thus their primary reason for forgiveness.

Help people experience the pain of the hurt rather than deny or minimize it. Encourage the person to reveal the extent of the hurt and the emotional feelings that went along with it. Don't allow excessive blaming of the partner. If a partner objects to the spouse's discussion of the hurt, saying that the spouse has blown the hurt out of proportion or is merely complaining, then suggest that hurts often don't look as bad to others as they feel to us. Hurts are subjective. Suggest that love is finding out the spouse's perspective and treating that as being what is *real* to the partner.

Help each partner empathize with the other. Empathy is one of the keys to forgiveness.[11] In fact, empathy is one of the keys to love. When people have been hurt, they will usually resist empathizing with the one who hurt them. To minimize resistance, approach the task indirectly. First, get partners to discuss how they were hurt and focus on the emotions. The partner who was hurt will probably display anger. Reframe it as *hurt.* Allow partners to discuss their emotions as long as they do not hurt each other again. If you don't let people share their emotional experience, it will be hard for their partners to empathize. However, remain in control of the session. If the partners get out of control, they won't return to counseling.

Sometimes you can promote empathy by telling a story about forgiveness. I have found two particularly helpful in producing a willingness to empathize with the partner (see intervention 9-5).

Intervention 9-5: Stories to Help People Empathize

Story 1: Corrie ten Boom and the guard.[12] Corrie ten Boom was in a concentration camp in Germany during World War II. She lost her sister, her father and her whole family to the cruelty of the Nazis, and she experienced the cruelty firsthand. After the war, she was speaking to a group about her experience. A man, whom she recognized as a guard in the very camp where she was incarcerated, approached her and asked for her forgiveness. He didn't recognize her as an individual. He felt guilty and was looking for her absolution.

Corrie was repulsed. She felt anger and hurt well up within her. She wanted to condemn. But she recognized how capable of hurt, anger and rage she was. When she saw how similar her heart was to the guard's, she was able to embrace and forgive him.

Story 2: The stones and the rock.[13] One woman hurt her friend. The friend gossiped widely about the hurt and repaid the hurt in a thousand slights and putdowns. Their relationship deteriorated, and they went to a wise woman in their village to get her help in restoring their relationship.

The wise woman sent the first woman into the field to bring back a boulder the size of a basketball. She sent the second woman into the field to bring back a thousand pebbles. When the women returned, the wise woman ordered the women to replace the stones exactly as they were before. The first woman could replace the boulder with great effort, but the second complained that it was impossible to restore the thousand pebbles to their original state.

The wise woman then told the first woman to repent for her large hurtful action. The wise woman told the second that she had the harder task: to repent for the thousand small hurts she had inflicted.

Strategy: Love, faith

Hope: Willpower to change, waypower to change, waitpower to let God work

---

As a homework assignment, have partners write a letter to themselves as if they were the partner (see intervention 9-6). Use this homework assignment when partners seem to show an inability to empathize with the partner's point of view. (This assignment was originally proposed by my son Jonathan in helping his sister Becca forgive a friend who had hurt her.)

Intervention 9-6 (Homework): Write a Letter from the Partner's Point of View

When a partner is apparently having difficulty empathizing with the partner's point of view, do not continue the frustrating task of trying to promote empathy during the session. Move to another intervention, but first assign a homework assignment that helps the partners reflect on the other person's viewpoint at a more leisurely pace. Here is an example.

> We all seem a bit frustrated now. Glenn, you seem to be having difficulty seeing things from Caitlin's perspective. I have found that it is sometimes difficult for people to see things from the other person's perspective when I put pressure on a person to feel empathy on the spur of the moment. So I want us to move away from this right now.
>
> Seeing each other's perspectives is vital to forming a healthier marriage. So let's try this. Let's take this at a slower pace. This week at home, I would like you each to write a letter expressing feelings around this hurt. However, instead of expressing your own feelings and your own perspective on the incident, I would like you to write the letter as if you were the other person writing to yourself. So Caitlin, you will write a letter as if you were Glenn, telling how he saw the events and how he felt and thought

about the events. Glenn, you write a letter as if you were Caitlin, giving her perspectives, thoughts and feelings. Each of you write in the first person. For instance, Caitlin, you might write, "I, Glenn, came home from work early because I was stressed out from dealing with my boss. As I walked in the door, . . ." Then, Caitlin, you would tell the entire incident as if you were Glenn writing a letter to you.

Do you each think you can do this sometime this week? The object is to write a letter so accurate that the other person might only make minor additions to the story. Are you each willing to write such a letter this week?
Strategy: Love
Hope: Waypower to change

Help each person reflect on his or her own capability of inflicting hurt. People can empathize with the partner and can still be unforgiving. To move from empathy to forgiveness, help the partner feel a sense of humility. Humility occurs when the person realizes in his or her spirit that he or she is capable of inflicting the same hurts or hurts that are just as deep and just as damaging as did the partner who hurt the person.

As people consider the hurts that they have inflicted, ask them to reflect on whether they have the capacity to inflict hurts of equal or greater emotional damage. Jesus said we do not have to murder another to be guilty of murder; rather we are guilty if we contemplate it in our heart (Mt 5:21-22). In the same way, people need not to have committed the same hurtful behavior as the partner—only judge themselves as capable of doing so.

To promote reflection on empathy and humility, use homework that helps each partner to consider his or her behavior in light of Scripture. Use two passages of Scripture to provoke thought in Christian couples (see intervention 9-7).

Intervention 9-7 (Homework): Bringing Scripture to Bear on Your Hurtfulness

Assign homework to promote empathy and humility. This assignment should be made prior to the week when forgiveness is to be the focus of counseling. At the subsequent session, discuss what the partners got from the devotionals during the week.

Assign partners to do a thirty-minute devotional every day for a week. Begin each devotional with a prayer for the Lord to work on the marriage. If a particular harmful act has been salient, the person should bring that act under God's care. Perhaps, in a particularly hurtful relationship, a different harm could be considered each day.

After the brief prayer, each partner is to spend five minutes reading the passage, ten minutes reflecting on it and writing any thoughts that seem pertinent, ten minutes worshiping God and five minutes praying for the mind of Christ in the marriage. Two passages will be used: one dealing with empathy (Mt 5:21-26, 38-47; 6:13-15; 7:1-12) and the other with humility (Phil 2:1-14). Have partners alternate days on which they read each. On the seventh day, they reread both passages, review their notes and write any lessons they learned that they might want to discuss in counseling. Finally, each is to pray for the partner.

Strategy: Faith
Hope: Willpower

Carrying out intervention 9-7 can lead to a conviction of one's own sinfulness in the context of God's grace and mercy. The central truths of Christianity are emphasized in the passages, so the passage can also help the person feel the wonder of forgiveness as well as the conviction of his or her own sin.

Help each person recall times that he or she has been forgiven. Every person can draw on a rich memory of having been forgiven. Parents, friends or employers might have forgiven an incident in which the person deserved punishment. The partner might have forgiven previous transgressions. If the person searches his or her memory, the person can remember several such incidents. (If the person is a Christian, God has forgiven him or her.) After an incident is recalled, the person should reflect on how grateful he or she felt at being forgiven.

Forgiveness is for giving. It is a gift that one gives. Forgiving is an act of altruism, of kindness, in which a person extends to the person who hurt him or her the same gift that he or she has experienced in other circumstances. Being grateful for having been forgiven is a precursor to forgiving. Stimulate that gratitude through homework (see intervention 9-8) or in-session interventions (see intervention 9-9).

Intervention 9-8 *(Homework):* Reflecting on Your Own Receiving of Forgiveness

Have the client do each of the following:

Step 1: Survey the following relationships and remember as many specific times as possible that he or she was granted forgiveness.

- ☐ client and mother
- ☐ client and father
- ☐ client and each sibling
- ☐ client and best friend growing up
- ☐ client and best adult friend
- ☐ client and partner during times when the relationship was going better
- ☐ client and boss
- ☐ client and coworker
- ☐ client and God

Step 2: Recall vividly specific incidents of offense and subsequent granting of forgiveness.

Step 3: Describe the client's behavior that offended or wronged someone.

Step 4: Recall what the other person did that let the client know he or she was forgiven.

Step 5: Describe as clearly as possible the gratitude and other feelings that the client felt at being forgiven.

Step 6: Ask the client whether he or she would like to give a similar gift of forgiveness to the partner.

Step 7: Write notes to bring back to the following session to describe two of the most vivid incidents of receiving forgiveness.

Strategy: Love

Hope: Waypower to change

Intervention 9-9: Reflecting on Your Own Forgiveness

Step 1: Have both partners survey a written list of relationships and recall one time that they experienced forgiveness in one of these contexts:

- ☐ person and mother
- ☐ person and father
- ☐ person and each sibling
- ☐ person and best friend growing up
- ☐ person and best adult friend
- ☐ person and partner during times when the relationship was going better
- ☐ person and boss
- ☐ person and coworker
- ☐ person and God

Step 2: Have each partner describe the experience.

Step 3: Ask each partner to describe the behavior that was offensive or wrong.

Step 4: Ask each partner to describe what the forgiver did that let the person know he or she was forgiven.

Step 5: Have each partner describe the gratitude and other feelings that he or she felt at being forgiven.

Step 6: Have each partner consider whether he or she would like to give a similar gift of forgiveness to the spouse. In early stages of counseling take the pressure off by asking each of the partners to consider this at home.

Strategy: Love

Hope: Waypower to change

Provide an opportunity for each person to say aloud that he or she forgives the partner. As counseling nears its conclusion, guide the couple through a forgiveness session,[14] aimed at promoting forgiveness of other wrongs that were uncovered throughout counseling (or perhaps hurts that were dealt with but the partners want to be sure are forgiven).

Generally, a forgiveness session stimulates spontaneous emotional forgiveness and genuine contrition. It is not the method of the forgiveness session that promotes forgiveness. Rather, the tenderness of the counselor in preparing the couple and the trust that has been rebuilt throughout counseling allows forgiveness to occur. The forgiveness session is not for all couples. It is indicated only when you sense that the couple is willing to forgive and wants to forgive past hurts. When it is needed and is appropriate for a couple, it should usually be used near the end of counseling. If you try to use the forgiveness session when the partners are blaming and hardhearted toward each other, you will do more harm than good.

To use the forgiveness session, prepare the couple in the prior session. Note aloud that the partners seem to have hurt each other, which needs to be dealt with through forgiveness. Ask if they perceive that to be the case. If they agree, suggest that each partner individually use the time between sessions to examine himself or herself to determine ways that he or she has hurt the partner and wishes to seek forgiveness from the partner. Caution both partners not to concern themselves with ways that the partner has hurt them. Instead they are to examine themselves before God, list their own actions for which they want to ask the partner for forgiveness and bring the list to the following session (see intervention 9-10).

Intervention 9-10 *(Homework):* Preparing for a Forgiveness Session

In preparing at home for a confession and forgiveness session, the partners should carry out the following acts independently of each other.[15] Preparation is in two parts: (1) recalling having been hurt by the partner and releasing those hurts and one's anger and (2) making a list of harmful acts that one has inflicted on the partner and examining one's regret over having hurt the partner.

Part 1: Recall How the Partner Hurt You and Release the Hurt and Anger

☐ List the hurts and write how each hurt affected you.

☐ Write an angry letter to the spouse, but do not mail it.

☐ Read the letter aloud to an empty chair in a place where you cannot be overheard.[16]

☐ Write a letter of forgiveness for the hurts your partner has inflicted on you, and include a vision of what you think the marriage should realistically be like.

☐ Read that letter aloud to the empty chair.

☐ Modify parts of the letter that didn't sound good when you read it aloud.

☐ Destroy the angry letter as a symbol of releasing your anger.

Part 2: List Your Own Hurtfulness and Examine Your Regret over Hurting Your Partner

☐ List times that you hurt your partner since marriage counseling began.

☐ Reflect on the recent history of the marriage and list any incidents that stand out as particularly hurtful, which you would like to confess to your partner and ask forgiveness for.

☐ Think of the more distant past of your relationship and add to your list incidents that were hurtful to your partner.

☐ Ponder your regret over such hurtfulness.

☐ Prioritize events that you want to seek forgiveness for.

☐ Examine your heart to see whether you can truthfully say that you will try not to perpetrate such hurts again.

Strategy: Love, faith

Hope: Waypower to change

At the beginning of the next session, assess the partners' moods to determine whether to conduct the forgiveness session. If blaming, criticism, condemnation, anger, contempt, defensiveness or emotional detachment is present in either partner, then suggest that the partners do not seem to be ready to proceed with a session on forgiveness. However, if the mood seems right to broach forgiveness, follow intervention 9-11 or your adaptation of it.

Intervention 9-11: Conducting the Forgiveness Session

Step 1: Have the partners face each other. They may or may not hold hands.

Step 2: Describe what you want the partners to do.

> In turn, I would like you each to mention one thing you have done to hurt your partner. If you feel sorry and if you want to seek forgiveness from your partner, express your feelings and ask your partner for forgiveness. If your partner confesses, you should recognize that it is not easy to ask for forgiveness. Furthermore, forgiveness should not easily be granted. Instead weigh what is heard and forgive only if the forgiveness is heartfelt. In most instances partners take time to think about the confession, its sincerity, the regret and the apology prior to granting forgiveness. So there may not be any granting of forgiveness today. It is more important that your confessions be sincere and heartfelt than that you receive forgiveness today. In most instances, forgiveness will eventually come—if not today, then sometime.
>
> Chances are that one of you will confess more hurts than the other. This isn't a contest. Your confessions should be prompted by the Holy Spirit's work in your own life and not by what the other person says or doesn't say. You are responsible for confessing your hurtfulness and for receiving your partner's confessions without gloating or defensiveness. Be attentive to the Spirit.

Step 3: Ask the husband to begin talking about a time in which he has hurt his partner. Try to stay out of the conversation unless there is active hurting going on. Do little (or no) coaching.

Step 4: After the husband has confessed a hurtful action and forgiveness has (usually) been granted, suggest that the wife confess a hurtful time.

Step 5: Alternate until one partner has exhausted his or her list. Allow the other partner to continue until he or she has exhausted his or her list. Generally, partners will have different numbers of hurts that they wish to confess.

Strategy: Love

Hope: Waypower to change

Discuss the maintenance of forgiveness and, under some conditions, the need to expand on forgiveness. Once people have granted forgiveness, they sometimes believe that they should never feel anger or bitterness over that hurt again. If they do feel anger, hurt, resentment or bitterness, they believe that the forgiveness was ineffective. That keeps them in a perpetual state of unforgiveness. However, once forgiveness has been granted, an act has truly been forgiven. That does not mean that negative feelings will not recur. Feelings may recur because (a) something new provokes the feelings, (b) some new unforgiven aspect of the incident needs attention, (c) the person is dwelling on the act and generating new anger, resentment and bitterness, (d) the person is hurt or rejected by someone else (which sensitizes the person to the old wound), (e) a similar situation arises, reminding the person of an old wound (even though no new hurt has occurred) or (f) the person is under high stress (which sensitizes him or her to old wounds). Caution the partners not to denigrate the forgiveness that they experienced. Forgiveness granted was real. Yet encourage them to deal with the new aspects of their unforgiveness and attempt to forgive the new aspects.

HELPING PEOPLE FORGIVE AFTER CONFLICT

Often conflicts have been heated and long-lasting. You may have worked with the couple to resolve some of those conflicts. Gary Rosberg has suggested that forgiveness "closes the loop" on conflict.[17] That is, forgiveness helps a couple put the conflict behind them. Intervention 9-12 describes one way to accomplish this.

Intervention 9-12: Forgiveness as a Finish to Conflict Resolution

Step 1: After a conflict is resolved, suggest that the conflict is not completely resolved until the partners have forgiven the hurts that might have been experienced around the disagreement.

Step 2: Invite partners to confess any hurtfulness that they believe they have caused (not to identify hurt they felt).

Step 3: Encourage partners to state their sincere sorrow at having hurt or offended their partner.

Step 4: Encourage partners to state their sincere intention not to hurt the partner in that way again—ever.

Step 5: Encourage partners to ask for forgiveness.

Step 6: If the partner grants forgiveness, the spouse is encouraged to accept the forgiveness and give up the guilt, maintaining his or her vow not to hurt the partner in the same way again.

Step 7: Repeat for the other partner.

Step 8: Tell the couple that the end point is to rebuild trust, and that can only be accomplished fully over a period of time. It won't happen simply because hurts are confessed and forgiven and the forgiveness is accepted.

Step 9: Suggest that while ideally such hurts will never happen again, in reality we are imperfect creatures and there is a possibility that such hurts will recur. Both partners are encouraged to maintain a tolerance based on an understanding of their own imperfections.

Strategy: Love, faith

Hope: Waypower to change, waitpower for God

SUMMARY

Forgiveness is a key step along the path toward reconciliation. Help promote the individual experience of forgiveness in each partner. Lead each partner through the steps of forgiveness beginning with recalling the hurt, passing through empathy and a sense of humility and gratitude for having been forgiven, and culminating in a forgiveness session. The forgiveness session links the individual experience of forgiveness with the beginning of the journey toward reconciliation.

Reconciliation after harmful actions is generally two-sided. It involves a softening of the partners' attitudes through confession followed by the granting of forgiveness. With that softening the partners are empowered to strengthen the relationship and the reconciliation through behaving like trustworthy lovers who treat each other as pearls of great value.

Chapter 10

Interventions
for Strengthening
Communication

People communicate to meet their needs. High on the list of needs is giving and receiving love. It is precisely that need in which troubled couples are deficient. Thus amid the need to exchange basic information, provide for children or get dinner on the table, the hope-focused marriage counselor zeroes in on promoting love. In this chapter we examine a few general considerations about treating problems in couple communication. First, I outline some general principles for training couples to communicate better. In that context I discuss how to help couples become aware of their communication patterns. Then I summarize interventions for helping couples communicate love directly; positively; by listening; by sharing information, their experiences, feelings and values; by creating time to communicate; and by avoiding devaluing communications.

PRINCIPLES FOR TRAINING THE COUPLE IN BETTER COMMUNICATION
Marital counselors must understand certain basic principles for training couples to communicate.

Easy-to-Make Errors

Counselors sometimes make errors in helping couples improve their communication.

☐ *Being too negative.* Don't correct all the time. Point out positive communications often.

☐ *Intervening too early.* Wait to intervene until the communication problem has developed enough that the couple is aware of it.

☐ *Getting sidetracked when dealing with another issue.* This is the easiest error to make. If your session is about closeness and a destructive communication occurs, don't change the focus of the session to communication. Instead, deal with the poor communication in a sentence or two and get back to the main problem.

☐ *Getting too content-oriented.* Don't get swept up in the content of the couple's communications. Change the patterns of communication.

☐ *Pursuing your agenda instead of attending to clients.* Don't be program-oriented. Tailor interventions to client needs.

☐ *Getting spread too thinly.* You can't make couples perfect communicators. Don't try. Focus only on the most important communication problems.

☐ *Giving up on the couple.* If counseling stalls, change *your* behavior. For example:

   * Try a session with each individual instead of continuing to meet conjointly.
   * Ask what is preventing the person from changing.
   * Address objections nondefensively.
   * When one spouse says that the partner is acting differently because you are forcing him or her and the partner has not *really* changed, suggest that the partner has chosen to behave in a particular way because he or she wants to do so and that you have only provided some suggestions about how the person can change.

An Effective Training Method

For best results use the following method to help partners change communication:

   1. Instruct specifically how partners can communicate.
   2. Demonstrate the communication or give an example.
   3. Have the partners employ your suggestions, usually with an issue that is involving but does not have high emotional significance. Give feedback about their communication.

4. Have the couple employ the suggestions on a hotter issue.

5. Assign the couple to try the behavior at home. Time homework carefully. Communication is often harmful when couples come to counseling. Don't assign at-home communication until the couple can avoid damage.

6. Over time, fade your feedback to the couple, making fewer direct suggestions as the partners become more adept at communicating. Couples will always be imperfect communicators. Don't hold such high standards for their behavior that you continually give feedback and never let the couple proceed independently.

Help Both Partners Know the Objective of Training

Before you try to help partners improve their communication, make sure partners understand that they need to change habit *patterns* of communication to better reflect their love for each other. Mention that the objective is not to change individual communications or even to resolve their differences. By stressing that partners should focus on patterns of communication that show love, you set up the expectations that (a) they are expanding on the strategy on which you have focused other interventions, (b) they need to practice at home (rather than thinking they "fixed" their problems during the session) and (c) you will mention the patterns repeatedly in counseling, not just once.

Emphasize that patterns of communication are habits, which date from early in the relationship and sometimes from as early as the family of origin. Thus partners can expect two things: (1) Patterns of communication will not be changed overnight—perhaps not by the end of counseling or even by the end of the first year after counseling. (2) Both partners may backslide. To discourage each partner from being self-critical or critical of the spouse, ask them both to give themselves or their spouse the benefit of the doubt.

Communicating Faith Working Through Love

Hope-focused marriage counseling seeks to improve marriage through building more love, faith and work. Center communication training on increasing ways that partners value each other and on decreasing ways they devalue each other.

Increasing ways partners value each other. Partners with healthy patterns value each other in many ways. First, they directly communicate their love for each other in ways that each partner can understand. Second, they communicate the aspects of their relationships that they value—the positive parts. Third, they listen to each other with respect. Fourth, they share their experience, including

(a) important information, (b) their thoughts, perceived needs and desires, (c) their feelings and (d) their values. Fifth, they make time and opportunities available for good communication.

Decreasing ways partners devalue each other. The ways that troubled couples insult, put down, ignore, talk over, disqualify and in numerous other ways devalue each other are not a mystery to marital counselors. You could spend all of counseling simply correcting the couple. To create a hope-focused environment, constant correction is counterproductive. While you cannot shy away from confronting a pathological pattern of communication—in fact, such confrontations are necessary—the balance of emphasis must remain clearly tipped toward the positive. That is reflected in my offering fewer interventions to correct devaluing than to promote valuing.

Before partners' communication can be changed, partners must become aware of how they are communicating—ways that are positive and should be continued, and ways that are negative and should be changed. Show partners clearly when they are not communicating love to each other.

Making Couples Aware of Their Communication Patterns

Interventions are aimed at making things sensible to the couples. Make communication patterns visible and audible.

Dramatize their behavior. After witnessing a conversation in which misunderstanding is profound, dramatize the misunderstanding by directing the partners to reverse roles. In a role reversal each partner takes the other person's perspective. Tell the couple, "You say you understand each other's point of view, but I don't see a lot of evidence that you do. Can you change roles briefly and show me by arguing the other person's side that you understand each other?"

Create a sculpture of communication. Further dramatize communication patterns by using a technique borrowed from family therapy: sculpting (see intervention 10-1), in which you arrange both partners' bodies as a sculpture to represent the communication physically.[1] Alternatively, have partners sculpt each other. Often partners are hurtful when they do this, so I usually avoid using it in this way.

Intervention 10-1: Use Sculpting as a Metaphor for Communication

If the couple is involved in a particular pattern of communication, sculpt them to represent that pattern.

a. "You both seem entrenched in your position. Turn your chairs away from each other and place your hands over your ears. Now continue your conversation."

b. "John, point your finger accusingly at Mary. Mary, hold up your hands defensively in front of you to ward off his attack. Now that's the way I see you communicating in the last few minutes."

Strategy: Love

Hope: Willpower to change

Create awareness of love busters. Willard Harley has written eloquently about "love busters," and I highly recommend his books.[2] A love buster is a habit that makes it likely that the spouse will be unhappy and lose love for the partner. Love busters are found in five categories:

☐ angry outbursts

☐ disrespectful judgments

☐ annoying behavior

☐ selfish demands

☐ dishonesty

Use intervention 10-2 to make partners aware of some of the love busters in their marriage. The intervention leads to a homework assignment that may improve the communication (see step five).

Intervention 10-2: Identifying Love Busters

Step 1: Introduce the concept of love busters. Describe the five categories.

Bill Harley, in his book *Love Busters*, has determined that there are five types of behaviors that can have a negative effect on your love. The five behaviors are angry outbursts, disrespectful judgments, annoying behavior, selfish demands and dishonesty.

Step 2: Help partners identify the love busters in their marriage. The best approach is to consider each category in turn.

I would like each of you to consider whether you do any of the "love busters." I'll consider each in turn. Identify whether you do it and, if so, how often. Don't tell me what your partner does, and don't nod enthusiastically when your partner admits to doing a "love buster." Consider only your own behavior and be responsible for what you can do to stop doing the "love busters" or do them less often.

Name the first category, angry outbursts, and ask each partner about his or her angry outbursts. Ask how the partner might stop those angry outbursts or do them less often. Move to the other partner and repeat. Write down on paper each partner's resolutions about how to improve.

Step 3: At the end of the session, summarize each's resolutions by referring to your paper.

Step 4: Photocopy the paper and give a copy to each partner (providing a tangible product to make change sensible).

Step 5: Assign each partner homework to put three resolutions into effect during the upcoming week.

Strategy: Love

Hope: Willpower to change, waypower to change

Use a miracle script. Direct each partner to write a description of what their marital communication would be like if it were perfect (see intervention 10-3). Alternatively, each can make an audiotape. This can function like the "miracle question" that was used in session one.[3] That is, by explicitly discussing aspects of "perfect" communication, partners can recognize that they can achieve much of this perfect communication with surprisingly little effort.

Intervention 10-3 (Homework): Miracle Script for Perfect Communication

Assign partners to either write a script or narrate into an audiotape recorder a script for how the marriage would function if a miracle occurred and communication were perfect. Each partner is urged to concentrate on how they would communicate more perfectly as well as discuss how the other partner specifically would communicate more perfectly. Partners are cautioned to minimize saying how each other would *not* communicate. For example, they should avoid statements like "If communication were perfect, Clarence would not communicate that he had a poor day at work by kicking down the front door and ripping the refrigerator door off its hinges with his teeth as he usually does." Instead they should be coached to say things like "Clarence would express that he had a rotten day by saying, 'Honeychile, I had a really rotten day, so my temper is a bit on edge right now. I think I need a little time to wind down before dinner.'"

Strategy: Love

Hope: Willpower to change, waypower to change

Get at the roots of communication. Habits learned in families of origin are often the root of communication difficulties. People grew up within a particular pattern of communication and they often revert to that pattern when uncertain or under stress. Sometimes, people were repulsed by the communication in their family of origin and they vow not to repeat those patterns. However, that doesn't mean they can or do carry out their vow.

Discuss with each partner the typical communication patterns in each's family of origin. Get input from the spouse. Ask whether the partners see themselves repeating those patterns in their own marriage. Ask how they can change some of those patterns. Following that session, assign homework to promote additional thinking about the roots of communication using construction of a genogram (see intervention 10-4).[4]

Intervention 10-4 *(Homework):* Getting Back to the Source

Have partners construct a genogram of as far back as they can remember. A genogram is a family tree with females represented by circles and males by squares. Ask partners to think about how couples communicated. Try to get a sense of where, in their family of origin and even beyond, their own communication patterns developed.

Strategy: Love

Hope: Willpower to change

TRAINING COUPLES TO BETTER COMMUNICATE LOVE

In training partners to better communicate love to each other, use interventions for helping them communicate love directly; positively; by listening; by sharing information, their experiences, feelings and values; by creating time to communicate; and by avoiding devaluing communications.

Helping Couples Communicate Love Directly

In Gary Chapman's bestselling *The Five Love Languages,* he identifies five primary languages by which people communicate and receive communications of love (see table 10.1).[5] The goal is to communicate to loved ones in ways they can receive rather than the ways that we prefer. The book has become popular because people easily understand and use its main ideas. We have used it successfully in marital counseling and marital enrichment workshops. The ideas fit beautifully with my central thrust: valuing the partner. Intervention

10-5 describes my adaptation and can be used as a homework assignment. Encourage couples to purchase and read the book. It will richly repay the investment.

Intervention 10-5: Discerning Languages of Love and Communicating in Ways the Partner Can Understand

1. Tell the couple the following:

According to Chapman's bestselling book, which you may want to purchase, people have at least five languages of love.[6] A language of love is a way that a person understands that someone loves the person. A language is also a way that the person shows love to others. At times, we all use each of the five languages to receive and express love.

We have a preferred language of receiving love. If the partner speaks in that language, we easily hear it. It is as if I were in France. People speak French all around me, but because I understand little French, it becomes a nondescript humming in my ears. However, if someone began to sing in English, I would immediately tune in. I focus on my primary language.

2. Teach the partners the five languages of love (see table 10.1 for an adaptation).

3. Have partners rank the languages of love for themselves. Have them guess at the partner's ranking. Couples with children can rank love languages for their children. Older children can predict each other's favorite love language.

4. Have the partners compare lists.

5. Have the partners discuss how each can show love more often in the other's primary language so the partner can receive the love.

Strategy: Love

Hope: Waypower for change

Use videotapes to make changes in communication sensible. Videocassette cameras and players are powerful technological aids to improving communication but are infrequently used by practicing counselors. To show couples the waypower to change their communication, though, videotaping their interaction is an excellent way to build their hope. It is concrete and reusable; it can provide a permanent record of their improvement and help couples recall what occurred in counseling. It makes change *sensible.* The creative counselor can use videotape to help clients in many ways (see interventions 10-6 and 10-7).

Table 10.1. Languages of love (adapted from Chapman[7])

☐ Words: Saying "I love you," sincerely admiring or praising the partner, sincerely complimenting the partner, expressing your positive feelings in words.

☐ Acts of service: Doing nice things for the other. Helping out. Serving the other says, "I care enough for you to go out of my way to spend my time to help you."

☐ Gifts: Buying a gift or making a gift for the other says, "I was thinking of you and I was willing to put my thoughts into action by getting something for you." The gift might be small or large.

☐ Physical touch or closeness: Touching, patting, rubbing, head rubs, back rubs, foot tickles and sexual caresses. Being near the other, bumping up against the other, putting an arm around the other.

☐ Quality time: Hanging out together, spending exclusive time together and talking about things that are important to each of you. By conversation, showing that you care for the partner.

Intervention 10-6 *(Homework)*: Make a Videotape of Excellent Communication

For couples with a video camera, have them record a conversation about some positive topic. Instruct them to make a videotape that illustrates excellent communication. Stress that the content of the discussion is of little importance. Rather they are concentrating on how to communicate in a way that values the partner and does not devalue the partner. They are to make an example of valuing love. If you have worked on communication in previous sessions, instruct them to incorporate some of the things they have learned.

Strategy: Love

Hope: Waypower to change

Intervention 10-7: Watch the Videotape of Good Communication and Process It

Step 1: Watch the tape of excellent communication with the couple. While you are watching the tape, make no corrections. Compliment each partner's behavior at least once.

Step 2: Ask about their reactions to the tape. Listen carefully. Reinforce them when they mention positive behaviors. Ask each what the partner did that showed valuing love.

Step 3: If the videotape was good, tell that to the couple and ask them to reflect on whether each can identify one thing that he or she could do to make the communication even better at showing love. Each should identify only something about his or her own behavior, not the behavior of the partner. Discuss those proposed changes.

Step 4: In the session, remake the conversation including the improvements. If you have access to videotape recording equipment, use the couple's videotape to record the improved version.

Step 5: Assign the couple to view the remake during the upcoming week and decide whether the remake is indeed an improvement.

Strategy: Love

Hope: Waypower to change

If you are videotaping a session, do not hesitate to use the videotape to repeat an important point. Call it an "instant replay." By showing the videotape replay, you give the partners a different perspective on the event.

If you have a particularly good session on communication that you have videotaped, allow the partners to take the tape home and assign them to view it. Instruct each to write at least two comments of aspects that they thought were the best in the session. In the following session, discuss the aspects of communication that seemed best to each partner.

Helping Partners Communicate Love Positively

Break up constant focus on the negative. Partners tend to focus on ways they are failing to communicate well as a couple or, perhaps more often, on ways the partner is failing to communicate well. Focusing on the negative is counterproductive. Break up the negative focus. When a partner frequently attributes negative motives to the spouse, ask, "How do you know he thinks that? . . . What evidence do you have? . . . How can your spouse assure you that she does not think those negative things?" After casting doubt on the partners' negative inferences several times, direct them to focus on behaving positively and on reaching the solutions they identified in the initial interview as being important.

Focus on the positive. When partners communicate well, call attention to it. As a counselor, you often see the dregs of communication. It is easy to get into the habit of noticing and correcting negative communication. Force yourself to make at least three positive comments about couples' communication for every correction. That will help the couples believe that they are doing good things, and it will help couples pay more attention to the corrections.

Only infrequently does a person intentionally set out to destroy the partner. Most people in counseling want the relationship to improve. When a poor communication occurs, assume that the person is trying to get the relationship

Table 10.2. Six steps to communicating better: a summary

Taken from Hope-Focused Marriage Counseling: A Guide to Brief Therapy. *Downers Grove, Ill.: InterVarsity Press, 1999.*

☐ Identify the difficulties.
☐ Don't try to change everything at once.
☐ Begin with the positive.
☐ Analyze situations carefully.
☐ Don't lose sight of the goal: to communicate valuing love in a positive way.
☐ Get a book that describes a structured way to change communication.

to improve and that the method is faulty, not the intention. Tell that to the couples. Over time, by attributing positive motives to the partners, you help them see more positive motives in each other.

Teach couples guidelines for communicating at home. When you begin to work on communication with the couple, they want to solve all their communication woes instantly. At the end of the first session concerning communication, hand each partner a summary of six guidelines for discussion at home (photocopy table 10.2).

Discuss each as described in intervention 10-8. Then suggest that they employ the guidelines at home for the next few weeks. Using those guidelines will concentrate their attention and might reduce some unrealistic expectations of instant recovery.

Intervention 10-8: Teach Couples Guidelines for Changing Their Communication

Following are six guidelines to teach couples about changing their communication:

First, identify the difficulty. In what kinds of communication do you fall down? Is it the ritual how-do-you-dos or the common courtesies? Is it failure to pass along important information about your life, your work, your children? Is it sensitivity to feelings and important issues? Is it failure to self-disclose about what is going on with your life? Or is it a failure to discuss your marital communication when that appears called for? Are your errors those of omission—simply failing to talk enough in one or more particular areas? Or are you talking too much—disclosing hurtful thoughts or past occurrences that hurt the partner?

Second, when you decide to communicate differently, don't try to change everything at once. Such large changes, especially if your partner is not aware of and in agreement with what you are trying to accomplish, can be disastrous. It is better to make small changes and take progress a step at a time.

Third, begin with positive reminiscences: times when the relationship was going well. Try to reexperience the feelings in those days. How did you communicate then? Determine what parts of your communication are worth trying to recapture. Then, try to bring the positive back into your life.

Fourth, analyze situations carefully. We may get into a bad mood because of disappointments experienced outside of the home. When a gripe about our spouse surfaces, we must ask ourselves, *Is the gripe legitimate or is it a product of a disappointment elsewhere; is it important or is it not really worth discussing; is it a chance to blow off steam or is it an issue that really needs discussion?* If the problem is worth discussing, warn your spouse of the outside pressures before you begin to get into the issue that bothers you. For example, you might say, "Look, honey, I have a problem. A lot happened today. I broke a filling in my tooth, the dog just bit a lawyer's son and my boss yelled at me, so I'm in a rotten mood. But I feel like we have to discuss something . . ."

Fifth, don't get so involved in the issues that you lose sight of your goal: communicating positively with your spouse as a demonstration that you value him or her.

Sixth, if other attempts to change your communication fail, get a book that provides a good structure for improving marriage communication, such as John Gottman and his colleagues' book *A Couple's Guide to Communication*[8] (which can be ordered from Research Press, 2612 North Mattis Avenue, Champaign, IL 61820).

Strategy: Love

Hope: Waypower to change

Helping Couples Communicate Love by Listening

When marriages begin to have trouble, partners stop listening to each other. They tune the spouse out, listen only for points to rebut or avoid communication altogether. The message is undeniable: I don't care enough about you to hear you.

To help partners change that message, help them listen carefully to each other and communicate that they understand the partner. Numerous programs have been developed to train couples in communication. I find few differences in any. Bernard G. Guerney, in Relationship Enhancement, focuses on empathy and draws from Rogerian counseling.[9] Some of the other good programs include those by Howard Markman (PREP)[10] and John Gottman.[11] The Interpersonal Communication Program (ICP), developed by Sherod Miller, uses two large canvas mats—one with the awareness wheel drawn on it and the other with the listening cycle.[12] The awareness wheel was derived from communication theories as an aid to helping people become aware of the important parts of their experience and communicate those aspects of their experience systematically. The listening cycle summarizes important aspects of active listening. Couples learn to use the mats individually. In the third phase of the ICP, couples use the listening mat and awareness wheel simultaneously to facilitate conflict resolution. In the full program, couples are carefully taught how to use each mat. Miller cautions that for best results, counselors who use the method should be trained by him or a certified trainer and should use the method exactly as the training prescribes.

In all effective programs that train people in listening, similar elements are taught. Partners learn to use minimal encouragers (that is, ums, head nods, uh-huhs), repeat words or phrases, reflect content, reflect feelings and summarize larger blocks of information.

Helping Partners Communicate Love by Sharing Information

Some people don't communicate enough. They don't share their thoughts, feelings, behaviors, goals, sensations and affirmations with the partner. They don't share important information about what occurred during the day. They don't communicate about their children, finances or plans.

When some important bit of information slips through the cracks and is not communicated, both partners can be embarrassed and angry. Have them set aside a time to share information each day. Besides being helpful as a communication exercise, this can promote a stronger sense of closeness by strengthening the couple boundary.

Helping Partners Communicate Love by Sharing Their Experiences

Teach leveling. Leveling is communicating truthfully, yet sensitively, about one's experiences.[13] Leveling is communicating "on the level." Tell couples when to level and not to level. Level when one feels isolated from the spouse, bored or unable to tell the spouse what one is feeling. Do not level if one feels very angry, often argues with the spouse, feels like one must have the last word in a disagreement, or often insults, puts down or devalues the spouse.

Help partners love by sharing (and refusing) requests graciously. Teach partners to ask directly for what they need from the other. While one of the benefits of marriage is getting to know the partner so well that the spouse can often know without asking what the partner needs or wants, often it is necessary to make direct requests. Partners are sometimes not skilled in making such requests. Their requests are perceived as demands, which are responded to by resistance or by argument.

Do not assume that partners are unskilled in making requests. Such an assumption can insult the partners. Rather, ask partners to demonstrate making a request; if they need improvement, offer it tactfully, as in intervention 10-9.

Intervention 10-9: Teach Partners to Make Direct Requests

Step 1: Discuss the importance of making requests at times and in ways that they will not be misperceived.

Step 2: Ask whether the couple can remember when one partner made a request and the other misperceived it. Discuss an example in their life in which a request was misperceived and negative consequences ensued.

Step 3: Ask each partner to demonstrate how he or she would make requests tactfully. Give a specific example, such as asking to be informed of the bank balance after the partner pays the bills each month (or some issue that you know is *not* an issue with the couple). If you determine that their technique could be improved, compliment each partner on the things that were done well and then suggest that they might add to their repertoire by making requests in the following way.

Step 4: Model making a direct request. Say, "Dear, I like the way you always pay the bills on time. I've spent too much on clothes for a couple of months, building up a credit-card balance that has put us too close to overdrawing our checking, and that embarrasses me. It would help me if you would let me know what our bank balance is after you finish the bills each month. Would you do that?"

Step 5: Ask partners how they would respond if their partner made the request like that.

Step 6: Have each partner make a request using the method you suggested.

Strategy: Love

Hope: Waypower to change

Partners should feel free to ask for whatever they want, but in each instance the giver will determine which requests will be granted.[14] If the giver decides not to grant a request, he or she should provide a reason. Relate a sample situation, such as a partner saying, "I appreciate your not wanting to overdraw the checking account. It isn't easy for me to look you up and tell you about the balance, and I don't always pay all the bills in a single sitting. What if we were to keep the checkbook on the shelf in the kitchen? Then I can get it when I need to pay the bills, and you can check the balance before you go shopping."

Ask couples how they would respond if their partner refused a request like that. Have each partner make a refusal using the method you suggested.

Helping Partners Communicate Love by Sharing Feelings

The necessity of mutual understanding of feelings. According to Daniel B. Wile, when a person needs to get across an immediate feeling (what Wile calls a "leading-edge" feeling) and is frustrated in that need, he or she may react in offensive, provocative, compulsive or impulsive ways.[15] Generally, if you notice a partner becoming more symptomatic—that is, exhibiting extreme behavior—look for the frustration of being unable to get a leading-edge feeling across. Ask yourself, *What is the ordinary adult feeling that the person is trying to get across and can't?* Once you have identified that feeling, say, for example, "It seems like what you might be trying to say to Tim is 'I'm afraid that you will leave me if you get to know me better.'"

If you do not effectively intervene, or if the partner does not show that the spouse has gotten across that leading-edge feeling, then there will be a new one: frustration or anger at not being understood. If that leading-edge feeling is not received, then the spouse will become increasingly symptomatic, and the cycle will continue.

This is one reason why it is helpful to teach couples to respond to their feelings of frustration at being misunderstood by active listening and especially by identifying the partner's feelings. Once the spouse feels understood, he or she will feel less compelled to be symptomatic and will be able to think more clearly and can try in turn to understand the partner.

This point works two ways. When we as counselors become frustrated because we can't get our point across to our clients, we too get frustrated and thus symptomatic. We are simply more sophisticated in how we become symptomatic: we do it by interpreting clients' behavior in negative ways, confronting clients, attributing negative personalities to them, thinking of them as "resistant" and the like. Thus when we sense ourselves becoming frustrated with our clients because they don't seem to understand us, we need to check the impulse to punish the client and seek to understand instead.

Dealing with negative emotions. As much as we may dislike it, we all feel the negative emotions at times.[16] Fear hovers over us, occupying our minds and taking away our breath. Anger stomps up to us and squeezes our guts, making us want to hit something and scream. Frustration seethes inside us, filling us to the bursting point. What do we do with those strong feelings?

Feelings are the power of human relationships, but expressions of feelings are more controllable than are emotional experiences. Emotions can usually be expressed in love. Insist that such expression happen in session and at home.

Larry Crabb identifies three responses to strong feelings.[17] We may stuff them inside of us and bear them in stoic martyrdom, dump them on the nearest receptacle (the dog, our coworker, the children and too often our spouse) or deal with the feelings.

Freud suggested that stuffing feelings was the most harmful. According to his theory, the feelings *would* pop out, usually at the most inopportune time, in ways that we might hate later. This catharsis theory has largely been discredited, but stuffing feelings still has its costs, which might include having a "hair trigger" for further provocation and perhaps even physical illness (though there is evidence that this happens more rarely than was previously thought). Besides, it's no fun to suffer alone. An old Chinese proverb says, "Even a piece of paper is lighter if two people pick it up." Even more, shared burdens seem lighter.

However, dumping feelings is no way to share them. When we become angry and let that anger out explosively, it will have negative effects. Anger vented on friends and family members boomerangs. Fear grows like a viral infection. Dumped anger provokes feelings in others, and we must deal with those feelings as well as our own feelings. In addition, expressing strong feelings doesn't really get rid of the feelings. To the contrary, according to psychologist Carol Tavris, who examined years of research on anger, expressing strong feelings multiplies them.[18] Hitting a pillow in rage usually makes us madder. Yelling in fury usually makes us more furious.

How then do we deal productively with negative emotions? Crabb recommends three ways. First, talk about them. Labeling our emotions provides a sense of control and confidence. Second, try to solve the problem. If the problem is interpersonal, try to change our own behavior, not the other person. Third, accept that we may not be able to solve the problem completely. Acceptance of the things over which we have no control helps us control our emotions. Crabb gives five guidelines for dealing with anger, which are summarized in table 10.3.[19]

While Crabb's guidelines help us train couples in explicit communication, the suggestions are certainly not complete. People handle negative feelings in many other ways. Crabb identified some of the methods of explicit reconciliation[20] but not any of the methods of implicit reconciliation. Implicit reconciliation involves calming negative feelings without directly discussing them. People calm themselves often by avoiding conflict, gently touching the partner, gift giving, making love and many other ways. Being counselors who value explicit communication, we tend to impose that approach on clients, sometimes clients who are not well suited to explicit reconciliation. Instead, through careful assessment, we must be alert to matching other methods to partners who cannot benefit by explicit reconciliation.

Table 10.3. Five guidelines for dealing with anger (adapted from Crabb[21])

☐ Be slow to anger.
☐ Acknowledge when you feel angry.
☐ Think through your goals and determine which goals are blocked by the spouse's behavior; seek to meet your spouse's needs.
☐ Assume responsibility for the goal of ministering to your spouse.
☐ Express negative feelings if doing so serves a good purpose (but edit out a hurtful style and hurtful comments).

Helping Couples Communicate Love by Sharing Their Values

One way to produce a sense of closeness is to have partners talk about things they value. Suggest such topics of communication when you are training the couple in good communication or when you are attempting to promote feelings of closeness and intimacy. Following is a list of topics that generally produce good feelings when partners discuss them, if the partners agree on their positions about the topics.

☐ pleasant shared memories (such as taking enjoyable vacations, eating at good restaurants, attending special events like concerts or sporting events)

☐ shared times of emotional bonding (such as being together at the birth of a child)

☐ memories of mutual accomplishment (such as building a bathroom together or planting a garden)

☐ memories of accomplishments of the children

☐ shared worship that was particularly moving

☐ each other's accomplishments

☐ exciting intellectual ideas

☐ good television shows or movies

☐ goals and dreams for each partner individually and for the couple

If partners can share their ideas about what they value in life, they can often talk excitedly for long periods. Partners may also enjoy simply being with each other in a common activity.

Helping Couples Communicate Love by Creating Time and Opportunities to Communicate

One important way that people feel loved is knowing that the partner is willing to devote time to being together—just the two of them. Chapman calls this quality time and suggests that spending quality time together is more important to some people than to others.[22] Generally, although people have varying demands on their time and have learned to expect and value time together differently, all relationships need bounded time to allow intimacy to grow.

Couples grow in intimacy by establishing bounded or protected time in which they reserve time for each other and do not permit interruptions from children, phone calls or other distractions. In addition, that bounded time (especially if it is regularly scheduled) permits an avenue for regular communication. Have couples establish time to devote exclusively to each other. Sometimes couples will object that they "cannot" have such time: small children constantly intrude or demands from work keep the partner away from home.

One structured activity to promote more conversation is an adaptation of Corsini's marriage conference, which was described by H. Norman Wright[23] and in my 1989 book[24] as a conflict-management strategy (see intervention 10-10). Adapt the intervention to pleasant discussion and follow the protocol described for resolving differences.

Intervention 10-10 *(Homework)*: Marriage Conference for Communication

Have people set four one-hour times to express their thoughts to each other. In each session, one person talks without interruption for thirty minutes. Then the other talks for thirty minutes. They should not discuss between conferences what went on at the previous conference. Alternate as to who speaks first in each session. Provide a list of suggested topics (see above in the section on sharing values for one list). Stress to the partners that they can discuss anything that they think would interest and please the partner.

Note: When you assign this, be sure to let people know that it is not a conflict-resolution exercise. It is a communication-of-your-experience exercise.

Strategy: Love

Hope: Waypower to change

Helping Couples Avoid Devaluing Communications

Teach editing. Editors cut words to make communication better. In communications training *editing* is cutting desired acts or statements to make communication better.

Teach couples to edit harmful communications, such as triggers that fire off conflict (for example, shooting off one's mouth), confrontation of every annoyance, or "love busters" (see intervention 10-2).[25] Partners don't have to say everything they think. Have them hold back on communications that will devalue the spouse.

Teach couples not to pull the triggers. Conflict usually doesn't come out of nowhere. Generally, there are triggers that set off conflict: a certain look that shows the partner that you don't care or are bored, a particular whine of voice, a glare, a sudden withdrawal from the conversation, constant complaining or even discussion of a particular topic. One way to prevent arguments and disagreements is to learn to recognize the triggers and divert a possible argument into more positive directions.

When a couple recognizes a trigger for conflict, tell them to unashamedly avoid it. It is no disgrace to avoid almost certain conflict. It isn't necessary to stand boldly and spit in the eye of the tiger to demonstrate courage. We avoid excess cholesterol, fat foods, harsh sunshine and a sedentary lifestyle to improve our health. We avoid riding our bicycle down the center stripe of a two-lane street, tugging on Batman's cape and insulting Mike Tyson (thus avoiding potential ear injury).

Teach couples not only to avoid the trigger situations but also to use the triggers to remind themselves to be more loving. Help them plan ahead how to deal with the triggers, letting triggers be reminders to put the plan into action.

Take care of the pressures as they build. When people are aggravated, they often let communication slide. This is especially true if the partners are under a lot of stress, perhaps with two jobs, several children and multiple responsibilities in work, home and community. The couple must balance their energies. They cannot confront every aggravation. There simply is not enough time and energy, and the marriage would become incredibly focused on the negative. On the other hand, they also cannot let every devaluing remark or action slide. The marriage would be based on denial, which works well in the short run but not always in the long run.

When negative things are said, they hurt like a small pinch.[26] Sometimes people store up a lot of pinches and then whomp the other person by recalling all the past pinches. Instead, tell partners to take care of each pinch as soon as possible after it occurs. People can deal with the pinches by (a) letting them pass and forgetting, (b) saying "ouch," letting them pass and forgetting, or (c) talking about them in a spirit of conveying that one has been hurt, not condemning the partner, and seeking forgiveness and assurances that the partner will try to avoid the pinches in the future.

Occasional pinches happen in all marriages. Most are never confronted (and shouldn't be!). Different couples will have widely different criteria for deciding when an issue must be confronted. Early communication theorists, basing their theories on the human potential movement of the 1960s, valued honest communication, straight from the hip. They theorized that couples with few conflicts must necessarily have a poor relationship, and if the marriage looked good, that was only frosting that hid a time bomb within the cake. They counseled people to confront every slight or harm directly. That turned out not to be helpful.

Gottman watched highly functional couples to determine how they actually communicated.[27] He dispelled the myth that all well-functioning couples immediately confront issues and disagree about several topics. About one-third of the well-functioning couples virtually never have conflict, one-third have a moderate amount of conflict, and one-third have frequent hot conflicts and reconcile just as passionately.

As counselors, we must respect couples' natural tendencies. While couples who come to marital counseling admit that their normal behavior is not working optimally, not all partners must be transformed into open, sensitive verbal processors. Assess the natural tendencies of the partners individually and as a couple. Then design a program that fits them.

BEYOND LEVELING AND EDITING

Leveling, editing, making requests and sharing feelings are not goals for communication. They are tools to achieve goals. One goal is to "speak the truth in love" (Eph 4:24). Couples who profess Christianity need to understand the reason editing and leveling are used. Help them understand through discussing Ephesians 4:24. Then say, "You each seem to be trying hard to get a truth across to your partner. I sense that you both want to 'speak the truth in love.' If true love is valuing the other person like a pearl of great value, then tell me how you can communicate truth in love to your partner." After each person has suggested ways to communicate in love, return to the issue they were previously discussing. Ask them, "Using the principles you have just suggested, how would you convey the truth you want your partner to hear in love?" Conveying love is communication's aim.

Chapter 11

Interventions for Aiding Conflict Resolution

Watch almost any modern movie and you will see abundant conflict between romantic partners. Usually the conflict ends in the mutual insight that the partners are in love, followed by passionate sex. If only it were that easy in real life.

In real life Bud and Cheri had not had sex in three weeks. Whenever they tried, Cheri got irritated by Bud's stimulation and Bud was turned off by Cheri's rejection. What began as making love ended in making war.

Most couples come to marital counseling in conflict over numerous issues, conflict they cannot seem to resolve. Usually you will spend several sessions helping couples apply different methods of resolving their differences. Note that I did not say that you would help them resolve their differences. To resolve specific differences might be the couple's goal but not the counselor's. Instead, help the couple (a) learn *how* to resolve whatever differences they encounter and (b) see conflict resolution in the bigger picture as an opportunity to act in faith and love. If you could do that every time, you'd win the Nobel Peace Prize.

You are interested primarily in helping couples act in love to build hope. Trying to resolve differences in a love that values the partner and does not devalue the partner provides one of the greatest challenges to any couple. That is especially true for troubled couples, who have already established many hurtful, devaluing strategies.

Conflict implies that differences and separateness strain the bonds of closeness. Of course, you usually want to help people become closer, but conflict resolution is more than learning bargaining techniques, compromising or avoiding hurtfulness during negotiation. Conflict resolution also involves reconciliation of the conflicted parties. Reconciliation generally means confession of one's hurtfulness and forgiveness of the other person's hurtfulness. Thus, conflict resolution is usually paired, in some way with techniques discussed in chapter nine ("Interventions for Promoting Confession and Forgiveness") and perhaps chapter thirteen ("Interventions for Stimulating More Closeness").

Differences between people in close relationships are inevitable. Some would argue that they are necessary, that life would be dull if it consisted of unmodulated harmony. In over twenty years, though, I have never had a couple come to marital counseling saying, "Doc, we are simply too close. You have to help us have more conflict." Most want fewer differences and less conflict over them. When people differ, help them to resolve some of the differences, to accept some of the differences, but above all to deal with the differences in love.

To help couples resolve conflicts, follow four general guidelines.

1. *Deal with the conflict as it is being acted out in the session.* When people discuss differences, don't interrupt until they have discussed a few minutes. If you jump on every little communication glitch, you won't get anywhere.

2. *Have one major focus per session.* Partners may discuss several issues, and you might point out several ways to resolve differences in love, but concentrate on only one theme.

3. *Point out the positive.* When a partner does something positive during a conflict, note it. If the husband rubs the wife's arm when she is crying, or if the wife stops yelling when she sees her husband is hurt, make a point of it as indicating that the partners are valuing each other.

4. *Create a joint platform from which to discuss a problem.* According to Daniel Wile a "joint platform" is a neutral, nonaccusing, nondefensive vantage point from which to view a problem.[1] Instead of rushing to try to solve the problem by compromising or by determining who is right and who isn't, try to help partners create a joint platform. Not all problems can be solved, but a marriage that approaches difficulties from a joint platform will be likely to succeed.

PREPARING THE COUPLE TO RESOLVE CONFLICTS

The goals of training couples in conflict resolution are threefold. The first and most important goal is to help partners practice faith working through love, in which partners strive to prevent any statement or implication of devaluing and try to positively value the spouse. The next most important is to teach a process of resolving conflict that will make it easier to practice faith working through love in future conflict-resolution situations. Partners develop a mindset in which they want to learn how to solve their problems more than they want to "win" the argument. Third, partners want to resolve the issues discussed in counseling to show that the conflict resolution skills that they have practiced there can work with other problems.

It is important that the couple know the goals. State them and review them at the start of each session that deals with conflict. Couples want you to referee their fights, and each partner wants you to validate him or her. You can't do that. Convince partners that the target for your intervention is *how* they communicate, not *what* they are disagreeing over. Imagine this conversation.

Counselor:	How long have you had this disagreement?
Henrietta:	About four years. It began in the summer.
Counselor:	What is the likelihood you'll resolve it in the next thirty minutes?
Billy-Bob:	'Bout as likely as it snowing this July Fourth.
Counselor:	Then our purpose isn't to resolve this conflict, but it is to help you develop different ways to resolve *any* conflict you have in a way that shows your love. Does that make sense?

INCREASING PARTNERS' AWARENESS OF THEIR CONFLICT AND RESOLUTION

Couples are usually aware that they have conflict, how frequently they have conflict and how severe the conflict is. Their judgments may not be the same as yours. Assess the level of conflict. According to a system developed by Philip Guerin and his colleagues, there are four levels of marital conflict (see table 11.1).[2] Use the four levels to make a rough prognosis of the couple. Then tailor your interventions to the couple's level of conflict.

Increasing Awareness of Topics of Disagreement

Partners know their main topics of disagreement but often cannot name all of

---

Table 11.1. Four levels of conflict (based on Guerin et al.'s model[3])

☐ Level 1: Occasional arguments, not much conflict. (Prognosis good. Couples respond to more educative interventions.)

☐ Level 2: Active conflict. Power struggle formed, but active conflict has lasted less than six months. (Prognosis good with therapy. Usually five to eight intervention sessions to reduce conflict and get back to more positive interactions.)

☐ Level 3: Chronic power struggle that has lasted longer than six months. (Prognosis mixed. Usually will make some progress in five to eight intervention sessions, but will still have significant problems. Best hope is to make progress in five to eight intervention sessions, direct the couple to try to continue progress for a period and perhaps return for more sessions at a later date.)

☐ Level 4: Chronic conflict and one or both spouses have engaged an attorney. (Poor prognosis. Chances are high that the marriage won't survive. Best bet is to limit the emotional damage each inflicts and try to help the marriage survive and improve; however, the couple probably will seek divorce, so you can help with separation and divorce when the partners give up. This is not a statement of fatalism, but a practical matter. People will not always respond to marital therapy.)

---

them on cue. This can mean trouble for the hapless counselor. You bring up a topic that you think is relatively benign only to find that the partners turn on you and rip out your heart. (Well, it *feels* that way sometimes.)

Use Richard S. Stuart's powergram as a homework assignment to determine the major topics of conflict (see intervention 11-1).[4] The powergram can be completed separately (or together) by the partners. The powergram does not require that partners discuss the topics, only identify the topics.

Intervention 11-1 (*Homework*): Powergram

Stuart has people identify topics about which they disagree by drawing two circles (labeled his and hers) with a space between them.[5] Partners identify disagreements and give each disagreement a letter. One partner (let's say the husband) places a capital letter at the distance between the circles representing how much power the partner thinks he has on that issue. The other partner places a small letter between the circles representing how much power she thinks the spouse has. Thus, if the partners think "holidays with the in-laws" is an important issue of conflict, the husband might place a capital *A* somewhere in the wife's circle, indicating he thinks his wife has most of the power to decide. The wife might place her small *a* between the circles, indicating that she thinks the power is shared equally.

Strategy: Love, Work

Hope: Willpower to change

Increasing Awareness of How Partners Try to Resolve Conflict

Partners generally have a limited ability to tell you how they attempt to resolve their differences. They describe their motives ("I try always to be understanding and never to hurt her"), some salient actions ("We end up yelling at each other") and some socially acceptable strategies ("We try to compromise"). However, they rarely have much insight into what triggers conflict and arguing, how they each try to reduce the conflict, what provokes the partner to escalate conflict and often how they make up after conflict dies down.

You cannot get the couple to understand fully all aspects of their effective and ineffective conflict strategies. Don't try. However, you can raise the couple's awareness of areas that you intend to work on. Namely, help them become aware of ways they devalue or fail to value each other. Show the couple how they fail to listen to each other, how they trigger opposition perhaps unwittingly and how they take positions that prevent achieving any resolution. Help partners see ways they fail to reconcile after the conflict passes. You will eventually intervene to help partners change each of those areas. Do not get sidetracked into pointing out aspects of conflict resolution that you do not intend to address. Partners might perceive you as wise, but they will not effectively deal with their differences if you spread their awareness too thinly. Stay focused.

Discovering What Happens When Partners Disagree

Suggest that it would be helpful to know how each person actually behaves during a disagreement. Direct the partners to re-create a recent disagreement. Couples don't like to argue, especially not in front of someone. They will *tell* you how they argue; however, this is not helpful. Direct them to act out a recent disagreement, and you'll be more likely to see what usually happens. Then say that it would be helpful to know how well each partner understands the other's viewpoint. Prescribe a role reversal. That will help them understand the other person's perspective and thus generate empathy for the other person.

Say, "Gordon, you are Kathy. Kathy, you are Gordon. Have the discussion you just completed but this time pretend that you are the other person." Sometimes partners depict each other's behavior in an exaggeratedly negative way. Redirect this hostility by labeling it as humorous or directly say that the point of the exercise is not to portray the partner negatively but is to show whether the partner knows the other person's perspective.

Another way to increase awareness of what happens during conflict is to assign partners to record on audiotape or videotape arguments at home (see intervention 11-2).

Intervention 11-2 *(Homework):* Videotape or Audiotape a Discussion of a Difference at Home

In session have the couple select an issue about which they disagree. Choose a topic about which there are definite differences of opinion but not too much emotional investment.

Have partners videotape or audiotape their discussion at home. Have them set a timer for ten minutes. After they discuss the issue for ten minutes in their normal way, they should try to discuss the issue again for ten minutes, with the conscious intention to always value the partner. Even if disagreements occur, the partners should try to value the partner and never to devalue the partner. Have the couple bring the tape with both discussions to the next session. Discuss the differences between the two conversations. Ask the partners to discern lessons they learned.

Important: You must be willing to watch the videotape (or listen to the audiotape) in session. If you do not watch (or listen to) at least part of each tape, you will undercut the couple's compliance with any later homework.

Strategy: Love, work

Hope: Waypower to change

Couples can be pessimistic about their relationship because they have differences. In fact, they may be almost unwilling to reveal to the counselor that they have conflict. Help them become less self-conscious (see intervention 11-3).

Intervention 11-3: Reducing a Couple's Negativity About Having Differences

Couples often believe that their differences are the major source of problems. They feel that any differences are evidence that they are not meant for each other. Attention to differences is heightened by frequent conflict. Sometimes a major intervention can be simply to get the couple to lighten up about their differences.

☐ When you mention that the couple have differences, say something like "Like all couples, you have differences. One of them is. . . ."

☐ Frame the problems in terms of the couple's interactions instead of their differences. Say, "All couples have differences. The difference between troubled and untroubled couples is the way the couples interact to handle the differences, not the presence or absence of differences. The two of you certainly have differences. [You might name a few.] But you have no more differences than any other couple. You do have a lot of difficulty dealing with your differences."

☐ Briefly describe a case in which a couple overcame a similar difference by changing their interactions or by simply accepting that they would be different in that area.

☐ When possible, note current conflictual differences that originally attracted the partners. Point out that a difference doesn't have to divide them, even though it currently is. After all, the same difference didn't divide them in the past.

☐ Take the sting out of differences by explaining the partners' behavior as something common among people and a spouse's reaction as understandable in light of personality, family of origin, or situational pressures.

☐ Characterize differences as a matter of degree rather than as a stark difference[6]. For instance, a couple defines an issue as one of responsibility versus irresponsibility. The wife is seen by the husband as a spendthrift who blows all their money on clothes, shoes and perfume—irresponsible but fun-loving. The husband is seen by the wife as a penny-pinching stick-in-the-mud—responsible but no fun. The counselor might frame the issue like this:

> Both of you seem to value both having fun and being responsible with your money. Over time, you have argued yourselves into extreme positions in which you see each other and perhaps even yourself in terms that are black and white. I'm willing to bet, though, that you [husband] like to have fun and would be willing to spend money if you thought the fun was justified and that you [wife] think it is important to have money for the things that are really important and would be willing to save on an immediate purchase for something you thought was more important. I bet that the disagreement is not all-or-nothing, like the two of you treat it, but one of degree. Let's work on understanding that both of you want the same important things—to have fun doing the things you think are fun and to save money responsibly for things you think are of major worth—but you differ on what items are worth spending on and what items are worth saving for. It's a matter of degree.

Strategy: Love, work
Hope: Waypower to change

HELPING COUPLES STOP DEVALUING EACH OTHER
Couples can devalue each other in many ways. You can help them reduce the number of these negative interactions by teaching them to stop pulling triggers, cross-complaining and personalizing issues.

Increasing the Ratio of Positive to Negative Interactions
Couples come to counseling with a low ratio of positive to negative interactions—often less than 1:1. Help them raise it.[7] You will make the most immediate impact on the ratio if you help the couple reduce the number of negative interactions. If a couple has five positive and five negative interactions each day, they have a 1:1 ratio. If they want to raise the ratio, would it be easier to have twenty additional positive interactions or to reduce the negative interactions by four? Obviously, there is less effort involved in doing four less-negative behaviors than in thinking up and doing twenty positive behaviors.

Increasing positive interactions is important, however, because they are usually easier to do and are more noticeable than are decreasing negative interactions. First, it is usually easier to do something nice (e.g., smile, say thank you, buy a present) than to reduce criticism or some other habitual negative act. Negative interactions usually occur in response to triggers, which are often automatic. Once the triggered sequence begins, much effort must be exerted to stop it. Second, if a partner completely ignores a provocation to a negative interaction, the avoided behavior is usually not noticeable simply because it did not happen. However, a positive interaction is noticeable. (What is noticeable is to look back over the day or the week and realize that few negative interactions occured.)

We want the couple to both reduce the negative and increase the positive. For example, suggest that the couple do three less negatives and five more positives, increasing the ratio to 10:2 (or 5:1). Approach the couple as follows.

First, explain Gottman's ratio (see chapter four): a five-to-one ratio of positive-to-negative acts predicts marital satisfaction of four years later. Then say, "As 1 Peter 3 says, do not repay insult with insult, but with blessing. For example, when you feel angry, don't just sulk in silence, but instead try a little tenderness. Say something that values rather than devalues your partner. Say, 'I want to understand you. I really do. What you are saying is important to me. I'm going to try to understand and repeat back what I understand you to be saying. I want you to tell me if I'm correctly understanding what you are saying.' "

By describing how to bless the partner, even in the face of provocation, you provide a model of the skills needed for the partners to change their positive-to-negative ratio.

Helping Couples Avoid Pulling Triggers

There are several common triggers for conflict. Help couples avoid pulling those triggers that start arguments.

Have partners avoid backing themselves into corners. Have couples resolve not to threaten divorce or separation or to take unilateral irrevocable actions. Threats are destructive because if the other person doesn't respond, a partner must either follow through or back down, which is especially hard to do in a power struggle. Have couples pledge aloud not to threaten separation or divorce during the agreed-upon duration of counseling.

Have partners avoid mutual traps. A mutual trap occurs when both partners are desperately trying to avoid having a conflict, but the things that they do to avoid the conflict are the very things that seem to set off the other person.[8] Help partners recognize and avoid mutual traps. After explaining the mutual trap to the couple, you might address the clients like this (if at all possible using an example from the clients' own lives):

> For instance, you, Marsha, described how you interpreted Ahmed's refusal to stay late as another instance of what you thought was a lack of ambition. To help Ahmed, you suggested that he not be so quick to turn down overtime pay. You, Ahmed, felt criticized, but you said that you didn't want to get into an argument, so you didn't respond. You, Marsha, said that you didn't want to get into an argument either and that you were afraid that if you let this simmer it would blow up later, so you kept after Ahmed. Eventually he yelled at you and you got into the fight you were both trying hard to avoid.

Label these mutual traps as triggers that partners should try not to pull.

Have partners avoid minefields and land mines. A "minefield" or "land mine," in the terminology of Andrew Christensen, N. S. Jacobson and J. C. Babcock, is an issue that, once addressed, almost always leads to a conflict.[9] Point out these too as triggers. Usually these issues are rooted in chronic conflict in the couple's history and even more deeply in an issue that has great personal significance to one or both partners.

Have partners avoid issues about which there are credibility gaps. A credibility gap is a violation of trust at some time in the past.[10] Whenever that violation is recalled, conversation ceases because the aggrieved partner cannot get past his or her unforgiveness of the violation of trust. Approach the credibility gap problem in two ways: (1) counsel couples to avoid issues that bring up a known credibility gap and (2) test to see whether the unforgiving partner can forgive and both partners can pledge to work on rebuilding trust.

Help partners avoid their own idiosyncratic triggers. All couples associate certain gestures, actions, phrases and topics addressed by each other with previous conflict. Seeing or hearing those immediately leads to an emotional response, which quickly leads to conflict if not stopped instantly.

Helping Couples Stop Cross-Complaining

Cross-complaining is answering a complaint with a complaint of one's own.[11] Cross-complaining devalues the partner because it communicates that the partner is self-centered and doesn't take one's complaint seriously enough to even respond. Further, the partner accuses the person of blameworthy acts—a double-whammy. For instance, Joan says, "You never take me out to eat." Greg says, "You don't keep the house clean."

One way to help couples stop cross-complaining is to use the listening and repeating intervention described in the next section (intervention 11-7). Another way is to challenge couples to make a radical assumption: that the partner might (perish the thought) be right. This helps break up the pattern and gets partners to focus on potential solutions.[12]

Helping Couples Stop Personalizing Issues

Personalizing an issue is treating every disagreement as a personal attack on one's identity. When the marriage has turned highly negative, people often personalize arguments. Personalizing arguments prevents them from addressing the merit of the partner's complaint and devalues the partner because it treats the partner as an attacker rather than treating the partner's complaint or suggestion as having any merit.

Help partners remove some of the pain from the way they construe their arguments. Help them talk about the arguments more objectively than emotionally after the argument is over. To do this, you can try an empty-chair intervention that originated in the integrative behavioral marital therapy approach.[13]

If an argument has recently taken place (either during the session or before the session), bring in a fourth chair. Say, "Imagine that the problem is in the chair. Let's discuss it. Whenever you mention the problem, treat it as if it were an object that is here in the room." Follow the empty chair intervention with a homework assignment (see intervention 11-4).

Intervention 11-4 *(Homework)*: Increase Objectivity

Use either of the following assignments to increase the objectivity with which partners treat their arguments, thus reducing the personalizing of issues.

☐ If an argument erupts at home, when the argument is finished, bring a chair in and talk about the problem again as "it." Imagine the problem is an impersonal object. Analyze it without getting each other upset again.[14]

☐ When an argument erupts at home, as it inevitably will some day, set a chair for the counselor. Pretend that the counselor is there with you, and discuss the argument after you have cooled down.[15]

Strategy: Love

Hope: Waypower to change

HELPING COUPLES VALUE EACH OTHER

Focus conflict-resolution training on resolving differences in love. To make that concept salient to couples, I organized the major interventions to promote conflict resolution in hope-focused marriage counseling into an acrostic: LOVE. Each letter stands for one focus of training. *L, O* and *E* stand for skills: *L* for listening and repeating, *O* for observing your effects and *E* for evaluating both partners' interests. *V* stands for the principle of value your partner (see table 11.2; feel free to photocopy).

Presenting the LOVE Acrostic

When you decide to deal with conflict, use the last ten minutes of the previous session to prepare the couple. Tell them that next session you intend to begin working on helping them resolve their differences in love with less conflict. Then present the LOVE acrostic (see intervention 11-5).

Intervention 11-5: Teaching the LOVE Acrostic

Tell the couple that you will use three skills and one general principle to help them resolve differences. Say that you have summarized those in an acrostic to deal with power struggles. Tell them that you want to give them a thumbnail sketch of the methods for about five minutes and then you'll provide a handout

Table 11.2. A summary of the LOVE acrostic for couples

Taken from Hope-Focused Marriage Counseling: A Guide to Brief Therapy. *Downers Grove, Ill.: InterVarsity Press, 1999.*

LOVE

L: **Listen and repeat.** Break up those patterns by listening to your partner and repeating a short summary of what he or she said before you make your point.

O: **Observe your effects.** What we intend for a communication to say is not always the impact the communication has. When you see that your partner has responded in a way that indicates a misunderstanding, stop and say, "I feel like I didn't communicate as clearly as I would like. What I meant to say was . . ." Notice the triggers that get you into conflicts or that make conflicts get suddenly worse. Avoid those triggers.

V: **Value your partner.** In whatever communication, always strive to value your partner and never devalue your partner.

E: **Evaluate both partners' interests.** Use the method of conflict resolution advocated by Roger Fisher and William Ury in *Getting to Yes: Negotiating Agreement Without Giving In.*[16] Go beyond the statement of your position in a conflict and identify the real interests you both are trying to meet. If you both identify your interests, then you can often find several solutions that meet both of your interests—not just one person's interests.

to read and think about. At the following session, you'll begin to use some of those ideas to help them more effectively resolve conflicts.

Then talk for no more than five minutes (less if possible) about the following.
Topic 1: Power Struggles

What is a power struggle? A power struggle is a chronic struggle not over an issue but over who has the say in an issue. Give an example of a couple who disagreed about an issue and the position they took changed without altering the intensity of the conflict. Tell them how to recognize if a person is in a power struggle: rehearsing conversations in one's mind and thinking that the other person is violating one's basic rights.
Topic 2: How Do Partners Get Out of Power Struggles?

I use four ways to help partners get out of power struggles. You can use these with your friends who are locked in deadly battles of their wills. I use an acrostic to organize these techniques: LOVE. Hand them the photocopy of table 11.2 and talk them through it.

L: *Listen and repeat.* When people get in power struggles, they stop listening to each other. You can help them break up those patterns by having each person listen and repeat a short summary of what the partner said before responding. Have the speaker pass either a dollar ("passing the buck"; "the buck stops here") or a Nerf ball ("the ball's in your court") to signify that it is the other partner's turn to talk.

O: *Observe your effects.* What we intend for a communication to say is not always the impact the communication has. When a person sees that the partner has responded in a way that indicated a misunderstanding, the person should stop and say, "I feel like I didn't communicate as clearly as I would like. What I meant to say was . . ." Then the partners need to get back on task at solving the problem or resolving the difference or whatever the task was.

V: *Value your partner.* In every communication, each partner must strive always to value and to never devalue the partner.

E: *Evaluate both partners' interests.* I teach partners the method of conflict resolution advocated by Roger Fisher and William Ury in *Getting to Yes: Negotiating Agreement Without Giving In.*[17] Partners are taught how to go beyond the statement of their position in a conflict and identify the real interests they are trying to meet with the solution they proposed. If both people identify their interests, then the couple can often find several solutions that meet both people's interests—not just one person's interests.

Assign couples the task of reflecting on each strategy between sessions.
Strategy: Love
Hope: Waypower to change

You might also find it helpful to assign couples (especially younger ones) to find out more about valuing love. Intervention 11-6 describes one assignment that will give couples an opportunity to learn about love outside of the counseling hour.

Intervention 11-6 *(Homework):* Learning About Love

Les and Leslie Parrott suggest that young couples seeking to marry should interview long-married couples.[18] I have adapted this to troubled couples.

Get partners to interview an older couple whom they believe to have a good marriage. (Each partner will interview the same-sex partner in the long-married couple.) Direct the troubled couple to discuss with the partners of the older couple how the older couple has handled differences successfully.

This assignment is based on two assumptions. The first assumption is that all marriages have some troubles, though about one-third of all marriages seem to have very few difficulties according to Gottman.[19] Happy couples have learned to roll with the punches and cope with life's jolts. The second assumption is that people learn by observing successful models who have coped successfully with difficulties.

In their interviews of the same-sex partner, have each partner find out from the partner he or she is interviewing:

☐ What difficulties have you and your spouse faced throughout your married life?
☐ When your spouse had problems, what did you do to support him or her?
☐ When you had problems, what did your spouse do that you particularly appreciated to help you deal with the struggles?
☐ How did you resolve your differences?
☐ What do you think is primarily responsible for your happy marriage?
Strategy: Love
Hope: Waypower to change

In subsequent sessions, select one or more of the three next interventions (listening and repeating [11-7], observing your effects [11-8] and evaluating both partners' interests [11-9]). Spend at least one session on whichever you select. Remember to emphasize the principle of valuing one's partner throughout. Depending on the couple, you might spend more than one session on these interventions.

Teaching Couples to Listen and Repeat

Partners don't have to listen to each other. Marriages are two-sided. When one person initiates a conversation, the other needs to listen to that request; but if the timing is not good for the conversation, the other partner should refuse the conversation nicely and suggest a time when he or she would like to talk, usually within a day. Model how to refuse a request to talk by saying, "I really want to talk with you. This isn't a good time right now. I'm doing X. How about if we talk in twenty minutes? Would that be okay?"

After conversations develop, people sometimes feel misunderstood. When people begin to feel misunderstood it usually is because they *are* misunderstood. When we feel this way, our natural response is to concentrate on how to be understood. So whenever we finish making a statement, we immediately begin to plan our next statement to help the spouse understand us. The obvious effect is that we stop listening to the spouse. The spouse rightfully feels misunderstood and begins to tune out the partner and concentrate on being understood himself or herself. Partners are caught in a cycle of misunderstanding. Neither partner is listening to the other. Neither is understanding the other.

For the person who wants to be understood, paradoxically, the road to being understood is to put aside the desire to be understood and replace it with both understanding and communicating that understanding to the spouse. If the partner can communicate to the spouse that he or she understands, the spouse can begin to listen and perhaps even to understand. Intervention 11-7 describes how I teach listening and repeating.

Intervention 11-7: Teaching Couples to Listen and Repeat Directly

Step 1: Tell the partners that valuing the partner requires that we listen. We must listen for what is said (whether we like to hear what is said or not) and for what the other person is feeling.

Step 2: Tell the couple about how to deal with misunderstandings by listening and repeating what the partner says until the partner knows you understand.

Step 3: Emphasize that it is not sufficient simply to understand the partner. The important part is to let the partner know that you understand.

Step 4: Have one partner speak. Ask the listener what was said. Ask the original speaker if that is correct. If so, ask the original listener to speak. If not, ask the original speaker to correct the listener's understanding.

Step 5: Once you have gone through this several times, have the couple try this on their own in the session while you observe.

Step 6: Process this sequence with the partners. Find what effect listening and repeating had on them. Usually, it makes them feel frustrated because they have a lot to say and this interrupts their flow; however, it also lowers emotion and prevents them from flying off the handle and saying hurtful things. Sometimes they will say that they feel more understood or more valued. If they don't spontaneously mention the positive, ask them.

Step 7: Get the partners to repeat the discussion with a new issue.

Step 8: Assign them to employ this listen-and-repeat method at home if they have a misunderstanding between sessions.

Strategy: Love, work

Hope: Waypower to change

Listening and repeating is a basic communication skill that is used by a number of counselors of different theoretical persuasions and virtually all communication training programs. Sherod Miller uses it in his listening cycle.[20] Scott M. Stanley, Daniel W. Trathen and Savanna McCain[21] use a version of listening and repeating adapted for Christians from Howard Markman's PREP model.[22] In their speaker-listener technique, the speaker holds a piece of tile flooring, speaks for the self (not the partner) and keeps the statements relatively short. The listener edits any tendency to rebut, focuses on the speaker's message and summarizes that message by paraphrasing. Listening and repeating is valuable for several reasons:

☐ Listening to the partner values him or her and communicates that valuing clearly to the partner. Thus, when couples practice listening and repeating, they are building love into their relationship.[23]

☐ Listening and repeating slows down hot responses, making interactions more likely to conform to biblical guidelines. In 1 Peter 3:9-10 (NIV) Scripture says, "Do not repay evil with evil or insult with insult, but with blessing, because to this you were called so that you may inherit a blessing. For, 'Whoever would love life and see good days must keep his tongue from evil and his lips from deceitful speech.' " (See also Prov 12:18, 15:1; 29:11; Eph 4:25-27.)

☐ Problems are not solved merely because a couple listen to each other, but sometimes problems are dissolved through listening. That is, the problem ceases to bother the spouse as much if the spouse feels understood.

☐ Listening and repeating, used when a partner feels stuck in trying to solve a problem, breaks the partners out of a rut.

☐ Listening and repeating is consistent with the biblical admonition "Be quick to listen, slow to speak" (Jas 1:19).[24]

☐ Listening and repeating has partners stop trying to be understood and instead focus on understanding the partner and reflecting that understanding to the partner.[25] To the extent that such a change in focus is apprehended by the partner, the partner will be more eager to listen.

Teaching Couples to Observe Their Effects

I teach the intent-impact connection (see intervention 11-8), also used by numerous counselors and communication training programs. The essence of this method is that what we intend to communicate is not always the impact our communication makes. Partners should observe their effects on each other. Partners are told to use their spouse's unexpected reaction as a signal to question whether they could communicate differently. If the spouse responds unexpectedly (perhaps reacting angrily or defensively) instead of following the flow of the conversation, the partner should immediately stop and see whether the spouse understood what the partner intended.

Intervention 11-8: Teaching Couples to Observe Their Effects Directly

Step 1: *Teaching the concept:* Draw two stick figures. One has a thought bubble that states her or his intent (for example, "I see you are under stress and I want to take pressure off of you by offering to do some things that you usually do around the house"). The other stick figure has a frown on his or her face with a thought bubble that shows that the impact of the first figure's offer to do a job did not have the impact that was intended (for example, "My partner wants to control me. My partner thinks I'm inadequate and can't handle my responsibilities. This means my partner thinks I'm a failure").

Step 2: *Teaching what to look for:* Observe the effects on your partner of what you say. The effects to look for include (a) a partner's emotional reactions that are out of line with your expectations, (b) puzzled looks, (c) defensiveness and (d) straightforward challenges.

Step 3: *Teaching what to do when you see effects that you didn't intend:* (1) Brainstorm with partners to find what they think they should do. Write down the strategies they come up with. (2) Teach directly that they can ask, "You aren't reacting as I thought you would to what I just said. How did you understand what I just said to you? . . . That's not what I meant to convey to you. I wanted to say . . ." Give each partner a copy of the list.

Strategy: Love

Hope: Waypower to change

Teaching Couples to Value Their Partners

Central to hope-focused marriage counseling is teaching love: valuing and not devaluing one's partner. Not surprisingly, it is one of the centerpieces of helping couples resolve conflicts in love.

Valuing is treating the other person with respect, with honor, as a pearl of great value. Valuing is not devaluing by putting down, using devaluing looks (like rolling the eyes), making fun of the other, saying anything negative about the other, pointing out negative aspects of the partner's character to other people (whether the partner is present or not), making jokes at the other's expense, criticizing the other, calling names, expecting the worst of the other. In short, devaluing is expressing contempt for the partner. Contempt is the poison of family relationships.[26]

Ask each partner to tell how he or she has devalued the partner. Insist that the partner not talk for anyone but himself or herself, and discourage the partner from agreeing nonverbally (or verbally) when the spouse describes a way he or she has devalued the partner.

After teaching the concepts of valuing and devaluing, teach the couple valuing strategies they can use during conflict: (1) Teach partners to listen and repeat what the other person said prior to defending himself or herself. (2) Teach partners to validate the other person's feelings before trying to solve the problem. (For example, "I can see that this issue means a lot to you and that you are angry about it. I can see that you really want to arrive at a solution that we both can live with. I'm sorry I've contributed to making you so angry. I don't want to hurt or fight with you. Let's see if we can solve this problem.") (3) Teach partners to think, *I need to value my partner,* especially during conflict.

Teaching Couples to Evaluate Both Partners' Interests

Regardless of how much a counselor might want couples to resolve differences on the basis of agape, other-oriented love (laying down one's life for the partner), there are times when partners simply need to negotiate solutions. Ury and Fisher have developed a strong method of conflict resolution that purports to help couples negotiate agreement without giving in.[27] Instead of focusing on partners' positions on a contentious issue, partners are taught to look behind their own position to what their real interests are. When both partners identify their interests, they can usually find a solution—not involving compromise—that satisfies both partners' interests. Thus a win-win situation is created instead of a partially win-partially win compromise.

Begin your intervention recalling that the agenda of the couple is not that of the counselor. Couples want the counselor to walk with them through the minefield and defuse each mine as it is uncovered. The counselor wants to help the couple to disarm a few mines to teach the more important skill that *the partners* can defuse *any* mine they discover. Repeat the agenda to the couple: to help them employ faith working through love to resolve *any* differences. Then employ Ury and Fisher's method (intervention 11-9). Effective conflict resolution will have four sequential steps. Don't skip a step because the partners do not seem to grasp the step or seem unable to apply it to their situation. Bolster your teaching by assigning couples to buy *Getting to Yes*[28] and read it. Some couples may want to read chapters aloud to each other.

Intervention 11-9: Teaching Couples to Evaluate Both Partners' Interests

Step 1: Define the problem. Initially, help the couple define the problem quickly and not get sidetracked from working on a single problem. One stumbling block to solving problems is failing to agree on what the problem is. When that occurs, the partners spend considerable effort and frustration trying to arrive at a single solution to two different problems.

Have each partner state what he or she thinks is the main problem *in no more than two sentences.* Help the couple determine whether the two statements of the problem are similar or are, in reality, different problems. If the problem statements are different, get the couple to address each problem separately. Both cannot be solved simultaneously.

Have partners state the problem clearly and concretely rather than vaguely and generally. Rather than allowing the husband to define the problem as "You've been a real pain since you got under stress at work," help him be specific. For example, he could say, "During the last two weeks, you have raised your voice, argued loudly or criticized me at least four times. It would be less hurtful if you would act that way less often. I would like it if you would try not to talk loudly and criticize me." Such a concrete statement of the problem tells exactly what he is complaining about and gives a clear statement of what he expects his wife to do to remedy the problem. Obviously, only the husband may think that the wife's behavior is problematic; she may not. Help both partners see that behaviors that bother their spouse will ultimately result in trouble for them if the bothersome behaviors are not dealt with.

Step 2: Help partners identify their spouse's position. Usually each person will have a position about how the problem might be solved. Each partner should identify his or her own suggested solution and then summarize the spouse's solution. In our example, the husband says that the wife needs to stop being so crabby. The wife says that the husband needs to be more considerate. If partners summarize their spouse's position, both spouses are sure that their partner values them enough to have heard them. Partners may in turn give reasons why they believe their solution is the one that the couple should adopt, but they may not rebut.

If a proposed solution is not quickly agreeable to both partners, which it will rarely be, say that prolonged discussion of their positions will not help. This is especially true if the issue is one in which incompatible positions have been discussed often.

Step 3: Help couples identify the interests behind their positions. Generally people do not want to achieve the particular position that they have offered, even though they might believe that they do. Rather, they want to satisfy their needs and meet the interests behind their position. For instance, in the example above, the husband complained about his wife's crabbiness and took the position that the problem would be solved if she would act less crabby and criticize him less. Behind that position are the interests that (1) he feels demeaned and devalued by his wife's criticism and (2) he feels angry and hurt by her complaints, which extract energy from him, making his life more miserable. His wife's position is that he should be more considerate of her. Her interests behind that position are that (1) she feels devalued by her husband's complaints and criticisms, (2) she does not feel understood by her husband and (3) she wants her husband to agree to help her with more of her chores during her stress at work.

Step 4: Help couples think of a different solution that will meet both people's interests. Let partners brainstorm for solutions that meet the needs of both.

Partners suggest solutions that come to mind without evaluating the solutions until brainstorming is complete. Each solution is then evaluated against how well it meets both partners' interests.

Usually, more effective solutions will be thought up if you suggest that each partner try to think of solutions that will meet the partner's interests. People usually find it easy to suggest solutions that meet their own interests and will arrive at those solutions with little difficulty. If the partners are prompted to think of the spouse, less selfish solutions will usually be suggested and final decisions among suggested solutions will be easier.

Strategy: Love, work

Hope: Waypower to change

If You Need More . . .

Conflict is so heated in many couples that you might need other interventions besides those in the LOVE acrostic. One way to help people think about other ways that they have resolved conflicts is to have them recall how they did that early in their marriage. Ask them what would need to happen for them to use those helpful strategies again. One other general problem-solving strategy that I have used, but usually save as a backup, is teaching couples guidelines for good conflict resolution (see table 11.3) and helping them apply those rules at home (see intervention 11-10).

DEALING WITH THE COUPLE'S FAILURES

When the couple has a poor interaction—either during the week or in session—help the couple process it. Wile calls these conversations about disagreements "recovery conversations."[29] They are common, so don't become discouraged when they occur. Partners need to try to figure out how they got into the argument (without looking to blame the other person), what the argument was about, what it reveals about the relationship and what they can do to reconcile. The couple most clearly remembers how the argument escalated and ended. Most of the time they will be discouraged and pessimistic about the potential success of counseling.

Do not treat the argument as if it signifies failure of counseling. Treat it as if it is a vital part of counseling that can reveal lessons to the partners, not the least of which is how the argument ended. Treating the argument as a learning experience keeps their hope high (see intervention 11-11).

How Couples Can Deal with a Partner's Perceived Attack

The partners are told that there are four common ways to protect oneself in the face of an attack: leaving the situation, seeking support from another person, confronting the partner and defining the situation differently. Partners are told how to use each defense productively.

Leaving the situation should only be used if the person who leaves sets a time to finish the discussion within twenty-four hours. The partner might say, "I'm feeling too upset to talk right now. I want to resolve this. I don't want to just leave you angry. Can we talk later when I'm less upset, maybe this afternoon after work?"

Seeking support from another person can help, but it can also magnify problems if the partner has not agreed ahead of time. For example, one husband continually phoned his mother whenever he and his wife had an argument. That phone call always made the wife furious because she perceived her mother-in-law as a gossip who spread rumors about her and about their marriage. When conflict is not active, partners should discuss who might be a support. Best friends of the same sex, relatives who live in another city, pastors and lay counselors often make good confidants.

Confronting the partner should be done without blame, if possible. Partners can be coached to say, "I see that you are upset, and I know how angry you are about this issue. But I get upset when you call me names. I think we'll be more likely to resolve this if we don't get back into name-calling."

Defining the situation differently through self-talk can defuse anger. Following are some examples of redefining the situation. The partner might think to himself or herself,

☐ *He's under a lot of stress with this car deal. He has a hair trigger to frustration. Don't let his shortness make you angry.*

☐ *This angry outburst probably won't last long. Hold on and don't get provoked.*

☐ *She's just angry at the kids and she's taking it out on me. Don't take it personally.*

Dealing with Your Own Disappointment as the Counselor

Working with couples in conflict can frustrate the counselor. The counselor tries valiantly to focus on the ways that the couple are arguing, stopping the couple repeatedly to help the partners express themselves better. Couples still get into emotional arguments. It is easy to become discouraged. In the midst of conflict, the content of the arguments tends to gain the partners' attention; it can

Intervention 11-10: Applying Rules for Resolving Conflict

The following rules for resolving conflict are summarized in many places throughout behavioral approaches.[30]

1. Provide a copy of the rules for each partner (see table 11.3).

2. Read the rules together and illustrate points that the partners question.

3. Have the partners select an issue on which to practice the rules. Usually the partners will learn faster if the issue is of low emotional valence.

4. Practice the rules on the issue.

5. Practice again with an issue of higher emotional involvement.

6. Assign the couple to practice on an issue at home.

Strategy: Love

Hope: Waypower to change

---

be almost impossible to wrest the attention back to a therapeutic direction in which the partners practice improved communication. If you become discouraged, do not despair. Remind yourself that such failures happen to every counselor.

At the end of the hour, sometimes it is best to admit to the clients that you are frustrated with what occurred during the session. For example, you might say:

I must tell you that throughout the session I felt frustrated. You each were very involved with the issue you were trying to solve, and you put each other down several times. I'm glad that you care so much about the issues that you passionately try to resolve them. However, I believe that it is in your best interest to value each other persistently, even when you argue. I was encouraged that at several times during your discussion, you tried to be more valuing, such as when you . . . I hope that we can work on communication and conflict resolution again next week, perhaps with another issue. Maybe we will have more success. If not, we'll try another route to help you be able to deal with these conflicts more productively without becoming so heated.

In hope-focused marriage counseling, try not to become discouraged with a single bad session. Almost every couple will have some bad sessions. On the other hand, you cannot afford to try a communication program week after week if the couple is not responding to it. A middle ground is to allow two consecutive

Table 11.3. Guidelines for resolving conflict (based on Christensen et al.[31])

General Guidelines

☐ Discuss one problem at a time.

☐ Take turns discussing your own views and do not speculate about your partner's view.

☐ Begin your talk with a paraphrase or summary of what the other person said.

Guidelines for Problem Definition

☐ Look for and mention some positive aspect of the problem (for example, "You usually are very neat, but one habit really bothers me").

☐ State problems in discrete behavioral terms, not as the spouse's personality problems or as general problems (for example, "It makes me angry when you spit tobacco juice on the carpet").

☐ Then state feelings about the problem (for example, "I feel disgusted, and the living-room carpet looks spotty").

☐ Acknowledge your own role in perpetuating the problem (for example, "I have contributed to the problem by not providing spittoons for us").

☐ After describing the problem, make a brief summary of the problem (for example, "So the problem is dealing with the problem of a wife's spitting her tobacco juice on the carpet").

Guidelines for Solving the Problem

☐ Discussion should be focused on solving the problem via brainstorming rather than on further elaborating the problem.

☐ Evaluate the potential solutions.

☐ Any agreement that is reached should be explicit and in writing. ("So we agree to decorate the living room in army camouflage.")

poor sessions to trigger a reanalysis of your plan for changing communication, conflict management or intimacy.

DEALING WITH THE COUPLE'S SUCCESSES

Encourage couples to bring up events in which they successfully dealt with a conflict and resolved it. That strengthens learning. With the couple feeling good about their conflict-resolution ability, say, "What if things don't work out so well the next time? Unfortunately, no couple can always communicate as well as you two did in this instance." This suggests that failures will inevitably happen and that all couples can expect failures in communication at times. That expectation can correct perfectionistic expectations and make lasting happiness in the relationship more likely.

Often, people in conflict hurt each other. They should try not to hurt each other, and they should not excuse their hurts or their partner's hurts. Nonetheless, the fact remains that married partners do hurt each other at times. To complete conflict resolution, reconciliation is necessary by seeking forgiveness for any hurts that one has wittingly or unwittingly inflicted on the partner:

☐ The person needs to admit freely that he or she hurt the partner. Anger and hurt are often interrelated, so if one partner is angry, he or she is probably feeling hurt. Instead of denying the legitimacy of the hurt and anger, talk about the depth of the anger and hurt in a way that is aimed at understanding, not blaming or making guilty.

☐ The person who inflicted the hurt needs to say that he or she is sorry *and mean it.*

☐ The person has to sincerely say that he or she does not ever intend to hurt the other person in that way again, and the person has to resolve in his or her mind to try never to hurt in that way again.

☐ The other person eventually needs to forgive the person who did the hurting.

☐ Rebuilding trust may take some time.

Intervention 11-11: What to Do If the Couple Reports a Severe Argument Occurred at Home

Let's assume that the partners had a serious argument two days before coming to counseling. They were so discouraged that they have not spoken to each other since the argument, and they have come to their session intending to terminate counseling.

What not to discuss. When you begin to discuss the argument, do not focus on the end of the argument—the emotional carnage. Discussing that will show little of benefit to the partners. Also don't get caught up in the couple's agenda, which usually is (a) to terminate counseling or (b) if they stay, to get you to determine who started the argument (both usually think the partner started it).

Acknowledge their disappointment. Say, "I know you are both extremely disappointed at having this argument. You both felt positive about the way counseling was going, and now it seems as if it has all been a waste. Let me tell you, though, that I have been through this many times with many couples. This is a part of counseling that often happens. Instead of sticking up the white flag, we can use this as a powerful aid to helping you improve. To use this event instead of having it use you, we must discover what you can learn from it. Are you willing to work with me to see what we can learn?"

Ask about the beginning of the argument to determine the triggers. If they want to quit immediately, appeal to fully using the therapy hour. When they agree to discuss the incident, say, "I want you to describe what happened. What were some of the things that were happening immediately before the problem broke out?" Rather than focus on the latter stages of the conflict, after both partners were angry and involved in the content of the conflict, you should focus on the early interactions.

Determine what caused the argument to escalate out of control. Try to discover (a) how the conflict spiraled out of control, (b) how the couple could have prevented the eruption from occurring by communicating more effectively, (c) whether there was a point at which either partner could have stopped the argument and (d) what the couple could have done to soothe themselves and the spouse. These are crucial points to discuss.

Determine what stopped the argument. The argument obviously ceased at some point. What stopped it? Sometimes the way couples stop arguments can be used earlier to head off arguments before they get severe.

Determine the state of reconciliation. This might be a time to discuss forgiveness and reconciliation (see chapter nine).

Stop and summarize what was learned. Consider what was learned that will benefit each partner.

Solidify the learning by putting some of the following strategies into effect.
☐ Tell the couple that you want them to determine ways that they can deal with such arguments. Record their suggestions (and perhaps a few of your own) on

a piece of paper or on a white board if you have it in your office.

☐ Tell the couple that you want them to practice some of these strategies.

☐ Have the couple role-play an argument that gets out of hand. Coach the couple to role-play their usual conflict-resolution strategies that lead to emotional arguments. Set up the role-play carefully to minimize the chances that the partners actually get emotionally involved in the role-play.

☐ After this halfhearted role-play, have the couple role play using the ways of processing the argument that they identified (perhaps with your help). This intervention allows the couple to practice dealing with an argument without being emotionally involved in it.

Strategy: Love, faith

Hope: Willpower to change, waypower to change

SUMMARY

Resolving conflicts must be done in love. Successful resolution of conflicts involves dissolving differences through understanding, working out differences and resolving the hurts that occurred as arguments and discussions took place. Thus resolution of conflict involves both communication skills and confession and forgiveness.

In conflict, emotions run hot and cold. Disappointment easily spreads from the couple to you. Relying on God's sovereignty is your hope for helping couples and keeping your own emotions on track.

Chapter 12

Interventions for Changing Cognition

Happy couples never have disagreements," said Maria.

I could easily see that Maria had a faulty assumption about marriage. It was clear to me that I should correct it. Perhaps I should show her how her *thinking* was making her miserable—not their disagreements. That would lead to helping her change her assumption, and then she could begin the long process of changing her habitual thinking patterns to more helpful ones. It looked like a six-week project. I'd be someone that cognitive therapist Aaron Beck could be proud of.[1]

Bobby interrupted my thinking. "You're crazy," he told Maria. "Isn't she crazy?" he asked me.

If I had been counseling Maria alone, I might have launched into cognitive therapy. In marital counseling I had more immediate problems. Bobby had put me on the hot seat. No matter how clearly I could see Maria's faulty assumption, I could not deal with it thoroughly. So after dodging the "isn't-she-crazy-Doc" bullet, I took a quick pass at Maria's cognition—but not as a cognitive therapist would have done. My approach was more like video clips than a video movie, sound bytes rather than sound cognitive therapy.

Cognition is mental activity. In its totality, cognition involves verbal and nonverbal mental activity, conscious and unconscious mental activity. However, this chapter focuses primarily on conscious verbal activity, referred to as "cognition" (even though an accurate definition of cognition is broader). In your counseling help couples change their cognition in four areas: negative thinking about the marriage, attributions that blame the spouse, expectations about the future of the marriage and assumptions about the marriage.[2]

GUIDELINES FOR CHANGING PARTNERS' COGNITION
Following are some guidelines to help you change couples' faulty cognition.

Should You Deal with Partners' Cognition?
As you probably guessed from my introduction, my answer to this question is not an automatic yes. My approach in 1989 was heavily influenced by the cognitive-behavioral therapy tradition, my individual psychotherapy of choice at that time.[3] I considered cognition a prime target of change. However, within the last ten years I have become less inclined to conduct cognitive interventions during marital counseling.

First, I found that in practice those techniques did not work nearly as well as other, more active techniques. (This was true for me and for many of the graduate students and professional counselors I trained.) Second, even when the techniques worked, they often required more time to make a large impact than was available in brief marital counseling, usually between six and twelve sessions. Third, couples often resisted the cognitive interventions to a greater degree than they resisted more active interventions.

I did not conclude from this experience that cognitive interventions were ineffective. Some couples respond well to cognitive interventions. Assessment of couples is again crucial. My experience has been (though I do not have research that substantiates this experience) that the couples who respond well to cognitive interventions are the ones in which neither partner is highly verbal or cognitively oriented. Couples in which one or both partners are already verbal and cognitively oriented may *say* they like and want cognitive interventions, but they usually resist them. One or both partners argue and defend cognitively. Cognitively naive couples, on the other hand, seem to be more in awe of the power of the cognitive interventions and take the gains on face value.

There is one other reason I continue to include cognitive interventions in hope-focused marriage counseling. Some counselors use cognitive interventions effectively. In hope-focused marriage counseling I want to encourage them to employ their strengths. I personally prefer more active, dramatic interventions that use manipulation of behavior, space and physical objects.

It heartened me to discover that other theorists were independently coming to the same conclusions as mine on the importance of cognitive therapy. For example, in early versions of cognitive-behavioral marital therapy,[4] including Christian versions,[5] theorists suggested that counselors concentrate on changing cognition over a series of consecutive weeks—usually three to six weeks. In a recent version of cognitive-behavioral marital therapy, Donald H. Baucom, Norman Epstein and L. A. Rankin advocated using cognitive interventions differently from behavioral interventions.[6] They suggested that cognitive interventions could be scattered throughout counseling, while being careful not to jump willy-nilly from intervention to intervention within a single session. They recommended that cognitive interventions not be viewed as supplemental interventions because they were used on more of an ad hoc basis than were behavioral interventions. Rather, cognitive interventions were essential to a cognitive-behavioral marital therapy that was effective and produced lasting effects. Yet cognitive interventions were best used at teachable moments instead of as a six-week package.

Integrative behavioral marital therapy, which had previously included cognitive interventions, has also modified its stance toward cognition—at least in the form that Jacobson and Christensen propose.[7] Many behavioral marital therapists will undoubtedly continue to include cognitive interventions.

Change Cognition by (First) Teaching the Cognitive Paradigm

If you use cognitive interventions, what is the most effective and efficient way? First and most important, teach the partners the cognitive paradigm (see the next section). The cognitive paradigm consists of two parts, the general and the specific. In general, get across two truths: (1) It is cognition that causes maladaptive behavior and feelings, not external events or people. (2) Changing cognition will change behavior and feelings.

Once the clients believe the general cognitive paradigm, they must apply it to themselves specifically: (1) The client's specific cognition is causing his or her maladaptive feelings or behavior. (2) The client can change his or her specific cognition and thus change feelings and behavior.

Change Cognition by (Second) Changing Specific Cognition

Once the cognitive paradigm is taught, then cognitive interventions can be inserted within counseling at convenient places. First, at the beginning of a session, the counselor almost always discusses the client's homework. That discussion could include an analysis of expectations and attributions about the cause of success or failure of the assignment. Second, if the couple reported that they were unsuccessful at carrying out an assignment, the counselor might inquire about the cognitive factors that might have been involved. Third, if a particular session has been planned to deal with a particular topic, the counselor might address relevant cognitive issues prior to getting into the session. Fourth, at the end of sessions, if the counselor leaves time to discuss the couple's experience of the session, the counselor might detect that some cognitive factors might need to be addressed. Fifth, in the midst of an intervention the counselor might detect that the couple is resisting it. That resistance might indicate that beliefs or expectancies are being violated and need to be explored. Sixth, sometimes a partner, like Maria, states beliefs or values that need to be addressed immediately, as soon as you escape Bobby's pressure to put you in the middle.

When dealing with a particular belief, thought, expectation or assumption, follow a set procedure. First, determine the content of the cognition (for example, the assumption that "Happily married people never have disagreements"). Second, ask how the cognition affects the marriage positively and negatively. (Inevitable disagreements are opposed to the assumption. The inconsistency indicates that the couple must not be happily married.) Third, discuss evidence that supports or refutes the cognition and speculate about the effects on the marriage of different cognitions (for example, "Happily married people sometimes disagree and may even become very angry, but they exhibit valuing love while they are disagreeing, forgive each other if they hurt each other and discuss the disagreement afterward to try to avoid similar disagreements in the future"). Fourth, assign homework that involves the new cognition (for example, "Discuss the old and new beliefs and see whether upon reflection you still agree that the new belief is better for your marriage").

Correcting Couples with Poor Actions and Cognition

Cognitive techniques—in fact, most recommended techniques in this book—involves correcting couples. You must repeatedly show couples their incorrect, negative or maladaptive thinking and help them replace that thinking with correct, positive and adaptive thinking. However, the danger is that frequent correction can intensify problems. The ego-analytic approach to marital therapy by Wile suggests that when people have problems they reproach themselves.[8] Self-reproach inhibits productive thinking and acting. Wile argues that when counselors correct clients, the correctives often contribute to the client's self-reproach, paradoxically making solution of the marital problems more difficult, not easier.

Deal with client self-reproach by (a) presenting a defense of the client's behavior, which attempts to free the client from self-reproach so the client can think, or (b) finding the hidden validity in the client's responses, which shows how the responses actually make sense in the present situation.

For example, suppose the counselor says, "Maria, you seem to be feeling negatively about the marriage again in spite of the progress you have made during the past three weeks. I couldn't help but notice that you just assumed things would never change and then you immediately blamed Bobby."

"You're right," says Maria. "I can't seem to stop these negative thoughts. I know we have worked on this. I can't help myself."

The counselor notices the self-reproach. To head off Maria's spiral of negative thoughts about herself, her partner, her marriage and even the prospect of successful counseling, the counselor (a) defends the client's behavior and (b) finds some validity in it. The counselor can say, "Maria, you seem discouraged. Yet I've seen many couples and, for this stage of counseling, I think you are doing remarkably well [your defense]. These negative patterns of thinking are burned into your mind and actions because of the pain you both have experienced. They are very difficult to change, and you'll probably have periodic negative thinking even after counseling is long completed. Everyone gets negative at times [the hidden validity]."

Negative Cognition Might Be True
Do not assume that negative cognition is necessarily incorrect or maladaptive. For instance, if a partner claims, "I yelled at him because he tried to embarrass me by asking a question he knew I couldn't answer in front of my boss," investigate the truth of the claim. If the claim turns out to be correct, then deal with the partner's reasons for wanting to embarrass his or her spouse. If the claim turns out to be unfounded, then deal with the distortion in the belief or selective negative attribution.

Changing Cognition to Focus on Love, Work and Faith
Changing people's thoughts can help other changes (behavioral or emotional) last longer. Help partners recognize and change negative thoughts and replace them with thoughts about how each values and loves the other. Help partners avoid blaming each other by getting them to think of being responsible for their own behavior and how they can improve it. Help them focus on living by faith working through love, which can help them develop a brighter expectation of

the future of their marriage. Finally, help them identify and change assumptions about the marriage that drag them down. As they change their way of viewing the marriage—from hopeless and negative to hopeful and positive—they will be able to avoid harmful devaluing of each other and of their marriage and to promote positive valuing.

TEACHING THE COGNITIVE PARADIGM

"Cognition causes feeling and behavior; external events or people are not the causes." Despite its common acceptance by cognitive therapists, this statement is not completely true. Cognitive therapies were formulated in the 1960s and 1970s when less was known about brain science. The statement that cognition causes feeling and behavior is true only for conscious memory. In fact, numerous memory systems in the brain are associated with emotion, and not all of them are conscious.[9]

Instead of explaining all of the results of modern mind science to clients, counselors oversimplify the science to make an impact on the client. Present the simplified version using several examples. To get across the idea that thinking causes us to feel and think certain thoughts, use this example: Two girls are scolded by their mother. One gets angry, the other sad. The mother's scolding did not cause each girl's emotion; instead each girl's thoughts caused her emotions (see intervention 12-3, step 1). To get across the idea that we can *change* thinking and we will feel and act differently, use this (or another common) example.

> Have you ever been fussing at the children, really steamed up, and the phone rings? What happens? You pick up the phone and calmly say, "Hello." As you think, *I need to be pleasant in answering the phone,* your anger subsides almost immediately. After you hang up, though, it is easy to work up the anger once again as your thinking focuses on the event that originally riled you. Changing thinking will change your emotion and behavior.

If you intend to use cognitive interventions throughout your counseling of a couple, you must teach them the cognitive paradigm before beginning to try changing their thoughts. One mistake that novice counselors commonly make is to challenge clients' thinking without having addressed the cognitive paradigm. In such cases, their challenges almost never produce positive results due to one of two reasons. One, clients might not understand what the counselor is trying to do, and they will feel criticized or condemned. Two, clients must believe that there is a relationship between changing thoughts and consequent behaviors, or they will contaminate any therapeutic effects by covertly arguing against the counselor.

REDUCING NEGATIVE THINKING

Unless troubled couples turn the marriage around, most of them reach the point where they perceive each other, virtually all of their partner's behavior, the partner's motives and the future of the marriage as negative.[10] Successful marital counseling helps them turn their emphasis back to positive. You can intervene actively and hope the negativity will abate, or you can address the negativity directly.

If you choose to address the negativity directly, help the couple reduce negative thinking that devalues each other and replace it by positive thinking in which they experience valuing love for each other. Be able to justify biblically your emphasis on cognition for Christian clients who question you. You might use the NIV marginal reading of Proverbs 23:7 ("As he thinks within himself, so he is") or Philippians 4:8 (essentially, "Whatsoever is true and positive, think about these").

Making Partners Aware of Their Negativity

Help the partners become aware of the specific negative interactions and the negative cognition that precedes and accompanies those interactions. Build awareness by interrupting patterns and discussing them. Follow up with homework directing partners to identify negative thinking involved in negative interactions. Intervention 12-1 summarizes several ways to enhance couples awareness of their negative patterns. In intervention 12-2 have couples keep a thought log, which will be used throughout counseling.

Intervention 12-1: Increasing Spouses' Awareness of Their Selective Attention to Negative Behavior

Following are several interventions for helping couples notice and label negative patterns of behavior:

☐ When the counselor notices a negative pattern of interactions, the counselor can summarize the pattern for the couple and suggest that the couple notice further instances of the pattern.

☐ Interrupt ongoing negative interactions and coach the spouses to identify the sequence.

☐ The counselor can interrupt the ongoing pattern and play back the audiotape or videotape recording of the interaction to help couples note the pattern.

☐ For homework, request that spouses keep daily logs of relationship behaviors, summarizing their interactions and perhaps writing their thoughts about the interactions.

☐ For homework, request that partners keep logs of marital interactions that are either negative or positive and write their thoughts about the interactions.

☐ Present anonymous case examples of couples who have made inaccurate inferences about their partner, faulty attributions about the cause of problems or inaccurate assumptions about marriage. This will help sensitize partners to those cognitive errors without challenging them directly about their own inferences, attributions and assumptions.

☐ During treatment look for sudden shifts in emotion or behavior and use those shifts as a cue to inquire about cognition.

☐ Develop an incomplete sentence form to assess partners' assumptions about marriage. Examples of stems of sentences might include things like "Each week, we should share our feelings and thoughts at least ____ hours"; "We should show appreciation for each other by ____"; "We can show love by ____"; "We could communicate better if only we would ____."

Strategy: Love

Hope: Waypower to change

Intervention 12-2 (Homework): Have the Partners Monitor Their Negative Thoughts for a Week

Keep a thought log of three columns—event, negative thoughts and outcomes (emotional and behavioral)—for a week. At the following session, you will try to discern with the partners the relationships between negative thinking and moods and behaviors.

Strategy: Love

Hope: Waypower to change

Focusing on the Positive Aspects of Negative Behavior

When you make partners more aware of their negativity, they can easily become discouraged. Prevent their discouragement by finding some positive aspects to some of the negative behavior. For instance, observe, "Sally, when you criticize Mike for not responding to you emotionally, you certainly engage him emotionally—even though you don't really like his anger when he feels you are criticizing him."

Making the Negative Thinking More Positive

Once partners have understood the cognitive paradigm and are aware of specific patterns of negative thinking, help them change those patterns. Intervention 12-3 summarizes how you might help partners know several ways to make their cognition more positive.

Intervention 12-3: Changing Each Partner's Negative Thoughts

Step 1: *Present the rationale.* Review the rationale that how people think controls how they feel and act. Give an example, such as the following. Suppose a mother sees two of her children, Mary and Ramona, arguing. She corrects them sharply. Mary thinks, *I'm embarrassed and ashamed.* She apologizes and feels sad. But Ramona thinks, *It makes me mad when she yells at me. She doesn't understand me. She always takes Mary's side.* Instead of being penitent, Ramona is angry, obstinate and combative. With identical events, different thoughts produced different emotions and behaviors.

Step 2: *Have partners monitor thoughts.* Tell partners to listen as if they had a third ear that could tune into the negative thinking. Encourage them to recognize the negative thinking early and interrupt its flow, replacing negative thinking about partner and marriage with positive thinking that emphasizes the partner's good qualities and the benefits of working to preserve the marriage.

Step 3: *Describe briefly three strategies for making thoughts more positive.* Teach clients to control negative thoughts by (a) thinking about the positive instead of the negative, (b) thinking about how to solve the problem instead of elaborating the problem and (c) noticing ways the partner values the person.

Strategy: Love

Hope: Waypower to change

Using Journals and Thought Logs

Making change sensible involves producing tangible records of change as often as possible. Produce such records by having partners keep written records, in either an unstructured or a structured format. If partners keep a journal while they attend counseling, the record of their experience can sometimes be heartening, producing faith and demonstrating the hard work that they have put into the marriage. Some people keep journals without being prompted. Others cannot seem to manage even if you assign them that task (and threaten them with electric shock). Ask partners whether they think they can keep a journal. If they are willing to experiment, assign the following homework (see intervention 12-4) and use it throughout counseling, especially as termination approaches.

Intervention 12-4 *(Homework):* Journal of Marital Improvements

Instruct the partners to carry out the following exercise:

> Write a journal over the next month describing the ways that your marriage has changed for the better and describing your feelings about those changes. Do not record complaints about the marriage. Usually if your marriage is in distress, you'll already be thinking about your complaints, but you won't as easily be able to detect the improvements. This exercise is to help you notice improvements when they happen. You might think that your marriage cannot improve very much, but it will. The real test will be whether you can notice the improvements. Please do not share your journal with your partner. Instead, bring your journal to each session, and I will look it over briefly at the beginning of the session without making any comments about it.

Each week review each partner's journal. Do not comment on it. As termination approaches, assign the partners to review their journals and identify improvements in their marriage. Tell them to write those improvements down to share aloud at the final session. In that session, ask each to describe the major improvements he or she has noticed in the marriage. During the course of that session, have the partners evaluate what still needs to be done to improve the marriage. In the final assessment report, you will provide your written and oral assessment of the strengths and weaknesses of the marriage and the actions that are needed to improve the marriage. Refer to some of the improvements the partners identified. Use those improvements to show that the couple can produce a positive impact on their marriage if they work. State that such evidence can give them hope that the improvements can continue until the couple reach their goals for the marriage.

Strategy: Work, love, faith

Hope: Willpower to change, waypower to change

Once partners begin to try changing their negative thinking, it helps them to document the results of their efforts. If they began keeping a thought log during the early part of counseling (when you were helping them become aware of negative thinking), use it again once the partners begin trying to change their thinking (see intervention 12-5). Success will increase their faith that counseling is working and increase their hope in the marriage.

Intervention 12-5 (*Homework*): Have Partners Change Negative Thinking

Have partners add two additional columns to their thought logs (see intervention 12-2). The three columns already being used were event, negative thoughts and outcomes (emotional and behavioral). Those columns were useful for making people aware of specific negative thinking associated with their negative emotions and behavior. The two columns to be added, actions and results, deal with how people are attempting to change their thinking and thus experience different results.

In session you will have described briefly three strategies for making thoughts more positive: (a) thinking about the positive instead of the negative, (b) thinking about how to solve the problem instead of elaborating the problem and (c) noticing ways the partner values the person. Have partners try to combat negative thoughts by using one of the strategies and monitoring the results on mood and behavior.

Strategy: Faith

Hope: Willpower to change, waypower to change

CHANGING ATTRIBUTIONS OF BLAME

It is natural to explain the causes of our behavior in terms of what we see. If I bump my head on the kitchen cabinet and slam the door in anger, I will probably say that the pain *caused* me to be angry. When marriage partners are in conflict, each sees the other's behavior. They are likely to explain their own behavior as being due to what the spouse has done to them, blaming the spouse for the marriage difficulties.

Empathy is the antidote to the poison of blaming. If partners can see things through the spouse's eyes, then the partners will be less likely to blame the spouse for the problems and will be more likely to take personal responsibility for improving the marriage. Creating such empathy is one of your goals of counseling.[11] Enhance empathy by dramatizing that each problem has multiple sides. Each person sees the problem from only one side, his or her own perspective. Build the awareness of both partners' different perceptions. Combat blame by promoting empathy.

First, from the beginning build the idea that each person has a different perspective. Don't just ask each person to describe the problem, ask each to describe the problem *from his or her point of view.* Also, throughout counseling encourage each partner to see things from the spouse's perspective. Have partners describe what they believe their spouse is thinking and feeling. Encourage partners to speculate about how they disturb their spouses. Finally, vigilantly help partners see how they can value each other. It is better to have partners think about what the spouse would like (that is, think empathically about the spouse) and how to give that to the spouse than to have the spouse tell the partner what he or she would like. (However, if one partner is unable to empathize well, it is better to have partners tell each other explicitly what they would like from the other than to suffer the miscommunication.)

Helping Partners Respond with Acceptance Rather than Blame
Integrative behavioral marital therapists teach clients the adage "Focus on the pain. Eliminate the blame."[12] When pain is high and one partner accuses the spouse of wrongdoing or harm, that accusation will escalate unhappiness. However, when empathic acknowledgment of the pain of the partner occurs without blame, then the partner will usually respond with acceptance. To teach this concept to the partners, use these equations:[13]

PAIN + ACCUSATION = MARITAL DISCORD
PAIN - ACCUSATION = ACCEPTANCE

Keeping a Record of Attempts to Change Attributions
The journal can provide a record of attempts to change blaming attributions. Through writing about attempts to change, partners keep their efforts fresh between sessions. Over time the written record provides evidence of effort at change and can document success, increasing both faith and hope. When a partner feels blame for the spouse, the partner should write in his or her journal (a) the blaming thoughts, (b) what he or she thinks the spouse's perspective is, (c) what the partner's own responsibility is in the problem or issue and (d) how he or she can value the spouse instead of blaming the spouse.

CHANGING NEGATIVE EXPECTATIONS ABOUT THE MARRIAGE
Troubled marriages are plagued by expectations of a dismal future. While perceiving only the negative, partners constantly devalue each other, keeping the marriage in an unloving state. Help partners begin to value each other and

develop faith in the future. Addressing their negative expectations directly affects their faith in the future of the marriage. Ask about expectations, and juxtapose them to a time when the expectations were higher.

One way to break this negative perceptual cycle is to have partners recall a time when their marriage was going positively. This is easy to do when you are taking the relationship history in the first session. Ask the partners what they did differently during those times of marital happiness than they currently do. Pose questions: "What would happen if you behaved that way again? Could you change things to be more like they were before? What would you have to do differently to get the marriage happy again?" Attention to differences in happy and unhappy times and to solutions (rather than problems) spurs partners to action.[14]

CHANGING NEGATIVE ASSUMPTIONS ABOUT THE MARRIAGE

For most people, underlying assumptions about the marriage are difficult to identify. Some common faulty assumptions are summarized in table 12.1. (Feel free to photocopy the table.) Have partners evaluate their own beliefs against the faulty assumptions (see intervention 12-6).

Intervention 12-6 *(Homework):* Identifying Faulty Assumptions About Marriage and Changing Them

Give the partners a copy of the assumptions about marriage and have them examine the list at home, determining the degree to which each person thinks the assumption is true of him or her. Have each partner focus on the self and not the spouse.

Maladaptive assumptions about the marriage can be changed by following six steps:

☐ First, make the couple aware that much of their behavior is governed by their assumptions about marriage. Give a copy of the ten faulty assumptions (table 12.1) and tell the partners why the assumptions may lead to marital problems. For ease in reproduction, the ten assumptions are printed on a page by themselves. Your mere description of the assumptions will *not* change the partners. It merely sets the stage.

☐ Second, help individuals identify whether any of the assumptions are operating in their own marriage. They usually identify most easily the partner's maladaptive assumptions. People are amazingly blind to their own assumptions. Ask about individuals' thoughts about the marriage, which may reveal assump-

Table 12.1. Common faulty assumptions

Taken from Hope-Focused Marriage Counseling: A Guide to Brief Therapy. *Downers Grove, Ill.: InterVarsity Press, 1999.*

1. To demonstrate love, my mate must tell me he or she loves me several times daily.

2. If I don't feel romantic with my partner, it means we aren't in love any longer.

3. My partner should meet all my needs, especially all my needs for intimacy.

4. My partner should support all my ideas.

5. When I've had a bad day, my mate should be able to sense it and should do something to cheer me up without my having to tell him or her.

6. My spouse should not expect me to be courteous and polite. That's what marriage is all about: being yourself and not having to put on some show.

7. My partner should be able to know how to stimulate me when we're making love. I shouldn't have to tell him or her what to do and when to do it.

8. My mate and I should do almost everything as a couple if we are to maintain a happy marriage.

9. I should be able to keep my partner from ever getting unhappy.

10. My partner and I should never argue or disagree if our marriage is good.

tions. For example, a wife who often thinks, *We're not in love any more,* might be asked, "How do you know that you aren't in love?" Her reply, "I don't feel any of the excitement I felt when we were in love," might reveal (upon continued discussion) that she believes that love is a feeling. She is confusing romance or passion with love. Love involves *more* than mere feeling. Feelings may be rebuilt if some of the other elements of love are still present, such as respect, caring, commitment, knowledge, responsibility and the will to value.

☐ Third, once faulty assumptions are identified, examine their consequences. Question the couple to see how holding to those assumptions of marriage affects their behavior toward each other. For example, if the partners believe that good marriage is characterized by such a close communion of mind and spirit that communication is not needed, they may fail to communicate about their sexual experiences. This might lead to the woman's failing to have orgasms because she can't tell her husband when to change angles, pressures or locations of stimulation. If the partners recognize negative consequences of their assumptions, they will be more motivated to change.

☐ Fourth, help individuals change assumptions that they want to change. When a partner recognizes that he or she is making an unwanted assumption, he or she should question the assumption. Avoid having spouses point out their partner's assumptions, regardless of how obvious. It is important that each partner take responsibility for his or her own thoughts, not the spouse's.

☐ Fifth, have partners write, or at least plan, rebuttals to the faulty assumptions that they hold but wish to change. Through discussions with the partners, partners can see you model how to reason in opposition to some of the faulty assumptions—as Maria observes her counselor doing below. Use the list of faulty assumptions to check off specifically which ones each partner should deal with at home.

☐ Sixth, experience has the most impact on changing assumptions. Try to provoke experiences that will make it easier to change assumptions. For example, Maria believed that a "good" marriage was one in which arguing never occurs and that any arguing was evidence of a poor marriage. She was eventually assigned homework, to interview at least ten couples whom she considered to be well adjusted. Her task was to ascertain whether they ever argued. All did. Her interviews made her more willing and able to change her assumptions.

Strategy: Love

Hope: Willpower to change, waypower to change

Maria and Bobby: A Case Study

In session, you can address the logic of assumptions. In the sixth step of intervention 12-6, Maria was found to assume that no arguing occurs in a good marriage. After she completed her homework (interviewing ten happy couples to find whether they ever argued), she and her counselor discussed her assumption further. Her counselor questioned the logic of her assumption. Here is a facsimile of their conversation.

Counselor: So, Maria, in a good marriage there is never any arguing.

Maria: Right.

Counselor: You and Bobby are having difficulty now, but have you always had such difficulties?

Maria: No, we had a lot of good years.

Counselor: And you never had a single disagreement during all those good years?

Maria: Of course we had some disagreements.

Counselor: But you were still happy, despite your disagreements. Hmm. Tell me, can you imagine any couple that could be so angry with each other that they never talked?

Maria: Yes. It wouldn't be a very good marriage.

Counselor: True. But if the couple never talked, they also could never disagree.

Maria: Right. I see what you're getting at. Disagreements don't always mean unhappiness, and unhappiness doesn't always mean disagreements.

Counselor: Right. So what does that tell you about your assumption?

Maria: It probably isn't correct. But still it isn't good to fight continually.

Counselor: That's true, and naturally you want to avoid fighting, arguing or even getting angry at each other. Still, saying that you want to resolve disagreements is far different than believing that you never can disagree with Bobby and that any disagreement means you have a poor marriage.

Maria: You're right. There is a big difference.

Faulty perfectionistic assumptions about marriage are often revealed by partners' habitual use of absolute statements, such as "Everyone makes love with the light out" or "You always whine." Most people occasionally use such absolutes; do not address an occasional use. However, if a partner uses such absolute statements frequently, look at what might be behind the statements (see intervention 12-7).

Intervention 12-7: Dealing with "Always," "Never" and "Everyone" Statements

Generally, statements that claim that one spouse "always" does something or "never" does something are inaccurate. They almost never produce the effect they were intended to produce. They challenge the partner to refute the statement, which often sidetracks the discussion into a did-too, did-not argument.

☐ When you spot a partner who habitually uses absolutistic statements, point out the use of the statements.

☐ Investigate with the partner the intent of the communication and its effect, showing that the communication did not achieve its hoped-for effect.

☐ Instead of simply suggesting that the partner avoid such absolutistic statements, suggest that the partner use the impulse to make such statements to analyze under what conditions the exceptions to the "always" or "never" behavior might occur and the times when such behavior does occur. Determining conditions for exceptions and instances might give a clue as to how to reduce the partner's unwanted behavior.

☐ Demonstrate how to do this with the most recent occurrence. For example, if the husband said, "You always criticize me for not paying the bills on time," you might inquire whether there were ever a time when the bills were not paid and the wife did not criticize the husband. That might lead to the discovery that the wife did not criticize the husband when she knew the husband to be under a lot of pressure at work. In turn, that might lead the couple to conclude that the wife, instead of being critical, was trying to be considerate of the husband when she saw his need.

Strategy: Love

Hope: Waypower to change

Changing Partners' Standards for the Marriage

Part of the assumptions about marriage are the standards against which partners measure the marriage. Not only are the standards that people hold sometimes unrealistically high, but also couples often disagree about standards that should govern the marriage even if both partners' sets of standards are realistic.

For example, one partner might believe that whenever a problem occurs, each individual is obligated to share the problem in detail with the partner, submitting the problem to mutual problem-solving efforts. The other partner might believe that to share one's problems is an indication of weakness and will erode trust in the marriage. Neither of the partners has the one and only correct standard. The standards each holds might work equally well for that partner. But their disagreement will obviously create tension and misunderstanding in the relationship because they will not discuss problems equally.

When partners disagree about standards for the marriage, there are four possible solutions to resolve the differences.

□ One partner can modify his or her standards to fit the other partner's standards.

□ Both partners can compromise and perhaps apply different standards to each partner.

□ Partners can negotiate agreed-upon standards for the relationship.

□ Partners can agree to disagree and can tolerate the differences.

Present the four possibilities to the partners and see which they would like to attempt. Usually they will want to negotiate agreed-upon standards. However, if they fail to negotiate the compromise and if neither person has modified his or her beliefs, then they should be presented again with the other alternatives.

SUMMARY

Depending on your own theoretical approach and your assessment of the couple, you may not focus on changing partners' cognition. If you do, teach the cognitive paradigm explicitly until the partners understand and buy into it. Then eliminate negative cognition as it shows up during counseling. Rather than focus two or three sessions on changing cognition, in hope-focused marriage counseling you will probably have more success if you integrate cognition interventions within the counseling at teachable moments but spend most of the time on other interventions that promote faith, work and love.

Chapter 13

Interventions for Stimulating More Closeness

In many ways closeness is the product of faith working through love in a marriage. When faith in the relationship and willingness to work are high, they can produce feelings of closeness, which eventually show up as love.

Dealing directly with couples' closeness can make a powerful impact on the marriage, if couples can accept the help. Couples in high conflict often cannot benefit from interventions to increase their closeness. Conflict creates fear, which stimulates self-protection. People protect themselves by either distancing or defensive fighting. Neither self-protective behavior is conducive to responding positively to a counselor urging closeness and vulnerability. Thus, interventions that are aimed at promoting closeness must be carefully timed. They depend on your assessment of the couple's readiness to lay down their weapons, stop running from each other, reduce the separation between them and open themselves to being vulnerable. Only when couples can receive interventions to help them become closer can feelings of closeness reemerge and love, faith and work find their culmination.

The interventions in this chapter are aimed mostly at helping to increase closeness, provide more intimacy, stimulate more pleasant coaction. Part of closeness is allowing each partner a sufficient amount of time apart from the spouse. People differ dramatically in how much time they require alone. However, for most troubled couples the needs are heavily tipped in favor of needing more intimacy and pleasant coaction, so this chapter focuses mostly on those interventions. (Occasionally couples will be overly involved with each other— that is, enmeshed—and require more separateness. Among couples who attend marital counseling, this is much rarer than the need for intimacy, so I focused less attention on it.) Before I get to specific interventions, let me discuss a couple of general guidelines for dealing with closeness.

SOME GUIDELINES FOR DEALING WITH CLOSENESS

Emphasize the softer emotions. Emotional expression often has mixtures of emotions within a single expression.[1] Generally a protective emotion obscures a more vulnerable emotion. Following are some examples:

☐ When a person is angry (protective), the person is usually also hurt or in pain (vulnerable).

☐ When a person is angry (protective), the person is often also sad, distressed or even depressed (vulnerable).

☐ When a person is bullying or intimidating (protective), the person is also often afraid, worried or insecure (vulnerable).

☐ When a person is sad (protective when dealing with a strong opponent), the person is also often fearful (vulnerable) or angry (vulnerable if the stronger opponent attacks).

☐ When the person is resentful (protective), the person is also often disappointed (vulnerable).

☐ When a person is hostile (protective), the person also cares enough to risk rejection (vulnerable).

☐ When a person acts like a martyr (protective), the person is being self-sacrificial (vulnerable).

☐ When a person is distressed (protective), the person also cares about the other (vulnerable).

Expression of the protective emotions by themselves create a wall that separates. Expression of the vulnerable emotions in each other's presence creates a tie that connects two people. Create a safe atmosphere, one that encourages revealing of the vulnerable emotions, by (a) preventing attacks on the partners' character, toxic arguments and devaluing and (b) noticing and labeling the positive aspects of the relationship, seeing the positive in both partners and maintaining control of the session.

When people disclose their feelings, they usually disclose the protective feelings first. Protective feelings arise in response to some threat.

☐ Anger usually signifies a boundary violation (loss of valuing love) and precipitates a reaction to defend.

☐ Fear often signifies threat of rejection (loss of love) and precipitates a reaction to withdraw.

☐ Sadness often signifies a loss of control (loss of love) and precipitates a reaction to recover the loss.

Help clients appreciate that negative emotions are fundamentally self-protective because the person feels vulnerable. Probe for the more tender, vulnerable feelings. Their expression can motivate partners to protect each other by sparing the other provocations of the negative emotions.

INCREASE PARTNERS' AWARENESS OF CLOSENESS PATTERNS

As in other areas good treatment depends on (a) assessment so you can effectively plan treatment and (b) increasing the couple's awareness of their patterns so they will be receptive to changes you might suggest. Use dramatic ways to demonstrate the patterns rather than merely to talk about them.

Emphasizing the Possibility of Improvement

Many couples who seek counseling have seen enormous erosion of closeness from their early marriage to the time they sought counseling. They feel that restoration of that intimacy is hopeless. They have lost faith in potential for the future, the partner, counseling and sometimes even God to restore feelings of closeness. "I don't doubt that God could renew our love," said one woman. "I doubt that he has chosen to. I don't think we are going to make it."

One way to make inroads into this lack of faith and resulting hopelessness is to incorporate assessments of emotional closeness (see intervention 13-1) and love (see intervention 13-2) into your initial assessment period. The idea to get across to the partners is that things can change: if things can go from good to bad (as they have recently), then they can also go from bad to good; if spirituality has been low in the past and yet has rebounded, so can closeness and love.

Intervention 13-1 *(Homework):* The Ups and Downs of Spirituality and Emotional Closeness Between Partners

Direct couples to draw two graphs.[2] On the top graph, each partner is to draw his or her perception of his or her relationship to the Lord. Below that graph, each partner draws his or her perception of closeness to the spouse since meeting the spouse. In processing the homework with the couple, the counselor makes three points. First, make a parallel between the covenantal commitment to the Lord and the covenantal commitment to the partner in marriage. Second, show the partners that there are substantial changes over time. There have been valleys before and most likely will be again in the future. Currently the couple is in a valley, but, as before, they can come out of the valley. Third, point out that the nature of relationships involves an ebb and flow. That should combat an unrealistic expectation that the relationship can be completely healed (never to have any tension ever again) by counseling. Fourth, ask about the low points and find out what caused those in their perception. Suggest that the partners try to avoid those negative interactions that resulted in low points. Ask about the high points. Often the high points occurred on special times when the partners were together, just the two of them. See if the partners would be willing to reinstitute any of those activities.

Strategy: Love

Hope: Willpower to change

Intervention 13-2: Use Graphs to Show That Love Changes over Time

According to Robert Sternberg's triangular theory of love, the three parts—passion, intimacy and commitment—can vary over the course of the marriage.[3] Tell couples about these three parts of love. Describe passion as the hot feelings that come and go in any marriage. Passion may ebb and flow from day to day. Passion is feeling. Intimacy is the warmth of companionship and unity that comes from sharing similarity of experience. Intimacy usually takes a long time to build and a long time to erode. Commitment is dedication and constraints that hold two people together. Commitment is like an on and off switch. It turns on. It can be turned up or turned down, but it tends to increase or decrease in jumps rather than smoothly.

Haye the partners chart the amount of passion, intimacy and commitment they have felt at different periods in their life:

☐ just before they married

☐ on their honeymoon

☐ after returning from their honeymoon

☐ after about three months of marriage

☐ at the end of the first year of marriage

☐ at the birth of their first child (if they have children)

☐ at other significant positive and negative experiences in their married life

☐ now

Make the following points:

☐ Love can change.

☐ Love has been low in the past and it has increased. Thus if it is poor now, it can get better.

☐ The components of love also change over time. If passion is low now, it can change. The same is true of intimacy and commitment.

Strategy: Faith

Hope: Willpower to change

Making Couples Aware of Their Intimacy Deficiency

Some couples aren't aware of their deficiency in intimacy. They focus on conflict and pay little attention to the emotional, intimate core of the relationship. Ask questions about the amount of time they spend together and about the amount of close intimate activity they have. Whenever a spouse expresses dissatisfaction with the intimacy, ask the spouse to talk more about that dissatisfaction. Obviously this should be done only early in the counseling, because you want to move the couple toward building more intimacy as counseling progresses, not focusing on their deficiency in intimacy.

Creating a Physical Representation of Intimacy

To make the intimate climate dramatically obvious, represent closeness physically. Sculpting, creating a physical "sculpture" of the dynamic relationship, uses the physical space of the office, making their dynamics seem more real to clients (see Intervention 13-3).

Intervention 13-3: Sculpting Intimacy

Have each partner in turn pose themselves as a couple, creating a sculpture of the two people to illustrate the status of intimacy in their relationship. For instance, the couple might complain about a lack of intimacy. You might ask the wife to illustrate by creating a sculpture of their intimacy.[4] She might pose the husband as running away from her and herself as kneeling and begging him for intimacy. After the wife has had an opportunity, have the husband create a sculpture from his point of view. After each spouse has sculpted, the counselor can discuss with the spouses the view of intimacy that is illustrated. Summarize by saying both partners seem unhappy with the pattern.

Have each spouse create an ideal sculpture. Ask, "What do you think you would have to do to move your relationship closer to the ideal? . . . What do you think your partner would have to do to move your relationship closer to the ideal?"

Strategy: Love

Hope: Willpower to change, waypower to change

CLEAVE: ORGANIZING INTERVENTIONS TO PROMOTE CLOSENESS

I have organized most interventions that promote closeness into six categories, which I summarize using the acrostic CLEAVE (see table 13.1). This is based on Genesis 2:24 (KJV), which says, "Therefore shall a man leave his father and mother, and shall cleave unto his wife: and they shall be one flesh." In the NIV, "cleave unto" is translated "be united to," suggesting high intimacy.

Teach the acrostic to the couple (see intervention 13-4). Then, depending on your assessment of their unique problems in closeness, focus on the aspects of CLEAVE that apply to them.

Intervention 13-4: Teach CLEAVE

Give both partners the handout explaining the CLEAVE interventions for building closeness. (Table 13.1 may be photocopied to use as the handout.) Give each partner a copy of the handout both when you begin to work on closeness and again at the end of the several sessions that you work on closeness.

Review the handout quickly (in less than five minutes) and describe each intervention. That five-minute discussion will end the teaching intervention. Then focus on the one intervention that you want the couple to address and spend the bulk of the session on that intervention. Use the handout to introduce additional interventions.

Strategy: Love, work, faith

Hope: Willpower to change, waypower to change

The goal of teaching the CLEAVE acrostic is to give the couple an overview of different interventions to improve intimacy. The overview helps them see intimacy in context. Sometimes partners will resonate with one of the areas that you had not intended to work on. By listening to their assessment, you can sometimes achieve high cooperation.

Use homework to help couples remember the six ways of creating closeness, represented in the CLEAVE acrostic. Make sure partners each have a copy of it. Direct partners to read the sheet at home each day for six days. Each day each partner is to make up one way he or she could contribute to the couple's closeness. By the

Table 13.1. CLEAVE: Building closeness

Taken from Hope-Focused Marriage Counseling: A Guide to Brief Therapy. *Downers Grove, Ill.: InterVarsity Press, 1999.*

C: Change actions to positive

Marriages tend to be satisfying and stable if the ratio of positive to negative interactions is at least 5:1. A positive interaction is any interaction that the partners feel good about. It can be large or small. It can be a communication, a light touch, a smile, a favor, a chore, an unexpected compliment, or anything. A negative interaction is likewise anything that the partners feel negative about. It can be large, such as a large emotional fight, or small, such as a slight, a forgotten birthday or a devaluing look.

If you want to build more intimacy, increase the more positive interactions and reduce the negative interactions. Simply stop acting negatively as much as possible. That will make a big change in your relationship. Yet it is hard for your partner to see what you are *not* doing. Doing positive things for each other is the easiest for your partner to observe. Try to do things that the other person likes.

L: Loving romance

How did you show romance to each other when things were going better? Try to show romance again. It is important to make an explicit agreement not to argue or have negative interactions when attempting to have a "date." Instead, *pretend* that you are dating for the first time.

E: Employ a calendar

We all adjust the amount of intimacy, distance and coaction we experience through arranging our activities. If you feel short of intimacy, then rearrange your calendar to do activities that meet that need. Simply using a calendar and planning positive events can increase the number of positive interactions and promote more intimacy.

A: Adjust intimacy elsewhere

Sometimes husbands and wives do not have the same needs for intimacy. One will require more intimacy and the other will be stifled by too much intimacy. We can have some of our needs for intimacy met outside of marriage—not sexual intimacy of course, which is reserved for the marriage bond, but other intimacy such as sharing plans, talking about important topics, recalling good times or praying together. For the person who needs more intimacy than his or her spouse is comfortable providing, a same-sex friend can provide for many intimacy needs. For the person who feels stifled by too much intimacy, often that person can cut back on intimate interactions with friends so that the partner can fill more of the person's intimacy needs.

V: Value your partner

Valuing love builds intimacy. When we feel valued, we feel closer to the one who values us. Try to value each other. Each spouse should look for and identify the partner's actions that value the spouse. To the extent you can value each other in tangible ways, you will feel closer to each other.

E: Enjoy yourselves sexually

Husbands and wives must go beyond the movie stereotypes of instant passion and immediate intercourse and must learn patiently to pleasure each other sexually. If there are sexual difficulties or if you aren't enjoying your sexual relations, learn to be better lovers. Communicate better during lovemaking, including talking to each other erotically (which is very individually determined). Don't rush into intercourse. Enjoy caressing each other's body. Have your partner show you (by guiding your hand) exactly how to caress him or her in a way that is exciting. A good lover is not one who knows exactly how to pleasure the partner. A good lover is one who tries to do what the partner wants (assuming it is not against your standards and is not harmful) each time they make love.

end of the week, each partner should have six ways: one each for each letter.

CHANGING ACTIONS TO POSITIVE

The goal of the series of interventions that follow is to increase positive interactions and decrease negative interactions (see chapter eleven). In fact, years of research on behavioral marital counseling have shown that such efforts help marriages become less troubled and more fulfilling, but that intervention alone is insufficient to change many troubled marriages into untroubled ones.[5] Such research was based on techniques that have since been improved upon, so it is likely that employing the techniques I have suggested in the following interventions might produce even stronger effects than early research showed.

The Love Bank and Associated Interventions

Explain the concept of "love bank." Intervention 13-5 describes how to explain the concept of a love bank to partners.[6] Beginning with a review of Gottman's ratio, make an analogy of storing up love to storing up money in a bank account.[7]

Intervention 13-5: Describe the Love Bank

To help people understand that they need to increase the positive and decrease the negative behavior, use Willard F. (Bill) Harley Jr.'s "love bank."[8] Tell the couple that the purpose of marriage counseling is to rebuild love. Ask why they married. (Answer: they were in love.) Ask why they were happy early in their relationship. (Answer: they were in love.) Ask why they are not happy now. (Answer: love has waned.)

Tell them to imagine that their relationship holds a love bank, which is like a bank account that they put money in. As they know from their checking account, when the balance is high, life is fun and worry-free. With ten thousand dollars in the bank, the threat of making a ten-dollar withdrawal this afternoon is hardly noticed. However, if the bank balance falls to negative, there is constant worry. When the bank balance is positive but near zero, the person also worries. It doesn't even take a withdrawal to set off the worry. Just the threat that a withdrawal might possibly happen is enough to set off alarm bells. Thus it is important to have a high bank balance.

In the same way, it is important for couples to build a high love-bank balance. Each time that one partner does something nice, positive or pleasing for the other, that action deposits love in the love bank. Whenever either person does something that is unpleasant, that withdraws love from the love bank. I incorporate Gottman's finding by saying that one negative act, regardless of how small, undoes the good of about five pleasing actions.

Each partner keeps attuned to the love-bank balance. As long as the love bank has a positive balance, the person says, "I'm in love." When the balance falls near zero, the person becomes uneasy and worried. When the balance falls below zero, the partner says, "I don't feel like I love my partner." Just as people fell out of love, people can fall back in love. To do so, they must deposit love in their love bank and they must avoid making withdrawals.

Strategy: Love

Hope: Waypower to change

Reduce negative acts. Direct partners to try as hard as they can to avoid provoking the partner and to avoid responding to provocations. This might be done early in counseling, even before you deal explicitly with closeness. Partners will usually say (or at any rate, think) that such a change will do no good because it will not change either partner's attitude. Anticipate that objection and say,

> I would like to ask you each to do something for the next few weeks. Try to reduce your number of negative interactions. You may think that might not do any good, but I have found that it actually can help the marriage when couples give it a wholehearted try.
>
> During the next few weeks, we are going to be trying to help you communicate better and resolve your differences with less conflict, so we will be working on a lot of the issues. I am not asking you to give up on discussing your differences. I am asking simply that you try to cut down on your negative interactions and save some of the discussions about the hot issues until we can work on them in session.
>
> That means that each of you will try consciously not to provoke the spouse to anger. It also means that you are to try as hard as you can not to respond in anger to any provocation by the spouse. You have two chances to avoid any argument: don't start it, and if the other person starts it, don't continue it.
>
> Do you understand what I want you to do? Do you think you can do it? Will you do it?

Determine what constitutes a positive act. After the love bank and reducing negative acts are explained, the third step is to determine what might constitute deposits in a couple's love bank. Have partners list things they could do to please the partner. Using the love-bank metaphor, you can call positive behaviors "love-bank deposits." The behavioral marital counseling traditionally called such behaviors "pleases." I use either term.

Have partners list what they could do to please the partner. You want partners to think about love—valuing the partner—rather than the more self-centered orientation that is produced by generating ideas about how the partner could please them. Both partners must be willing to consider each other (1 Cor 13; Eph 5:30-31; 1 Pet 3:7). Getting partners to think of how they can please the other person builds empathy and promotes taking responsibility for one's actions. Have partners come up with three lists of pleasing acts they can do: his (generated by the wife), hers (generated by the husband) and ours (generated by both partners). Do this in session (see intervention 13-6) or assign it as homework (see intervention 13-7).

Intervention 13-6: Identifying Deposits in the Love Bank ("Pleases")

Direct each partner to think of many acts he or she could do to please the other—acts the other would consider deposits in the love bank. (Check the results with the partner.) Record the lists and photocopy them after the session, giving a copy of all lists to each partner.

After partners have generated lists of how they could deposit love in their partner's love bank, ask them together to suggest ways they could deposit love in their joint love bank through doing pleasant things together. Record that list and provide photocopies at the end of the session.

Strategy: Love

Hope: Waypower to change

Intervention 13-7 (Homework): Identifying Deposits in the Love Bank (Pleases)

Have each partner as homework list twenty-five things he or she could do to please the spouse. In the next session, trade lists. Have the partners read the lists and ask questions to clarify activities. Check for agreement on whether each activity would be considered pleasing by the spouse.

Strategy: Love

Hope: Waypower to change

You can also have partners identify positive behaviors that they would like the spouse to do for them. That approach has been successful in much behavior counseling and is recommended by Harley.[9] However, I have found the approach I recommend (think of how you can please your partner) not only more congruent with my theory (promoting value-your-partner love) but also better at helping partners think of each other rather than themselves. In addition, Jacobson and Christensen[10] and Christensen, Jacobson and Babcock,[11] in the most recent version of integrative behavioral marital counseling, have recommended getting partners to think of ways they could please each other. Their recommendation is based on a practical justification: it works better.

Get partners to do more positive acts. Once love-bank deposits are identified, several homework assignments can be used to help partners increase the frequency of deposits. These include free-form instructions simply to increase deposits and more structured interventions, called love days[12] and caring days.[13] Current versions of integrative behavioral marital counseling direct the partner to increase the spouse's daily marital satisfaction by increasing the positives at any time that the giver chooses.[14]

Here are some other ways couples can increase their deposits in their love bank.

☐ Have couples reminisce about good times in their marriage.[15] Ask them how they could reacquire those feelings.

☐ Have couples make up a progressive story. Each talks for a minute, leaving the two in peril. End the story happily.

☐ Have couples go out to dinner and pretend to be something they aren't. For example, they could pretend to be British spies. Allow the couple to create their own silliness.[16]

☐ Couples may break a social norm together, such as singing on a city bus or facing the wrong way in an elevator.

☐ Have each partner make a jar with fifty-two ideas for special activities or presents.[17] Each partner draws one idea each week and does it for the spouse.

☐ The "up deck" is 85 activities to help the partner feel more cheerful. The "fun deck" is 126 activities that might be fun for couples. Both can be found in *A Couple's Guide to Communication* by Gottman et al.[18] Have couples screen both decks for activities they would consider fun, then draw cards and do the activities.

☐ Have the partners establish three cookie jars: his, hers and ours,[19] with activities that are agreeable to both (policy of joint agreement).[20] At a prescribed schedule, draw an activity from whatever jar is appropriate. For instance, on three days a week, she might draw from his jar; on another three, he might draw from her jar; and on the seventh, they draw from the "ours" jar.

☐ This is more radical than identifying pleases. Have each person create a wish list of behaviors that the partner could do as the ultimate in positive interactions. Don't give any expectations that any activities will ever be done. In fact, insist that most likely none will ever be done. Have the partners exchange lists. These are merely to plant seeds in the partners' minds about intimacy.

Have partners acknowledge each other's positive behavior. Partners are told that love involves noticing when the partner does positive acts. Those acts might indicate that (a) the partner is trying to work on the marriage, (b) the partner is trying to value the spouse and (c) the number of negative interactions has decreased. There are three parts to increasing the Gottman ratio: identifying and reducing negative acts; identifying and checking out positive acts with the partner and doing them; and helping clients recognize and acknowledge when they receive a positive.

Dealing with Objections to Love-Bank Homework

Some partners will object to the intervention of reducing negative interactions and increasing positive interactions by saying, "This is too easy. We've tried all this before." Like all counselors, you will need to deal effectively with objections to your interventions. The following can be used when couples object to the love bank interventions. More generally, you'll find that objections are common and the responses can be used with objections to many interventions.

"It's too simple," they object. You might respond by saying,

☐ "The real test is: will it work? Let's try and see."

☐ "I once took five strokes from my golf game by merely holding my thumb a different way when I swung the driver. Sometimes a simple but fundamental change is what's needed, not a complicated change."

☐ "It might be simple, but it isn't always easy to do."

"It will just deal with the symptoms and not the real problem," they object. Possible responses include

☐ "You may be right. Let's put it to the test by giving a wholehearted try."

☐ "Some people make these changes and find that their marriage improves so much that they don't need anything else."

☐ "If we find that it only changes the symptoms and doesn't affect the deeper attitudes, we can work on the deeper attitudes then. First, let's take the simple approach. If it works, it will save you time, money and heartache. Isn't that worth a try?"

"It feels unnatural," they object. Examples of responses include

☐ "Almost anything new feels unnatural at first."

☐ "It *is* unnatural. It's too structured to use for your next fifty years of marriage.

It's like putting a cast on a broken arm for a while. The cast, which is unnatural, is used only briefly to help the arm heal. But after the cast is taken off, the arm will probably be well the rest of the person's life."

LOVING ROMANCE

Remember what it feels like to be romanced? Each person devotes lots of thought, time, energy and creativity to making the other feel special or valued. Romance is emotional. Romance touches the deep feelings and stirs them up.

Draw on the Couple's Memories of Romance

Brainstorm with partners ways to be romantic.[21] Ask them to recall how they were romantic during their early marriage. Ask them to describe their favorite mutual experiences. Their memories are their greatest resource, but following are some other ideas to help them recall their romance.

☐ Prescribe a date.[22] Have them pretend that they are wooing the partner. Challenge them to come up with the most creative date possible.

☐ Have each partner pick a day and do things to make the partner feel special.

☐ Suggest that the couple need to have some fun playing. Charge the partners to carry out your instructions with fidelity, not allowing themselves to make a single devaluing remark or to act negatively a single time. Give the couple the following instructions: Put a "Just Married" sign on your car. Go to a nice restaurant. Tell the waiter or waitress that you are just married. The waiter or waitress doesn't have to know that you were just married ten years ago. Look lovingly into each other's eyes. Celebrate with champagne or sparkling cider. Talk intimately about love and sex. Never slip out of character. Sit close as you drive home and caress each other. Kiss passionately at traffic lights. When you get home, have wild sex.

☐ Have the partners write love letters to each other.[23]

You can also create more romance with more structured interventions (see intervention 13-8).

Intervention 13-8: Take Steps Toward Building Romantic Love

Harley recommends five steps to building romantic love.[24] Following this intervention might take several weeks or an abbreviated version might be accomplished in a session. If the couple responds, supplement your work in session and at home with readings from *His Needs, Her Needs*[25] and *Love Busters*.[26]

Step 1. Have the couple sign an agreement that commits the husband and wife to three things: (a) avoid doing actions that are likely to cause the partner to lose love (that is, avoid "love busters"), (b) meet each other's important emotional needs and (c) spend at least fifteen hours per week giving each other undivided attention.

Step 2. Have the couple identify the "love busters" that operate in their marriage. Use the checklist on the cover (or lists in the text) of *Love Busters* to assess which apply most directly to the couple.

Step 3. Eliminate the "love busters" identified in Step 2.

Step 4. Identify each partner's five most important emotional needs. Consult *His Needs, Her Needs*.

Step 5. Learn how to meet those emotional needs of the partner and try to meet them.

Have the couple spend about fifteen hours a week outside of therapy working on the target step for the week or in other ways giving each other undivided attention.

Strategy: Love

Hope: Waypower to change

Using the Office to Explore Emotional Closeness

One family counseling technique developed by Salvador Minuchin, founder of structural family counseling, is particularly effective at dealing with issues of intimacy.[27] The office is used as a metaphor for emotional closeness or distance. Minuchin moves the couple into a room to deal with the executive subsystem. He moves a parent and child together to deal with that subsystem. Minuchin is interested in revealing and changing the structure of relationships, hence the name for his approach. Solution-focused therapy approaches use a version of this, which they call scaling.[28] In scaling, the partners imagine that the room represents a ten-point scale of closeness. They are asked where they would be on the scale. They are then asked what it would take to move them one unit closer.

I use this technique differently from either, by using the space as a metaphor (like Minuchin) and creating a scale (like solution-focused therapy) but having partners communicate in ways that physically move them closer (see intervention 13-9). Using the space in the office as a metaphor for closeness is one of the most powerful techniques I have seen. It has multiple purposes.

☐ It allows a quick assessment of closeness.

☐ It reveals patterns like the emotional distancer-pursuer pattern.

☐ It allows you to use scaling interventions (such as those used in solution-focused therapy).

☐ It powerfully demonstrates that partners can make themselves emotionally closer through having positive interactions and emotionally more distant through having negative interactions. Thus it shows

　＊ that partners can change

　＊ that partners have a choice in creating more or less intimacy

　＊ How to make the marriage emotionally closer (acting positively) or more distant (acting negatively)

☐ It can change the emotional climate.

I have demonstrated this technique and others in a case study[29] and videotape.[30] Terry Hight (see appendix) provides a transcript of a marital counseling session in which he used this intervention.

Intervention 13-9: Use the Space in the Office as a Metaphor for Closeness

The partners are asked to imagine that the distance from one side of the office to the other represents points of maximum emotional separation. Direct couples to stand at some distance apart that represents how emotionally close they feel at the present. Say, for example, "So if this were a scale from 1 (the farthest apart emotionally you can imagine being) to 10 (the closest together emotionally you can imagine being), you would be about 3. Is that right?"

After that, direct the partners to stand at the distance that represents how close together emotionally they *ideally* would like to be. Usually they hug, but sometimes the emotional distancer pursuer pattern surfaces dramatically as one wants extreme closeness and the other wants some emotional distance between them. If partners disagree about how close they ideally should be, have one stand firm, say the husband, and let the wife show how close she would like to be. Discuss with each how it feels, one partner at a time. For example, you might ask the wife, who says, "It feels great. I feel happy and loved. I only wish we could achieve this." You would reflect her feeling and probe for anything additional she would like to say. Then ask the husband how he feels if they are this close. He might say, "It feels like we are too close. I feel hemmed in, constricted. I need fewer demands to make me feel less pressured." Reflect his feelings and probe. Then repeat the procedure by letting the wife stand firm and the husband move to his desired level of intimacy.

Finally, direct them to move to the distance they feel right now. Say, "You said earlier, before we had this discussion about the ideal closeness, that you were about 3 in closeness. You might not be at 3 now. Where are you now?" By suggesting that they might rate their closeness differently now, you plant, for the first of several times, the suggestion that emotional closeness can change as a result of their interactions, which is the main point of the exercise.

Direct partners to pull their chairs to the distance apart that they currently feel. Have them discuss a pleasant shared memory. When you sense that they are more emotionally connected than they were at the beginning of the discussion, have them move their chairs closer together to represent the intimacy they now feel. Ask each to speculate about why they feel emotionally more intimate as a couple. You hope one or both will say that each is feeling valued by the partner.

Repeat these discussions with other intimacy-producing topics, such as their goals, dreams or memories of a time when they were particularly close. At critical points in each discussion, direct partners to move their chairs closer. With this exercise, show them, in about twenty-five minutes, that they can get closer to each other by having discussions that show love to each other. At the end of the discussion, ask whether each person feels valued by the partner.

At some point during the discussions, negative interactions will occur. (This has never failed to happen.) Let it go on for a brief period. When you sense the mood getting negative, stop the interaction and say, "You are not as close now. Move your chairs back." After they move their chairs to the new level, say, "Do you see that you each have the power to determine to some degree how close you feel toward each other? If you focus on positive memories and pleasant events, you will feel close. If you focus on your differences and act negatively, you will feel more distant. You have a lot of control over your emotional closeness."

Strategy: Love

Hope: Waypower to change

STRUCTURING TIME TOGETHER
Scheduling time together is essential for maintaining a healthy marriage and healing a troubled one. Yet busy schedules often conspire to keep partners apart.

Adjusting Time Schedules
People attempt to meet their needs for intimacy, coaction and distance by apportioning their activities (see chapter four). Suggest that people change their time schedules to meet their needs for closeness.

Prepare for resistance. It is difficult to change time schedules, and changes must be gradual rather than sudden. Furthermore, once changes are initiated, the effects may ripple through the marriage for months or years, leading to other needed adjustments. If the couple perseveres, both partners' needs for intimacy, coaction and distance may be satisfied. Changing time schedules is difficult and costly. Characterize a partner's willingness to make such modifications as indicating that the partner loves and values his or her spouse enough to change.

Establishing Bounded Couple Time

Having bounded time, as a couple, strengthens marriages and families (see also chapter ten; intervention 10-10). Numerous theorists have recognized this, including Minuchin, pioneer in structural family counseling, who suggests that couples act as an executive subsystem to strengthen the entire family system.[31] Mara Selvini-Pallazoli, who developed her own approach to family counseling and then worked collaboratively with Minuchin for a while, suggests that troubled families strengthen the parental subsystem by having the parents go on a regular date night without telling the children where they are going or when they will return.[32] Pastor Gary Ezzo, in *Growing Kids God's Way*, recommends that couples have nightly "couch time" in which they discuss the events of the day without allowing children to interrupt.[33] Some couples take walks (which my wife Kirby and I do), stay up late and talk, or use the last hour of the day to treat as exclusively their time.[34]

Bounded couple time provides the structure for partners to talk and share experiences.[35] It also defines clear boundaries around the marriage subsystem[36] and provides a shared experience. Describe the need for protected couple time. Describe how couples create such time together and what it does for the marriage. For homework assign couples to have some protected time during the course of the upcoming week.

Reading Together

Some couples like to read together. They pick a book that each likes and during a trip read it aloud. Or they read together each night (or several nights per week).[37] Early in counseling, assign the couple to buy the book *Getting to Yes: Negotiating Agreement Without Giving In*[38] and read it together without discussing it. This assignment promotes intimacy by spending positive time together and prepares the couple for dealing with conflict.

ADJUSTING INTIMACY ELSEWHERE

Many troubled couples would like to experience more intimacy in their marriage. That often is revealed when you use space in the office as a metaphor for closeness (see intervention 13-9). Partners do not necessarily agree on what increased intimacy would consist of. Before you intervene to adjust intimacy, discuss the specific meaning of intimacy for each partner (see intervention 13-10).

Intervention 13-10: Discuss Intimacy

Ask both partners, "What do you mean when you say that you want more intimacy in your marriage?" Answers will differ. Some partners focus on sexual intimacy and others on emotional intimacy. Regardless of the type of intimacy people prefer, guide the discussion to what it means to have more intimacy. Usually people mean that in intimacy they have a sense of unity or shared positive experience. Sexual intimacy is a sense that they share sexual good times together. Spiritual intimacy usually means that there is a sense of shared spiritual experiences. Emotional intimacy usually means that partners frequently share a sense of emotional closeness.

Ask, "How do you specifically make those shared experiences happen?" Answers usually boil down to several steps:

☐ Let your partner know what makes you feel more intimate. Is it taking a walk, taking a shower together, feeling really listened to? If partners share what are their feelings, they can more likely know whether they share similar feelings.

☐ Search for activities in which similarities are greatest and do more of them. This could involve trying new sexual experiences; experimenting with new forms of worship, praise, prayer or Scripture study; seeking common emotional experiences (attending concerts, going dancing, attending plays); or searching for other shared experiences.

☐ Talk about the positive experiences. The couple that talks about their positive experiences will be likely to seek other similar experiences.

After a discussion of intimacy, assign the couple to agree on and try some new experience (or some experience that they do not regularly do) and talk about their reactions to it. The experience might be sexual, emotional, social, recreational, intellectual or spiritual. If immediate agreement is not reached, they are to search until they find an activity that both partners enthusiastically agree to (Harley's principle of mutual agreement).[39] Tell the couple you will ask for a report at the following session. Next week, of course, ask what they did and how they reacted to it.

Strategy: Love

Hope: Willpower to change, waypower to change

Breaking Up the Emotional Distancer-Pursuer Pattern
A common pattern of conflict over intimacy occurs with the emotional distancer-

pursuer pattern.[40] One spouse, usually the wife, demands more closeness than the husband feels he can provide. So he demands more distance. (Sometimes the pattern is reversed, but not often.)

At advanced stages the pursuer may give up, erect an emotional barrier and lob insults and criticisms over the barrier. "I've been hurt for years and won't make myself vulnerable again," she might whine. The distancer, after initially feeling free from ever-present demands for intimacy, may attempt to revive the relationship; however, encountering a barrage of criticism, he may erect his own barrier and commence his own hostilities.

The ironic part of the emotional distancer-pursuer pattern, and the part that fuels the pattern at all stages, is that usually *neither* spouse wants a lot of intimacy. Both are comfortable with moderate intimacy. They merely have different ways of keeping the other moderately distant. The pursuer pursues so strongly that she drives the distancer away. The distancer runs away, but not too far away. Neither partner feels valued by the other. Over counseling, help each to value the other, even if each must change his or her strategy of distancing or pursuing.

Break up the emotional distancer-pursuer pattern through different interactions with each partner. To deal with an emotional distancer-pursuer pattern, spend most of your time talking to the emotional pursuer; don't pursue the emotional distancer. If you demand that an emotional distancer husband be more intimate with his wife, he will likely respond to you as he does to his wife: running away and perhaps ending counseling. On the other hand, pay close attention to the emotional pursuer, thus meeting some of her desire for attention and reducing some pressure on the distancer. Help the emotional pursuer meet some of her needs for intimacy elsewhere (except for sexual intimacy, of course). Help her avoid criticizing her spouse, and help her value her husband.

As the pursuer lessens her pressure on the husband, he will probably feel more need for intimacy. Suggest (but don't order or demand) that he initiate some intimate activity that he thinks his wife would enjoy. Help her accept whatever intimacy is offered without criticizing or demanding more. As the partners change these deep-seated patterns of behavior, commend them for their willingness to value each other above their own needs.

Break up the emotional distancer-pursuer pattern through using homework. Use a homework assignment that accounts for the differences between emotional distancers and pursuers. For years I have used intervention 13-11, which has proven effective with emotional distancer-pursuer couples.[41] I assign appropriate homework to each with additional instructions that neither partner tell the other what his or her assignment is and that they try to guess what the other's assignment is.

Intervention 13-11 *(Homework):* Breaking up the Emotional Distancer-Pursuer Pattern Through "Sealed Orders"

Prepare two envelopes before beginning the session. In one (for the pursuer) write: "Do not ask for any intimacy all week, and avoid criticizing your partner either aloud or to yourself if your partner does not meet your expectations." In the other (for the distancer) write: "Initiate some activity of your choosing at a time of your choosing that you know your partner likes and that will help the two of you become a little closer."

During the session, draw out from the couple a description of their emotional distancer-pursuer pattern. You might do this by using the physical space of the office (see intervention 13-9) or by discussion. Explain the emotional distancer-pursuer pattern to the couple, referring frequently to their own behavior. The intervention works best if you have drawn a chart prior to the session showing the stages of the emotional distancer-pursuer pattern. When you pull out the predrawn chart, the couple gain confidence that others have gone through this pattern, and they more readily believe that you indeed have an intervention that will help break up the pattern.

Announce that you'd like them to do something at home and that you don't want to discuss the assignment until after they have tried it. If they agree to try as hard as they can to carry out the assignment, give them the appropriate envelopes. Ask them not to mention what is in each's envelope until next session.

At the following session, process how the assignment went.

Strategy: Love

Hope: Waypower to change

Helping Develop Spiritual Intimacy

Discuss spiritual intimacy. Ask the couple, "What is spiritual intimacy?" After they respond and discuss the issue, suggest that intimacy is a feeling of like-mindedness, like-feeling or unity of experience. Spiritual intimacy is feeling that partners experience a sense of unity in things spiritual—such as worship, prayer, private devotions, how much they talk about spiritual issues, ways they react emotionally to spiritual things, ways they use their faith to cope with adversity, ways they use religious beliefs and values in daily life and the amount of emphasis they place on religion in their family and in their private life. Spiritual intimacy may also include experiences that are not explicitly Christian, because people can feel reverence and awe at God's creation. Thus partners might feel spiritually intimate when they share a sight of the mountains, the ocean or a flower garden. It might involve hearing praise music or a great symphony.

Spiritual intimacy may have more to do with sharing feelings and thoughts about what is important spiritually than it has to do with such things as time studying Scripture together, time reading the Bible together, whether partners attend the same church, whether they have devotions or pray together. It isn't necessarily theology, Bible study or church life that makes a couple spiritually intimate, though differences in these areas can contribute to *not* feeling intimate spiritually.

Of course, spiritual intimacy can occur in shared religious experiences, through unifying with each other and focusing together on God. Uniting with each other might involve experiences like sacrificing for the other,[42] valuing the other, building the other up, blessing the other, confessing to the other, forgiving the other, praying together, and reading and studying the Bible together. Focusing together on God might include experiences like praying together, sharing a quiet time, reminding each other that God is in control or ministering to others.

Discern whether partners want to be more spiritually intimate. Ask the couple, "Do you want to be more spiritually intimate?" If both do, ask, "If you are not as spiritually intimate with your partner as you would like to be, what stops you?"

Donald Harvey suggests that you might get answers like these: [43]

☐ "I'm not spiritual enough to share."
☐ "I'm uncomfortable to share the spiritual."
☐ "Lack of time."
☐ "My mate won't share."
☐ "I feel bad about my spiritual life and don't want to look bad to my mate."
☐ "I feel good about my spiritual life and don't want to share."
☐ "My mate won't listen to me with interest."

Direct the couple in creating more spiritual intimacy in their marriage. Ask whether the partners would like to commit to try one of the ways to feel more spiritually intimate. Partners should not settle on a way unless both partners enthusiastically agree.[44]

Direct the couple to have patience while waiting for change. Each should state his or her needs for more spiritual intimacy and suggest a way for the partner to participate. Each should give the partner space, not harassing the partner to perform the behavior. Each should demonstrate what he or she wants; for example, if the wife wants a prayer time, she should not expect it unless she is having a private prayer time. Admonish both partners to continue to invest in other areas of intimacy. While waiting for spiritual intimacy to develop, each partner should take care not to become resentful if the partner does not want to engage in a particular spiritual experience.

VALUING ONE'S PARTNER

Closeness is not only built by sharing experiences. It is also built by partners' treating each other as pearls of great value. When a person feels valued, he or she also feels secure and attached to the partner. When a person does not feel that the partner values him or her, the person is apprehensive and vigilant to receive rejection. That anxiety and vigilance produces avoidance and distancing from the partner. Obviously, having a sense of being valued should produce firm attachment and an increased sense of closeness.[45]

Two homework assignments can produce an increased sense of valuing and being valued. In the first, direct the partners to perform at least three random acts of tenderness in the ensuing week. Give a few examples, such as leaving a note taped to the bathroom mirror, looking tenderly at the partner when he or she isn't looking at you and then letting the partner catch you looking, admiring the partner's body when you see him or her undressed, whispering endearments or sexual suggestions to the partner when you are in public, or mailing a steamy love letter to your partner's workplace. In the second, direct each partner to keep a log that describes every situation in which he or she consciously tried to value the partner. At the following session, examine the logs and discuss the exercise.

ENJOYING ONESELF AND ONE'S PARTNER SEXUALLY

Couples may present in marital counseling with or without sexual problems and with or without general marital problems. Sometimes sexual problems are a result of other marital difficulties. Usually this is discernible when the couple reports a history of good sexual relations but reports a recent deterioration in their sexual happiness that coincides with a deterioration in their marital relationship. Deal with both marital and sexual problems. Improving the marriage will not automatically result in a better sexual relationship.

Other couples may never have had a good sexual relationship. Their marital problems may have developed later in their marriage, apart from their sexual relationship. They may assume that because of their history of sexual unhappiness they are destined to be unfulfilled sexually. Their marital and sexual difficulties are unrelated to each other (as seen by their being maritally happy but sexually unfulfilled for years). Each must be treated separately.

Some couples may have both sexual and general marital problems, with the sexual problems causing the marital problems. Sometimes couples never adjust to each other sexually during early marriage, though most couples work out their sexual problems in the first year of marriage. At other times, sexual problems develop because of a life transition, such as having a child, experiencing extreme stress or developing a physical problem. Because the couple cannot work out the new sexual relationship, they might become unhappy with their marriage in general.

Other couples might have few marital problems. They might seek counseling because their sexual relationship is not fulfilling. Generally, of all couples who have sexual problems, couples who have a good marriage but a troubled sex life stand the best chance of successful treatment.

Assessing Sexual Functioning

Assess the type of sexual problems that a couple might be experiencing during the first session by asking directly about their sexual relationship. Ask,

☐ "How frequently do you make love?"

☐ "Are you each satisfied with the frequency?"

☐ "When you make love, are you satisfied with what happens?"

☐ (If not) "Why not?"

☐ "Would you each say whether you think there are problems with your sexual relationship?"

☐ (If so) "What do you see as the problems?"

If the couple report sexual problems, advise an appointment with a physician to discuss the possibility of physical causes (unless the partner has already seen a physician). If no physical problems are found and if the couple identify the problem as one they want to work on in counseling, assess your competence to deal with the problem. Training in sex therapy is needed prior to attempting to treat couples who have sexual problems. In today's climate of litigation and awareness of sexual harassment and abuse, counselors who deal explicitly and directly with sexual difficulties must not only be competent in sex therapy but also be able to adduce hard evidence of their training in sex therapy. Competence in marital counseling does not imply competence in sex therapy. If you do not have adequate training specifically in sex therapy, refer the couple to a qualified sex therapist.

Treating Sexual Problems

Doug Rosenau has suggested that treatment for sexual problems involves one of three levels of intervention: dialogue, education or coaching.[46]

☐ Couples who need dialogue generally either are newly wedded or have never talked openly about their sex life and have developed some behaviors that bother each other.

☐ Couples who need education are those who subscribe to many common myths about sexuality, regardless of where they picked up the false beliefs. Sometimes serious sexual problems can disappear when a myth is challenged effectively by a counselor. In several couples I counseled, both man and woman were frustrated with their sex life, believing the woman to be difficult to arouse because she was not very lubricated. They had each tried one of the commercial lubricants with little success. I suggested that saliva could be an effective, easy-to-access lubricant; when the man took the suggestion, the frustrations soon ceased and orgasms were forthcoming.

☐ Couples who need coaching are treated using common sexual therapy techniques. The foundation technique for most sex therapy is sensate focus exercises. In sensate focus, the partners explore each other's bodies with the objective of giving and receiving pleasure rather than with the objective of intercourse or orgasm. Hour-long sessions proceed slowly over a period of weeks, as the partners forgo intercourse and concentrate on touching, stroking and caressing each part of the body, proceeding from nongenital touching to genital caressing. After several weeks, the partners usually are more than eager to have intercourse and are primed for orgasm.

Sex therapy interventions can be found in many texts. For information about how to perform the techniques, I will trust the trained counselor to consult appropriate sources. One source for your own reading is Joyce and Clifford Penner's *Counseling for Sexual Disorders*.[47] I have compiled other reading for the trained counselor concerning sexual therapy (see table 13.2).

Needed: Good Information About Sex

Sexual problems often occur within marriages that are troubled. Most of the time they seem to be a result of other relationship difficulties that suggest failures in love and valuing, such as lack of emotional intimacy, poor communication, constant conflict, bitter blaming and the like. They usually indicate a failure of partners to value the other person.

This is not always true, though. Sometimes a marriage is excellent but partners

---

Table 13.2. Some recommended books on sex therapy for therapists

Kaplan, Helen S. 1974. *The New Sex Therapy.* New York: Brunner/Mazel.
———. 1979. *Disorders of Sexual Desire.* New York: Brunner/Mazel.
Lieblum, S. R., and R. C. Rosen, eds. 1989. *Principles and Practice of Sex Therapy.* 2nd ed. New York: Guilford.
Penner, Clifford L., and Joyce J. Penner, 1990. *Counseling for Sexual Disorders.* Dallas: Word.
———. 1993. *Restoring the Pleasure: Complete Step-by-Step Programs to Help Couples Overcome the Most Common Sexual Barriers.* Dallas: Word.
Schnarch, D. M. 1991. *The Sexual Crucible: An Integration of Sexual and Marital Therapy.* New York: W. W. Norton.
Wahking, Harold, and Gene Zimmerman. 1994. *Sexual Issues: A Short-Term Structured Model.* Grand Rapids, Mich.: Baker.

---

may (a) be ill-informed about maintaining a good sexual relationship, (b) have faulty ideas about how to stimulate each other sexually, (c) hold beliefs that are harmful such as "the male should know how to bring his wife to orgasm without her needing to tell him what feels good and what doesn't" or "the only good sex is simultaneous orgasm," (d) disagree over acceptable sexual positions or behavior or (e) have physical problems that make sexual enjoyment difficult or impossible for one or both of the partners. Many of such difficulties may be solved if you provide accurate information or good reading material. The book I recommend most often to couples is Rosenau's *Celebration of Sex.*[48]

SUMMARY

Although most couples cannot benefit from therapeutic attempts to produce increased closeness until they have dealt with communication and conflict, the area of closeness offers extraordinary potential to affect couples. Careful assessment is needed throughout marital counseling to determine when couples are likely to be receptive to interventions that aim at producing more closeness. By helping people value each other and strive for shared experiences, counselors can help many couples create more intimate marriages.

Chapter 14

Interventions for Cementing Commitment

Marriage counseling should help couples gain a sense of increased commitment. But should you address commitment explicitly? Some therapists believe that if the counselor can help couples become happier, there is no need to address commitment.[1] I disagree.

Commitment is multifaceted. It includes partners' long-term fidelity to each other, but other commitments are also important—commitments to trying to change, attending counseling as one way they will try to change, following most of the counselor's suggestions about how to try to change, preventing competitors from encroaching into the relationship, and loving God. Dealing with this multitude of commitments involves different therapeutic skills because the partners are in different places with many of the commitments. You help couples build new commitments (to change, to therapy, to work at home), restore weak commitments (to each other, to not allow competitors) and maintain strong commitments (to God). All levels of commitment require promoting willpower (motivation) to rebuild, change or maintain commitment. All involve augmenting couples' waypower to change by using concrete interventions that make change sensible. Maintaining commitments also requires waitpower as the couple, knowing God cares for them (1 Pet 5:7), waits for him to work increased levels of commitment.

This chapter outlines some guidelines for helping couples build or rebuild commitment. I then consider the biggest threat to commitment in marriage—divorce—and suggest some ways to confront that threat when it arises. Because counselors and partners may differ in their view of whether marriage is a contract or a covenant, I discuss that issue. Finally, I suggest some interventions for strengthening the components of commitment.

GUIDELINES FOR PROMOTING COMMITMENT
Following are some basic guidelines for helping couples build or rebuild commitment.

Minimizing Heavy-Handed Emphasis on Shoulds
Marriage was designed by God as a permanent relationship that mirrors the permanent faithfulness between a Christian and God. Many verses describe God's desire for the permanence of marriage (Mal 2:16; Mt 5:32; Mk 10:6-9; 19:9; 1 Cor 7:15). It is tempting to quote verses to partners whose commitments are wavering and to command that they obey.

At times that may be the very tack to take. Probably, though, that approach should be taken less often than it is. There are several reasons for this. First, Christian commitment is based on covenant, not law.[2] Commanding obedience to law reinforces a contractual view of marriage, which can undermine covenantal commitment in the long run. Second, people inevitably make attributions about why they remain together. When obedience to God's laws is stressed people think, *We are staying together only because we must, according to God's law.* Such thoughts make it more difficult for them to see that they are also staying together because they love each other.[3] Third, people do not usually respond well to coercion.[4] Some may rebel, especially if the counselor's style is heavy-handed. The loving approach is usually (not always) to build a heartfelt desire (rather than a feeling of obligation) to maintain commitment.

Assuming a Lifelong Commitment
Once a couple, Christian or non-Christian, express their verbal commitment to each other, strengthen their resolve to work on the marriage by pointing out instances of their commitment. Assume they will be together forever and therefore need to find solutions to their differences. One powerful means of helping solidify commitment is presupposing their lifelong commitment.

Securing an Explicit Commitment to Try

Just because people attend a counseling interview does not mean they are committed to try to change. Any marriage counselor can name countless cases in which one or both partners seemed to attend counseling simply to prove that they had tried everything before divorce. It is not usually productive to assume naively that couples have committed to try to help the marriage survive.

One paradox of therapy is that people usually come implicitly saying, "Fix the problem but don't make me change."[5] Troubled couples hate their marriage but usually believe that they are responding in the only sane way to their bad situation. They might resist your suggestions to do things differently. Ask them, "If what you are doing isn't working and is leading you to an unhappy marriage, then why not try doing it a different way? What have you got to lose?"

Adapt this approach to your clients.[6] For a physician you might ask, "If you'd tried the same operation on fifteen patients and they all died, wouldn't you try something else?" For a lawyer, "If you'd tried the same type of argument in fifteen cases and had lost all of them, wouldn't you take a different approach?" For a salesperson, "If you tried the same sales technique fifteen times and didn't make a sale, wouldn't you change your approach?"

Promoting a Commitment to Therapy

If commitment to therapy wanes, DeLoss and Ruby Friesen recommend explaining to the couple their doubt model.[7] I have adapted that model (see intervention 14-1) to show its connection to reestablishing hope. To see the way the Friesens use the model, consult their article.

Intervention 14-1: Promote a Commitment to Therapy

First, describe the erosion of hope. Point out that when things began to go wrong in the marriage, it did not instantly deteriorate. Instead, the behaviors got less and less positive, but hope was maintained. Eventually, though, the behaviors pulled hope down until it was at low ebb. Partners became pessimistic about the marriage and about its future. Partners were discouraged.

Second, remind partners that instead of giving in to lack of hope, they came to therapy and worked to make their marriage better. (Name several concrete things they did to make their marriage better and describe the results, or ask them to name several of the things they found helpful about the therapy.)

Third, acknowledge low hope. Say that at present hope is low, but—as the couple have just described—behaviors have become positive more often than when they entered therapy.

Fourth, describe the insidiousness of doubt and its constantly changing nature. Doubt keeps hope low. Describe several types of doubt.

Doubt of sincerity. The doubt in early stages of therapy is about whether the partner is sincere about changing. In fact, each person might doubt his or her own sincerity, wondering whether the relationship actually has a future.

Doubt of ability. If that doubt of sincerity is overcome by faithful attempts at change, despite some setbacks, then a second doubt arises: doubt about the partner's (and perhaps one's own) ability to actually change the ingrained patterns of poor marital interaction. Doubt of ability is usually associated with the middle part of therapy. With faithful behavior, despite periodic setbacks, that doubt is overcome and the couple believes that change can happen and indeed has happened.

Doubt of permanence. Near the end of therapy the person might doubt whether the change is meaningful and permanent. With faithful behavior, despite some setbacks, that doubt of permanence can also be overcome. It is important that the couple knows that periodic setbacks will occur, so they do not invalidate their progress whenever those difficulties occur.

On a white board or piece of paper, draw a figure with three boxes, labeled "doubt of sincerity," "doubt of ability" and "doubt of permanence." Use the figure to accompany your explanation.

Fifth, place the couple accurately at one of the stages of doubt, whichever is appropriate for them at the moment of your discussion. Be specific as to why you think they are at that stage. Most likely they are not in a low stage of doubt (such as doubt about sincerity) but are in one of those periodic setbacks, which is why you are discussing doubt.

Sixth, caution the couple about having unrealistically high expectations about what the marriage will be like after things are better. Draw on the initial hope-focused interview in which the couple identified ways they would know that things were better. Usually those changes were quite modest and help the couple see that they have indeed made progress.

Strategy: Work

Hope: Willpower to change

Promoting a Commitment to Work Outside of Therapy

Therapists often assume that partners will carry out the homework that has been assigned; they are often surprised when partners can't seem to find the time. Address the importance of working on the marriage outside of therapy before you assign homework. Once partners get into a pattern of noncompliance with homework assignments, the pattern is hard to break. Conduct intervention 14-2 within the first three minutes of the first session; its impact will usually last throughout marital therapy.

Intervention 14-2: Promote a Commitment to Work Outside of Therapy

Ask how important the marriage is to the partners. Ask whether it is important enough to spend a week on. (I've never had anyone say no.) Say,

> While you are attending marital therapy during the next two to three months, I am going to ask you to spend a work week of forty hours working on the marriage. Is the possibility of saving your marriage important enough for you to commit to that? (Let them answer.)
>
> Let's see what this is going to mean in practice. Suppose that after we complete today's assessment session, we decide to meet for seven additional sessions over about eight weeks. Follow me on this arithmetic. Attending today's session is about two hours, and attending the next seven sessions will be about seven more, for a total of nine hours. Suppose I ask you to do something between sessions that takes you three hours each week, starting last week when you completed the instruments at home. That would be last week, this week and the next seven weeks, for a total of nine weeks. At three hours per week, that's twenty-seven hours. If we add the nine hours for attending sessions and the twenty-seven hours working at home, that's thirty-six total hours—less than a work week. Even if you add travel time to and from the sessions, that's probably less than forty hours you will have devoted to possibly saving your marriage.
>
> Think about all the things you do at your work or at school or at home that you spend forty hours on. Is it worth forty hours of hard work to try to save your relationship? You have invested so much of your life and self into this marriage. Are you willing to put one more work week into it?

Get the commitment from them.
Strategy: Work
Hope: Willpower to change

AVOIDING DIVORCE

Divorce is the biggest threat to commitment in marriage. This section explores that threat and how to confront it when it arises.

Threats of Divorce

Troubled couples may not want to divorce at first, but the worse marriage gets, the more they entertain ideas about what life would be like if they divorced. They might wrestle with theological questions over the scriptural permissibility of divorce as well as being concerned about what people in their church might think and do if divorce became a reality. They certainly will consider reactions of family members to news of divorce. While the contemplation is occurring, the marriage usually will limp along.

At some point, though, one of the partners may utter the first suggestion that divorce is possible. Whether uttered like a threat or mused as a remote possibility, those words usually strongly affect the marriage. Partners are threatened. Fear circuits are activated in the brain, producing defensiveness and self-protection, which loosens the bonds between the partners. Suddenly divorce seems to be a real possibility, and that utterance accelerates the slide toward divorce.

Couples' Beliefs on Divorce

During the assessment session, if couples bring up the possibility of divorce, ask about their beliefs regarding divorce. To the extent that they believe that divorce is not a viable option, or is to be considered only under extreme circumstances, the couple is empowered to love each other unconditionally.

Discussing divorce can at times precipitate a theological defense, in which a partner might try to debate you about the scriptural permissibility of divorce. I usually refer them to a book that outlines positions on divorce, such as *Divorce and Remarriage: Four Christian Views*,[8] and say that they need to wrestle with that question before the Lord themselves. If couples do not mention divorce in the assessment session, I usually do not ask.

When the Threat of Divorce Goes Public

When divorce has been explicitly threatened, do not try to argue them out of it.

Meet the threat head-on. When couples come to therapy having already threatened divorce, the prognosis for their recovering is poor. Make a four-pronged attack on the problem.

1. Teach couples that they should consider a paradox: Never let the threat of the possibility of divorce escape from your lips, but if you do consider divorce, be realistic about what you expect.

2. Threatening divorce is a coercive strategy that negatively affects one's partner and one's own marital satisfaction and stability. Once the threat of divorce is mentioned, it is irreversible. The damage might be repaired, but scar tissue will remain. Threatening divorce sets people thinking about the possibility, and what people think about can become a reality. People pay attention to the negative aspects of their relationship selectively once they begin to think about divorce, and they look for alternatives and selectively focus on the positive aspects of the alternatives. On the other hand, if partners simply assume that they will never divorce, they may still experience troubles in their marriage, but their attention will be more directed to working out the troubles and solving the problems than escaping the troubles and fleeing to an alternative.

3. Once a couple begins to entertain ideas of divorce, they usually succumb to four myths about divorce. Make those myths explicit and counter them with facts (see table 14.1).

4. When divorce considerations become serious, don't try to talk partners out of it. Instead, say that you want them to be sure that they understand what they will be getting into. To help them understand divorce, use the strategy adapted from one recommended by H. Norman Wright (see intervention 14-3).[9]

Intervention 14-3: Helping Couples Understand Divorce

As suggested by Wright, discuss the difficulty of working on the marriage with divorce hanging over both partners' heads.[14] Suggest that partners throw themselves into trying to make the marriage work for a limited period of time, giving it their highest effort. If they are unable to make the marriage work after that time, they can consider divorce seriously. If they agree, ask the partners to

☐ not threaten divorce for six months

☐ commit to completing at least three months of marital therapy

☐ devote their energies to a good-faith effort to improve their marriage through marital therapy and working on the relationship at home

Table 14.1. Facts to combat myths leading to divorce

Myth 1: If we divorce, my pain will end.

Fact: If you divorce, your pain will change. It will not end. There is evidence that pain will increase after divorce for most people.[10] After a period of relief, other pains begin. Divorced or separated people may be lonely, financially strained or troubled about getting into the singles scene, may experience difficulties in child care and may experience rejection from date partners, members of their family and the church community. In addition, there is substantial research that relates poorer physical health with people who have divorced.[11] This is especially true of men, but it is also true of women. From the research point of view, we don't know whether (1) people who divorce feel more stress and thus divorce causes health problems, (2) people who have poorer health cause strains on their marriage relationship and thus poor health causes divorce, or (3) people who divorce and who have poor health do so because some other variable causes both—for example, drinking, drug abuse, chronic anger, narcissism or chronic depression might each affect health and simultaneously affect marital satisfaction and stability. Most likely each of the three is happening with different people.

Myth 2: If we divorce, my conflict with my spouse will end.

Fact: In about half of the cases, the conflict stays virtually the same. In about one-fourth of the cases, the conflict lessens but remains substantial. In the remaining one-fourth of the cases, the conflict virtually ends. It is more likely that after divorce the conflict will continue rather than end.[12]

Myth 3: If I divorce and marry another person, the other person won't have the negative qualities of my partner.

Fact: Often the other person will have the same qualities. People are often attracted to a particular type of partner. They substitute one for the other. Even if a person is determined not to make the same mistake again, the partner will inevitably have his or her own poor habits and negative qualities. Everyone does. The task is not finding the perfect partner who doesn't have any flaws; it is living with a human being who (by virtue of being human) has flaws.

Myth 4: If I divorce and remarry, I'll be happier because I will have learned what I like and don't like and will be able to avoid the mistakes I made in the first marriage.

Fact: The divorce rate is at least ten percentage points higher in remarriage than in first marriage.[13]

☐ attend a divorce recovery group to get a realistic sense of what divorced people are struggling with

☐ read at least two books about divorce to find out what one might expect for the self and the family (I recommend *The Divorce Decision* by Gary Richmond and *Second Chances* by Judith Wallerstein and Sandra Blakeslee)[15]

Strategy: Faith, work, love

Hope: Willpower to change, waypower to change

Staying Together for the Sake of the Kids

Tom Whiteman suggests an answer to the frequently asked question "Should we divorce or should we stay together in our bad marriage for the sake of the kids?"[16] He answers that in fact, both are bad. But why must those be the only two alternatives? Another way out is marriage counseling, which allows partners to change the marriage relationship or accept each other without conflict rather than divorcing (which is painful) or continuing in conflict (which is also painful).

Whiteman argues that there is nothing wrong with staying together for the sake of the kids, or for church, or for other constraints. Commitment, according to Scott M. Stanley and Howard J. Markman, involves both constraints and dedication.[17] The therapist can use those constraints as barriers to divorce, trying to build the partners' dedication to each other.

COMMITMENT TO MARRIAGE: COVENANT OR CONTRACT?

What is a commitment and how can couples strengthen it? Marriage counselors (and partners) take two distinctly different views of commitment.[18] It may be seen as an implicit or explicit contract between partners that as long as one person carries out his or her part of the contract, the other person will carry out his or hers. Or commitment is seen as a covenantal joining of people into one flesh, one body, one blood, in which a person willingly treats the spouse as having the same status as the self.

Promoting Covenantal Commitment to God

I believe that marriage is most fruitfully (and scripturally) viewed as a covenant. Viewing marriage as a covenant provides some ways to deal with problems in commitment and strengthen the covenantal commitment. The foundation of the covenantal perspective on marriage is the individual Christian commitment of the spouses. To the extent that individuals can understand the covenants of God and can apply that perspective to their own marriage, the commitment can be strengthened. Covenantal commitment is based on married partners' being "one flesh" (Gen 2:24). (See also chapter four.) It involves treating each other as pearls of great value, promoting faith and expecting that work on the marriage will occur.

Not all Christian marriage counselors agree that commitment should be treated as a covenant. For example, the Friesens[19] and Willard F. Harley Jr.[20] each advocate a contractual understanding of marriage commitment. The contractual model has the advantage of allowing people to see that they can change their own behavior and eventually expect to get a different response from the partner. On the other hand, it has the disadvantage of presenting an understanding of marriage that is not rooted in Scripture and that promotes a wait-and-see mentality on the part of spouses. Further, it implies a commitment that is fragile in that if one person stops living up to the "contract," or even if a mate thinks the other is not, then the commitment might abruptly end.

If you see the benefits in treating marriage as a contract, then you will want to consult the Friesens' and Harley's works in that area. I personally treat marriage as a contract when counseling couples, often non-Christians, who understand their marriage as a contract. Work by behavior marital therapists on contractual commitment has been shown to have validity in years of practice.[21]

Matching Your Rationale to Your Clients
From my perspective, contracts are not necessarily to be shunned. Instead, match your intervention to your assessment of the couple. For the couple in which at least one partner is not Christian, the contract can often bring harmony and stability to troubled relationships. Duties and expectations can be made clear through the negotiation of a contract. In one couple, the wife (a new Christian) agreed not to make the husband (a non-Christian) feel guilty or morally inferior by bringing judgments on him for failing to attend church, drinking and swearing. Even though she was worried about her husband's salvation, she was willing to trust God with his eternity. The husband promised not to belittle the wife's faith, prevent her from attending church or judge her as mentally inferior due to her profession of faith. In that case, the contract prevented the lack of valuing that had emerged since the wife's recent conversion to Christianity.

Consider not only the partners' perspectives (on contractual or covenantal commitment) but also the level of their commitment. Christensen, Jacobson and Babcock suggest presenting different rationales for treatment to couples who evidence different levels of commitment.[22] For couples with high commitment the counselor might say, "I see that you are highly committed to your marriage despite the problems you have mentioned." For couples of moderate commitment the counselor might say, "I see that both of you seem to want the relationship to work, even though you see the problems as severe." For couples with low commitment the counselor might say, "This therapy seems to be a last try at making the marriage work, even though neither of you seems to have much hope that therapy will succeed."

Christensen et al. offer these rationales to reassure some couples, to underscore the seriousness of the problems for other couples and to challenge poorly committed couples by informing them that they are responsible for whether their marriage improves—not the therapist. Christensen et al. find that the success of therapy depends more on whether the couple is willing to work than on the skills of the therapist.

Teaching Directly About Covenantal Commitment

The mere fact that a couple embraces a view of commitment that is rooted in contracts does not mean that you must treat the marriage as if commitment were contractual. If couples are not familiar with covenants, you can teach them. Keep your explanation brief—less than three minutes. Draw on the discussion in this chapter and in chapter four.

Correcting Commitment Drift

Successful marriage requires love, faith and work. When couples do not actively work on their marriage, it deteriorates.

Using Donald Harvey's notion of commitment drift, we can visualize the marriage as one flesh, one body, which is allowed to run downhill.[23] When I allow myself regularly to eat beyond what I need, my weight creeps upward. When I sit at the computer all day and my major form of exercise is dinnertime fork-lifts (heavy loads, many repetitions) instead of getting good exercise, my muscles atrophy. Commitment drift is the functional equivalent. When energy is not added to the marriage, it gets fat, flabby and flaccid.

Call attention to patterns of commitment drift early in counseling. In the assessment report, characterize it as a failure to put sufficient work into the marriage to maintain its vitality. In counseling you will encounter the drifting marriage, usually because a crisis has erupted like a volcano, spewing the lava of distress and anger throughout the landscape. First deal with the crisis. Then deal with the underlying commitment drift.

The marriage might not be irretrievably damaged, and you might be able to prevent further deterioration by pointing out the drift. Suggest to the couple that the real temptation on their part will be to alleviate the crisis and return to their pattern of drifting. Intervention 14-4 describes a method suggested by marital expert Donald Harvey for dealing with the drift of commitment.

Intervention 14-4: Deal with Commitment Drift

This intervention is based on suggestions by Don Harvey, who has written extensively about drifting commitment in relationships.[24]

Step 1: Teach about commitment drift.

◻ According to Harvey drifting of marital commitment is a gradual, subtle, often unintentional, sometimes intentional severing of the emotional ties between a husband and wife. From the outside the marriage looks fine. From the inside it functions well. However, when a crisis hits the marriage that has drifted apart, the crisis is often met with hostility.

Step 2: Teach about the causes of commitment drift. For example, Harvey lists five common causes.

◻ Some couples become overwhelmed by the demands of life. With lots of external demands, the home is seen as the place partners go to collapse, the place they don't have to be nice. That leads to unintentional drift.

◻ The drive to succeed makes it hard to invest in the home relationships. That too leads to unintentional drift.

◻ More intentional drift occurs when a partner decides to keep one's distance.

◻ Another intentional way to contribute to drift is when one or both partners seek out and invest in outside interests as a way of avoiding home.

◻ Finally, default, or investing little effort in the relationship, will contribute to drift.

Step 3: Teach partners ways to recognize whether their relationship is drifting. They should prayerfully ask themselves several questions.

◻ Are patterns of insensitivity becoming evident?

◻ Has there been a progressive disengagement and increase of activity elsewhere?

◻ Is there anything that should be happening in the marriage but isn't?

◻ Have they felt some disturbing feelings?

◻ Is there a sense of dissatisfaction with what is happening in the relationship?

◻ Are feelings of resentment evident?

Step 4: In counseling, deal with commitment drift while you are doing other therapy.

Strategy: Love, work

Hope: Willpower to change, waypower to change

STRENGTHENING THE COMPONENTS OF COMMITMENT

Recall that according to Caryl Rusbult,[25]

Commitment = Marital Satisfaction - Satisfaction with Alternatives to the Marriage + Joint Investments in the Marriage

To strengthen commitment, each of the components can be changed.

Helping Partners Become More Satisfied with Their Marriage

People usually feel more committed if they feel their needs are met and they are valued as loved ones. The counselor can help strengthen commitment by helping the couple see how they meet each other's needs and how they value each other.

Anything that promotes more satisfaction with the marriage will strengthen commitment to it. Marriage counseling is aimed at increasing satisfaction, which should bolster commitment. As you help the couple build faith working through love in all areas of the marriage, the partners will strengthen their commitment.

Eliminating Competitors to the Marriage

Similarly, eliminating competitors to a relationship will strengthen commitment to the relationship. Competitors may be other romantic interests, but may also be other activities that interfere with the couple's relationship. This might include work, hobbies or even church activities.

Reduce temptation to affairs by counseling those who are tempted that God will provide a way out. The way out is usually not to get into the tempting situation in the first place.[26] Teach the partner that when tempted by an affair, he or she should mentally look for the problems with the alternative relationship. The partner should ask himself or herself, *Why won't the grass be greener on the other side?*[27] This puts into effect Malachi 2:16 (" 'I hate divorce,' says the LORD God") and the preceding passage that says, "Guard yourself in your spirit, and do not break faith with the wife of your youth."

Sharing Investments

Sharing resources strengthens commitment because neither person wants to give up the resources held in common. In marriage, resources held in common include anything in which a couple invests time, energy or money, such as a jointly owned house or property, children, mutual hobbies and leisure activities. Even a couple's identity as a couple is a resource.

SOLIDIFYING A STRENGTHENED COMMITMENT

By the end of counseling we hope to have strengthened the couple's commitment. Generally the most effective way of strengthening commitment is to increase their satisfaction (which all of therapy is aimed at doing) through promoting more love, faith and work on the marriage. By engaging central values, sharpening the core vision, helping build more confession and forgiveness, inducing better communication, promoting more conflict resolution and reconciliation, changing blaming cognition and promoting more secure closeness, you contribute to higher marital satisfaction, making commitment stronger.

Still, the couple has gone through an ordeal by the end of counseling, and they should celebrate. One way to do that is to retake their marriage vows. Some couples like to retake their vows in a public ceremony, others in front of family or therapist, and yet others with no one else present. (See Guernsey for an elaboration of this idea and some model vows.)[28] Guernsey's recommended vows emphasize affirming that the partners will love each other despite the certainty of failures in love by the spouse.

SUMMARY

Commitment is a covenantal agreement in which partners treat each other like one flesh. Relative to the other aspects of marriage, commitment receives less direct attention. As other areas of marriage are strengthened, though, the effects usually show up as stronger commitment.

15

Interventions for Promoting Couple Commencement from Counseling

---

"Termination" sounds so final. It conjures images of Arnold Schwarzenegger saying, "Hasta la vista, baby."

Termination has been traditionally the term used by counselors to talk about ending counseling. With brief counseling, though, *termination* might be less accurate than when it is used to describe the last session or more of five-times-per-week-for-three-or-four-years psychoanalysis. People might well return for additional counseling (perhaps months later, perhaps years later) if they have had a good experience with brief counseling.

PROMOTING COMMENCEMENT

I prefer the term *commencement*, which conjures images of graduating from formal education and beginning life without the educators in the foreground. Commencement from high school, or even from a doctoral program, does not signify that the person knows it all. Commencement from hope-focused marriage counseling, likewise, suggests that the couple will continue to learn.

Commencement signifies that something important has been accomplished.

In hope-focused marriage counseling, the couple entered marital counseling with little hope and reaches commencement with renewed hope. Partners began marital counseling without a strategy for making the marriage thrive and reach commencement with an effective strategy that they can use throughout their marriage: promoting faith working through love. They began marital counseling unsatisfied with their marriage and reach commencement with higher marital satisfaction and strengthened commitment. In the best outcome partners began marital counseling with less faith in God than when they reach commencement.

Commencement involves rituals. Rituals create strong images in memory. They embody lessons learned in the ordeal that rituals signify. They make accomplishments more tangible.

Commencement has six objectives. First, help partners prepare for commencement by developing independence from regular counseling sessions. After this preparation, conduct a solid final session, which will embody five other objectives.
□ Suggest that partners create a memorial to remember what they and the Lord have accomplished in their marriage.
□ Discuss what the partners learned during counseling.
□ Solicit from partners how they intend to continue to improve the marriage.
□ Present a final assessment report that (a) takes stock of the status of the marriage in light of the initial assessment report and (b) suggests areas where the partners should exert additional effort.
□ Open the door to additional counseling if needed in the future.

DEVELOPING INDEPENDENCE AS COMMENCEMENT APPROACHES
Ending counseling can be difficult for both clients and counselors. Developing the couple's independence is crucial to successful commencement.

Difficulties of Ending Counseling
It is difficult to end counseling. Clients are usually ambivalent as the end of counseling approaches. Partners want to be told they have succeeded at repairing their marriage. They want to be independent. Yet clients who are anxious about being abandoned may perceive the last session as abandonment by the counselor. Ending counseling signifies moving into a new phase of marriage. Partners are back on their own and have natural concerns about whether their gains will last. Sometimes people have crises near the time of the last session in an unconscious attempt to prolong counseling. Some professional counselors rigidly insist that additional counseling not be offered in crisis. However, most counselors see

clients in crisis for an additional session to control the crisis, but they will not extend their regular sessions.

Counselors are usually ambivalent too as counseling ends. They want their clients to succeed, but they also hate to give up the known client for the next, unknown one. Worse, what if they end up with no new client to fill the time slot?

Both couples and counselor desire independence from each other and simultaneously are dependent on each other. The counselor must face his or her ambivalence, as counselors repeatedly do successfully, and push for independence.

Encouraging Independence

How do you encourage the couple's independence? Throughout counseling, foster an independent mindset. In each session, encourage active participation by clients in role playing and interacting under your guidance. The more active partners can be, the more they will feel that they made changes rather than that changes happened to them. Also, use homework, which allows the clients to initiate change and carry out tasks at home.

Several methods can help promote additional independence as counseling nears completion. First, become less active in the later stage of counseling, "weaning" the client from your direction.

Second, as clients learn the interventions, talk less and use more questions. For instance, near the beginning of counseling you might interrupt a mutually devaluing interchange by saying, "Stop. Our goal in here is always to treat each other like a pearl of great value. Just now, you each devalued the other. Let's try that communication again while valuing each other." Near the end of counseling interrupt a similar exchange with questions like "What could you do differently to keep yourselves from being swept into conflict?" Or simply say, "Stop," and wait for one partner to tell the counselor what would have been a better way to communicate. Ideally, by the end of counseling, the couple will avoid poor behavior altogether or quickly interrupt themselves and change their behavior.

Third, promote more independence by having the last session a couple of weeks after the next-to-last session. Clients get used to meeting regularly with you. They begin to store their discussions to air during sessions. That is partly because you might, early in counseling, reduce their negative interactions by encouraging them to refrain from negative interactions between sessions. As commencement approaches, though, the couple nears the time when you will not be available to contain conflict. Ease the transition between ongoing counseling and no therapeutic contact by spacing the last sessions. During the week of an omitted session, you could prescribe a session at home at the regular time of counseling in which the counselor's empty chair can serve as a proxy for the counselor in helping the clients discuss the issues. Alternatively, merely say that partners could use more opportunity to practice their skills at home.

HAVING PARTNERS SUMMARIZE WHAT THEY LEARNED
As couples prepare for the commencement session, ask them to reflect on what they learned. Have them write five positive things they learned during the course of counseling about themselves, five about their partner and five about their marriage.

In the commencement session have partners share what they received from counseling. Reflect the content of their statements. Stay alert to reinforce points they make in the final assessment report, which you will go over with them at the end of the session. Also reinforce ways they built love and faith, and learned to work on the marriage.

HAVE PARTNERS PLAN WHAT THEY WILL DO NEXT
Direct partners to discuss specific ways they intend to continue working on their marriage. Help couples create specific plans. Vague plans such as "keep working on our marriage" won't be carried out. Have partners agree on one area to change and stick with it for several weeks.

Don't feel threatened if the few sessions of counseling did not revolutionize the marriage. Problems that have been built up over many years will take a long time to be completely solved. You may feel pressured to move into long-term marriage counseling, but under most conditions resist the urge. Let people try to make changes on their own rather than try to keep them in counseling. However, if they cannot change on their own, encourage them to return to counseling, not to give up.

CREATING A JOSHUA MEMORIAL
In the final session, cement commitment by creating a "Joshua memorial," which is any physical remembrance of the progress made in counseling.[1] Some couples write letters of commitment to each other and frame them. Some take trips and frame the plane or boat tickets. Other couples create a symbol to remind them of what God has done in their marriage. Some couples set up ritual events to commemorate what the Lord has done. For instance, one couple established the tradition of an annual ski trip to celebrate their successful counseling, and another took a weekend vacation away from the children to renew their love. One couple

bought a beautiful box in which they each placed a small scroll stating their desire to honor God by making their marriage a reflection of his ever-faithful covenantal love for Christians and for the church. After explaining the Joshua memorial to the couple (see intervention 15-1), provide time during the session for them to discuss what they might do.

Intervention 15-1: The Joshua Memorial

Following is a script you can approximate to present the Joshua memorial to the couple. You can use this for couples who are not Christian as well as for those who are; however, you usually need to phrase it in a way that nonreligious couples can accept.

> The progress you have made in your marriage during the past weeks is really something. When we make an important change in our lives, it is often helpful to create a physical reminder of that progress. When Joshua eventually led the people of Israel across the Jordan River into the land God had promised them, God parted the water (Josh 4:5-9). Joshua retrieved stones from the bed of the Jordan River and made a memorial to the Lord to celebrate what God had done in their lives.
>
> I believe God has worked in your lives during the past weeks. In the same way that Joshua built a memorial to God, I would encourage you to create a memorial for what he has done in your marriage. You can do whatever you want to remember what has happened in your marriage. I could give you some examples of what other couples have done to get you started thinking about what you want to do. Or you might want to create your own memorial without knowing what other couples have done. Would you like some ideas?

If couples want ideas, provide examples from those listed in the text. If not, let them discuss the memorial in your office or at home.

Strategy: Love, faith, work

Hope: Waitpower

DISCUSSING THE FINAL ASSESSMENT REPORT

Prior to the last session, write an assessment report based on the initial report you wrote after the first session. Much of the initial report can be cut and pasted into the final report. For example, directly copy the couple's presenting problem and goals for treatment.

Briefly summarize the progress of treatment. Describe each intervention thoroughly. While that sounds time consuming, it doesn't have to be. You can create a file that summarizes each of the interventions that you commonly use; cut and paste these files directly into your report. Your description of the intervention refreshes the couple's memory of it and makes the report more comprehensive.

Assess the current status of the couple's marriage and suggest no more than five practical goals for the couple to continue to work on. After you have done this several times, you can cut and paste much of this. You can probably write a comprehensive final assessment report, tailored specifically to the couple, in twenty to thirty minutes.

OPENING THE DOOR TO ADDITIONAL COUNSELING

Marital counseling is not expected to be a once-in-a-lifetime experience. Nor is it expected to be interminable. Through hope-focused marriage counseling you will have, we hope, set the marriage on a path toward improvement rather than deterioration. It is trite to mention it, but life is filled with adjustments. As partners move from stage to stage, they face the possibility of a poor adjustment at each stage. Generally, over three-fourths of all couples will have virtually no problems at each new stage of life.[2] Some will have difficulties adjusting at almost every stage. Leave open the possibility of seeking future counseling. Tell the couple,

> I have enjoyed working with you these last few months. You have worked hard, have been open to the Lord's intervention in your life together and have made important changes in your marriage. As we wrap up counseling, I hope you feel that you got a lot from it. If in the future you need counseling, I hope you'll seek me out so we can build on what you have already done. If I am not available, if you've moved or if you simply want to see someone with a different perspective, then I hope you'll seek counseling from some other counselor. My door is always open to you.

TAKING STOCK OF WHAT YOU LEARNED AS A COUNSELOR

Another important aspect of commencement is assessing what you as a counselor have learned from your experience with the clients.

Learning from Failures

Couples are not the only beneficiaries of counseling. The counselor often benefits as well. In fact, the couples from whom I have benefited most have been the ones who failed to improve. When I have carried out my therapeutic interventions as well as I could and people still did not improve, I have to pause and ask why. The easy answer is to chalk up the failure to the clients. I have heard myself repeatedly say, "They were resistant . . . passive-aggressive . . . obviously toilet trained way too early . . . already decided they were going to divorce . . . unwilling to work." And those were the charitable attributions.

But were they really nasty, resistant clients? Or were they simply being themselves and I could not connect with them for some reason? Perhaps I had been under stress and was too short-tempered with them. Maybe I assessed them inaccurately and couldn't match my interventions well to their patterns of interaction and learning styles. Perhaps I selected ineffective interventions. Perhaps my approach was inappropriate for the couple. The reasons counseling was unsuccessful are legion, but unless I honestly ask questions of my own performance, I will not learn from my mistakes.

Learning from Successes

I have also learned much from successes. Sometimes counseling has coasted on automatic pilot. I was frustrated at being stuck in a rut. Then, an intervention would turn counseling around. When that occurs, I ask myself what happened. What was the turning point?

Sometimes the intervention that created a leap forward was one I had used for years. (I might wonder whether I could have predicted earlier that the intervention might have worked, and if so what would have allowed me to predict that.) At other times, the intervention that made a difference was one I simply created on the spot because it seemed to me that the couple would benefit. (I might ponder about what made me think the intervention would work with that couple.)

At still other times, the intervention that caused a breakthrough came from another counselor: learned from a book, a continuing education seminar or a workshop. (I might consider how that intervention fits with my theory. In fact, I find that not all interventions fit with my theory, which places me in the uncomfortable position of either using an intervention that is inconsistent with what I believe or not using an intervention I have found to be effective. That dilemma makes me ponder even more.)

Being More Creative as a Counselor and Theorist

My creativity has been stimulated by seeking and trying new experiences. Creativity often occurs because incongruous events are juxtaposed. I look at the marriage through a hope-focused filter. By continually exposing myself to other approaches, I occasionally find that the filter needs to be rotated.

Don't expect astounding progress in the few sessions of any brief marital counseling. The canoe of the marriage has been floating downstream toward the waterfall for a considerable time prior to counseling. In only a few sessions, you can feel satisfied if you merely help turn the canoe around. Many paddle strokes will be required to move the canoe upstream.

Chapter 16

Essentials of Hope-Focused Marriage Counseling

I have now discussed the hope-focused marriage counseling model in detail, and I have described well over one hundred discrete interventions—many drawn from other theorists. So what makes hope-focused marriage counseling a separate approach?

This chapter lists twelve of the components I have recommended in previous chapters as those that are essential to hope-focused marriage counseling. Currently all twelve appear to be necessary. Research is needed to determine which, if any, might be omitted without affecting the integrity and effectiveness of the approach. I have described twelve additional "semi-essential" interventions, selected from the many interventions I recommended. Research is also needed to determine whether any of those are actually essential, that is, whether their inclusion will markedly increase the effectiveness of hope-focused marriage counseling.

The effectiveness of a counseling can be supported by unsystematic application within the clinic—as my students, my trainees and I have done—but validation requires rigorous research. I have made some efforts to investigate a hope-focused approach with couples who are not clinically troubled. Those studies are encouraging and show that the approach works in a marriage-enrichment context. The approach still needs testing by me and by independent investigators in clinical trials. I hope this chapter makes it easier to do research on the efficacy and effectiveness of hope-focused marriage counseling.

TWELVE ESSENTIAL COMPONENTS THAT DEFINE THE APPROACH

1. On the phone, suggest that sometimes improvement occurs before the first interview and direct partners to look for it.

2. Have couples complete written assessments before the first session begins. At present, I recommend two instruments: the Personal Assessment of Intimacy in Relationships (PAIR) and the Marital Assessment Inventory (MAI). I use the brief marital assessment battery, which measures marital satisfaction with the Couple's Assessment of Relationship Elements (CARE),[1] marital hope, intimacy (via intimacy thermometers) and degree of marital forgiveness. I hope the brief marital battery will be available, with initial psychometric data, soon after the publication of this book. (That battery has not been investigated well enough psychometrically to recommend it as a first choice at this point; however, when our psychometric studies are complete, I hope the evidence will support its use instead of the two longer instruments.) Written assessment is necessary; it contributes to making change sensible and has been shown in controlled research to account for substantial change in relationship enrichment.[2]

3. Prior to the first interview have both partners read "Benefiting from the Marital Counseling You Are About to Receive" (table 5.2), watch a precounseling videotape (table 5.1) or both.

4. Conduct the initial hope-focused first assessment session (ninety minutes) in which you focus on solutions through (a) taking a relationship history and asking especially about the positive events during the history, (b) asking about the times in the past when the relationship was good and how those good times might be recaptured, (c) asking about good times in the current interactions, (d) asking about the future (perhaps using a version of the miracle question)[3] and (e) pursuing descriptions of how the other person would know that the relationship was better. That solution-focused assessment should build hope.

5. Throughout the initial hope-focused interview, call attention to some salient failures to value the partner. Identify a greater number of successes in valuing love. Call attention to instances of loss of faith in the partner (and if appropriate in the Lord) and more frequently instances in which the partners had high faith in each other (usually during the good times revealed in their marital history). Call attention to ways that the partners have stopped working

on the marriage (probably as they have lost hope that things can get better) and more frequently to the many ways they have worked to better the marriage and solve the problems. Conclude the interview by summarizing the problems and framing them in terms of problems in love, faith, work and therefore hope.

6. Between first and second sessions, write an assessment report (two pages; see table 6.4). Give to both partners and place it in their file. Characterize the cause of their marital problems in terms of failures in valuing love, faith in each other (and for Christian couples faith in the Lord, if appropriate) and work on the relationship, culminating in a loss of hope in the future of the marriage. The assessment report works best if the couples have already completed their written assessment (see number 2 above) so you can use its results.

7. Begin the second session by giving the written report to each partner, reviewing it and agreeing on an approximate number of sessions needed to achieve the goals identified in the report.

8. Focus each session on a single theme. The potential themes are central values, core vision of marriage, confession and forgiveness, closeness, communication, conflict resolution, cognition, complicating problems and commitment. Structure counseling to the clients' needs. Use as many sessions as are needed for each theme relevant to each couple.

9. Throughout counseling, use the strategy of increasing love, faith and work, and keep a focus on rebuilding hope. Show partners repeatedly how to value their mate.

10. Use interventions that make change sensible, and thus increase hope. Those interventions involve physical manipulations, behavioral actions or interactions or making physical products (such as reports, written lists or tapes) that are completed and verbally processed. These interventions may be drawn from any theory of marital counseling you wish, using your own favorite techniques. The requirements are that they (a) increase hope (willpower, waypower or waitpower), (b) fit within the strategic framework and (c) make change sensible to clients.

11. Assign homework at the end of every session and, at the beginning of the following session, check to see whether the couple did it.

☐ Even the most resistant clients can be assigned observe-and-report assignments, in which they observe instances where things went well (or less badly) and report back.

☐ Most partners can be assigned active homework.

12. When counseling is completed, present a written assessment report,

similar to the initial assessment report, that examines the couple's progress in light of their initial goals. The report must use the strategy of increasing valuing love, faith and work; keep a focus on rebuilding hope; and suggest ways that the couple can continue to improve their marriage.

TESTABLE PROPOSITIONS

If you use these twelve essential components, I believe you will find four statements true in your practice or research.

Proposition 1: Use of hope-focused marriage counseling that involves all twelve essential components will help troubled marital couples improve marital satisfaction and will reduce the likelihood of divorce relative to the absence of marital counseling, self-help alone and bibliotherapy alone.

Proposition 2: Use of hope-focused marriage counseling will not be worse at improving marital satisfaction than (a) counselors' choice of their own eclectic theory or (b) any recognized validated theoretical approach; it will be more effective than some approaches.

Proposition 3: All twelve essential components will contribute positively to the effectiveness of the approach.

Proposition 4: Some counselors will have better outcomes using hope-focused marriage counseling than will others. Namely, marital counselors who form working alliances with clients quickly and strongly will have better outcomes than marital counselors who are slower to form alliances or form weaker alliances. Also, counselors who prefer and have experience using brief approaches will have more success than will counselors who prefer long-term approaches or who have less experience with brief approaches. All counselors, regardless of speed and depth of working alliance formed and regardless of preference and experience with brief approaches, will have success no worse than their preferred approach if they conduct hope-focused marriage counseling according to the procedures outlined in this book (including the twelve essential interventions and as many of the twelve semi-essential interventions as are appropriate for the couple).

These propositions are not facts. They are hypotheses to test in the clinic and laboratory.

TWELVE SEMI-ESSENTIAL INTERVENTIONS

The following interventions are used with a large majority of all couples. Because couples differ in their problems and because assessment is the cornerstone of intervention planning, the following twelve semi-essential interventions are not used for all clients (as are the twelve essential components listed above). I have listed the intervention numbers in parentheses after each. The interventions marked with an asterisk have been included in the research on hope-focused relationship enhancement.[4]

1. Creating and revising a vision for marriage (interventions 8-6 and 8-8)

2. Conducting a forgiveness session[5] (interventions 9-10 and 9-11)

3. Using forgiveness to complete conflict resolution[6] (intervention 9-12)

4. Ranking Chapman's five love languages[7] (intervention 10-5)

5. *Teaching the LOVE acrostic (intervention 11-5)

6. *Using listening and repeating to deal with miscommunications (intervention 11-7)

7. *Training partners to observe their effects to short-circuit triggers (intervention 11-8)

8. *Training partners to evaluate both partners' interests[8] (intervention 11-9)

9. Employing the CLEAVE acrostic (table 13.1 and intervention 13-4)

10. *Teaching Harley's love bank[9] (interventions 13-5 and 13-6)

11. *Using physical space as a metaphor for closeness[10] (intervention 13-9)

12. *Using a Joshua memorial in the last session (intervention 15-1)

DRAWING FROM MANY APPROACHES

Hope-focused marriage counseling draws from many approaches to marital or couple counseling, and yet it is not merely one version of any of those approaches.

□ Emotionally focused marital therapy has contributed a sense of the importance of emotional experience.[11] It evokes emotional expression, particularly of tender emotions, which helps partners see each other's vulnerability. I have appreciated and used that.

□ Behavioral marital therapy, integrative behavioral marital therapy and cognitive behavioral marital therapy have affected my approach strongly.[12] I particularly like the findings of Gottman concerning the minimum ratio of five positive to negative behaviors in untroubled couples.[13] I also like the ways that such approaches treat communication and conflict, help couples focus on the positive and (in integrative behavioral marital therapy) accept what they cannot change.

□ Structural family therapy's underlying theory of changing the structure of marriages has shaped the way I think about counseling.[14] I appreciate the ways

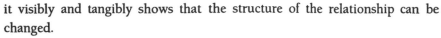

it visibly and tangibly shows that the structure of the relationship can be changed.

☐ Solution-focused therapy promotes straightforward identification of goals.[15] The concreteness of the solutions appeals to me.

☐ The Interpersonal Communications Programs (ICP)[16] uses an awareness wheel and listening mat to teach communication systematically and concretely. A focus on concrete communication that is similar to the ICP approach (but does not use the awareness wheel or listening mats) has been fruitful for hope-focused marriage counseling. (Counselors using the ICP approach will achieve their best success by following the ICP with high fidelity.)

☐ Scripture contributes a framework through which I see life and thus see marital counseling. It provides a strategy (faith working through love; Gal 5:6), goal (building hope) and focus beyond mere skill building (to aim at forgiveness and reconciliation after hurtful interactions—not just teaching communication, managing conflict and restoring intimacy—and to promote covenantal commitment and spiritual intimacy).

What is common to the various parts of theoretical approaches that have attracted me? All have attempted to make change real, tangible and concrete to the partners: to make change sensible. There is an extraordinary value to tangible manipulations that exceeds mere verbal methods of counseling.

SOME THEOLOGICAL MUSINGS

If we look at Scripture, we see numerous examples of the importance of physical evidences of God's presence. Let me list a few.

When Jesus rose from the dead, he appeared several times in bodily form to the disciples. On one occasion he invited Thomas to physically put his fingers in the wounds. On another, he appeared to the disciples as they were fishing, and he didn't just appear and then vanish. He cooked fish for them to eat.

Paul appeals to readers not merely to have faith that Jesus rose bodily. He appeals also to their senses. He points to over five hundred witnesses of the resurrection (1 Cor 15:6). He implies, "Ask the witnesses, because they physically saw Jesus." In two places Paul argues that it is better to walk by sight than by faith (1 Cor 13:12; 2 Cor 5:8). His argument in both passages is that when all Christians are united with Jesus, we will walk by sight and that will be glorious. However, for now, on earth, we walk by faith and not by sight. Now we see through a mirror dimly. Then we will see face to face. Now we have lots of temporary gifts such as tongues of men and angels, prophecy and the like.

Then, when we walk face to face, we will have no need of such things because we will see Jesus face to face. Paul concludes his argument in 1 Corinthians 13 by proclaiming that faith, hope and love abide, but the greatest of these is love (1 Cor 13:13). Why is love the greatest? Because when we walk face to face with Jesus, faith and hope will be unnecessary but love will be experienced in full glory.

The church universal observes two sacraments: Communion and baptism. (Of course some denominations add other sacraments; however, all Christian churches observe these two common sacraments.) In Communion Jesus called the bread and wine his body and blood, and he invited Christians henceforth to celebrate his resurrection until he comes again by taking the physical elements. In baptism he has us apply water in obedience. Hot debates occur about what actually happens during the sacraments, but everyone agrees that in Communion and baptism we use physical elements to engage in a spiritual act.

I am not arguing that verbal methods of counseling are somehow unscriptural. Rather, I am arguing that somehow God blesses physical demonstrations of faith, hope and love that supplement the verbal. As John says, "The Word became flesh" (Jn 1:14).

In hope-focused marriage counseling I have tried to mirror that scriptural balance. I have emphasized physical as well as verbal interventions. I believe counseling can be powerful with both. I consider the physical interventions powerful. I want to make change as sensible as possible for couples who have a difficult time hoping for change.

GOD IS IN CONTROL

At the outset of this book I described the difficulties of conducting effective marital counseling. Throughout the book I have attempted to show you exactly how (and why) to conduct one type of brief Christian-oriented marital counseling. This book can serve as a manual for practice (and as a guide to research for those who are inclined in that direction). I have been encouraged with the success that graduate students and professional counselors have had with the method. However, being an obsessive-compulsive scholar-researcher, I want to see the approach put to empirical tests that show how well it works relative to other approaches, and I want to know which parts of the approach are essential and which are fluff.

While we await controlled research, though, you can continue to contribute to field testing the approach with your clients—modifying, picking and choosing the parts that fit your style and your clients. Many of the techniques and interventions that make up hope-focused marriage counseling have actually received empirical support. Still, I believe that the entire package will be an exceptionally strong combination, and we won't know whether that is correct until the approach as a whole is thoroughly tested. Any approach needs to demonstrate both effectiveness in the clinic and efficacy in the laboratory.

One Christmas I was taking a long walk when I saw a woman walking toward me at great speed. Because I was moving right along myself, I expected we would quickly pass each other. As we passed, though, she reversed her direction and walked alongside me. I looked at her. I had no clue who she was.

"You're a runner," she said.

I nodded

She said, "I used to run marathons, but now I can't. The doctor won't let me. I have a bladder problem. When I try to run, I leak."

Intriguing. It isn't often that a stranger uses the leaky bladder conversational opening. I surreptitiously lengthened my stride, but she was younger and in better shape, and she easily matched my pace.

"My husband doesn't understand me," she continued.

Ho-boy, I thought.

As the conversation continued, I quickly shared some things (we were walking fast) about how she could improve her marriage. (I couldn't help much with the leaky bladder problem.) When we parted ways at the corner, I walked across the highway pondering the social significance of a conversation with someone who appears out of the mist, describes her bladder and marital problems, receives some advice and disappears into the mist. Then I realized that I was wearing my Richmond Marathon hat. She had seen the hat, immediately identified me as a kindred spirit and sought help. (I blush at the irony of it. I have never run in a marathon in my life. Kirby bought that hat for me at a yard sale—for a quarter. I felt like such an impostor.)

Then my head cleared. I realized that it was no accident that, of my ten hats, I had worn that one. God had given me training in marital counseling, dressed me up in a uniform so I would be easily recognized and brought that woman to walk beside me for a brief period. Such a metaphor for counseling. The Lord trains us, brings the people he wants us to help across our path and gives us the privilege of walking side by side with them for a while. God is in control, and he will train each of us for the ministry he has ordained for us. I hope that this book will become part of your training that he can use to bless your clients.

Appendix

Hope-Focused Marriage Counseling with a Young Professional Couple
A Case Study

Terry L. Hight

INTRODUCTION

It is mind-boggling how many spouses embark on their marriage relationships with great anticipation of happiness, only to see their hopes and dreams shattered by separation and divorce. How can these marriages change from sources of immense satisfaction to crucibles of pain and disillusionment? Over the past several years, we at Virginia Commonwealth University (VCU) have worked with over one hundred couples to help empower their relationships and to inoculate them against destructive patterns of relating. Most of our research has been marital enrichment rather than marital therapy because we have been working with couples who have relatively minor marital troubles.

However, many of the hope-focused interventions, which have worked so well in our research on enrichment, are effective with couples who have more serious marital difficulties and have been used by numerous counselors throughout the United States and in other countries where Ev Worthington has conducted training. In the following pages I describe my efforts to use hope-focused marriage counseling with a couple who had marital problems. I worked with Jeff and Valerie (their names and identifying information have been changed to protect their confidentiality) while a doctoral practicum therapist at a secular university counseling center (at VCU). It is noteworthy that during my work with Jeff and Valerie I was supervised by an independent licensed psychologist who was not associated with our research. That argues well for the generalizability of hope-focused marriage counseling.

THE COUPLE

Neither Jeff nor Valerie spoke as they sat in the reception room nervously completing the necessary paperwork before their first session. It was apparent, even to the untrained eye, that their relationship was in turmoil. The two chairs they occupied did not seem to allow them enough distance, so they sat with their backs to each other. Each spouse leaned forward to increase the physical separation. Without speaking or making eye contact, they hurriedly recorded their responses. After a few minutes they indicated that they were ready to begin counseling.

Reason for Seeking Therapy

Jeff and Valerie reported wanting to improve their relationship, which was characterized by increased levels of conflict, lessened emotional intimacy and increased dissatisfaction with sexual activity. During the first session they were able to discuss calmly their reasons for seeking therapy. Although they maintained relatively good eye contact with each other and the therapist, their posture continued to reflect an emotional wall between them.

They reported that their entrance into therapy was precipitated by Valerie's discovery that Jeff had misrepresented his membership in a local gym. Prior to joining the athletic program, Jeff was concerned that he was not in tiptop shape. He desired to improve himself (physically and emotionally) and was particularly interested in the gym's aerobics program. Jeff enrolled without discussing it—and the subsequent financial requirements—with Valerie. He signed a contract allowing a monthly deduction from their checking account. However, Jeff quickly lost interest in the gym and stopped going after a month.

When Valerie asked Jeff about the organization that was drafting money from their banking statement, Jeff led her to believe that it was a retirement account that he had established for their future. Several months later Valerie, concerned about their finances because of the impending costs associated with her pregnancy, stopped payment to the account. Because Jeff had signed a contract guaranteeing a two-year membership, the gym turned their case over to a collection agency, which contacted Valerie requesting payment. At that time Valerie discovered Jeff's misrepresentation. She blanched at the nearly two thousand dollars they owed. She felt angry at and betrayed by Jeff, who described feeling embarrassed, frustrated and angry. They were unable to put the offense in the past and avoided discussing the situation, lest they argue. Thus their relationship continued to deteriorate as they reactively distanced themselves emotionally.

Background Information

Jeff and Valerie were gifted students at VCU and had been married for six years at the time they entered counseling. Jeff, a thirty-six-year-old Caucasian male, was pursuing a law degree with plans for a career in corporate law. Valerie, a thirty-three-year-old Caucasian female, was taking courses in preparation for graduate studies in chemistry. Together they had one child, Elizabeth, who was three years old, and were expecting a second.

Valerie, the second of three daughters, was reared in upstate New York. Her older sister committed suicide when Valerie was eighteen years old. Her parents were retired and lived in Arizona. Valerie described her childhood as "relatively happy" and viewed herself as the "responsible one" of the sisters. Valerie was married for the first time when she was twenty-three years old. However, she divorced after a few months because her "husband was emotionally abusive."

Jeff, the second of three sons, was reared in Ohio, where his mother, a retired attorney, and his father, the president of a small bank, remained. As a child, Jeff had a learning disability (dyslexia) and his parents "indulged" him. He described their doting as instrumental in the development of his general sense that "things will turn out fine" and "others will take care of me."

Valerie and Jeff met when both were members of a small music group. Valerie had just divorced her first husband. She and Jeff became friends. After several months of dating they began living together; they were married several years later. They described the first years of their relationship in globally positive terms, noting that they shared many values and interests.

Valerie was reluctant to begin a family, and they waited nearly four years before attempting to get pregnant. In 1995 she became pregnant and gave birth to Elizabeth. A year later Jeff entered law school, and Valerie too began taking classes.

Valerie first noticed difficulties in their relationship when she became pregnant. She began to have less energy and interest in sexual interactions. These difficulties were exacerbated when she became pregnant a second time, two months prior to entering therapy. Jeff attributed the onset of their difficulties to transitions associated with reentering school. He indicated that he would focus on school and "neglect his duties" at home (for example, forgetting to buy groceries or pick up Elizabeth from daycare). Valerie said she felt like she was raising two children: Jeff and their daughter. She also felt jealous of Jeff's career development, because she perceived her career to be "on hold." She felt bitter because she saw herself as the one who made "all the sacrifices" so that Jeff could get a degree.

Initially, Valerie attributed her "trust issues" to Jeff's failure to disclose his involvement with the gymnasium. However, during the fifth session Valerie disclosed (with Jeff's consent) that five years earlier she had discovered Jeff and a mutual female friend (Leigh Anne) in a "passionate" moment while the couples were on a vacation together. She described feeling bewildered and betrayed. After that incident Valerie experienced episodes of depression, and the couple attended five sessions of couples counseling. Both Jeff and Valerie reported that they "worked through" the incident and rarely discussed it.

HOPE-FOCUSED TREATMENT PLAN

The treatment plan of their hope-focused marriage counseling consisted of three stages: encounter, engagement and disengagement.

Encounter Stage

Because hope-focused marriage counseling is predicated on an early, quick assessment of couple functioning, the immediate goal of counseling was (a) to establish rapport with both partners and (b) to assess the "Nine Cs" (central values, core vision, confession and forgiveness, communication, conflict resolution, cognition, closeness, complicating problems and commitment). The assessment was to consist of a clinical interview and a brief assessment battery.

Engagement Stage

The second goal was (a) to help Jeff and Valerie see their difficulties as problems in faith, work and love and (b) to begin to effect change in their relationship by targeting the Nine Cs. Because the hope-focused approach is modular, treatment was tailored to address the couple's presenting concerns. Valerie and Jeff indicated that difficulties in communication and closeness (sexual problems) were most salient, that they shared many central values for their relationship and that their level of commitment to the relationship was strong. Therefore, early sessions were to focus on developing and enhancing communication skills, which would facilitate later discussions about closeness, especially their sexual interactions. Later sessions were to help Valerie and Jeff explore their experiences of conflict resolution, cognition, and confession and forgiveness. As their relationship improved, the topic of termination (or commencement) was to be discussed.

Disengagement Stage

The goal of the final phase of therapy was to consolidate the improvements that Jeff and Valerie had effected. Additionally, after the final session they would complete a posttreatment assessment battery.

COURSE OF TREATMENT

Over six months, Jeff and Valerie participated in thirteen weekly sessions of marital counseling, their final session occurring after a three-week interim. After the first session they canceled or rescheduled six sessions but never missed a session without notification.

Encounter Phase: Sessions One and Two

Delivery. Prior to the first session, two "precounseling" interventions were made. During the call to schedule their initial appointment, Jeff and Valerie were asked to attend to any positive changes in their relationship that might occur prior to the first session. Second, while in the waiting area Jeff and Valerie individually completed a brief assessment battery, which included the Dyadic Adjustment Scale (DAS),[1] three intimacy "thermometers"[2] and two single-item measures of forgiveness.[3]

Valerie's score on the DAS was 99 and Jeff's was 100. Thus, at the time of the first session, Jeff and Valerie were experiencing relationship difficulties sufficient to warrant clinical attention.[4] Their DAS scores, which were consistent with their style of presentation during the first session, indicated that they were experiencing relationship problems that were consistent with those of couples considered "clinically distressed." Additionally, the consistency of their responses were noteworthy and indicated that Jeff and Valerie had similar views of their troubled marriage. Their responses on the intimacy measure indicated that although they felt relatively close emotionally, Valerie and Jeff were experiencing significant distance in their level of sexual intimacy. Both Valerie and Jeff indicated that they desired greater levels of sexual closeness. As with the DAS, they shared similar assessments of the intimacy in their relationship. On the forgiveness scales, both Jeff and Valerie indicated that they had experienced hurtful actions, which led to emotional distance in their relationship. They had not completely resolved the hurtful action that would allow them to move beyond their emotional pain.

In the initial session I aimed to establish rapport and to explore their presenting concerns. I asked both Jeff and Valerie to describe their perceptions of the problems. Additionally, I obtained a history of the couple's relationship, inquiring about positive as well as negative aspects of their marriage. To flesh out the couple's core vision of their marriage, Jeff and Valerie described how each would know when their marriage had improved (that is, the "miracle question").[5]

After the first session, the couple was given the Couple's Precounseling Inventory (CPI),[6] which they completed and returned. The results of the CPI indicated that, as with their scores on other instruments, Jeff and Valerie had similar views of both their problems and their strengths. The problem areas, consistent with those reported in session, included communication, division of household responsibilities and sexual interactions. Both Valerie and Jeff were highly committed to each other and to making their marriage better and shared similar positive assessments of their child-care practices

Valerie and Jeff canceled the second session because Valerie miscarried the night prior to the session. Consequently the feedback session was postponed, and the second session focused on having them discuss their experience of the miscarriage. Valerie and Jeff held hands throughout the session and demonstrated the capacity to respond empathically and comfort each other.

From a hope-focused marriage counseling perspective, Valerie and Jeff's presenting concerns were viewed as problems in faith, work and love. Their greatest area of difficulty appeared to be that of problems in *faith*. Although their commitment to each other appeared high, their sexual problems and problems in communication appeared to be related to violations of trust. Second, in the area of *work*, they seemed to be focusing considerable energy into work and school, which (a) left little energy for working on their marriage aside from parenting and (b) was associated with mutual feelings of neglect. Valerie appeared to desire more emotional, nonsexual connection, whereas Jeff appeared to desire more frequent sexual interactions. Finally, problems in *love* were evident. They sometimes misinterpreted each other's actions as devaluing. For example, when they were discussing their financial situation, Jeff and Valerie justified their respective positions rather than listening empathically. This tendency was most apparent in their sexual interactions and in their inability to communicate and resolve conflict effectively.

Evaluation. When asked whether they had noticed any changes in their relationship prior to the first session, Jeff and Valerie stated that things were unchanged. They generally agreed on the parameters of their problems and were able to discuss their relationship in session without heated exchanges. The flow of the encounter phase was affected by Valerie's miscarriage, which changed the tone of the sessions. For example, during the first session after the miscarriage, their mood was somber and they held hands throughout the session. They remarked that the urgency of resolving their presenting problems had lessened and that they were able to approach each other less defensively. I interpreted this as a positive sign in that they could support each other emotionally (evidencing love and work), and they voiced a renewed commitment to improve their relationship (evidencing work and faith).

Engagement Phase: Sessions Three Through Ten

Delivery. The engagement stage focused on helping Jeff and Valerie systematically address their marital problems. Jeff and Valerie participated in a feedback session; here they received information about their marriage, including a brief report that was given to each partner. Their difficulties were framed as problems in faith, work and love, which led to a deterioration of hope. A copy of the brief report is summarized in table A.1.

Sessions three through six focused primarily on developing communication skills and addressing issues of faith and trust. During these sessions Jeff and Valerie faced each other and alternated speaking and listening roles. The speaking role was developed through Sherod Miller's awareness wheel, which identifies five components of one's experience: sensations, thoughts, feelings, desires and actions. Each spouse used "I statements" to describe his or her experiences. The listening role was facilitated through Miller's listening cycle, which identifies five active listening components: attending, acknowledging, inviting, summarizing and asking questions. (I had received training in the Couples Communication Program[7] from Miller in my previous training in the marital and family therapy master's degree program at Reformed Theological Seminary in Jackson, Mississippi.) The awareness wheel and listening cycle provided structure to the couple's communication as well as increased their ability (a) to identify and communicate accurately their experiences and (b) to empathize with each other. Jeff and Valerie practiced this method of communication in session and identified issues for discussion during homework assignments.

Sessions seven through ten built upon improved communication skills to address issues of closeness. A variety of interventions were used to improve the couple's sexual and emotional intimacy. To improve sexual intimacy I obtained a full sexual history of both Jeff and Valerie to assess for sexual dysfunction and to develop interventions to improve sexual satisfaction. Neither Jeff nor Valerie had sexual difficulties that met DSM-IV criteria. However, Jeff desired sexual

Table A.1. Brief report describing Jeff and Valerie's relationship, provided in session three

CONFIDENTIAL

Jeff and Valerie

Personal Information
Jeff (36) and Valerie (33), married six years, have sought counseling because they want to improve a marriage that has recently been characterized by increased levels of conflict and lessened intimacy. They met approximately ten years ago and have one child, Elizabeth (3).

Relationship Strengths
Jeff and Valerie, you have a multitude of strengths in your marriage. Both of you are intelligent and share similar values about life, people and relationships. You place a high value on cooperation and mutual participation in making decisions about your home life and careers.

Most notably, you each have a high degree of commitment to each other and place a high priority on having your marriage work. You each have invested much into your relationship and appear to value each other. Although you experience periods of disagreement and emotional distance, you seem to have the willingness and energy to negotiate mutually satisfying outcomes. You are both invested in supporting each other's individuality and independence, which means you have the ability to respect each other's views, even when you do not agree.

Another area in which you have tremendous investment and agreement is with Elizabeth. Your relationship with her appears to be a source of happiness and satisfaction for each of you. Because you share similar values on child management, you have little conflict with each other over how you wish to raise your daughter.

Furthermore, you have a similar understanding of your marriage. You have tremendous agreement with each other about strengths as well as areas that need improvement.

Areas for Potential Change
Jeff and Valerie, most relationship difficulties can be related to problems in one or more of the following areas:
☐ love: being willing to value and refusing to devalue each other
☐ work: putting energy into maintaining and improving your relationship
☐ faith: trust in each other and in your ability to resolve differences in mutually satisfying ways

Although you do not appear to engage routinely in actions that openly devalue each other, you sometimes seem to misinterpret each other's actions as devaluing. This is most apparent both in your sexual interactions and in your ability to communicate and resolve conflict effectively, which you both indicate as areas that you would like to improve.

Each of you focuses considerable energy on your career. Because demands from work and school are extensive at this time, your ability to focus on each other has been diminished. You indicate feeling neglected by each other. Valerie, this appears to be evident in your desire for emotional connection with Jeff, whereas, Jeff, this appears to be evident in your desire for more frequent sexual interactions.

Your greatest difficulty appears to be problems in faith. Although your commitment to each other is high, your trust in each other has been shaken. You each identified how past events make it difficult to trust openly and to be emotionally available to each other.

Suggestions for Improving Your Relationship
Jeff and Valerie, a key to improving your marriage will be developing a "partner-centered" heart or mindset. Strengthening love involves valuing each other more and devaluing each other less. It also requires effort by both partners and faith that you each have the best interests of your relationship foremost in your minds.

You identified several goals for resolving your marital difficulties. When asked how you would know when your relationship was better, you indicated that you would resolve conflict positively, communicate better and improve your sexual intimacy. In your ideal marriage, you would like to discuss your thoughts and feelings without feeling criticized or misunderstood. You both want to feel acknowledged and appreciated for your unique points of view. One way to accomplish this is, whenever you disagree, to make sure your partner feels understood before you express your own opinion. It will also help to resist using "you" statements in disagreements and instead stick to "I feel . . ." or "I think . . ." statements. Ideally, you would both like to show more patience with each other and feel more understood and appreciated for the efforts you put into the relationship.

As you work to understand your partner's experience, you will learn new ways to value each other. You will have the opportunity to "try on" several techniques to improve your ability to communicate and to resolve conflict in relationship-enhancing ways. You will have the opportunity to discuss specifics to improve the intimacy you feel emotionally and sexually.

Furthermore, you will gain insight into how past actions have intentionally and unintentionally devalued each other. In all emotionally important relationships, partners hurt one another. You will be given the opportunity to put your hurtful actions into the past by exploring the role of forgiveness in your relationship.

Summary

Valerie and Jeff, you have a special relationship and appear well-suited for each other. You appear to love each other and share many common values. You appear to have the commitment and willingness to work on your marriage even through the hard times still to come. You have both expressed a great deal of love for each other that can be enhanced by efforts to achieve a partner-centered focus and to value one another more actively.

Although you both identified problems in your marriage, these problems can be resolved *if you are willing to work hard on your marriage*. The lasting changes in your marriage depend largely on how hard you are willing to work and on whether you are able and willing to cherish one another in many ways. I encourage you to draw on the investments you have made in each other to help you to *work with high energy on your marriage*. Your marriage will be successful to the extent that you put the effort into continuing to strengthen it.
Terry L. Hight, M.S., M.A.
Practicum Therapist

---

intercourse more frequently than did Valerie. They appeared entrenched in an "emotional pursuer-distancer" interactional pattern,[8] in which Jeff initiated sexual intercourse and Valerie determined when the couple would have sex. Valerie rarely initiated sexual interaction and frequently declined Jeff's advances. Although he would feel rejected, he would increase his efforts at pursuing Valerie sexually.

This pattern was addressed on three levels. First, a metaphor of a "soft-drink machine versus a slot machine" was used to name the couple's pattern of initiating sexual intercourse. At present, requesting sex was as variable as a slot machine. Both desired a "soft-drink machine" love life, in which they could depend on each other's responses to their requests. Second, the couple was asked to agree in advance on a time for them to have sexual interactions. This intervention allowed Jeff to decrease his advances and allowed Valerie not to feel as if every caress from Jeff was an invitation for sexual intercourse. Finally, the couple used active listening to express emotional experiences surrounding sexual interactions, namely Jeff's feeling of rejection and Valerie's feelings of emotional neglect.

Three interventions were used to improve emotional intimacy. First, a "scaling" technique was used to have Jeff and Valerie demonstrate the level of intimacy each felt. In this technique, the couple used the physical space in the therapy room as a gross scale representing closeness. Jeff and Valerie identified their perceptions of closeness at various periods in their relationship. This intervention (like the pursuer-distancer intervention discussed above) also examined the couple's cognition about their relationship. Second, John Gottman's[9] research on couples was discussed along with the concept of the love bank.[10] Each spouse identified positive behaviors that he or she would like the partner to perform. Gottman's research suggests that couples who maintain a 5:1 ratio of positive interactions to negative interactions tend to have lasting relationships. Jeff and Valerie practiced "valuing" behaviors at home and reported the effects in subsequent sessions. Finally, Richard S. Stuart's caring day intervention[11] was discussed, and they set aside one day as a "caring" day. On this day a partner did as many valuing behaviors as he or she could for the other.

Sessions eleven and twelve were used to reevaluate progress in therapy and to address issues of confession and forgiveness. Jeff and Valerie reported significant improvements in their relationship, and an empathy-humility-commitment (or pyramid) model of forgiveness[12] was briefly discussed as a way to put and keep hurtful actions in the past. Jeff and Valerie prepared for a forgiveness session, in which each confessed prior offenses and apologized for previous hurts.[13]

Session transcript. The following excerpt is from session ten, in which the "scaling" technique was discussed. The intervention is designed to provide the couple with a concrete representation of the closeness by using the physical space of the office to represent their intimacy. This intervention also helps the couple to identify ways to increase their closeness. The excerpt begins with all parties seated in a nine-by-twelve-foot room (J = Jeff, V = Valerie and T = Terry).

T: I'd like for you to think of this room from here [counselor stands near a wall] to here [counselor moves to the opposite wall] as being a gauge of how close you feel. If one of you were standing right here [counselor stands at wall] and the other at that wall, that would be as far away as you could possibly feel. And if you both were standing right here in the middle [counselor stands in the middle of the room], perhaps hugging, that would be as close as you could feel. And, thinking along those lines, why don't you guys stand up and . . . *[Hope-focused marriage counseling attempts to find concrete ways for couples to think about both their current relationship and how their relationship might be when improved. Here I attempted to have Jeff and Valerie become physically active in session and to have them think about the closeness in their relationship.]*

J: You mean like the center being close.

T: As you stand up and face one another.

J: Oh, I see. [J and V stand and face one another.]

V: So, if we're both standing here and hugging, that would be close.

T: Yeah, and if you were at opposite walls, that would be emotionally distant. [They face one another in the center of the room, standing approximately five feet apart.] And so, right now, this moment, how close do you feel to one another? [Brief pause.]

V: Well, what if I really feel close to him and he didn't feel close to me? [V laughs nervously.]

T: Oh, you are so insightful. That is what this is supposed to get at. *[Couple has spoken in previous sessions about their differing views about how they manage intimacy. This intervention allows them to discuss this issue directly. V's comment and nervous laughter appear to be because of (a) the change in therapy format and the novelty of the intervention and (b) a recognition of an uncomfortable issue.]*

V: OK.

T: You're doing very well. [Brief pause.] So how close? [J stands in the middle of the room. V stands on her "side" of the room approximately four feet from J. Both smile.]

V: [Directed to J] Well, then, get over here.

J: [J looks down at the floor as if to assess the dimensions of the room.] I was waiting on you to come over here . . . [to himself] You always make me . . .

V: Oh, oh . . . [Each steps toward the other and they embrace each other in a hug.]

T: OK, hmmm. Standing right there, you [J] said something interesting. . . . *[In the opening moments of the intervention, the couple represents concretely two dynamics of their relationship: a sense of inequity of emotional investment and the tendency to avoid emotionally laden issues. J stands in the center of the room, while V is on her side. Each wishes the other would take the first step to move closer.]*

V: [interrupts] Oh, I don't think it's perfect yet. [V takes two very small steps backward and they continue to hold hands.] OK.

T: OK. Right here, the way that you are now, does this capture it for you [V]? Would you move J back? Would you move back? *[Therapist wishes to assess each partner's perception of closeness.]*

V: I think this is pretty good.

T: So, that pretty much captures it. OK. J, from your standpoint, would you change anything about this?

J: No, I think this captures it.

T: OK. *[Couple now has a baseline, upon which they agree and from which they can discuss issues of closeness in their relationship.]* You said something earlier, "I've gone halfway." [V laughs nervously.]

J: Oh, well. No, I guess it's a matter of, well, I don't want to step in the middle if you're not going to.

V: Oh, OK.

T: Say more about that. Is that something that applies in general, perhaps? [pause] *[Therapist is attempting to obviate hope-focused marriage counseling's goal of making relationship dynamics concrete.]*

V: Yeah. [Both laugh.]

T: Say more about that. Tell me about it.

V: Well, I think we've discussed this before. But, like, when we're having problems, we both sulk like children in our little corners . . . and it's usually me who comes forward first and I know I have to do it because he's not going to do it. *[Couple realizes this is a pattern in their relationship. In later sessions, the couple would reference a change in this pattern as evidence that they are improving their relationship.]*

T: OK.

V: I mean that's not why I do it. It's uncomfortable and I want to resolve it. But . . . I always sense that J's not going to . . . like . . . put his neck out there really.

T: OK. Very good. It sounds like you've noticed a difference between the times when you're like today—not a lot of conflict—and the times when there is conflict. I want to get to that in just a second. I'm curious as to how it might be if you could have it exactly like you want. *[I was at a choice point. I had three goals for this portion of the intervention. The first goal was to have them see and discuss their marriage in concrete terms. The second goal was to have them discuss how they might like for it to be. The third goal was to have them see that marital intimacy ebbs and flows and that they could effect changes in their intimacy level by what they focus on.]*

V: Well, it'd be more like this. [V takes two steps to J and they embrace for several seconds.]

J: That's nice.

T: J, would you change anything about that, or is that pretty much . . .

J: Hmmm. Good. *[J and V embrace and smile genuinely. They seem to be interacting in a manner different—and more positive—from when they entered therapy.]*

V: Or would this be just as good if you'd come over here? [V takes two steps back and pulls J to embrace her.]

J: [backing up] You made me come over to your side.

T: Say more about that. What about that move right there? *[Jeff and Valerie have an opportunity to discuss a dynamic in their relationship, which is a difference in the perceived level of work in the relationship.]*

V: Well, I was just kinda, just talking . . . responding to what we were talking about earlier. This is good [V stands next to J] and so is this [she takes two steps back and pulls J closer].

J: [to V] Oh, I mean . . . so like pressing out a little bit further, right? You mean venturing.

V: Yeah, maybe it was an equity thing too. Like, you know, can we be as close when things aren't ideal for you? I mean can we have that feeling?

T: So, how can you move toward each other in ways that would be well received by the other? [To J] Sounds like you were concerned about stepping into that area.

J: Yeah, sort of not sure exactly what to do.

T: Let's try something a bit different with this. Go back to a time when you first married. How close was it then? Represent that right here. *[Begin working on establishing a positive experience in therapy as well as focus them on what first attracted them to each other.]* [J and V move to each other and embrace for a brief period.]

T: All right. Now, think of a time when you had your first conflict. Your first time of real disagreement. How did it feel then? What would change? *[I wanted the couple to focus on a negative time in their relationship so that they could see that intimacy ebbs and flows.]*

V: I don't even know what it was.

J: I don't remember what it was either . . . but I can understand [J steps back 3 feet.]

T: All right, go back to a time of conflict. It may not have been the first or
      the most recent, and agree on what that time is. Represent that time right
      now. [pause]

J: Well, the worst would be with Leigh Anne.

V: Yeah, that's true. [V moves to the far wall.] Can't get far enough back.

T: OK. So you [V] would back way up pretty much to the wall. J, what about
      you?

J: Um. [pause] I'm not really sure.

V: Actually, I think I would be doing a two-step against the wall and going,
      um [V steps away from the wall and back several times].

T: Leigh Anne? Talk more about the situation. *[This is a major issue in their
      relationship—and the first time in therapy that they have used the woman's
      name. The incident represented a major violation of faith in their relationship.
      This broaching of the topic leads to discussions in future sessions of forgiveness
      and reconciliation.]*

V: That was the girl I caught J with.

T: So that was a time when you could not feel farther away from each other.
      And how did it move back to a time when you were more like you were
      when you started this thing today?

V: I don't know.

J: I guess it was a while . . . it was a while. But I think . . . um . . . one thing
      was a pragmatic concern about having a family. So I think that caused us
      to pull together. We went to France and were blissed out after that . . . V
      got pregnant a couple of months later.

T: So there was a lot going on, it sounds like, at that time. And it sounds like
      a period of a fair amount of distance emotionally. *[On later reflection, I
      probably missed a good opportunity by not asking what they did that "blissed
      them out." That could have led into a discussion about how to be more
      intimate.]* Go back to the time when you first came in [for counseling].
      This was shortly after you discovered the financial situation with the
      gymnasium, and that was the thing that drove you guys here. How would
      you represent that picture—how close you felt at that time? [Pause.
      Couple moves to stand approximately seven feet apart.] *[This issue of the
      gym is another issue of faith violation. This issue was strategically selected by
      the therapist so that presenting concerns could be linked to future discussions
      of putting the hurts in the past.]*

V: I guess this is a good spot.

J: I think that maybe just a little, well, closer.

T: This may be an odd question, but who typically moves? [pause] *[I attempted to focus their attention on their patterns of reconciliation in a concrete way.]*

V: I think I'm the mover. Usually . . . I think.

T: [To J] How do you get V to move closer to you? [pause] *[I attempt to get the couple to see that although Valerie is typically the emotional pursuer and seeker of emotional reconciliation, Jeff's actions affect Valerie's patterns.]*

T: Building on this concept we've been discussing in counseling of valuing and refusing to devalue, do you see it as having a direct bearing on the closeness that you feel? What could you say to each other that would communicate to your partner that you value them? Even right here today. In other words, if I gave you a task and your goal is to end up in the middle of the room hugging one another, what would you say to bring you together? *[I again hit the concept of love and empathically appreciating each other's experience.]*

J: Um, I think one thing is . . . mutually valuing each other's struggles. Particularly now with each other being in school.

V: Yeah, that's what it is—valuing the other person's struggles.

T: I think that's great, getting into your partner's mind and heart. With that, let's try something. J, say something to V that you value about her. *[I try to get the couple to see that they become more intimate by focusing on the positive aspects of each other and their relationship. I also wanted them to see that small sensible and tangible changes can and do have positive ramifications.]*

J: [pause] Well, I'm thinking . . . well, I value the way you hold down the fort . . . like with all the insurance paperwork. I appreciate all that.

V: My turn? I really value what you do with Elizabeth. You're a great dad.

T: How close do you feel right now? [Each takes a step toward the other.]

Jeff and Valerie took turns saying positive things to each other. After each interaction they moved closer to each other, reflecting the increasing positive emotions that they felt. As the intervention ended, Jeff and Valerie tearfully stood embracing each other in the middle of the room.

Evaluation. Jeff and Valerie responded well to the feedback session. They commented that describing their presenting concerns as problems in faith, work and love captured the gist of their problems and "made sense [to them]." (Neither partner considered himself or herself a Christian, but neither partner was put off by the word *faith*.) They resonated most with the concept of valuing and refusing to devalue as a way to increase their love.

Because both had identified communication as problematic, Jeff and Valerie were motivated to work on improving their communication skills. Valerie noted that although she liked the concept of empathic listening, she found the speaking portion of the awareness wheel to be too cumbersome for practical use. Thus rather than using the entire wheel, the couple used "I statements" to express thoughts, feelings and desires.

The couple said they had significantly improved in their communication and closeness during the middle portion of the engagement phase. The tone of their sessions improved relative to the initial sessions, and the couple could speak nondefensively and playfully laugh during session.

Disengagement Phase: Sessions Eleven Through Thirteen

Delivery. The possibility of commencement was discussed in session eleven, when Jeff and Valerie reflected on their progress in counseling. During session twelve they indicated that they had reached their goals for counseling and were ready for termination. Specifically, they noted that they (a) were able to communicate and resolve conflict effectively, (b) felt closer emotionally and sexually and (c) felt hopeful about the future of their marriage. They also noted that Valerie was again pregnant.

A final session was scheduled after a three-week interim. Jeff and Valerie used the interim to discuss their relationship and the progress they had made in therapy and to represent that progress symbolically in a physical memorial. Jeff was excited about the idea. They were asked to bring the symbol with them to their final session.

During the final session both Jeff and Valerie reiterated their readiness to end counseling. They reported continued ability to communicate and resolve conflict. Although they noted that their schedules were more hectic and they felt somewhat less close that they had a month earlier, they were not alarmed by this and had adjusted their schedules to ensure acceptable feelings of closeness. They symbolized the improvement in their relationship by taking two marble slabs and leaning them on each other in the shape of an inverted V. They said that this memorial represented their renewed trust in each other and also symbolized the shelter of their marriage, to which they could turn during difficult times. Both Jeff and Valerie tearfully spoke words of confession and apology during the final session.

Evaluation. Valerie and Jeff's relationship had improved significantly since the initial sessions of therapy. This improvement did not appear to be a "flight into health." They had several disagreements throughout the course of therapy, but the manner in which they resolved the issues suggested that they were indeed ready for commencement. Specifically, they had been able to resolve the issues without falling into old patterns of resentment and withdrawal. Jeff and Valerie could apologize and seek forgiveness. They appeared to understand that forgiveness is a choice and reconciliation, a process. They were willing to work on their marriage through the final session, as evidenced by their return for the final session, the monument symbolizing their relationship and the willingness to seek forgiveness.

Overall Evaluation of Jeff and Valerie's Progress

Formal. Jeff and Valerie completed a brief assessment battery prior to the first session. After the final session, they completed a posttherapy assessment battery to measure their improvements. They demonstrated significant improvement in their relationship adjustment at the time of termination. Jeff's DAS score improved from 100 (clinically distressed) at the initial session to 121 at termination. Valerie's DAS score improved from 99 (clinically distressed) at the initial session to 122 at termination. Additionally, the couple's emotional intimacy and sexual intimacy scores on the intimacy thermometers moved closer to their ideals at termination than they had been at intake. Finally, Jeff's score on the single-item measure of forgiveness indicated that he had been able to put hurtful actions into the past (6/6 on the measure). Likewise, Valerie's score on the forgiveness measure improved from 4/6 at the initial session to 5/6 at termination.

Informal. Additionally, Jeff and Valerie's progress was monitored throughout the therapeutic process. From the first session, they began thinking about how they would know when their marriage had improved. They began to report improvement in their relationship beginning with the sixth session. Jeff reported increased awareness of his tendency to withdraw defensively during periods of conflict. He noted that he was able to express his feelings directly rather than withdraw. The first improvements in their sexual relationship were reported in session eight. Valerie reported that she had initiated sexual intercourse rather than Jeff. She attributed her increased desire to Jeff's increased attention to her and his performing household responsibilities. In a subsequent session, they reported having sexual intercourse approximately twice weekly (improved from less than once a month, which they had reported at intake). Valerie described an increased level of trust in Jeff as well as a decreased level of hurt and resentment. By session twelve they reported being able to quickly resolve minor disagreements in mutually satisfying ways, without global, stable and negative attributions about their relationship.

Notes

Chapter 1: Brief Marital Counseling

[1]Matthew 5:31-32; 19:5; Luke 16:18; 1 Corinthians 6:16; 7:1-39; Ephesians 5:25-33; 1 Timothy 5:14; Hebrews 13:4.

[2]I have elected to use the words *counseling* and *counselor* instead of *therapy* and *therapist*. I treat counseling as a more general category that includes therapy. Many professionals might disagree, preferring to define therapy as treatment that is appropriate for more serious disturbances than is counseling. I regard hope-focused marriage counseling as applicable to couples who have a wide range of serious and not-so-serious marital troubles.

[3]Everett L. Worthington Jr., "Marriage Counseling: A Christian Approach," *Journal of Psychology and Christianity* 13 (1994): 166-73; Everett L. Worthington Jr., "Marriage Counseling: A Christian Approach," in *Christian Marital Counseling: Eight Approaches to Helping Couples*, ed. Everett L. Worthington Jr. (Grand Rapids, Mich.: Baker, 1996), pp. 159-85.

[4]T. M. Hammonds and Everett L. Worthington Jr., "The Effect of Facilitator Utterances on Participant Responses in a Brief ACME-Type Marriage Enrichment Group," *American Journal of Family Therapy* 13, no. 2 (1985): 39-49; Everett L. Worthington Jr., B. G. Buston and T. M. Hammonds, "A Component Analysis of Marriage Enrichment: Information and Treatment Modality," *Journal of Counseling and Development* 62 (1989): 555-60; Everett L. Worthington Jr., Terry L. Hight, Jennifer S. Ripley, Kristin M. Perrone, Taro A. Kurusu and Dawn R. Jones, "Strategic Hope-Focused Relationship-Enrichment Counseling with Individual Couples," *Journal of Counseling Psychology* 44 (1997): 381-89; Everett L. Worthington Jr. et al., "Can Marital Assessment and Feedback Improve Marriages? Assessment as a Brief Marital Enrichment Procedure," *Journal of Counseling Psychology* 42 (1995): 466-75.

[5]"Mental Health: Does Therapy Help?" *Consumer Reports*, November 1995, pp. 734-40.

[6]J. F. Alexander, A. Holtzworth-Munroe and P. Jameson, "The Process and Outcome of Marital and Family Therapy: Research Review and Evaluation," in *Handbook of Psychotherapy and Behavior Change*, 4th ed., ed. Allen E. Bergin and Sol L. Garfield (New York: Wiley, 1994), pp. 595-630; R. Bean and D. R. Crane, "Marriage and Family Therapy Research with Ethnic Minorities: Current Status," *American Journal of Family Therapy* 24 (1996): 3-8; J. H. Bray and E. N. Jouriles, "Treatment of Marital Conflict and Prevention of Divorce," *Journal of Marital and Family Therapy* 21 (1995): 461-73; R. L. Dunn and A. I. Schwebel, "Meta-analytic Review of Marital Therapy Outcome Research," *Journal of Family Psychology* 9 (1995): 58-68; A. S. Gurman and N. S. Jacobson, "Therapy with Couples: A Coming of Age," in *Clinical Handbook of Couple Therapy*, ed. N. S. Jacobson and A. S. Gurman (New York: Guilford, 1995), pp. 1-10; N. S. Jacobson and M. E. Addis, "Research on Couple Therapy: What Do We Know? Where Are We Going?" *Journal of Consulting and Clinical Psychology* 61 (1993): 85-93; B. R. Karney and T. N. Bradbury, "The Longitudinal Course of Marital Quality and Stability: A Review of Theory, Method and Research," *Psychological Bulletin* 118 (1995): 3-34; J. L. Lebow and A. S. Gurman, "Research Assessing Couple and Family Therapy," *Annual Review of Psychology* 46 (1995): 27-57; W. M. Pinsof and L. C. Wynne, "The Effectiveness and Efficacy of Marital and Family Therapy: An Introduction to the Special Issue," *Journal of Marital and Family Therapy* 21 (1995): 341-43; W. M. Pinsof and L. C. Wynne, "The Efficacy of Marital and Family Therapy: An Empirical Overview, Conclusions and Recommendations," *Journal of Marital and Family Therapy* 21 (1995): 585-613; S. E. Prince and N. S. Jacobson, "A Review and Evaluation of Marital and Family Therapies for Affective Disorders," *Journal of Marital and Family Therapy* 21 (1995): 377-401; W. R. Shadish, K. Ragsdale, R. R. Glaser and L. M. Montgomery, "The Efficacy and Effectiveness of Marital and Family Therapy: A Perspective

from Meta-analysis," *Journal of Marital and Family Therapy* 21 (1995): 345-60.

[7]Everett L. Worthington Jr. and H. DeVries, "Individual, Marital and Family Therapy: Empirical, Pragmatic and Value Considerations," *Journal of Couple Therapy* 1 (1990): 77-90.

[8]A. S. Gurman and D. P. Kniskern, "Family Therapy Outcome Research: Knowns and Unknowns," in *Handbook of Family Therapy*, ed. Alan S. Gurman and David P. Kniskern (New York: Brunner/Mazel, 1981), pp. 742-75; A. S. Gurman and D. P. Kniskern, "Commentary: Individual Marital Therapy—Have Reports of Your Death Been Somewhat Exaggerated?" *Family Process* 25 (1986): 51-62; R. A. Wells and V. J. Gianetti, "Individual Marital Therapy: A Critical Reappraisal," *Family Process* 25 (1986): 43-51; R. A. Wells and V. J. Gianetti, "Rejoinder: Whither Marital Therapy?" *Family Process* 25 (1986): 62-65.

[9]V. Shoham, M. Rohrbaugh and J. Patterson, "Problem- and Solution-Focused Couple Therapies: The MRI and Milwaukee Models," in *Clinical Handbook of Couple Therapy*, ed. Neil S. Jacobson and Alan S. Gurman (New York: Guilford, 1995), pp. 142-63.

[10]N. S. Jacobson and G. Margolin, *Marital Therapy: Strategies Based on Social Learning and Behavior Exchange Principles* (New York: Brunner/Mazel, 1979).   .

[11]D. A. Bagarozzi, *The Couple and Family in Managed Care: Assessment, Evaluation and Treatment* (New York: Brunner/Mazel, 1996); Bruce Ecker and Laurel Hulley, *Depth Oriented Brief Therapy: How to Be Brief When You Were Trained to Be Deep—And Vice Versa* (San Francisco: Jossey-Bass, 1996); Michael F. Hoyt, *Brief Therapy and Managed Care: Readings for Contemporary Practice* (San Francisco: Jossey-Bass, 1995); Harville Hendrix, *Getting the Love You Want* (New York: Harper, 1988); Wade Luquet, *Short-Term Couples Therapy: The Imago Model in Action* (New York: Brunner/Mazel, 1996); Gary J. Oliver, M. Hasz and M. Richburg, *Promoting Change Through Brief Therapy in Christian Counseling* (Wheaton, Ill.: Tyndale House, 1998); Gene Pekarik, *Psychotherapy Abbreviation: A Practical Guide* (New York: Haworth, 1996); Ellen K. Quick, *Doing What Works in Brief Therapy: A Strategic Solution Focused Approach* (San Diego: Academic Press, 1996); Michelle Weiner-Davis, *Divorce Busting: A Revolutionary and Rapid Program for Staying Together* (New York: Simon & Schuster, 1992).

[12]M. P. Koss and J. Shiang, "Research on Brief Psychotherapy," in *Handbook of Psychotherapy and Behavior Change*, ed. Allen E. Bergin and Sol L. Garfield, 4th ed. (New York: Wiley, 1994), pp. 664-700.

[13]Simon H. Budman and Alan S. Gurman, *Theory and Practice of Brief Therapy* (New York: Guilford, 1988); Bagarozzi, *The Couple and Family in Managed Care*; Quick, *Doing What Works in Brief Therapy*.

[14]D. Shapiro, M. Barkham, G. Hardy and L. Morrison, "The Second Sheffield Psychotherapy Project: Rationale, Design and Preliminary Outcome Data," *British Journal of Medical Psychology* 63 (1990): 97-108; M. Talmon, *Single Session Therapy: Maximizing the Effect of the First (and Often Only) Therapeutic Encounter* (San Francisco: Jossey-Bass, 1990).

[15]Everett L. Worthington Jr., ed., *Christian Marital Counseling: Eight Approaches to Helping Couples* (Grand Rapids, Mich.: Baker, 1996).

[16]J. S. Ripley and Everett L. Worthington Jr., "Exploring Christian Marital Counseling," in *Christian Marital Counseling: Eight Approaches to Helping Couples*, ed. Everett L. Worthington Jr. (Grand Rapids, Mich.: Baker, 1996), pp. 211-40.

[17]Koss and Shiang, "Research on Brief Psychotherapy," pp. 664-700.

[18]G. Oliver and H. N. Wright, "Solution-Based Brief Therapy: One Approach to Helping Couples Change," *Marriage and Family: A Christian Journal* 1 (1997): 17-27; Dan B. Allender, "Commentary on Oliver and Wright," *Marriage and Family: A Christian Journal* 1 (1997): 28-30; K. J. Edwards, "Commentary on Oliver and Wright," *Marriage and Family: A Christian Journal* 1 (1997): 33-35; Ruby M. Friesen and DeLoss Friesen, "Commentary on Oliver and Wright," *Marriage and Family: A Christian Journal* 1 (1997): 31-32; G. Oliver and H. N.Wright, "The Authors Respond," *Marriage and Family: A Christian Journal* 1 (1997): 36-37.

[19]Kenneth I. Howard, Mark Kopta and David E. Orlinsky, "The Dose-Effect Relationship in Psychotherapy," *American Psychologist* 41 (1986): 159-64.

[20]Jay Haley, *Ordeal Therapy: Unusual Ways to Change Behavior* (San Francisco: Jossey-Bass, 1984).

[21]Neil S. Jacobson and Andrew Christensen, *Integrative Couple Therapy: Promoting Acceptance and Change* (New York: W. W. Norton, 1996).

[22]Everett L. Worthington Jr., *Marriage Counseling: A Christian Approach to Counseling Couples* (Downers Grove, Ill.: InterVarsity Press, 1989).

[23]Jennifer S. Ripley and Everett L. Worthington Jr., "What the Journals Reveal About Christian Marital Counseling: An Inadequate (but Emerging) Scientific Base," *Marriage and Family: A Christian Journal* 1 (1998): 375-96.

Chapter 2: Bird's-Eye View of Hope-Focused Marriage Counseling

[1]J. F. Alexander, A. Holtzworth-Munroe and P. Jameson, "The Process and Outcome of Marital and Family Therapy: Research Review and Evaluation," in *Handbook of Psychotherapy and Behavior Change*, ed. Allen E. Bergin and Sol L. Garfield, 4th ed., (New York: Wiley, 1994), pp. 595-630.

[2]A. S. Gurman and D. P. Kniskern, "Family Therapy Outcome Research: Knowns and Unknowns," in *Handbook of Family Therapy*, ed. Alan S. Gurman and David P. Kniskern (New York: Brunner/Mazel, 1981), pp. 742-75; Stanley R. Strong, "Counseling: An Interpersonal Influence Approach," *Journal of Counseling Psychology* 15 (1968): 215-24.

[3]G. B. Spanier, "Measuring Dyadic Adjustment: New Scales for Assessing the Quality of Marriage and Similar Dyads," *Journal of Marriage and the Family* 38 (1976): 15-28; G. B. Spanier and E. E. Filsinger, "The Dyadic Adjustment Scale," in *Marriage and Family Assessment: A Sourcebook for Family Therapy*, ed. Erik E. Filsinger (Beverly Hills, Calif.: Sage, 1983), pp. 156-68.

[4]N. S. Jacobson, W. C. Follette and D. Revenstorf, "Psychotherapy Outcome Research: Methods for Reporting Variability and Estimating Clinical Significance," *Behavior Therapy* 15 (1984): 336-52.

[5]"Mental Health: Does Therapy Help?" *Consumer Reports*, November 1995, pp. 734-40.

[6]C. R. Snyder, *The Psychology of Hope: You Can Get There from Here* (New York: Free Press, 1994).

[7]Gabriel Marcel, *Homo Viator: An Introduction to the Metaphysics of Hope* (New York: Harper & Row, 1962).

[8]C. S. Lewis uses this analogy in a letter to Vanauken, in Sheldon Vanauken, *A Severe Mercy* (New York: Bantam, 1979).

[9]Gary W. Moon, *Homesick for Eden: Confessions About the Journey of a Soul* (Atlanta: LifeSprings Resources, 1996).

[10]M. Rohrbaugh, V. Shoham, C. Spungen and P. Steinglass, "A Systematic Couples Therapy for Problem Drinking," in *Foundations of Psychotherapy: Theory, Research and Practice*, ed. B. Bongar and L. Beutler (London: Oxford University Press, 1995), pp. 228-53; V. Shoham, M. Rohrbaugh and J. Patterson, "Problem- and Solution-Focused Couple Therapies: The MRI and Milwaukee Models," in *Clinical Handbook of Couple Therapy*, ed. Neil S. Jacobson and Alan S. Gurman (New York: Guilford, 1995), pp. 142-63; Paul Watzlawick, Janet Beavin Bavelas and Don D. Jackson, *Pragmatics of Human Communication: A Study of Interactional Patterns, Pathologies and Paradoxes* (New York: W. W. Norton, 1967); Paul Watzlawick, J. H. Weakland and R. Fisch, *Change: Principles of Problem Formation and Problem Resolution* (New York: W. W. Norton, 1974).

[11]S. de Shazer, *Clues: Investigating Solutions in Brief Therapy* (New York: W. W. Norton, 1988).

[12]Leslie S. Greenberg and Susan M. Johnson, *Emotionally Focused Therapy for Couples* (New York: Guilford, 1988); Susan M. Johnson, *The Practice of Emotionally Focused Marital Therapy: Creating Connection* (New York: Brunner/Mazel, 1996).

[13]See Everett L. Worthington Jr. and D. McMurry, *Marriage Conflicts* (Grand Rapids, Mich.: Baker, 1999).

[14]Josh McDowell, *Evidence That Demands a Verdict* (San Bernadino, Calif.: Campus Crusade for Christ, 1972).

[15]John Mordechai Gottman, *What Predicts Divorce: The Relationship Between Marital Processes and Marital Outcomes* (Hillsdale, N.J.: Lawrence Erlbaum, 1994).

[16]Everett L. Worthington Jr., et. al., "Can Marital Assessment and Feedback Improve Marriages? Assessment as a Brief Marital Enrichment Procedure," *Journal of Counseling Psychology* 42 (1995): 466-75.

[17]D. G. Benner, *Strategic Pastoral Counseling* (Grand Rapids, Mich.: Baker, 1992).

[18]Worthington et. al., "Can Marital Assessment and Feedback Improve Marriages?" pp. 466-75.

[19]I originally picked up the idea of such tailored interventions from behavioral marital therapy.

[20]E. A. Locke, "Motivation Through Conscious Goal Setting," *Applied and Preventive Psychology* 5 (1996): 117-24.

[21]Worthington and McMurry, *Marriage Conflicts.*

Chapter 3: Using the Strategy to Promote Hope

[1]Mike Mason, *The Mystery of Marriage: Iron Sharpens Iron* (Portland, Ore.: Multnomah Press, 1985).

[2]See Everett L. Worthington Jr., ed., *Psychotherapy and Religious Values* (Grand Rapids, Mich.: Baker, 1993), for several discussions of religious values and their inclusion (or not) in counseling.

[3]D. H. Baucom and N. Epstein, *Cognitive Behavioral Marital Therapy* (New York: Brunner/Mazel, 1990).

[4]John Mordechai Gottman, *What Predicts Divorce: The Relationship Between Marital Processes and Marital Outcomes* (Hillsdale, N.J.: Lawrence Erlbaum, 1994).

[5]Everett L. Worthington Jr., *Marriage Counseling: A Christian Approach to Counseling Couples* (Downers Grove, Ill.: InterVarsity Press, 1989).

[6]Larry Crabb, *Understanding People: Deep Longings for Relationship* (Grand Rapids, Mich.: Zondervan, 1988).

[7]S. M. Johnson and L. S. Greenberg, "The Emotionally Focused Approach to Problems in Adult Attachment," in *Clinical Handbook of Couple Therapy,* ed. Neil S. Jacobson and Alan S. Gurman (New York: Guilford, 1995), pp. 121-41.

[8]C. Hazan and P. Shaver, "Conceptualizing Romantic Love as an Attachment Process," *Journal of Personality and Social Psychology* 52 (1987): 511-24; C. Hazan and P. Shaver, "Attachment as an Organizational Framework for Research on Close Relationships," *Psychological Inquiry* 5 (1994): 1-22; R. J. Paterson and G. Moran, "Attachment Theory: Personality Development and Psychotherapy," *Clinical Psychology Review* 8 (1989): 611-36; C. Hazan, P. Shaver and D. Bradshaw, "Love as Attachment," in *The Psychology of Love,* ed. R. J. Sternberg and M. L. Barnes (New Haven, Conn.: Yale University Press, 1988), pp. 68-99.

[9]G. Lynch and U. Staubli, "Possible Contributions of Long-Term Potentiation to the Encoding and Organization of Memory," *Brain Research Reviews* 16 (1991): 204-6; G. E. Matt, C. Vazquez and W. K. Campbell, "Mood-Congruent Recall of Affectively Toned Stimuli: A Meta-analytic Review," *Clinical Psychology Review* 12 (1992): 227-55.

[10]Gottman, *What Predicts Divorce.*

[11]V. Shoham, M. Rohrbaugh and J. Patterson, "Problem- and Solution-Focused Couple Therapies: The MRI and Milwaukee Models," in *Clinical Handbook of Couple Therapy,* ed. Neil S. Jacobson and Alan S. Gurman (New York: Guilford, 1995), pp. 142-63.

[12]Gottman, *What Predicts Divorce.*

[13]P. J. Guerin Jr., L. F. Fay, S. L. Burden and J. G. Kautto, *The Evaluation and Treatment of Marital Conflict: A Four-Stage Approach* (New York: BasicBooks, 1987); Gottman, *What Predicts Divorce;* Baucom and Epstein, *Cognitive Behavioral Marital Therapy.*

[14]Gottman, *What Predicts Divorce.*

[15]Ibid.

[16]W. F. Harley Jr., *His Needs, Her Needs: Building an Affair-Proof Marriage* (Grand Rapids, Mich.: Revell, 1994); W. F. Harley Jr., *Love Busters: Overcoming the Habits That Destroy Romantic Love* (Tarrytown, N.Y.: Revell, 1992).

[17]Everett L. Worthington Jr. and D. McMurry, *Marriage Conflicts* (Grand Rapids, Mich.: Baker, 1994).

[18]DeLoss D. Friesen and Ruby M. Friesen, *Counseling and Marriage* (Dallas: Word, 1989).

[19]Steve de Shazer, *Patterns of Brief Family Therapy* (New York: Guilford, 1982); Steve de Shazer, *Keys to Solution in Brief Therapy* (New York: W. W. Norton, 1985); Steve de Shazer, *Clues: Investigating Solutions in Brief Therapy* (New York: W. W. Norton, 1988); Steve de Shazer, *Putting Differences to Work* (New York: W. W. Norton, 1991).

[20]Johnson and Greenberg, "Emotionally Focused Approach to Problems in Adult Attachment," pp. 121-41; J. S. Scharff, "Psychoanalytic Marital Therapy," in *Clinical Handbook of Couple Therapy*, ed. Neil S. Jacobson and Alan S. Gurman (New York: Guilford, 1995), pp. 164-93.

[21]Neil S. Jacobson and Andrew Christensen, *Integrative Couple Therapy: Promoting Acceptance and Change* (New York: W. W. Norton, 1996).

[22]R. Bandler and J. Grinder, *The Structure of Magic: A Book About Language and Therapy* (Palo Alto, Calif.: Science and Behavior Books, 1975).

[23]Friesen and Friesen, *Counseling and Marriage*.

Chapter 4: Applying the Strategy to Eight Areas of Marriage

[1]There are four common complicating factors: affairs, alcohol or drug abuse, physical abuse, emotional or psychological problems. Whenever you encounter one of them, the complicating factor like a disease that eats its way through the skin of the marriage into its heart—usually will eventually disrupt the marriage and marital counseling itself if it is not dealt with. Trying to treat a marital problem when one or more of these complicating problems exist will frustrate counselor and client. Ask about the presence of each of these during the initial interview. If you uncover one, design treatment to deal specifically with the complicating problem as well as to treat the marriage discord. Each of these difficulties has had volumes written about it. Due to practical space limitations, I cannot give each the attention it deserves in the present book. If you want more information about the complicating factors, here are some references to use as a starting place. For affairs: F. Pittman, *Private Lies: Infidelity and the Betrayal of Intimacy* (New York: W. W. Norton, 1989); H. A. Virkler, *Broken Promises: Healing and Preventing Affairs in Christian Marriages* (Dallas: Word, 1992). For alcohol and drug abuse: P. J. Wakefield, R. E. Williams, E. B. Yost and K. M. Patterson, *Couple Therapy for Alcoholism: A Cognitive-Behavioral Treatment Manual* (New York: Guilford, 1996). For marital violence: A. Holtzworth-Munroe, S. Beatty and K. Anglin, "The Assessment and Treatment of Marital Violence: An Introduction for the Marital Therapist," in *Clinical Handbook of Couple Therapy*, ed. Neil S. Jacobson and Alan S. Gurman (New York: Guilford, 1995), pp. 317-39. For depression: I. H. Gotlib and S. R. H. Beach, "A Marital/Family Discord Model of Depression: Implications of Therapeutic Intervention," in *Clinical Handbook of Couple Therapy*, ed. Neil S. Jacobson and Alan S. Gurman (New York: Guilford, 1995), pp. 411-36; S. E. Prince and N. S. Jacobson, "A Review and Evaluation of Marital and Family Therapies for Affective Disorders," *Journal of Marital and Family Therapy* 21 (1997): 377-402.

[2]W. M. Goldsmith and B. K. Hansen, "Boundary Areas of Religious Clients' Values: Target for Therapy," *Journal of Psychology and Christianity* 10 (1991): 224-36.

[3]P. Cushman, "Why the Self Is Empty: Toward a Historically Situated Psychology," *American Psychologist* 45 (1990): 599-611.

[4]Kenneth Gergen, *The Saturated Self* (New York: BasicBooks, 1991).

[5]Robert N. Bellah et. al., *Habits of the Heart: Individualism and Commitment in American Life* (Berkeley, Calif.: University of California Press, 1985).

[6]Mike Mason, *The Mystery of Marriage: Iron Sharpens Iron* (Portland, Ore.: Multnomah Press, 1985).

[7]See Everett L. Worthington Jr. and D. McMurry, *Marriage Conflicts* (Grand Rapids, Mich.: Baker, 1994), for a similar but different discussion.

[8]Enright and the Human Development Group, "Piaget on the Moral Development of Forgiveness: Identity or Reciprocity?" *Human Development* 37 (1994): 63-80; M. E. McCullough and Everett L. Worthington Jr., "Encouraging Clients to Forgive People Who Have Hurt Them: Review, Critique and Research Prospectus," *Journal of Psychology and Theology* 22 (1994): 3-20; M. E. McCullough, S. J. Sandage and Everett L. Worthington Jr., *To Forgive Is Human: How to Put Your Past in the Past*

(Downers Grove, Ill.: InterVarsity Press, 1997).

[9]M. E. McCullough, "Marriage and Forgiveness," *Marriage and Family: A Christian Journal* 1 (1997): 81-96; E. L. Worthington Jr., "Empathy-Humility-Commitment Model of Forgiveness Applied to Family Dyads," *Journal of Family Therapy* 20 (1998): 59-76.

[10]M. E. McCullough and Everett L. Worthington Jr., "Promoting Forgiveness: A Comparison of Two Psychoeducational Group Interventions with a Waiting-List Control," *Counseling and Values* 40 (1995): 55-68; M. E. McCullough, Everett L. Worthington Jr. and K. C. Rachal, "Interpersonal Forgiving in Close Relationships," *Journal of Personality and Social Psychology* 73 (1997): 321-36.

[11]Everett L. Worthington Jr., *Marriage Counseling: A Christian Approach to Counseling Couples* (Downers Grove, Ill.: InterVarsity Press, 1989) Everett L. Worthington Jr., "Marriage Counseling: A Christian Approach to Counseling Couples," *Counseling and Values* 35 (1990): 3-15; Everett L. Worthington Jr., "Marriage Counseling: Worthington's Reply to Responses," *Counseling and Values* 35 (1990): 21-23; Everett L. Worthington Jr., "Marriage Counseling with Christian Couples," in *Case Studies in Christian Counseling,* ed. Gary R. Collins (Dallas: Word, 1991), pp. 72-97; Everett L. Worthington Jr. and F. A. DiBlasio, "Promoting Mutual Forgiveness Within the Fractured Relationship," *Psychotherapy* 27 (1990): 219-23.

[12]Jay Haley, *Strategies of Psychotherapy* (New York: Grune & Stratton, 1963); Cloe Madanes, *Sex, Love and Violence: Strategies for Transformation* (New York: W. W. Norton, 1990).

[13]P. J. Guerin Jr., L. F. Fay, S. L. Burden and J. G. Kautto, *The Evaluation and Treatment of Marital Conflict: A Four-Stage Approach* (New York: BasicBooks, 1987).

[14]D. H. Baucom and N. Epstein, *Cognitive-Behavioral Marital Therapy* (New York: Brunner/Mazel, 1990).

[15]J. Alexander and B. V. Parsons, *Functional Family Therapy* (Monterey, Calif: Brooks/Cole, 1982).

[16]M.T. Schaefer and D. H. Olson, "Assessing Intimacy: The PAIR Inventory," *Journal of Marital and Family Therapy* 7 (1981): 47-60.

[17]D. G. Bromley and B. C. Busching, "Understanding the Structure of Contractual and Covenantal Social Relations: Implications for the Sociology of Religion," *Sociological Analysis* 49 (1988): 15-32; D. G. Bromley and C. H. Cress, "Beyond Corporal Punishment Debate Rhetoric: The Logic of Child Discipline in Two Social Worlds," *Marriage and Family: A Christian Journal* 1 (1998): 152-64; D. S. Browning et al., *From Culture Wars to Common Ground: Religion and the American Family Debate* (Louisville, Ky.: Westminster John Knox, 1997); J. S. Ripley, "Marital Social Values, Marital Enrichment, and Forgiveness and Reconciliation," unpublished dissertation, Virginia Commonwealth University, Richmond, 1999; John Witte Jr., *From Sacrament to Contract: Marriage, Religion and Law in the Western Tradition* (Louisville, Ky.: Westminster John Knox, 1997); J. M. Adams, J. S. Spain and K. Hunt, "The Measurement of Exchange and Communal Attitudes in Marriage: Scale Development and Initial Validation," paper presented at the meeting of the American Psychological Society, Washington, D.C., May 1998.

[18]Paul A. M. Van Lange et al., "Willingness to Sacrifice in Close Relationships," *Journal of Personality and Social Psychology* 72 (1997): 1373-95.

[19]Caryl E. Rusbult, "A Longitudinal Test of the Investment Model: The Development and Deterioration of Satisfaction in Heterosexual Involvements," *Journal of Personality and Social Psychology* 45 (1983): 101-17.

[20]Browning et al., *From Culture Wars to Common Ground.*

[21]Ken Pargament (personal communication, July 1997) is currently involved in exciting research showing that when couples view marriage as sacred, many benefits accrue. See also Annette Mahoney et al., "Sacred Vows: The Sanctification of Marriage and Its Psychosocial Implications," paper presented at the meeting of the American Psychological Association, Chicago, August 1996.

[22]Rusbult, "Longitudinal Test of the Investment Model."

[23]Van Lange et al., "Willingness to Sacrifice in Close Relationships," pp. 1373-95.

[24]S. M. Stanley and H. J. Markman, "Assessing Commitment in Personal Relationships," *Journal of*

Marriage and the Family 54 (1992): 595-608.

Chapter 5: Precounseling Interventions
[1]Steve de Shazer, *Clues: Investigating Solutions in Brief Therapy* (New York: W. W. Norton, 1988).
[2]D. E. Orlinsky and K. I. Howard, "Process and Outcome in Psychotherapy," in *Handbook of Psychotherapy and Behavior Change,* ed. S. L. Garfield and A. E. Bergin, 3rd ed. (New York: Wiley, 1986), pp. 311-81.
[3]L. E. Beutler, M. Crago and T. G. Arizmendi, "Research on Therapist Variables in Psychotherapy," in *Handbook of Psychotherapy and Behavior Change,* ed. S. L. Garfield and A. E. Bergin, 3rd ed. (New York: Wiley, 1986), pp. 257-310.
[4]Taro A. Kurusu, "The Effectiveness of Pretreatment Intervention on Participants of a Forgiveness Promoting Psychoeducational Group in Various Stages of Change," unpublished dissertation, Virginia Commonwealth University, Richmond, 1999.
[5]J. O. Prochaska, J. C. Norcross and C. C. DiClementi, *Changing for Good: A Revolutionary Six-Stage Program for Overcoming Bad Habits and Moving Your Life Positively Forward* (New York: Avon, 1995).

Chapter 6: Assessment Interventions
[1]G. B. Spanier, "Measuring Dyadic Adjustment: New Scales for Assessing the Quality of Marriage and Similar Dyads," *Journal of Marriage and the Family* 38 (1976): 15-28. Be sure to cite this source (i.e., Spanier's scale) when using this item.
[2]C. F. Sharpley and D. G. Cross, "A Psychometric Evaluation of the Dyadic Adjustment Scale," *Journal of Marriage and the Family* 44 (1982): 739-41.
[3]Everett L. Worthington Jr., *Marriage Counseling with Christian Couples* (videotape). Master's Counselors Videotape Series 3. (New Braunfels, Tex.: Christian Association for Psychological Studies, 1995). Write CAPS, P.O. Box 310400, New Braunfels, TX 78131-0400. Phone (210) 629-2277.
[4]Michelle Weiner-Davis, *Divorce Busting: A Revolutionary and Rapid Program for Staying Together* (New York: Simon & Schuster, 1992); Steve de Shazer, *Clues: Investigating Solutions in Brief Therapy* (New York: W. W. Norton, 1988).
[5]Everett L. Worthington Jr. et al., "Religious Commitment Inventory: Studies of Validity," unpublished manuscript, Virginia Commonwealth University, 1998. This manuscript is currently under editorial review. Additional validity studies are being conducted. Anyone interested in using the ten item measure of religious commitment should write to me for the items and psychometric support for the instrument. P.O. Box 842018, Richmond, VA 23284-2018; e-mail: eworth@vcu.edu
[6]Everett L. Worthington Jr. and J. W. Berry, "Marital Forgiveness," unpublished measure, 1998.. We are using this measure in research with couples and simultaneously collecting psychometric data to support its use. The measure is available from me upon request.
[7]D. H. Baucom and N. Epstein, *Cognitive Behavioral Marital Therapy* (New York: Brunner/Mazel, 1990).
[8]The concept is based partially on M. T. Schaefer and D. H. Olson, "Assessing Intimacy: The PAIR Inventory," *Journal of Marital and Family Therapy* 7 (1981): 47-60. The visual presentation as a thermometer I used in Everett L. Worthington Jr., *Hope for Troubled Marriages: Overcoming Common Problems and Major Difficulties* (Downers Grove, Ill.: InterVarsity Press, 1993).
[9]F. Pittman, *Private Lies: Infidelity and the Betrayal of Intimacy* (New York: W. W. Norton, 1989); H. A. Virkler, *Broken Promises: Healing and Preventing Affairs in Christian Marriages* (Dallas: Word, 1992).
[10]P. J. Wakefield, R. E. Williams, E. B. Yost and K. M. Patterson, *Couple Therapy for Alcoholism: A Cognitive-Behavioral Treatment Manual* (New York: Guilford, 1996).
[11]A. Holtzworth-Munroe, S. B. Beatty and K. Anglin, "The Assessment and Treatment of Marital Violence: An Introduction for the Marital Therapist," in *Clinical Handbook of Couple Therapy,* ed. Neil S. Jacobson and Alan S. Gurman (New York: Guilford, 1995), pp. 317-39.

[12]I. H. Gotlib and S. R. H. Beach, "A Marital/Family Discord Model of Depression: Implications of Therapeutic Intervention," in *Clinical Handbook of Couple Therapy*, ed. Neil S. Jacobson and Alan S. Gurman (New York: Guilford, 1995), pp. 411-36.

[13]John Mordechai Gottman, *What Predicts Divorce: The Relationship Between Marital Processes and Marital Outcomes* (Hillsdale, N.J.: Lawrence Erlbaum, 1994).

[14]H. Norman Wright. *Marital Assessment Inventory* (MAI, 1995) can be purchased for $10 per package of 10 (for five couples), with additional shipping costs of $2 for the first package (of 10) and $.50 per each additional package. (These prices are subject to change.) The MAI can be used with both Christian and non-Christian couples. A few items are specific to Christianity, so people who are strongly opposed to Christianity should be given other assessment instruments. You can get copies of the MAI from

Dr. H. Norman Wright
Christian Marriage Enrichment
P.O. Box 2468
Orange, CA 92859-0468
(800) 875-7560
(714) 544-8153 (F)

[15]Schaefer and Olson, "Assessing Intimacy: The PAIR Inventory," pp. 47-60. You can purchase quite inexpensive copies of the PAIR, manual, scoring template, profile sheets and answer sheets from

David H. Olson, Ph.D.
Family Social Science
290 McNeal Hall
University of Minnesota
St. Paul, MN 55108

[16]M. D. Nugent and L. L. Constantine, "Marital Paradigms: Compatibility, Treatment and Outcome in Marital Therapy," *Journal of Marital and Family Therapy* 14 (1988): 351-69.

[17]William Zinsser, *Writing to Learn* (New York: Harper & Row, 1988).

[18]Everett L. Worthington Jr. et al., "Can Marital Assessment and Feedback Improve Marriages? Assessment as a Brief Marital Enrichment Procedure," *Journal of Counseling Psychology* 42 (1995): 466-75.

Chapter 7: Interventions for Drawing on Central Values

[1]Everett L. Worthington Jr., T. A. Kurusu, M. E. McCullough and S. J. Sandage, "Empirical Research on Religion and Psychotherapeutic Processes and Outcomes: A 10-Year Review and Research Prospectus," *Psychological Bulletin* 119 (1996): 448-87.

[2]L. E. Beutler, "Convergence in Counseling and Psychotherapy: A Current Look," *Clinical Psychology Review* 1 (1981): 79-101; Everett L. Worthington Jr., ed., *Religious Values and Psychotherapy* (Grand Rapids, Mich.: Baker, 1993); A. E. Bergin, "Values and Religious Issues in Psychotherapy and Mental Health," *American Psychologist* 46 (1991): 394-403; A. E. Bergin, I. R. Payne and P. S. Richards, "Values in Psychotherapy," in *Religion and the Clinical Practice of Psychology*, ed. Edward P. Shafranske (Washington, D.C.: American Psychological Association, 1996), pp. 297-325.

[3]Kathleen N. Lewis and Douglas L. Epperson, "Values, Pretherapy Information and Informed Consent in Christian Counseling," *Journal of Psychology and Christianity* 10 (1991): 113-31; K. N. Lewis and D. A. Lewis, "Pretherapy Information, Counselor Influence and Value Similarity: Impact on Female Clients' Reactions," *Counseling and Values* 29 (1985): 151-63.

[4]Jennifer S. Ripley and Everett L. Worthington Jr., "Married Partners' Perceptions of Christian and Non-Christian Marital Therapists Who Use (or Don't Use) Explicitly Christian Techniques," unpublished manuscript under editorial consideration, 1998.

[5]Michael E. McCullough and Everett L. Worthington Jr., "College Students' Perceptions of a Psychotherapist's Treatment of a Religious Issue: Partial Replication and Extension," *Journal of Counseling and Development* 73 (1995): 626-34; M. E. McCullough, Everett L. Worthington Jr., Jennifer L. Maxey and Kenneth C. Rachal, "Gender in the Context of Religious Counseling: An

Example of the Interactive Framework for Gender in Counseling," *Journal of Counseling Psychology* 44 (1997): 80-88; David Morrow, Everett L. Worthington Jr. and M. E. McCullough, "Observers' Perceptions of a Psychotherapists' Treatment of a Religious Issue," *Journal of Counseling and Development* 71 (1993): 452-56.

[6]See for example, Donald Meichenbaum and Dennis C. Turk, *Facilitating Treatment Adherence: A Practitioner's Guidebook* (New York: Plenum, 1987).

[7]Judith S. Wallerstein and Sandra Blakeslee, *Second Chances: Men, Women and Children a Decade After Divorce* (New York: Ticknor & Fields, 1990).

Chapter 8: Interventions for Revisioning a Core Vision

[1]William James, *Psychology* (New York: Fawcett, 1963; original, 1892).

[2]Neil S. Jacobson and Andrew Christensen, *Integrative Couple Therapy: Promoting Acceptance and Change* (New York: W. W. Norton, 1996).

[3]Many approaches to the healing of memories are available. Doug McMurry and I have described an approach in Everett L. Worthington Jr. and Doug McMurry, *Marriage Conflicts* (Grand Rapids, Mich.: Baker, 1994). Other recent approaches include Wade Luquet, *Short-Term Couples Therapy: The Imago Model in Action* (New York: Brunner/Mazel, 1996); see also Siang-Yang Tan, *Cognitive Psychotherapy and Healing of Memories* (videotape; New Braunfels, Tex.: Christian Association for Psychological Studies, 1994). You can order from CAPS, P.O. Box 310400, New Braunfels, TX 78131-0400; phone (210) 629-2277.

[4]Steven de Shazer, *Clues: Investigating Solutions in Brief Therapy* (New York: W. W. Norton, 1988).

[5]M. Rohrbaugh, V. Shoham, C. Spungen and P. Steinglass, "A Systematic Couples Therapy for Problem Drinking," in *Foundations of Psychotherapy: Theory, Research and Practice,* ed. B. Bongar and L. Beutler (London: Oxford University Press, 1995), pp. 228-53; V. Shoham, M. Rohrbaugh and J. E. Patterson, "Problem- and Solution-Focused Couple Therapies: The MRI and Milwaukee Models," in *Clinical Handbook of Couple Therapy,* ed. Neil S. Jacobson and Alan S. Gurman (New York: Guilford, 1995), pp. 142-63.

[6]Gary J. Oliver and H. Norman Wright, "Solution-Based Brief Marital Therapy," *Marriage and Family: A Christian Journal* 1 (1997): 17-27; also Gary J. Oliver, M. Hasz and M. Richburg, *Promoting Change Through Brief Therapy in Christian Counseling* (Wheaton, Ill.: Tyndale House, 1997).

[7]Everett C. Worthington Jr., *Christian Marital Counseling* (videotape; New Braunfels, Tex.: Christian Association for Psychological Studies, 1994). You can order from CAPS, P.O. Box 310100, New Braunfels, TX 78131-0400; phone (210) 629-2277.

[8]John Mordechai Gottman, *What Predicts Divorce: The Relationship Between Marital Processes and Marital Outcomes* (Hillsdale, N.J.: Lawrence Erlbaum, 1994); John Mordechai Gottman, "Psychology and the Study of Marital Processes," *Annual Review of Psychology* 49 (1998): 169-97.

[9]Jacobson and Christensen, *Integrative Couple Therapy,* pp. 60-61.

[10]David A. Seamands, *Healing of Memories* (Wheaton, Ill.: Victor, 1985).

[11]A shortened version of this appeared in Everett L. Worthington Jr., "Counselor's Notebook," *Marriage Partnership* 14, no. 3 (1997): 33.

[12]Neil Clark Warren, "Baby, We're Going Places!" *Physician,* November/December 1995, pp. 9-11.

[13]Ibid.

[14]Robert Beavers and Robert Hampson, *Successful Families: Assessment and Intervention* (New York: W. W. Norton, 1990); Fran C. Dickson, "The Best Is Yet to Be: Research on Long-Lasting Marriages," in *Understudied Relationships: Off the Beaten Track,* ed. Julia T. Wood and Steve Duck (Thousand Oaks, Calif.: Sage, 1995), pp. 22-50; Paul Faulkner, *Achieving Success Without Failing Your Family* (West Monroe, La.: Howard, 1994); Florence W. Kaslow and H. Hammerschmidt, "Long-Term 'Good' Marriages: The Seemingly Essential Ingredients," *Journal of Couples Therapy* 3 (1992): 15-38; Florence Kaslow and James A. Robison, "Long-Term Satisfying Marriages: Perceptions of Contributing Factors," *American Journal of Family Therapy* 24 (1996): 153-70; F. Klagsbrun, *Married People: Staying Together in an Age of Divorce* (Toronto: Bantam, 1985); J. C. Lauer and R. H. Lauer, *Till Death Do Us Part: A Study Guide to Long-Term Marriage* (New York: Harrington Park, 1986); J. J.

Ponzetti Jr. and E. Long, "Healthy Family Functioning: A Review and Critique," *Family Therapy* 16 (1989): 43-49; Nicholas Stinnett and K. H. Sauer, "Relationship Characteristics of Strong Families," *Family Perspective* 11, no. 4 (1977): 3-11; N. Stinnett and J. DeFrain, *Secrets of Strong Families* (New York: BasicBooks, 1985).

[15]Diverse counselors from behavioral marital therapists (for example, Gottman, *What Predicts Divorce*; Jacobson and Christensen, *Integrative Couple Therapy*, pp. 60-61) to emotionally focused marital therapists (for example, Susan M. Johnson, *The Practice of Emotionally Focused Marital Therapy: Creating Connection* [New York: Brunner/Mazel, 1996]) recommend this.

[16]Neil S. Jacobson and Andrew Christensen, *Integrative Behavioral Couple Therapy: Promoting Acceptance and Change* (New York: W. W. Norton, 1996).

[17]Gottman, *What Predicts Divorce*; John M. Gottman, James Coan, Sybil Carrere and Catherine Swanson, "Predicting Marital Happiness and Stability from Newlywed Interactions," *Journal of Marriage and the Family* 60 (1998): 5-22.

[18]L. S. Greenberg and S. M. Johnson, *Emotionally Focused Therapy for Couples* (New York: Guilford, 1988); S. M. Johnson and L. S. Greenberg, "The Emotionally Focused Approach to Problems in Adult Attachment," in *Clinical Handbook of Couple Therapy*, ed. Neil S. Jacobson and Alan S. Gurman (New York: Guilford, 1995), pp. 121-41; Johnson, *Practice of Emotionally Focused Marital Therapy*.

[19]M. Deneneau and S. M. Johnson, "Facilitating Intimacy: A Comparative Outcome Study of Emotionally Focused and Cognitive Interventions," *Journal of Marital and Family Therapy* 20 (1994): 17-33; L. S. Greenberg, P. James and R. Conry, "Perceived Change Processes in Emotionally Focused Couples Therapy," *Family Psychology* 2 (1988): 4-23; Jan Gordon Walker, Susan Johnson, Ian Manion and Paula Cloutier, "Emotionally Focused Marital Intervention for Couples with Chronically Ill Children," *Journal of Consulting and Clinical Psychology* 64 (1996): 1029-36.

[20]Letter writing in counseling has a long history. See A. Burton, "The Use of Written Productions in Psychotherapy," in *The Use of Written Communications in Psychotherapy*, ed. L. Pearson (Springfield, Ill.: Charles C. Thomas, 1965), pp. 3-22; Michael White and David Epston, *Narrative Means to Therapeutic Ends* (New York: W. W. Norton, 1990).

Chapter 9: Interventions for Promoting Confession & Forgiveness

[1]M. E. McCullough, Everett L. Worthington Jr. and K. C. Rachal, "Interpersonal Forgiving in Close Relationships," *Journal of Personality and Social Psychology* 73 (1997): 321-36; M. E. McCullough, K. C. Rachal, S. J. Sandage, Everett L. Worthington Jr., S. W. Brown and T. L. Hight, "Forgiveness in Close Interpersonal Relationships II: Theoretical Elaboration and Measurement," *Journal of Personality and Social Psychology* 75 (1998): 1586-603; Everett L. Worthington Jr., "The Pyramid Model of Forgiveness: Some Interdisciplinary Speculations about Unforgiveness and the Promotion of Forgiveness," in *Dimensions of Forgiveness: Psychological Research and Theological Perspectives*, ed. Everett L. Worthington Jr. (Philadelphia: Templeton Foundation Press, 1998), pp. 107-37.

[2]Andrew Murray, *Humility: The Beauty of Holiness* (Old Tappan, N.J.: Revell, no date).

[3]Everett L. Worthington Jr., "An Empathy-Humility-Commitment Model of Forgiveness Applied within Family Dyads," *Journal of Family Therapy* 20 (1998): 59-76.

[4]Lewis Smedes, *Forgive and Forget: Healing the Hurts We Don't Deserve* (New York: Simon & Schuster, 1984).

[5]M. E. McCullough, S. J. Sandage and Everett L. Worthington Jr., *To Forgive Is Human: How to Put Your Past in the Past* (Downers Grove, Ill.: InterVarsity Press, 1997).

[6]DeLoss D. Friesen and Ruby M. Friesen, *Counseling and Marriage* (Dallas: Word, 1989).

[7]David Augsburger, *Caring Enough to Forgive and Caring Enough Not to Forgive* (Ventura, Calif.: Regal, 1981).

[8]M. E. McCullough and Everett L. Worthington Jr., "Encouraging Clients to Forgive People Who Have Hurt Them: Review, Critique and Research Prospectus," *Journal of Psychology and Theology* 22 (1994): 3-20.

[9]Worthington, "Empathy-Humility-Commitment Model of Forgiveness," pp. 59-76; Worthington, "Pyramid Model of Forgiveness."

[10]McCullough and Worthington, "Encouraging Clients to Forgive People," pp. 3-20.

[11]M. E. McCullough and Everett L. Worthington Jr., "Promoting Forgiveness: A Comparison of Two Brief Psychoeducational Group Interventions with a Waiting-List Control," *Counseling and Values* 39 (1995): 2-14; McCullough, Sandage and Worthington, *To Forgive Is Human*; McCullough, Worthington and Rachal, "Interpersonal Forgiving in Close Relationships," pp. 321-36; McCullough et al., "Forgiveness in Close Interpersonal Relationships II."

[12]Corrie ten Boom and Jamie Buckingham, *Tramp for the Lord* (New York: Jove, 1974).

[13]Smedes, *Forgive and Forget*.

[14]Everett L. Worthington Jr. and F. A. DiBlasio, "Promoting Mutual Forgiveness Within the Fractured Relationship," *Psychotherapy* 27 (1990): 219-23.

[15]Ibid.

[16]H. Norman Wright, "Marital Counseling," in *Christian Marital Counseling: Eight Approaches to Helping Couples*, ed. Everett L. Worthington Jr. (Grand Rapids, Mich.: Baker, 1996), pp. 187-210.

[17]Gary Rosberg, *Love in Difficult Relationships* (audiotape; Lynchburg, Va.: American Association for Christian Counseling, AACC Counsel Tapes, 1995).

Chapter 10: Interventions for Strengthening Communication

[1]Virginia Satir, *Conjoint Family Therapy* (Palo Alto, Calif.: Science and Behavior Books, 1964).

[2]Willard F. Harley Jr., *Love Busters* (Old Tappan, N.J.: Revell, 1993); Willard F. Harley Jr., "My Approach to Marriage Counseling," *Journal of Psychology and Christianity* 13 (1994): 125-32.

[3]Steve de Shazer, *Clues: Investigating Solutions in Brief Therapy* (New York: W. W. Norton, 1988).

[4]Monica McGoldrick and R. Gerson, *Genograms in Family Assessment* (New York: W. W. Norton, 1985).

[5]Gary Chapman, *The Five Love Languages: How to Express Heartfelt Commitment to Your Mate* (Chicago: Northfield, 1995).

[6]Ibid.

[7]Ibid.

[8]John M. Gottman, James Coan, Sybil Carrere and Catherine Swanson, "Predicting Marital Happiness and Stability from Newlywed Interactions," *Journal of Marriage and the Family* 60 (1998): 5-22.

[9]Bernard G. Guerney Jr., *Relationship Enhancement* (San Francisco: Jossey-Bass, 1977).

[10]Howard Markman, Scott Stanley and Susan L. Blumberg, *Fighting for Your Marriage: Positive Steps for Preventing Divorce and Preserving a Lasting Love* (San Francisco: Jossey-Bass, 1994), Scott Stanley, Daniel Trathen, Savanna McCain and Milt Bryan, *A Lasting Promise: A Christian Guide to Fighting for Your Marriage* (San Francisco: Jossey-Bass, 1998).

[11]John Gottman, Cliff Norarius, Jonni Gonso and Howard Markman, *A Couple's Guide to Communication* (Champaign, Ill.: Research Press, 1976); John Gottman with Nan Silver, *Why Marriages Succeed or Fail . . . And How You Can Make Yours Last* (New York: Simon & Schuster, 1994).

[12]Sherod Miller, Daniel Wackman, Elam Nunnally and Phyllis Miller, *Connecting: With Self and Others* (Littleton, Colo.: Interpersonal Communications, 1988).

[13]Gottman, Norarius, Gonso and Markman, *Couple's Guide to Communication*.

[14]A. Christensen, N. S. Jacobson and J. C. Babcock, "Integrative Behavioral Couple Therapy," in *Clinical Handbook of Couple Therapy*, ed., Neil S. Jacobson and Alan S. Gurman (New York: Guilford, 1995), pp. 31-64.

[15]Daniel B. Wile, "The Ego-Analytic Approach to Couple Therapy," in *Clinical Handbook of Couple Therapy*, ed. Neil S. Jacobson and Alan S. Gurman (New York: Guilford, 1995), pp. 91-120.

[16]Antonio Damasio, *Descartes' Error: Emotion, Reason and the Human Brain* (New York: Grosset/Putnam, 1994).

[17]Lawrence J. Crabb Jr., *Marriage Builder: A Blueprint for Couples and Counselors* (Grand Rapids, Mich.: Zondervan, 1982).

[18]Carol Tavris, *Anger: The Misunderstood Emotion* (New York: Touchstone, 1989); also see Howard Kassinove, ed., *Anger Disorders: Definitions, Diagnosis and Treatment* (Washington, D.C.: Taylor &

Francis, 1995).

[19]Crabb, *Marriage Builder.*

[20]Ibid.

[21]Frans de Waal, *Peacemaking Among Primates* (London: Penguin, 1989); also see Everett L. Worthington Jr. and D. T. Drinkard, "Promoting Reconciliation Through Psychoeducational and Therapeutic Interventions," 1999, unpublished manuscript, Virginia Commonwealth University.

[22]Chapman, *Five Love Languages.*

[23]H. Norman Wright, *Marital Counseling: A Cognitive, Behavioral, Biblical Approach* (San Francisco: Harper & Row, 1981).

[24]Everett L. Worthington Jr., *Marriage Counseling: A Christian Approach to Counseling Couples* (Downers Grove, Ill.: InterVarsity Press, 1989).

[25]Harley, *Love Busters.*

[26]John J. Sherwood and John C. Glidewell, "Planned Renegotiation: A Norm-Setting OD Intervention," in *Contemporary Organizational Development: Approaches and Interventions,* ed. Warner Burke (Washington, D.C.: NTL Learning Resources, 1972).

[27]Gottman with Silver, *Why Marriages Succeed or Fail.*

Chapter 11: Interventions for Aiding Conflict Resolution

[1]Daniel B. Wile, "The Ego-Analytic Approach to Couple Therapy," in *Clinical Handbook of Couple Therapy,* ed. Neil S. Jacobson and Alan S. Gurman (New York: Guilford, 1995), pp. 91-120.

[2]P. J. Guerin Jr., L. F. Fay, S. L. Burden and J. G. Kautto, *The Evaluation and Treatment of Marital Conflict: A Four-Stage Approach* (New York: BasicBooks, 1987).

[3]Ibid.

[4]Richard B. Stuart, *Helping Couples Change: A Social Learning Approach to Marital Therapy* (New York: Guilford, 1981).

[5]Ibid.

[6]Neil S. Jacobson and Andrew Christensen, *Integrative Couple Therapy: Promoting Acceptance and Change* (New York: W. W. Norton, 1996).

[7]John Gottman with Nan Silver, *Why Marriages Succeed or Fail . . . and How You Can Make Yours Last* (New York: Simon & Schuster, 1994); Howard Markman, Scott Stanley and Susan L. Blumberg, *Fighting for Your Marriage: Positive Steps for Preventing Divorce and Preserving a Lasting Love* (San Francisco: Jossey-Bass, 1994); Scott Stanley, Daniel Trathen, Savanna McCain and Milt Bryan, *A Lasting Promise: A Christian Guide to Fighting for Your Marriage* (San Francisco: Jossey-Bass, 1998).

[8]A. Christensen, N. S. Jacobson and J. C. Babcock, "Integrative Behavioral Couple Therapy," in *Clinical Handbook of Couple Therapy,* ed. Neil S. Jacobson and Alan S. Gurman (New York: Guilford, 1995), pp. 31-64; Jacobson and Christensen, *Integrative Couple Therapy.*

[9]Christensen, Jacobson and Babcock, "Integrative Behavioral Couple Therapy"; Jacobson and Christensen, *Integrative Couple Therapy.*

[10]Christensen, Jacobson and Babcock, "Integrative Behavioral Couple Therapy"; Jacobson and Christensen, *Integrative Couple Therapy.*

[11]John M. Gottman, *Marital Interaction: Empirical Investigations* (New York: Academic Press, 1979).

[12]H. Norman Wright, "Marital Counseling," *Journal of Psychology and Christianity* 13 (1994): 174-81.

[13]Christensen, Jacobson and Babcock, "Integrative Behavioral Couple Therapy."

[14]Ibid.

[15]Ibid.

[16]Roger Fisher and William Ury, *Getting to Yes: Negotiating Agreement Without Giving In* (New York: Penguin, 1981).

[17]Ibid.

[18]Les Parrott III and Leslie Parrott, "Growing a Healthy Marriage: Seven Questions to Ask Before You Start," *Christian Counseling Today* 4, no. 2 (1996): 16-20.

[19]Gottman with Silver, *Why Marriages Succeed or Fail.*

[20]Sherod Miller, Daniel Wackman, Elam Nunnally and Phyllis Miller, *Connecting: With Self and Others* (Littleton, Colo.: Interpersonal Communications, 1988); Henry A. Virkler, "Building Communication and Conflict-Resolution Skills in Marital Counseling," *Marriage and Family: A Christian Journal* 1 (1998): 341-54.

[21]Scott M. Stanley, Daniel W. Trathen and Savanna McCain, "Christian PREP: An Empirically Based Model for Marital and Premarital Intervention," *Journal of Psychology and Christianity* 13 (1994): 158-65; Stanley, Trathen, McCain and Bryan, *Lasting Promise.*

[22]Markman, Stanley and Blumberg, *Fighting for Your Marriage.*

[23]Everett L. Worthington Jr. and D. McMurry, *Marriage Conflicts* (Grand Rapids, Mich.: Baker, 1994).

[24]Scott Stanley, Daniel Trathen and Savanna McCain, "Christian PREP: An Empirically Based Model for Marital and Premarital Intervention," in *Christian Marital Counseling: Eight Approaches to Helping Couples,* ed. Everett L. Worthington Jr. (Grand Rapids, Mich.: Baker, 1996), pp. 135-58; Stanley, Trathen, McCain and Bryan, *Lasting Promise.*

[25]Christensen, Jacobson and Babcock, "Integrative Behavioral Couple Therapy."

[26]John M. Gottman, Lynn Fainsilber Katz and Carole Hooven, *Meta-emotion: How Families Communicate Emotionally* (Mahwah, N.J.: Lawrence Erlbaum, 1997).

[27]Fisher and Ury, *Getting to Yes.*

[28]Ibid.

[29]Wile, "The Ego-Analytic Approach to Couple Therapy," pp. 91-120.

[30]Christensen, Jacobson and Babcock, "Integrative Behavioral Couple Therapy"; Jacobson and Christensen, *Integrative Couple Therapy.*

[31]Ibid.

Chapter 12: Interventions for Changing Cognition

[1]Aaron T. Beck, A. John Rush, Brian F. Shaw and Gary Emery, *Cognitive Therapy of Depression* (New York: Guilford, 1979).

[2]Donald H. Baucom and Norman Epstein, *Cognitive-Behavioral Marital Therapy* (New York: Brunner/Mazel, 1990).

[3]Everett L. Worthington Jr., *Marriage Counseling: A Christian Approach to Counseling Couples* (Downers Grove, Ill.: InterVarsity Press, 1989).

[4]Baucom and Epstein, *Cognitive-Behavioral Marital Therapy.*

[5]DeLoss D. Friesen and Ruby M. Friesen, "Our Approach to Marriage Counseling," *Journal of Psychology and Christianity* 13 (1994): 109-16; Worthington, *Marriage Counseling;* H. Norman Wright, *Marital Counseling: A Biblical, Behavioral, Cognitive Approach* (New York: Harper & Row, 1981).

[6]D. H. Baucom, N. Epstein and L. A. Rankin, "Cognitive Aspects of Cognitive-Behavioral Marital Therapy," in *Clinical Handbook of Couple Therapy,* ed. Neil S. Jacobson and Alan S. Gurman (New York: Guilford, 1995), pp. 65-90.

[7]Neil S. Jacobson and Andrew Christensen, *Integrative Couple Therapy: Promoting Acceptance and Change* (New York: W. W. Norton, 1996).

[8]Daniel B. Wile, "The Ego-Analytic Approach to Couple Therapy," in *Clinical Handbook of Couple Therapy,* ed. Neil S. Jacobson and Alan S. Gurman (New York: Guilford, 1995), pp. 91-120.

[9]Antonio Damasio, *Descartes' Error: Emotion, Reason and the Human Brain* (New York: Grosset/Putnam, 1994); Joseph LeDoux, *The Emotional Brain: The Mysterious Underpinnings of Emotional Life* (New York: Simon & Schuster, 1996); Robert Plutchik, *The Psychology and Biology of Emotion* (New York: HarperCollins, 1994).

[10]Thomas N. Bradbury and Frank D. Fincham, "Attributions in Marriage: Review and Critique," *Psychological Bulletin* 107 (1990): 3-33; Frank D. Fincham and Thomas N. Bradbury, "The Impact of Attributions in Marriage: A Longitudinal Analysis," *Journal of Personality and Social Psychology* 53 (1987): 510-17; Frank D. Fincham and Thomas N. Bradbury, "Marital Satisfaction, Depression and Attributions: A Longitudinal Analysis," *Journal of Personality and Social Psychology* 64 (1993): 442-52.

[11]M. E. McCullough, "Marital Forgiveness: Theoretical Foundations and an Approach to Prevention," *Marriage and Family: A Christian Journal* 1 (1997): 81-96.

[12]A. Christensen, N. S. Jacobson and J. C. Babcock, "Integrative Behavioral Couple Therapy," in *Clinical Handbook of Couple Therapy*, ed. Neil S. Jacobson and Alan S. Gurman (New York: Guilford, 1995), pp. 31-64; Jacobson and Christensen, *Integrative Couple Therapy.*

[13]Christensen, Jacobson and Babcock, "Integrative Behavioral Couple Therapy."

[14]Gary J. Oliver, Monte Hasz and Matthew Richburg, *Promoting Change Through Brief Therapy in Christian Counseling* (Wheaton, Ill.: Tyndale House, 1997); Willyn Webb, *Solutioning: Solution-Focused Interventions for Counselors* (Philadelphia: Accelerated Development, 1999).

Chapter 13: Interventions for Stimulating More Closeness

[1]L. S. Greenberg and S. M. Johnson, *Emotionally Focused Therapy for Couples* (New York: Guilford, 1988); Susan M. Johnson, *Creating Connection: The Practice of Emotionally Focused Marital Therapy* (New York: Brunner/Mazel, 1996).

[2]Everett L. Worthington Jr., *Marriage Counseling: A Christian Approach to Counseling Couples* (Downers Grove, Ill.: InterVarsity Press, 1989), p. 305.

[3]Robert Sternberg, "A Triangular Theory of Love," *Psychological Review* 93 (1986): 119-35.

[4]Virginia Satir, *Conjoint Family Therapy* (Palo Alto, Calif.: Science and Behavior Books, 1964).

[5]John M. Gottman, *What Predicts Divorce: The Relationship Between Marital Processes and Marital Outcomes* (Hillsdale, N.J.: Lawrence Erlbaum, 1994); Neil S. Jacobson, "A Component Analysis of Behavioral Marital Therapy: The Relative Effectiveness of Behavior Exchange and Problem-Solving Training," *Journal of Consulting and Clinical Psychology* 52 (1984): 295-305; N. S. Jacobson and W. C. Follette, "Clinical Significance of Improvement Resulting from Two Behavioral Marital Therapy Components," *Behavior Therapy* 16 (1985): 249-62; N. S. Jacobson, K. B. Schmaling and A. Holtzworth-Munroe, "Component Analysis of Behavioral Marital Therapy: Two-Year Follow-Up and Prediction of Relapse," *Journal of Marital and Family Therapy* 13 (1987): 187-95; N. S. Jacobson, K. B. Schmaling and A. Holtzworth-Munroe, "Research-Structured vs. Clinically Flexible Versions of Social Learning-Based Marital Therapy," *Behavioural Research and Therapy* 27 (1989): 173-80; Patti L Johnson and K. Daniel O'Leary, "Behavioral Components of Marital Satisfaction: An Individualized Assessment Approach," *Journal of Consulting and Clinical Psychology* 64 (1996): 417-23; W. R. Shadish et al., "Effects of Family and Marital Therapies: A Meta-analysis," *Journal of Consulting and Clinical Psychology* 61 (1993): 992-1002.

[6]Willard F. (Bill) Harley Jr.'s "love bank" (*His Needs, Her Needs: Building an Affair-Proof Marriage* [Grand Rapids, Mich.: Revell, 1994]) and "love busters" (*Love Busters* [Old Tappan, N.J.: Revell, 1993]).

[7]Stuart presented the analogy of banking "pleases," but Harley named it "love bank" and expanded its use. (In fact, Stuart advises therapists not to use the word *love* with troubled couples because of the excess meaning of the term.) I recommend that couples buy and use Harley's books, and like Harley, I frequently use the word *love* because it is the language most people are familiar with. Richard B. Stuart, *Helping Couples Change* (New York: Guildford, 1980).

[8]Harley, *His Needs, Her Needs*, and Harley, *Love Busters.*

[9]Harley, *His Needs, Her Needs*, and Harley, *Love Busters.*

[10]Neil S. Jacobson and Andrew Christensen, *Integrative Couple Therapy: Promoting Acceptance and Change* (New York: W. W. Norton, 1996).

[11]A. Christensen, N. S. Jacobson and J. C. Babcock, "Integrative Behavioral Couple Therapy," in *Clinical Handbook of Couple Therapy*, ed. Neil S. Jacobson and Alan S. Gurman (New York: Guilford, 1995), pp. 31-64.

[12]N. S. Jacobson and G. Margolin, *Marital Therapy: Strategies Based on Social Learning and Behavior Exchange Principles* (New York: Brunner/Mazel, 1979); R. L Weiss and G. R. Birchler, "Adults with Marital Dysfunction," in *Behavior Therapy in the Psychiatric Setting*, ed. M. Hersen and A. S. Bellack

(Baltimore: Williams & Wilkins, 1978), pp. 331-64; R. L Weiss, H. Hops and G. R. Patterson, "A Framework for Conceptualizing Marital Conflict, Technology for Altering It, Some Data for Evaluating It," in *Behavior Change: Methodology, Concepts and Practice*, ed. L. A. Hamerlynck, L. C. Hardy and E. J. Mash (Champaign, Ill.: Research Press, 1973), pp. 309-42.

[13]Richard B. Stuart, *Helping Couples Change: A Social Learning Approach* (New York: Guilford, 1980).

[14]Christensen, Jacobson and Babcock, "Integrative Behavioral Couple Therapy."

[15]Everett L. Worthington Jr., "Marriage Counseling: A Christian Approach to Counseling Couples," *Counseling and Values* 35 (1990): 3-15; Everett L. Worthington Jr., "Marriage Counseling with Christian Couples," in *Case Studies in Christian Counseling*, ed. Gary R. Collins (Dallas: Word, 1991), pp. 72-97.

[16]Worthington, *Marriage Counseling*.

[17]Ibid.

[18]John Gottman, Cliff Norarius, Jonni Gonso and Howard Markman, *A Couple's Guide to Communication* (Champaign, Ill.: Research Press, 1976), chap. 10, n. 11.

[19]Worthington, *Marriage Counseling*.

[20]Willard F. Harley Jr., "Technique: Marital Intervention," *Marriage and Family: A Christian Journal* 1 (1997): 65.

[21]Gregory J. P. Godek, *1001 Ways to Be Romantic* (Boston: Casablanca Press, 1991).

[22]Prescribing a date is an almost universal homework assignment across types of marital therapies. It is justified according to theoretical perspective. For an early example, see Richard Simon, "Good-Bye Paradox, Hello Invariant Prescription: An Interview with Mara Selvini Palazzoli," *Family Therapy Networker* 11 no. 5 (1987): 16-33.

[23]Love letters have been recommended by various marital enrichment theorists, including D. R. Mace and V. C. Mace, "Marriage Enrichment—Wave of the Future," *The Family Coordinator* 24 (1975): 131-35; for an article on marriage encounters, see W. J. Doherty, P. McCabe and R. G. Ryder, "Marriage Encounter: A Critical Appraisal," *Journal of Marriage and Family Counseling* 4 (1978): 99-107.

[24]Willard F. Harley Jr., *Five Steps to Romantic Love: A Workbook for Readers of "Love Busters" and "His Needs, Her Needs"* (Grand Rapids, Mich.: Revell, 1994).

[25]Harley, *His Needs, Her Needs*.

[26]Harley, *Love Busters*.

[27]Salvador Minuchin and H. Charles Fishman, *Family Therapy Techniques* (Cambridge, Mass.: Harvard University Press, 1981).

[28]M. Rohrbaugh, V. Shoham, C. Spungen and P. Steinglass, "A Systematic Couples Therapy for Problem Drinking," in *Foundations of Psychotherapy: Theory, Research and Practice*, ed. B. Bongar and L Beutler (London: Oxford University Press, 1995), pp. 228-53.

[29]Worthington, "Marriage Counseling with Christian Couples," pp. 72-97.

[30]Everett L. Worthington Jr., clinical demonstration, *Theories and Techniques of Counseling I*, videotape 5 (Lynchburg, Va.: Liberty School of Lifelong Learning, 1991).

[31]Minuchin and Fishman, *Family Therapy Techniques*.

[32]Simon, "Good-Bye Paradox, Hello Invariant Prescription," pp. 16-33.

[33]Gary Ezzo and Anne Marie Ezzo, *Growing Kids God's Way: Biblical Ethics for Parenting* (Chatsworth, Calif.: Growing Families International, 1993).

[34]Jane Rosen-Grandon, "Time for Ourselves," *Marriage Education News* 7 no. 4 (1994/1995): 4.

[35]James F. Alexander and B. V. Parsons, *Functional Family Therapy* (Monterey, Calif.: Brooks/Cole, 1973).

[36]Minuchin and Fishman, *Family Therapy Techniques*.

[37]Sam Hamburg, "Reading Aloud as a First Homework Task in Marital Therapy," *Journal of Marital and Family Therapy* 9 (1983): 81-87.

[38]William Ury and Roger Fisher, *Getting to Yes: Negotiating Agreement Without Giving In* (New York: Penguin, 1981).

[39]Harley, "Technique: Marital Intervention," p. 65.

[40]P. J. Guerin Jr., L. F. Fay, S. L. Burden and J. G. Kautto, *The Evaluation and Treatment of Marital Conflict: A Four-Stage Approach* (New York: BasicBooks, 1987).

[41]Worthington, *Marriage Counseling.*

[42]Paul A. M. Van Lange et al., "Willingness to Sacrifice in Close Relationships," *Journal of Personality and Social Psychology* 72 (1997): 1373-95.

[43]Donald Harvey, "When Commitment Drifts," *Christian Counseling Today* 4, no. 2 (1996): 34-38.

[44]Harley, "Technique: Marital Intervention."

[45]C. Hazan and P. Shaver, "Romantic Love Conceptualized as an Attachment Process," *Journal of Personality and Social Psychology* 52 (1987): 511-24; Andrew D. Lester and Judith L. Lester, *It Takes Two: The Joy of Intimate Marriage* (Louisville, Ky.: Westminster John Knox, 1998).

[46]Douglas E. Rosenau, "Sex Therapy Made Simple: 8 Sexual Concepts to Teach Couples," *Christian Counseling Today* 4, no.2 (1996): 30-32, 33 (sidebar).

[47]Joyce J. Penner and Clifford L. Penner, *Counseling for Sexual Disorders* (Dallas: Word, 1990); see also Douglas McMurry, "The Song of Solomon: A Celebration of Sexual Love for a Time of Sexual Confusion," *Marriage and Family: A Christian Journal* 1 (1998): 167-76.

[48]Douglas E. Rosenau, *A Celebration of Sex* (Nashville: Thomas Nelson, 1993).

Chapter 14: Interventions for Cementing Commitment

[1]Willard F. Harley Jr., "My Approach to Marriage Counseling," *Journal of Psychology and Christianity* 13 (1994): 125-32.

[2]Dennis B. Guernsey, *The Family Covenant* (Elgin, Ill.: David C. Cook, 1984).

[3]Jay Haley, *Strategies of Psychotherapy* (New York: Grune & Stratton, 1962).

[4]Gerald R. Patterson, *Coercive Family Process* (Eugene, Ore.: Castalia, 1982).

[5]Sheldon B. Kopp, *If You Meet the Buddha on the Road, Kill Him!* (New York: Bantam 1972).

[6]H. Norman Wright, "Marital Counseling," *Journal of Psychology and Christianity* 13 (1994): 174-81.

[7]DeLoss D. Friesen and Ruby M. Friesen, "Our Approach to Marriage Counseling," *Journal of Psychology and Christianity* 13 (1994): 109-16.

[8]H. Wayne House, ed., *Divorce and Remarriage: Four Christian Views* (Downers Grove, Ill.: InterVarsity Press, 1990).

[9]Wright, "Marital Counseling."

[10]Susan S. Larson, David B. Larson and James P. Swyers, "Does Divorce Take a Clinical Toll? A Research Review of Potential Physical and Emotional Health Risks for Adults and Children," *Marriage and Family: A Christian Journal* 2 (1999).

[11]Ibid.

[12]Peter G. Jaffe and R. Geffner, "Child Custody Disputes and Domestic Violence: Critical Issues for Mental Health, Social Service and Legal Professionals," in *Children Exposed to Marital Violence: Theory, Research and Applied Issues*, ed. George W. Holden, Robert Geffner and Ernest N. Jouriles (Washington, D.C.: American Psychological Association, 1998), pp. 371-408.

[13]Andrew Cherlin, *Marriage, Divorce, Remarriage*, rev. ed. (Cambridge, Mass.: Harvard University Press, 1992).

[14]Wright, "Marital Counseling."

[15]Judith S. Wallerstein and Sandra Blakeslee, *Second Chances: Men, Women and Children a Decade After Divorce* (New York: Ticknor & Fields, 1990).

[16]Tom Whiteman, "What About Us? Should We Stay Together for the Sake of the Kids?" *Christian Counseling Today* 4, no. 2 (1996): 48-52.

[17]Scott M. Stanley and Howard J. Markman, "Assessing Commitment in Personal Relationships," *Journal of Marriage and the Family* 54 (1991): 595-608.

[18]D. S. Browning et al., *From Culture Wars to Common Ground: Religion and the American Family Debate* (Louisville, Ky.: Westminster John Knox, 1997); D. G. Bromley and B. C. Busching, "Understanding the Structure of Contractual and Covenantal Social Relations: Implications for the Sociology of Religion," *Sociological Analysis* 49 (1988): 15-32; D. G. Bromley and C. H. Cress, "Beyond Corporal Punishment Debate Rhetoric: The Logic of Child Discipline in Two Social

Worlds," *Marriage and Family: A Christian Journal* 1 (1998): 152-64; John Witte Jr., *From Sacrament to Contract: Marriage, Religion and Law in the Western Tradition* (Louisville, Ky.: Westminster John Knox, 1997).

[19]Friesen and Friesen, "Our Approach to Marriage Counseling," pp. 109-16; Friesen and Friesen, *Counseling and Marriage* (Dallas: Word, 1989).

[20]Harley, "My Approach to Marriage Counseling," pp. 125-32.

[21]N. S. Jacobson and G. Margolin, *Marital Therapy: Strategies Based on Social Learning and Behavior Exchange Principles* (New York: Brunner/Mazel, 1979); Richard B. Stuart, *Helping Couples Change: A Social Learning Approach to Marital Therapy* (New York: Guilford, 1980); Neil S. Jacobson and Andrew Christensen, *Integrative Couple Therapy: Promoting Acceptance and Change* (New York: W. W. Norton, 1996); A. Christensen, N. S. Jacobson and J. C. Babcock, "Integrative Behavioral Couple Therapy," in *Clinical Handbook of Couple Therapy*, ed. Neil S. Jacobson and Alan S. Gurman (New York: Guilford, 1995), pp. 31-64.

[22]Christensen, Jacobson and Babcock, "Integrative Behavioral Couple Therapy."

[23]Donald Harvey, "When Commitment Drifts," *Christian Counseling Today* 4, no. 2 (1996): 34-38.

[24]Donald R. Harvey, *Love Secured: How to Prevent a Drifting Marriage* (Grand Rapids, Mich.: Baker, 1994); Donald R. Harvey, *When the One You Love Wants to Leave: Guidance and Comfort for Surviving Marital Crises* (Grand Rapids, Mich.: Baker, 1993).

[25]Caryl Rusbult, "Commitment and Satisfaction in Romantic Associations: A Test of the Investment Model," *Journal of Experimental Social Psychology* 16 (1981): 172-80; C. E. Rusbult, "A Longitudinal Test of the Investment Model: The Develoment (and Deterioration) of Satisfaction and Commitment in Heterosexual Involvements," *Journal of Personality and Social Psychology* 45 (1983): 101-17; C. E. Rusbult, V. L. Bissonnette, X. B. Arriaga and C. L Cox, "Accommodation Processes During the Early Years of Marriage," in *The Developmental Course of Marital Dysfunction*, ed. Thomas N. Bradbury (New York: Cambridge University Press, 1998), pp. 74-113; C. E. Rusbult and B. P. Buunk, "Commitment Processes in Close Relationships: An Interdependence Analysis," *Journal of Social and Personal Relationships* 10 (1993): 175-204.

[26]Bill Gillham and Anabel Gillham, *Marriage Takes More Than Two* (Brentwood, Tenn.: Wolgemuth & Hyatt, 1989).

[27]Scott M. Stanley, "Back from the Brink," *Christian Counseling Today* 4 no. 2 (1996): 39-43; Scott M. Stanley and Daniel W. Trathen, "Christian PREP: An Empirically Based Model for Marital and Premarital Intervention," *Journal of Psychology and Christianity* 13 (1994): 158-65; Frank Pittman, *Private Lies: Infidelity and the Betrayal of Intimacy* (New York: W. W. Norton, 1989); Henry A. Virkler, *Broken Promises: Healing and Preventing Affairs in Christian Marriages* (Dallas: Word, 1992).

[28]Guernsey, *Family Covenant.*

Chapter 15: Interventions for Promoting Couple Commencement from Counseling

[1]Everett L. Worthington Jr., "Marriage Counseling: A Christian Approach to Counseling Couples," *Counseling and Values* 35 (1990): 3-15; Everett L. Worthington Jr., "Marriage Counseling with Christian Couples," in *Case Studies in Christian Counseling*, ed. Gary R. Collins (Dallas: Word, 1991), pp. 72-97.

[2]Lynne A. Bond and B. M. Wagner, ed., *Families in Transition: Primary Prevention Programs That Work* (Newbury Park, Calif.: Sage, 1988); Celia Jaes Falicov, ed., *Family Transitions: Continuity and Change over the Life Cycle* (New York: Guilford, 1988); Charles R. Figley and Hamilton I. McCubbin, ed., *Stress and the Family*, vol. 2, *Coping with Catastrophe* (New York: Brunner/Mazel, 1983); Hamilton I. McCubbin and Charles R. Figley, eds., *Stress and the Family*, vol. 1, *Coping with Normative Transitions* (New York: Brunner/Mazel, 1983); Frank S. Pittman III, *Turning Points: Treating Families in Transition and Crisis* (New York: W. W. Norton, 1987).

Chapter 16: Essentials of Hope-Focused Marriage Counseling

[1]The CARE (Couples Assessment of Relationship Elements) has been described and psychometric evidence of its reliability and validity has been presented in Everett L. Worthington Jr. et al.,

"Strategic Hope-Focused Relationship-Enrichment Counseling with Individual Couples," *Journal of Counseling Psychology* 44 (1997): 381-89. The CARE assesses relationship satisfaction across seven areas, using seven items. It is part of the brief marital assessment battery, which is not yet available for general use.

[2]Everett L. Worthington Jr. et al., "Can Marital Assessment and Feedback Improve Marriages? Assessment as a Brief Marital Enrichment Procedure," *Journal of Counseling Psychology* 42 (1995): 466-75.

[3]Michelle Weiner-Davis, *Divorce Busting: A Revolutionary and Rapid Program for Staying Together* (New York: Simon & Schuster, 1992).

[4]Worthington et al., "Can Marital Assessment and Feedback Improve Marriages?"; Worthington et al., "Strategic Hope-Focused Relationship-Enrichment Counseling."

[5]Everett L. Worthington Jr. and F. A. DiBlasio, "Promoting Mutual Forgiveness Within the Fractured Relationship," *Psychotherapy* 27 (1990): 219-23.

[6]Gary Rosberg, *Love in Difficult Relationships* (audiotape; Lynchburg, Va.: American Association for Christian Counseling, (AACC Counsel Tapes, 1995).

[7]Gary Chapman, *The Five Love Languages* (Chicago: Northfield, 1995).

[8]William Ury and Roger Fisher, *Getting to Yes: Negotiating Agreement Without Giving In* (New York: Penguin, 1981).

[9]Willard F. (Bill) Harley Jr., *Love Busters* (Old Tappan, N.J.: Revell, 1993); Willard F. (Bill) Harley Jr., *His Needs, Her Needs: Building an Affair-Proof Marriage* (Grand Rapids, Mich.: Revell, 1994).

[10]Salvador Minuchin and H. Charles Fishman, *Family Therapy Techniques* (Cambridge, Mass.: Harvard University Press, 1981); Steve de Shazer, *Clues: Investigating Solutions in Brief Therapy* (New York: W. W. Norton, 1988).

[11]L. S. Greenberg and S. M. Johnson, *Emotionally Focused Therapy for Couples* (New York: Guilford, 1988); Susan M. Johnson, *Creating Connection: The Practice of Emotionally Focused Marital Therapy* (New York: Brunner/Mazel, 1996).

[12]N. S. Jacobson and G. Margolin, *Marital Therapy: Strategies Based on Social Learning and Behavior Exchange Principles* (New York: Brunner/Mazel, 1979); Richard B. Stuart, *Helping Couples Change: A Social Learning Approach to Marital Therapy* (New York: Guilford, 1980); Neil S. Jacobson and Andrew Christensen, *Integrative Couple Therapy: Promoting Acceptance and Change* (New York: W. W. Norton, 1996); Donald H. Baucom and Norman Epstein, *Cognitive-Behavioral Marital Therapy* (New York: Brunner/Mazel, 1990).

[13]John M. Gottman, *What Predicts Divorce: The Relationship Between Marital Processes and Marital Outcomes* (Hillsdale, N.J.: Lawrence Erlbaum, 1994).

[14]Minuchin and Fishman, *Family Therapy Techniques.*

[15]De Shazer, *Clues: Investigating Solutions in Brief Therapy*; Weiner-Davis, *Divorce Busting.*

[16]Sherod Miller, Daniel Wackman, Elam Nunnally and Phyllis Miller, *Connecting: With Self and Others* (Littleton, Colo.: Interpersonal Communications, 1988).

Appendix
[1]G. B. Spanier, "Measuring Dyadic Adjustment: New Scales for Assessing the Quality of Marriage and Similar Dyads," *Journal of Marriage and the Family* 38 (1976): 15-28.

[2]Everett L. Worthington Jr., *Hope for Troubled Marriages: Overcoming Common Problems and Major Difficulties* (Downers Grove, Ill.: InterVarsity Press, 1993). See also chapter six, note 8.

[3]Everett L. Worthington Jr. and J. W. Berry, "Marital Forgiveness," 1998, unpublished measure. We are using this measure in research with couples and simultaneously collecting psychometric data to support its use. The measure is available from me upon request.

[4]G. B. Spanier and E. E. Filsinger, "The Dyadic Adjustment Scale," in *Marriage and Family Assessment: A Sourcebook for Family Therapy*, ed. Erik E. Filsinger (Beverly Hills, Calif.: Sage, 1983), pp. 156-68.

[5]Steve de Shazer, *Clues: Investigating Solutions in Brief Therapy* (New York: W. W. Norton, 1988).

[6]Richard B. Stuart, *Couple's Precounseling Inventory* (Champaign, Ill.: Research Press, 1983). (This

instrument is no longer in print.)

[7]Sherod Miller, Daniel Wackman, Elam Nunnally and Phyllis Miller, *Connecting: With Self and Others* (Littleton, Colo.: Interpersonal Communications, 1988).

[8]P. J. Guerin Jr., L. F. Fay, S. L. Burden and J. G. Kautto, *The Evaluation and Treatment of Marital Conflict: A Four-Stage Approach* (New York: BasicBooks, 1987).

[9]John M. Gottman, *What Predicts Divorce: The Relationship Between Marital Processes and Marital Outcomes* (Hillsdale, N.J.: Lawrence Erlbaum, 1994).

[10]Willard F. (Bill) Harley Jr., *His Needs, Her Needs: Building an Affair-Proof Marriage* (Grand Rapids, Mich.: Revell, 1994).

[11]Richard B. Stuart, *Helping Couples Change: A Social Learning Approach to Marital Therapy* (New York: Guilford, 1980).

[12]Everett L. Worthington Jr., "An Empathy-Humility-Commitment Model of Forgiveness Applied Within Family Dyads," *Journal of Family Therapy* 20 (1998): 59-76; Everett L. Worthington Jr., "The Pyramid Model of Forgiveness: Some Interdisciplinary Speculations about Unforgiveness and the Promotion of Forgiveness," in *Dimensions of Forgiveness: Psychological Research and Theological Perspectives,* ed. Everett L. Worthington Jr. (Philadelphia: Templeton Foundation Press, 1998), pp. 107-37.

[13]Everett L. Worthington Jr. and F. A. DiBlasio, "Promoting Mutual Forgiveness Within the Fractured Relationship," *Psychotherapy* 27 (1990): 219-23.

Author Index

Adams, J. M., 290
Addis, M. E., 285
Alexander, James F., 285, 287, 290, 299
Allender, Dan B., 286
Anglin, K., 289, 291
Arizmendi, T. G., 80, 291
Arriaga, Ximena B., 301
Augsburger, David, 134, 294

Babcock, J. C., 176, 223, 247, 295-99, 301
Bagarozzi, Dennis A., 286
Bandler, R., 56, 289
Barkham, M., 286
Barnes, M. L., 288
Baucom, Donald H., 197, 288, 290, 291, 297, 302
Bavelas, Janet Beavin, 287
Beach, Steven R. H., 289, 292
Bean, R., 285
Beatty, S. B., 289, 291
Beavers, Rovert, 293
Beck, Aaron T., 195, 297
Bellack, A. S., 298
Bellah, Robert N., 289
Benner, David G., 10, 288
Bergin, Allen E., 285-87, 291, 292
Beutler, Larry E., 80, 287, 291-93, 299
Birchler, G. R., 298
Bissonnette, V. L., 301
Blakeslee, Sandra, 246, 293, 300
Blumberg, Susan L., 295-97
Bond, Lynne A., 301
Bongar, B., 287, 293, 299
Bradbury, Thomas N., 285, 297, 301
Bradshaw, D., 288
Bray, J. H., 285
Bromley, David G., 290, 300
Brown, S. W., 294
Browning, Donald S., 290, 300
Bryan, Milt, 295-97
Buckingham, Jamie, 295
Budman, Simon H., 286

Burden, S. L., 288, 290, 296, 300, 303
Burton, A., 294
Busching, B. C., 290, 300
Buston, Beverly G., 285
Buunk, B. P., 301

Campbell, W. K., 288
Carrere, Sybil, 294, 295
Chapman, Gary, 153-55, 164, 264, 295, 302
Chartrand, Judy M., 288
Cherlin, Andrew, 300
Christensen, Andrew 176, 191, 197, 223, 247, 248, 287, 289, 293-98, 301, 302
Clinton, Tim, 10
Cloutier, Paula 294
Coan, James, 294, 295
Collins, Gary R., 10, 290, 299, 301
Conry, R., 294
Constantine, L. L., 292
Corsini, Rammond, 165
Cox, Chante L., 301
Crabb, Lawrence J., Jr., 163, 164, 288, 295
Crago, M., 80, 291
Crane, D. R., 285
Cress, C. H., 290, 300
Cross, D. G., 87, 177, 291
Cushman, Philip, 61, 289

Damasio, Antonio, 295, 297
DeFrain, John, 294
Deneneau, M., 294
de Shazer, Steven, 115, 287, 289, 291, 293, 295, 302
DeVries, Helen M., 286
de Waal, Frans, 296
DiBlasio, F. A., 290, 295, 302, 303
Dickson, Fran C., 293
DiClementi, Carlo C., 80, 81, 291
Doherty, W. J., 299
Drinkard, Dewitt T., 9, 296
Duck, Steve, 293

Dunn, R. L., 285

Ecker, Bruce, 286
Edwards, Keith J., 286
Epperson, Douglas L., 292
Epstein, Norman, 197, 288, 290, 291, 297, 302
Epston, David, 294
Ezzo, Anne Marie, 299
Ezzo, Gary, 299

Falicov, Celia Jaes, 301
Faulkner, Paul, 293
Fay, L. F., 288, 290, 296, 300, 303
Figley, Charles R., 301
Filsinger, Erik E., 287, 302
Fincham, Frank D., 297
Fisch, R., 287
Fisher, Roger, 179, 180, 185, 186, 296, 297, 299, 302
Fishman, H. Charles, 299, 302
Follette, W. C., 287, 298
Freud, Sigmund, 163
Friesen, DeLoss, 57, 134, 240, 247, 286, 288, 289, 294, 297, 300, 301
Friesen, Ruby, 57, 134, 240, 247, 286, 288, 289, 294, 297, 300, 301

Garfield, Sol L., 285-87, 291
Geffner, Robert, 300
Gergen, Kenneth, 61, 289
Gerson, R., 295
Gianetti, V. J., 286
Gillham, Anabel, 301
Gillham, Bill, 301
Glaser, R. R., 285
Glidewell, John C., 296
Godek, Gregory J. P., 299
Goldsmith, W. Mack, 289
Gonso, Jonni, 295, 299
Gotlib, I. H., 289, 292
Gottman, John Mordechai, 47, 50, 124, 159, 167, 181, 220, 221, 223, 224, 264, 277, 287, 288, 292-99, 302, 303

Greenberg, Leslie S., 287-89, 294, 298, 302
Grinder, J., 56, 289
Guerin, Philip J., Jr., 170, 171, 288, 290, 296, 300, 303
Guerney, Bernard G., Jr., 159, 295
Guernsey, Dennis B., 251, 300, 301
Gurman, Alan S., 285-89, 291-98, 301

Haley, Jay, 287, 290
Hamburg, Sam, 299
Hamerlynck, L. A., 299
Hammerschmidt, H., 293
Hammonds, T. M., 285
Hampson, Robert, 293
Hansen, Betty K., 289
Hardy, G., 286
Hardy, L. C., 299
Harley, Willard F., Jr., 151, 220, 223, 225, 230, 247, 264, 288, 295, 298-300, 302, 303
Harper, Charles, 11, 286, 287, 292, 296, 297
Harvey, Donald R., 233, 248, 249, 300, 301
Hasz, Monte, 286, 293, 298
Hazan, C., 288, 300
Hendrix, Harville, 286
Hersen, M., 298
Hight, Terry L., 9, 227, 268, 276, 285, 294, 302
Holden, George W., 300
Holtzworth-Munroe, A., 285, 287, 289, 291, 298
Hooven, Carole, 297
Hops, H., 299
House, H. Wayne, 177, 184, 251, 286, 293, 298, 300
Howard, Kenneth I., 70, 80, 159, 183, 246, 286, 291, 293, 295, 296, 299, 300
Hoyt, Michael F., 286
Hulley, Laurel, 286
Hunt, K., 290

Jackson, Don D., 274, 287
Jacobson, Neil S., 19, 176, 197, 223, 247, 285-89, 291-99, 301, 302

Jaffe, Peter G., 300
James, P., 294
James, William, 111, 297
Jameson, P., 285, 287
Johnson, Patti L., 298
Johnson, Susan M., 287, 288, 289, 294, 298, 302
Jones, Dawn R., 9, 285
Jouriles, Ernest N., 285, 300

Kaplan, Helen S., 237
Karney, B. R., 285
Kaslow, Florence W., 293
Kassinove, Howard, 295
Katz, Lynn Fainsilber, 297
Kautto, J. G., 288, 290, 296, 300, 303
Klagsbrun, F., 293
Kniskern, David P., 286, 287
Kopp, Sheldon B., 300
Kopta, Mark, 286
Koss, M. P., 286
Kurusu, Taro A., 9, 80, 285, 291, 292

Larson, David, B., 300
Larson, Susan S., 300
Lauer, J. C., 293
Lauer, R. H., 293
Lebow, J. L., 285
LeDoux, Joseph, 297
Lester, Andrew D., 300
Lester, Judith L., 300
Lewis, C. S., 287
Lewis, David A., 292
Lewis, Kathleen N., 292
Lieblum, S. R., 237
Locke, E. A., 288
Long, E., 294
Luquet, Wade, 286, 293
Lynch, G., 288

Mace, D. R., 299
Mace, V. C., 299
Madanes, Cloe, 290
Mahoney, Annette, 290
Manion, Ian, 294
Marcel, Gabriel, 31, 287
Margolin, Gayla, 286, 298, 301, 302
Markman, Howard J., 70, 159, 183, 246, 290, 295, 296, 299,

300
Mash, E. J., 299
Mason, Michael, 288, 289
Matt, G. E., 288
Maxey, Jennifer L., 292
McCabe, P., 299
McCain, Savanna, 183, 295-97
McCubbin, Hamilton I., 301
McCullough, Michael E., 10, 131, 289, 290, 292-95, 298
McDowell, Josh, 287
McGoldrick, Monica, 295
McMurry, Douglas, 10, 287-89, 293, 297, 300
Meichenbaum, Donald, 293
Miller, Phyllis, 295, 297, 302, 303
Miller, Sherod, 159, 160, 183, 274, 295, 297, 302, 303
Minuchin, Salvador, 226, 229, 299, 302
Montgomery, L. M., 285
Moon, Gary W., 287
Moran, G., 288
Morrison, L., 286
Morrow, David, 293
Murray, Andrew, 130, 294

Norarius, Cliff, 295, 299
Norcross, John C., 80, 81, 291
Nugent, M. D., 292
Nunnally, Elam, 295, 297, 302, 303

O'Leary, K. Daniel, 298
Oliver, Gary J., 10, 113, 286, 293, 298
Olson, David H., 290-92
Orlinsky, David E., 80, 286, 291

Pargament, Kenneth I., 290
Parrott, Les, III, 10, 181, 296
Parrott, Leslie, 181, 296
Parsons, B. V., 290, 299
Paterson, R. J., 288
Patterson, Gerald R., 299, 300
Patterson, J. E., 286, 287, 288, 293
Patterson, K. M., 289, 291
Payne, I. R., 292
Pearson, L., 294
Pekarik, Gene, 286

Penner, Clifford, L., 237
Perrone, Kristin M., 9, 285
Pinsof, W. M., 285
Pittman, Frank S., III, 289, 291, 301
Plutchik, Robert, 297
Ponzetti, J. J., Jr., 294
Prince, S. E., 285, 289
Prochaska, James O., 80, 81, 291

Quick, Ellen K., 22, 25, 27, 184, 195, 226, 271, 286

Rachal, Kenneth Christopher, 290, 292, 294, 295
Ragsdale, K., 285
Rankin, L. A., 197, 297
Revenstorf, D., 287
Richards, P. S., 292
Richburg, Matthew, 286, 293, 298
Richmond, Gary, 246, 267, 290, 291
Ripley, Jennifer S., 9, 22, 103, 285, 287, 290, 292
Robison, James A., 293
Rohrbaugh, M., 286-88, 293, 299
Rosberg, Gary, 145, 295, 302
Rosen, R. C., 237, 299
Rosen-Grandon, Jane, 299
Rosenau, Douglas E., 236, 237, 300
Rusbult, Caryl E., 250, 290, 301
Rush, A. John, 219, 297
Ryder, R. G., 299

Sandage, Steven J., 9, 131, 289, 292, 294, 295
Satir, Virginia, 295, 298
Sauer, K. H., 294
Schaefer, M. T., 290, 291
Scharff, J. S., 289
Schnarch, D. M., 237
Schmaling, K. B., 298
Schmitt, Michelle, 9
Schwebel, A. I., 285
Scott, E., 183, 246, 295, 296, 301
Seamands, David A., 293
Selvini-Palazzoli, Mara, 229,

299
Shadish, W. R., 285, 298
Shafranske, Edward P., 292
Shapiro, David, 286
Sharpley, C. F., 291
Shaver, P., 288, 300
Shaw, Brian F., 297
Sherwood, John J., 296
Shiang, J., 286
Shoham, V., 286-88, 293, 299
Simon, Richard, 51, 286, 294-97, 299, 302
Smedes, Lewis, 131, 294
Snyder, C. R., 30, 31, 44, 287
Spain, J. S., 290
Spanier, Graham B., 30, 287, 291, 302
Spungen, C., 287, 293, 299
Stanley, Scott M., 183, 246, 287, 290, 295-97, 300, 301
Staubli, U., 288
Steinglass, P., 287, 293, 299
Sternberg, Robert J., 216, 288, 298
Stinnett, Nicholas, 294
Strong, Stanley R., 24, 104, 162, 163, 185, 214, 238, 267, 271, 287, 294
Stuart, Richard B., 171, 277, 296, 298, 299, 301-3
Swanson, Catherine, 294, 295
Swyers, James P., 300

Talmon, M., 286
Tan, Siang-Yang, 293
Tavris, Carol, 163, 295
Templeton, Jack, 11
Templeton, Sir John, 11
ten Boom, Corrie, 137, 295
Trathen, Daniel W., 183, 295-97, 301
Turk, Dennis C., 293

Ury, William, 179, 180, 185, 186, 296, 297, 299, 302

Van Lange, Paula M., 290, 300
Vazquez, C., 288
Virkler, Henry A., 289, 291, 297, 301

Wackman, Daniel, 295, 302,

303
Wade, Nathaniel 9, 286, 293
Wagner, B. M., 301
Wahking, Harold, 237
Wakefield, P. J., 289, 291
Walker, Jan Gordon, 294
Wallerstein, Judith S., 246, 293, 300
Warren, Neil Clark, 121, 293
Watzlawick, Paul, 287
Weakland, John H., 287
Webb, Willyn, 298
Weiner-Davis, Michelle, 286, 302
Weiss, R. L., 298, 299
Wells, R. A., 286
White, Michael, 174, 193, 194, 241, 294
Whiteman, Tom, 246, 300
Wile, Daniel B., 162, 169, 188, 198, 295-97
Williams, R. E., 289, 291, 299
Witte, John, Jr., 290, 301
Wood, Julia T., 293
Worthington, Everett L., Jr., 77, 82, 95, 131, 268, 285, 286, 287-90, 291-99, 301-3
Wright, H. Norman, 115, 244, 286, 292, 293, 295-97
Wynne, L. C., 285

Yost, E. B., 289, 291

Zimmerman, Gene, 237
Zinsser, William, 292

Subject Index

abuse, 37, 66, 90, 93, 129, 235, 245, 289
  drug, 90, 93, 245, 289
  physical, 90, 289
acceptance, 48, 113, 163, 200, 206, 287, 289, 293, 294, 296-98, 301, 302
affair, 53, 99, 107, 250, 288, 298, 302, 303
always, never and other absolutes, 210; Intervention 12-7
apologize, apology, 63, 80, 144,

283, 284
areas of change (target areas),
18, 28, 36-38
assessment (assess), 13, 14, 21,
22, 26, 28, 29, 36, 41, 64,
71, 75-78, 80, 84-88, 96-
98, 100, 105, 106, 111, 116,
119, 127, 135, 143, 163,
167, 170, 196, 202, 212,
213, 215, 218, 226, 237,
242, 243, 247, 255-57, 261-
63, 271, 272, 284-89, 291-
93, 295, 298, 301, 302;
Table 7.1
assessment report, 37, 90, 92-
94, 96, 131, 204, 248, 253,
255-57, 262, 263; Table 6.4
assumptions, 22, 67, 90, 135,
181, 196, 200, 202, 207-11;
Interventions 12-6, 12-7;
Table 12.1
attachment, 48, 49, 234, 288,
289, 294, 300
attributions, 47, 67, 90, 124,
196, 197, 202, 205, 206,
239, 258, 284, 297
awareness wheel, 159, 265,
274, 283
barriers, 135, 136, 237, 246
behavioral couple therapy, 294-
99, 301
Bible, biblical, 10, 13, 118, 184,
233, 296, 297, 299
brief counseling, brief therapy,
14, 22, 23, 43, 82, 88, 92,
157, 179, 208, 219, 252,
286, 287, 289, 291, 293,
295, 298, 302
calendar, 79, 219
CAPS, 116, 291, 293
caring days, 223
central beliefs, 60, 89
central values, 26, 37, 101-5,
110, 129, 251, 262, 271,
292
Christ, 17, 24, 32, 35, 69, 118,
140, 287
Christian, Christianity, 10, 13,
14, 20, 22, 26, 27, 31, 33-
35, 45, 46, 48, 53, 55, 61,
70, 88, 89, 92, 93, 95, 101,
103, 115, 116, 139, 140,

167, 197, 201, 233, 239,
243, 246, 247, 256, 262,
266, 282, 285-93, 295, 296-
302
CLEAVE acrostic, 107, 108,
218, 219, 264; Intervention
13-4; Table 13.1
closeness, 26, 37, 40, 43, 50, 60,
64, 68, 77-79, 90, 123, 125,
129, 148, 155, 160, 164,
169, 213-19, 221, 226-31,
234, 237, 251, 262, 271,
272, 274, 277-79, 282, 283,
298
closing the loop by forgiveness,
145; Intervention 9-12
coaction, 37, 68, 69, 213, 214,
219, 228, 229
cognition, 26, 32, 37, 40, 60,
64, 67, 90, 129, 195-203,
212, 251, 262, 271, 277,
297
cognitive paradigm, 197, 200,
203, 212
cognitive-behavioral marital
therapy, 26, 197, 290, 297,
302
commencement or termination
session, 126, 252, 255, 271,
283, 284
commitment, marital, 24, 70,
249
commitment drift, 248-50; Intervention 14-4
commitment to therapy, 240
communication, 26, 30, 32, 36,
37, 40, 43, 49, 60, 64-66,
77, 79, 80, 90, 91, 97, 105,
119, 123, 129, 133, 147-
160, 163-67, 169, 179, 180,
183, 184, 190, 192, 194,
209, 211, 219, 223, 236,
237, 251, 254, 262, 264,
265, 271, 273, 274, 283,
287, 290, 295, 297, 299
community, 56, 94, 118, 123,
166, 245; Table 6.2
competing values, 105; Interventions 7-2, 7-3
competitors to marriage, 238,
250
complicating problems, 26, 37,

40, 262, 271, 289
compromise, 67, 107, 172, 186,
212
confession, 26, 36, 37, 40, 49,
60, 62, 63, 89, 109, 118,
128-31, 133-35, 143, 144,
146, 169, 194, 251, 262,
271, 277, 283, 294
conflict resolution, 26, 37, 40,
60, 64, 90, 91, 119, 168-70,
186, 190, 251, 262, 271,
296
confront, 10, 63, 102, 107, 132,
166, 167, 239, 243; Interventions 7-1, 7-4
contract, 69, 70, 239, 246, 247,
269, 290, 301
control, 44, 48, 66, 91, 94, 125,
133, 136, 137, 163, 184,
193, 203, 214, 215, 228,
233, 254, 266, 267, 290,
295
core vision, 26, 37, 60, 61, 89,
111-13, 116, 117, 127, 129,
251, 262, 271, 273, 293
Couples Assessment of Relationship Elements (CARE),
301, 302
covenant, 24, 46, 69, 70, 239,
246, 247, 300, 301
crisis, 41, 43, 60, 65, 248, 249,
253, 254, 301
cross-complaining, 175, 177
date (romance), 219, 225, 229,
243, 299; Intervention 13-8
devalue, 33, 36, 40, 46, 47, 51,
66, 77, 79, 82, 91, 99, 118,
149, 150, 155, 165, 168,
172, 173, 175, 179, 180,
206, 275, 282
devaluing, 33, 46, 47, 62, 66,
78, 82, 83, 91, 99, 100, 112,
118, 124, 147, 150, 153,
165, 166, 169, 170, 175,
185, 200, 214, 219, 225,
254, 273, 275
differences, 25, 33, 66, 69, 77,
79, 80, 83, 86, 91, 105, 106,
114, 131, 149, 159, 165,
168, 169, 169, 172, 173,
174, 178, 181, 185, 186,
194, 207, 212, 221, 228,

231, 233, 239, 275, 289;
    Intervention 11-3
discipleship, 32, 45
disengagement, 36, 39, 40, 44,
    51, 249, 271, 272, 283
distancing, 213, 231, 234
divorce, 18, 20-22, 30, 34, 51,
    71, 84, 86, 88, 93, 104, 110,
    171, 176, 239, 240, 243-46,
    250, 258, 263, 268, 286-88,
    291-96, 298, 300, 302, 303;
    Intervention 14-3; Table
    14.1
doubt model, 240
Dyadic Adjustment Scale, 30,
    87, 99, 272, 284, 287, 291,
    302
eclectic, 26, 263
editing, 91, 165, 167
effectance, 48, 49
effectiveness, 18, 20, 30, 35, 42,
    63, 125, 260, 261, 263,
    267, 285, 291, 298; Tables
    6.3, 6.5
effort, 30, 35, 36, 41, 42, 55, 63,
    65, 81, 95, 98, 110, 123,
    124, 136, 138, 152, 175,
    186, 206, 244, 249, 253,
    275, 276
ego analytic marital therapy,
    198, 295, 296, 297
emotion, 25, 32, 79, 91, 135,
    183, 200, 202, 214, 295,
    297; Table 8.2
emotional distancer-pursuer,
    54, 226, 227, 230-32; Inter-
    vention 13-11
empathy, 9, 130, 131, 135, 137-
    40, 146, 159, 172, 205,
    222, 277, 290, 294, 303
empty chair, 143, 178, 255; In-
    tervention 11-4
encounter, 36, 39, 44, 80, 84,
    122, 168, 248, 271-73, 286,
    289, 299
engagement, 36, 39, 40, 44,
    271, 274, 283
expectations, 20, 22, 66, 67, 90,
    106, 149, 158, 184, 192,
    196, 197, 206, 207, 224,
    232, 241, 247
evaluate both partners' inter-

ests, Intervention 11-9
faith, 10, 13, 17, 18, 20, 24-26,
    28, 32-38, 40, 42, 44-52,
    54, 55, 57, 58, 62, 67, 69,
    71, 75, 77, 78, 80-83, 92,
    94, 95, 100, 103, 112-14,
    118, 123, 124, 132, 138,
    140, 143, 146, 149, 168,
    170, 186, 194, 199, 203-7,
    212, 213, 215, 217, 218,
    232, 244, 246-48, 250, 251,
    253, 255, 256, 261-63, 265,
    266, 271, 273-75, 281, 282
family systems theory, 25, 27
feedback, 9, 10, 26, 37, 92, 97,
    148, 149, 273, 274, 282,
    285, 288, 292, 302
feelings, 29, 40, 45, 49, 51, 54,
    62, 68, 70, 79, 82, 91, 94,
    98, 108, 110, 117, 123-26,
    134, 136, 138, 139, 141,
    142, 144, 145, 147, 150,
    153, 155, 158, 160, 162-64,
    167, 185, 191, 197, 202,
    204, 209, 213-16, 223, 225,
    227, 230, 233, 249, 273,
    274, 276, 277, 283, 284
flexible, 14, 29, 30, 43, 90, 298
focusing people on their
    part/responsibility, Inter-
    vention 9-1
forgiveness, 9-11, 26, 36, 37,
    40, 46, 49, 53, 60, 62, 63,
    78, 80, 89, 118, 120, 128-
    31, 134-37, 139-45, 146,
    166, 169, 192-94, 251, 261,
    262, 264, 265, 271, 272,
    276, 277, 281, 284, 289-91,
    294, 295, 298, 302, 303;
    Intervention 9-4
forgiveness session, 142-44,
    146, 277; Interventions 9-
    10, 9-11
FREE (Forgiveness and Recon-
    ciliation through Experi-
    encing Empathy), 9, 287
genogram, 153; Intervention
    10-4
goals (plans), 20, 22, 25, 30, 31,
    33, 36, 41, 42, 43, 44, 80,
    81, 92, 95, 96, 98, 116, 122,
    123, 126, 127, 133, 160,

164, 167, 170, 204, 205,
    219, 228, 255, 256, 257,
    262, 263, 265, 270, 275,
    279, 283
God, 18, 23, 25, 31-33, 35, 40,
    44, 45, 47, 48, 54-56, 70,
    96, 100, 102, 118, 123,
    130, 138, 140-42, 146, 194,
    215, 229, 233, 238, 239,
    246, 247, 250, 253, 255,
    256, 265-67, 299
Gottman's ratio, 124, 175, 220,
    224
grace, 47, 107, 130, 140
graph of love, Intervention 13-
    2
gratitude, 130, 140-42, 146; In-
    terventions 9-8, 9-9
guidelines, 28, 41, 112, 127,
    158, 163, 164, 183, 188,
    191, 196, 214, 239
    for communicating better, In-
    tervention 10-8; Tables
    10.2, 11.3
    for conflict resolution, Inter-
    vention 11-10; Table 11.3
    for dealing with anger, 163,
    164; Table 10.3
    for dealing with closeness,
    214
    for promoting commitment,
    239
guilt, 130, 133, 136,
healing of memories, 40, 114,
    120, 134, 293
histories, 48, 112, 113, 134; In-
    terventions 8-1, 8-2, 10-4
Holy Spirit, 13, 34, 46, 55, 107,
    144
homework, 18, 25, 40-44, 53,
    54, 85, 97-100, 105, 106,
    109, 110, 117, 119-21, 125,
    126, 135, 136, 138-40, 143,
    149, 151-55, 165, 171, 173,
    178, 181, 197, 198, 201,
    202, 204, 205, 207, 209,
    210, 215, 216, 218, 222-24,
    229, 231, 232, 234, 242,
    254, 262, 274, 299; Inter-
    ventions 7-5, 14-2
hope, 9-11, 13, 14, 17-19, 21-
    33, 35, 36, 38-50, 52-58,

60, 62, 67, 71, 75, 76, 78, 80-82, 92, 93, 96, 100, 103, 105, 106, 109-15, 117, 120, 124, 126, 127, 132-34, 136, 138-44, 146, 147, 149-57, 159, 161, 165, 168, 171, 173, 175, 178, 179, 181, 183, 185, 188, 190, 194, 196, 201-6, 208, 209, 211, 212, 216-19, 221, 222, 226, 228, 230, 232, 240, 241, 243, 246, 248, 250-53, 256, 257, 259-69, 271, 273, 274, 279, 285, 287, 288, 291, 301, 302

hope-focused marital counseling, 23, 24

humility, 97, 123, 130, 135, 139, 140, 146, 277, 290, 294, 303

independence, 253, 254, 275

intake form, 86-88, 90, 93, 98, 103; Table 6.1

integrative behavioral couple therapy, 294-99, 301

intent-impact, 184; Intervention 11-8

Interpersonal Communication Program (ICP), 159, 265

intimacy, 20, 26, 33, 36, 37, 43, 48-50, 54, 64, 68, 69, 77-80, 90, 92, 93, 94, 116, 119, 123, 126, 127, 164, 165, 192, 208, 213-19, 224, 226-30, 231-34, 236, 261, 265, 269, 272, 274, 276-78, 280, 284, 289-92, 294, 301; Intervention 13-10
emotional, 68, 93, 230, 236, 269, 274, 277, 284; Intervention 13-1
sexual intimacy, 68, 69, 219, 230, 231, 272, 274, 276, 284; Table 13.2
spiritual intimacy, 20, 69, 90, 230, 232-34, 265; Intervention 13-1

investments in marriage, 37, 70, 110, 154, 173, 250, 275

Jesus, 11, 17, 23, 24, 32-35, 46, 70, 95, 101, 102, 139, 265, 266

joint platform, 169

journal, 203, 204, 206, 285, 285-303

justice, 63, 130

lay counselor, 20

letter, love, Intervention 8-7
empathy-promoting, Intervention 9-6

leveling, 91, 160, 167

listen and repeat, 79, 179, 182, 185; Intervention 11-7

listening cycle, 159, 183, 274

Lord, 36, 53, 56, 69, 100, 109, 136, 139, 215, 216, 243, 250, 253, 255-257, 261, 262, 267, 295

LOVE acrostic, 79, 178-80, 188, 264; Intervention 11-5; Table 11.2

love bank, 43, 220-24, 277, 298; Interventions 13-5, 13-6, 13-7

love busters, 151, 225, 226, 288, 295, 296, 298, 299, 302; Intervention 10-2

love languages, 153, 154, 295, 296, 302; Intervention 10-5; Table 10.1

marital interactions, 49, 202

marital therapy, 13, 26, 88, 115, 124, 125, 171, 177, 197, 198, 237, 242, 244, 264, 268, 286-94, 296-99, 301-3

marriage
successful, Table 8.1
troubled, 24, 33, 34, 52, 63, 64, 82, 105, 111, 113, 124, 272

Marriage Assessment Inventory (MAI), 92, 261, 292

marriage conference, 165; Intervention 10-10

marriage vows, 251

meaning, 48, 123, 230, 298

memorial, Joshua or physical, 255, 256, 264, 283; Intervention 15-1

Mental Research Institute, 31, 286-88, 293

mercy, 130, 140, 287

miracle question, 89, 115, 116, 152, 261, 273; Interven-

tions 8-3, 8-4, 10-3

misunderstandings, 64-67, 79, 130, 135, 182

mutual trap, 176

negative thinking, 67, 90, 196, 199, 201-5; Interventions 12-1, 12-2, 12-3, 12-4

objections, 40, 148, 224

observe your effects, Intervention 11-8

office, 11, 30, 75, 85, 86, 194, 217, 226, 227, 229, 232, 256, 277, Intervention 13-9

Personal Assessment of Intimacy in Relationships (PAIR), 92, 261, 290-292

pamphlet, 75, 81, 82

pastor (clergy), 10, 20, 30, 46, 84, 229

patterns, 23, 40, 49-51, 55, 62, 90, 91, 113, 114, 147-50, 153, 179, 195, 199, 201, 203, 215, 226, 231, 241, 248, 249, 258, 268, 282, 284, 287, 289

personalizing issues, 175, 177, 178

phone, 75, 76, 85, 165, 189, 200, 261, 291, 293

planning each session, 42

positive focus, Intervention 8-5

power, power struggle, 31, 43, 64-66, 91, 99, 130, 134, 162, 171, 176, 178, 196, 228

powergram, 171; Intervention 11-1

pray, prayer, 55, 109, 120, 139, 140, 230, 232, 233, 234

precounseling, 75-77, 80, 81, 261; 272, 273, 291, 302

PREP, 159, 183, 297, 301

promote a desire to change hurtful behavior, Intervention 9-3

psychoanalysis, 252

psychological problems, 90, 289

Pyramid Model of Forgiveness, 294, 303

reconciliation, 9, 11, 24, 30, 62, 63, 128, 129, 131, 134-36,

146, 163, 169, 192, 193, 251, 265, 281, 282, 284, 290, 296

recovery conversations, Intervention 11-11

regret, 80, 143, 144

Relationship Enhancement, 159, 264, 295

religion, 55, 233, 290, 292, 300, 301

religious, 14, 55, 69, 70, 89, 94, 103, 106, 107, 120, 123, 232, 233, 288, 289, 291-93

remember, 78, 79, 84, 86, 127, 140, 153, 161, 181, 218, 225, 253, 256, 280

respect, 97, 101-3, 123, 132, 149, 167, 185, 209, 275; Intervention 7-1

restitution, 134

revenge, 46, 128, 129, 134, 135

rituals, 253

role play, 194

role reversal, 150, 172

sacrifice, 69, 70, 108, 123, 290, 300

scaling, 226, 277

script, 76, 152, 256

Scripture, 13, 17, 24, 110, 117, 134, 139, 183, 230, 233, 247, 265

sculpting, 150, 217; Interventions 10-1, 13-3

self-reflection, 132, 133; Interventions 9-2, 9-7

sensible, 18, 28, 38, 39, 44, 52, 99, 100, 150, 152, 154, 203, 238, 261, 262, 265, 266, 282

separation, 21, 50, 129, 176, 213, 227, 268, 269

sex therapy, 235-37, 300

sharing (and refusing) requests, Intervention 10-9

stages, 32, 39, 44, 81, 105, 142, 193, 231, 232, 241, 271, 291

stonewalling, 50,

stories, 112, 113, 137; Intervention 9-5

strategy, strategic, 13, 18, 24-29, 32, 33, 36, 40, 42, 44,

45, 52, 54, 57-59, 67, 71, 81, 92, 103, 105, 106, 109, 110, 113-15, 117, 120, 126, 127, 132-34, 136, 138-44, 146, 149, 151-56, 159, 161, 165, 173, 175, 178, 181, 183, 185, 188, 190, 194, 202-5, 209, 211, 216-18, 221, 222, 226, 228, 230-32, 241, 243, 244, 246, 250, 253, 256, 262, 263, 265, 285, 286, 288, 289, 302

strengths, 38, 54, 76, 92, 94, 119, 196, 204, 273, 275

stress, 13, 62, 88, 145, 153, 155, 165, 166, 184, 186, 187, 189, 235, 245, 258, 301

structural family therapy, 264

support, 11, 20, 51, 56, 60, 63, 88, 93-95, 99, 104, 107-9, 123, 181, 189, 208, 261, 267, 274, 291, 302

tailoring (matching), 40, 41, 77, 163, 247

thought log, 201, 202, 204; Interventions 12-2, 12-4, 12-5

time limits, 41, 42

time together, 95, 106, 123, 155, 164, 228, 229; Interventions 7-3, 10-10

transtheoretical model of change, 80, 81

triggers, 165, 166, 172, 175, 176, 179, 193,

trust, 33, 34, 49, 53, 55, 63, 86, 93, 99, 123, 128, 129, 135, 142, 192, 212, 236, 247, 271, 273-275, 283, 284

unforgiveness, 33, 82, 135, 145, 294, 303

value, valuing, 28, 29, 32, 33, 36, 40, 41, 46, 47, 51-53, 60, 61, 62, 63, 65, 66, 67, 77-79, 82, 83, 92, 93, 95, 96, 100, 101-5, 107-10, 112, 113, 114, 118, 123, 124, 133, 146, 149, 150, 155, 157, 159, 163, 164, 167, 169, 170, 172-74, 178, 179, 180, 181-83, 185, 190, 196, 198, 200, 201, 206,

209, 215, 219, 223, 222, 224, 231, 233, 234, 236, 237, 247, 250, 254, 261-63, 265, 275, 276, 277, 282, 286, 292

videotape, 75-77, 80, 88-90, 116, 154-56, 173, 202, 261, 291, 293, 299; Interventions, 10-6, 10-7, 11-2; Tables 5.1, 6.2

Virginia Commonwealth University (VCU), 9, 10, 11, 77, 268, 270, 290, 291, 296

vision, written, Interventions 8-6, 8-8

withdrawal, 50, 78, 166, 220, 284

work, 9, 10, 17, 18, 21-26, 28-30, 32, 35-37, 40, 42, 43, 45-50, 52-54, 56-58, 62, 66, 71, 75, 77, 78, 80-83, 91, 92, 94, 95, 96, 99, 100, 104-7, 109, 110, 112-14, 116, 118, 119, 120, 124, 126, 129, 130, 134, 138, 139, 144, 149, 152, 158, 165, 166, 171-75, 183, 186-90, 193, 196, 199, 200, 203, 204, 211-13, 218, 221, 224, 225, 235, 238, 239, 241-44, 246-48, 250, 251, 255-58, 262, 263, 268, 271, 273-76, 280, 282-284, 289, 301

Scripture Index

Genesis
2, *108*
2:18, *24*
2:24, *107, 218, 247*
15:9-11, *24*
15:17-18, *24*

Joshua
4:5-9, *256*

Psalms
16:11, *122*

Proverbs
12:18, *183*

15:1, *183*
23:7, *201*
29:11, *183*
29:18, *120*

Jeremiah
31:32, *24*

Hosea
2:16, *24*
3:1, *24*

Malachi
2:14, *24*
2:16, *239, 250*

Matthew
5:9, *24*
5:21-22, *139*
5:21-26, *140*
5:31-32, *285*
5:32, *239*
5:38-47, *140*
6:13-15, *140*
7:1-12, *140*
19:4-6, *24, 293*
19:5, *285*
28:19, *45*

Mark
10:6-9, *239*

19:9, *239*

Luke
16:18, *285*
22:20, *24*

John
1:14, *266*
13:34-35, *102*
15:12-13, *102*

Romans
12:3, *128*
12:9-21, *24, 106*

1 Corinthians
6:16-17 *21, 285*
7:1-39, *285*
7:15, *239*
13, *24, 222, 266*
13:12, *265*
13:13, *266*
15:6, *265*
16:16, *285*

2 Corinthians
5:8, *265*

Galatians
5:6, *32, 118, 265*
6:5, *24*

Ephesians
4:15, *118*
4:22, *118*
4:22—5:2, *24, 123, 173, 189*
4:23, *118*
4:24, *118, 167*
4:25-27, *183*
5:25-33, *24, 229*
5:30-31, *222*
5:32, *17*

Philippians
2:1-14, *140*

1 Timothy
5:14, *285*

Hebrews
10:25, *24*
11:1, *33*
13:4, *285*

James
1:19, *184*
5:14, *24*
5:16, *24*

1 Peter
3:7, *222*
3:9-10, *175, 183*
5:7, *238*